DATE DUE

A New Southern Woman

Women's Diaries and Letters of the South
Carol Bleser, Series Editor

A New Southern Woman

The Correspondence of
ELIZA LUCY IRION NEILSON
1871–1883

Edited by Giselle Roberts

THE UNIVERSITY OF SOUTH CAROLINA PRESS

© 2013 University of South Carolina

Published by the University of South Carolina Press
Columbia, South Carolina 29208

www.sc.edu/uscpress

Manufactured in the United States of America

22 21 20 19 18 17 16 15 14 13
10 9 8 7 6 5 4 3 2 1

Library of Congress Cataloging-in-Publication Data
Neilson, Eliza Lucy Irion, 1843–1913.
A new Southern woman : the correspondence of Eliza Lucy Irion Neilson,
1871–1883 / edited by Giselle Roberts.
p. cm. — (Women's diaries and letters of the South)
Includes bibliographical references and index.
ISBN 978-1-61117-103-7
1. Neilson, Eliza Lucy Irion, 1843-1913—Correspondence.
2. Neilson, Eliza Lucy Irion, 1843–1913—Family. 3. Sisters—Mississippi—
Correspondence. 4. Women—Mississippi—Correspondence. 5. Families—
Mississippi—History—19th century—Sources. 6. Mississippi—Social life and
customs—19th century—Sources. 7. Reconstruction (U.S. history, 1865–1877)—
Mississippi—Sources. I. Roberts, Giselle, 1974– II. Title. III. Series.
F341.N45 2012
976.2'05—dc23
2012028937

This book was printed on a recycled paper with
30 percent postconsumer waste content.

For Glenn, with love

CONTENTS

ILLUSTRATIONS

A New Southern Woman: The Correspondence of Eliza Lucy Irion Neilson, 1871–1883 is the twenty-eighth volume in this series, now titled Women's Diaries and Letters of the South. This series includes a number of never-before-published diaries, collections of unpublished correspondence, and a few reprints of published diaries—a wide selection of nineteenth- and twentieth-century southern women's informal writings. This may be the largest series of published works by and on southern women.

The goal of the series is to enable women to speak for themselves, providing readers with a rarely opened window into southern society before, during, and after the American Civil War and into the twentieth century. The significance of these letters and journals lies not only in the personal revelations and the writing talent of these women authors but also in the range and versatility of the documents' contents. Taken together these publications tell us much about the heyday and the fall of the Cotton Kingdom, the mature years of the "peculiar institution," the war years, the adjustment of the South to a new social order following the defeat of the Confederacy, and the New South of the twentieth century. Through these writings the reader will also be presented with firsthand accounts of everyday life and social events, courtships, and marriages, family life and travels, religion and education, and the life-and-death matters that made up the ordinary and extraordinary world of the American South.

Carol Bleser

OTHER BOOKS IN THE SERIES

A Woman Doctor's Civil War: Esther Hill Hawks' Diary
Edited by Gerald Schwartz

A Rebel Came Home: The Diary and Letters of Floride Clemson, 1863–1866
Edited by Ernest McPherson Lander, Jr., and Charles M. McGee, Jr.

The Shattered Dream: The Day Book of Margaret Sloan, 1900–1902
Edited by Harold Woodell

The Letters of a Victorian Madwoman
Edited by John S. Hughes

A Confederate Nurse: The Diary of Ada W. Bacot, 1860–1863
Edited by Jean V. Berlin

ACKNOWLEDGMENTS

In a world where "pen and ink confabs" are largely things of the past, I feel privileged to have edited Eliza Lucy Irion Neilson's beautifully crafted and heartfelt letters.

Documentary editing requires considerable assistance from dedicated archivists, historians, and genealogists, and I am glad to have the opportunity to extend my thanks. Mattie Abraham from the Special Collections Department at Mississippi State University has provided me with help on a variety of queries since my graduate days. I am indebted to her for her expertise and generosity. The Lowndes County, Mississippi, History and Genealogy website was a wonderful resource; one that proved indispensible to me throughout this project. Lowndes County genealogist Carolyn Giles helped me on several occasions to piece together the complex web of Columbus family relations, as did Mona Vance from the Columbus Public Library and Bridget Smith Pieschel from the Mississippi University for Women. Their wealth of knowledge added immeasurably to this project, and I thank them kindly for helping me dig deeper into Eliza's community. Many others shared their family histories with me, and while their ancestors may appear only briefly in the context of this book, I feel privileged to have become acquainted with their life stories. Anne Webster and Alanna Patrick at the Mississippi Department of Archives and History, and Nan Prince at the Museum of Mississippi History assisted with copying papers and photographs. At the Mary Baldwin College, William Pollard and Sean Crowley generously consulted school records, and at the Borchardt Library at La Trobe University, Jonelle Bradley expertly tracked my numerous interlibrary requests. Michele Mooney kindly assisted with the proofreading.

The history department at La Trobe University supported my research efforts, for which I am most grateful. The late Charles East, my mentor and friend, truly understood and appreciated the joy of documentary editing. I will never forget our correspondence or his guidance. Warren Ellem and Elizabeth Dunn have offered similar support, and I have benefited greatly from their words of encouragement and practical assistance.

William Adams, Alexander Moore, and the wonderful team at the University of South Carolina Press have been exemplary. I am a great admirer of Carol Bleser's work and her series on southern women, and I can think of no better place for this book. I also thank the anonymous readers for their insightful comments and suggestions.

Fran, Marie, and William Fenamore have always treated me like family, and my life is richer because of them. Shaun Perry is both a dear friend and an adopted member of our family circle, and I am thankful for his encouragement and support.

My parents, Ron and Tricia Myers, have always reminded me that this is my path and have made sure I stayed true to all that I believe. My father taught me to look at things differently, and my mother helped me to see with my heart. My work is an expression of their belief in me.

My husband, Glenn, is my mainstay, balancing me in ways that no one else can. He and our cats Katie, Jermima, and Barney remind me daily of the simple pleasures of home life. My beloved fifteen-year-old cat, Snabby—who spent so much of his life sitting on my desk—passed in the last weeks of working on this manuscript. Writing, and indeed my heart, can never be the same without him.

The Irion Neilson Family Papers held at the Mississippi Department of Archives and History contain fourteen boxes of journals, correspondence, photographs, newspaper clippings, scrapbooks, and sheet music covering the period 1813–1924. The collection includes the six volumes of Eliza Lucy Irion Neilson's journal, written and compiled from 1860 to 1911.

Lucy began her diary on a clear winter's night in December 1860. After preparing "a little Christmas surprise, for one of our <u>faithful servants</u>," she sat down with a notebook and a "<u>sacred volume of memory</u> before my 'mind's eye'" and began writing her life story. "I do not pretend to be an excellent composer," she wrote; "therefore <u>these instances</u> shall be written in a simple style: & as <u>no</u> '<u>public eye</u>' is to <u>criticise</u> them [I] make the selection & write them, as they are recalled [by] the <u>magical</u> word, Memory" (Eliza Lucy Irion Neilson diary, undated recollections, December 1860). While Lucy remained committed to recording her story, she lacked the discipline needed for diary writing. She wrote daily entries for one- or two-week periods but always found her way back to sketches of seasonal highlights and family milestones, material that was supplemented by letters she had penned to family and friends. In her adulthood Lucy's compendium of correspondence replaced her fleeting romance with journalizing. Carefully saving the letters she had sent to family members along with a few penned to her by her sisters and her husband, John, Lucy found her own way to document her life in the time-strapped world of the New South.

From her wedding day in April 1871 until September 1883, Lucy collected over 130 letters. Most were written to her sister Elizabeth Irion Barron Watt and her niece Elizabeth Parthenia Irion Miller. Some were penned to her husband, brother, and brother-in-law. Of these I have selected 80 that provide a representative sample of the correspondence. Lucy also saved a select group of letters composed by other family members. This material is neither voluminous nor evenly distributed throughout Lucy's journals, and so I have included it in a supportive role only. Excerpts from these letters appear in chapter overviews and introductory passages.

Lucy regarded letter writing as a literary conversation with family and friends. She believed that "some rule & system" should govern the art of corresponding; adhering to conventions and etiquette, she noted, was just as important in print as it was in person. "Never write, unless compelled, in a <u>hurry</u>," she once instructed her niece. "Don't disgrace yourself, nor insult a friend, by sending off a letter that cannot be read! . . . Better have two pages well written, well spelt—than a dozen otherwise!" (Eliza Lucy Irion to Elizabeth Parthenia Irion, September 1, 1869). Unlike diary writing—which charted the spiritual, intellectual, and emotional growth of the writer—Lucy's correspondence documented an immediate exchange of news and ideas and the evolution of her most intimate relationships with family and friends.

The majority of Lucy's letters are included here in their entirety. On occasion I have omitted sentences or paragraphs, marked by [. . .]. Illegible words and sentences and paragraphs blackened out by Lucy or one of her descendants are marked by <. . .>. I have preserved inconsistencies such as variations in spelling and punctuation and irregularities in capitalization, but Lucy's own crossing out of the occasional word has been ignored. Lucy wrote dynamic letters and was fond of using dashes instead of full stops. While her style was slightly unusual, Lucy's offbeat punctuation and love of underlining give her words rhythm and energy, and so I have preserved her style. I have replaced Lucy's use of "+" and "+c" with "&" and "&c" and have lowered raised letters so that "7th" appears as "7th." Spelling mistakes have not been corrected, and I have refrained from using [sic]. More substantial errors are annotated. Where necessary I have inserted missing words to clarify meaning, inserted approximate dates for all undated letters, and provided state information on geographical locations outside Mississippi, marked by []. The general layout and paragraphing of Lucy's correspondence have also been preserved. Lucy often left space at the end of a paragraph and began a new topic on the same line. In such cases, I have placed the new paragraph on a new line.

I have attempted to identify all the people, places, and quotations mentioned in the correspondence by consulting family histories, court records, land records, newspapers, census material, maps, concordances, and genealogical sources. Where possible, I have included brief biographical sketches outlining the family relationships, military histories, and the professional backgrounds of cited individuals. Where a reference is not included, I have been unable to make an identification. If an exact date of birth or death could not be established, I have estimated one based on the census material, indicated by [b. ca.]. Bibliographical references are included for quotations cited by Lucy.

Working on Lucy's correspondence prompted me to think about the characteristics of documentary editing, one of which is the editor's tendency to present a subject's complete biography in the introduction. I adopt a different approach, setting the correspondence within a tight narrative so that Lucy's life story is revealed over the course of the book. The introduction covers Lucy's biography up to the time of her marriage to John Abert Neilson, and each chapter addresses a theme in the correspondence. My analyses of these materials are embedded within this narrative structure and in the four interludes devoted to the Irion women. The interludes do not address the overarching themes for the chapters that follow; rather they serve as points of interpretation—about both the narrative and southern womanhood more generally—at specific junctures within the correspondence. Chapter introductions and the notes before each letter also connect Lucy's story to the historiography and the wider political, economic, and social events of the period.

KEY TO FAMILY NAMES
AND FAMILY TREES

Eliza Lucy Irion Neilson used familiar or shortened names for the following family members:

IRION FAMILY

Eliza Lucy Irion Neilson
  Ida, T'Ida, Lute
Cornelia A. Parthenia Irion (Lucy's sister)
  Cordele, Miss, Nela, Neana, Neanie
James William Gray Irion (Lucy's brother)
  Jim, Brother, Marse, Jeemes
McKinney Irion Jr. (Lucy's brother)
  Brother Mc
Elizabeth Parthenia Irion Miller (Lucy's niece)
  Bess, Brooks
Elizabeth Charlotte Irion Barron Watt (Lucy's sister)
  Trot, Lizzie, Sis Lizzie

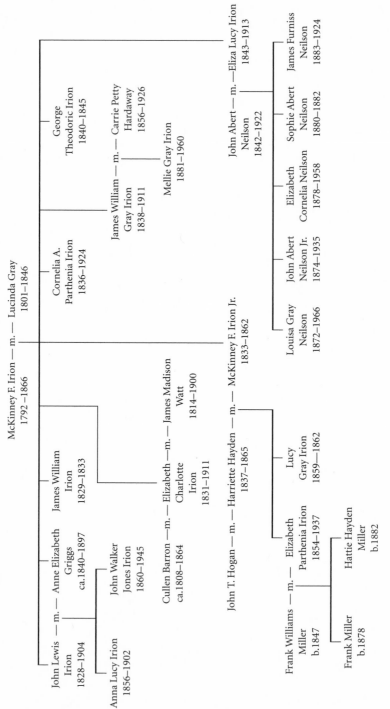

THE IRION FAMILY TREE

McKinney F. Irion — m. — Lucinda Gray
1792–1866   1801–1846

George
Theodoric Irion
1840–1845

James William — m. — Carrie Petty
Gray Irion   Hardaway
1838–1911   1856–1926

Mellie Gray Irion
1881–1960

Cornelia A.
Parthenia Irion
1836–1924

John Abert — m. — Eliza Lucy Irion
Neilson   1843–1913
1842–1922

James William
Irion
1829–1833

Louisa Gray   John Abert   Elizabeth   Sophie Abert   James Furniss
Neilson   Neilson Jr.   Cornelia Neilson Neilson   Neilson
1872–1966   1874–1935   1878–1958   1880–1882   1883–1924

John Lewis — m. — Anne Elizabeth
Irion   Griggs
1828–1904   ca.1840–1897

John Walker
Jones Irion
1860–1945

Anna Lucy Irion
1856–1902

Cullen Barron — m. — Elizabeth — m. — James Madison
ca.1808–1864   Charlotte   Watt
                    Irion   1814–1900
                    1831–1911

John T. Hogan — m. — Harriette Hayden — m. — McKinney F. Irion Jr.
                    1837–1865   1833–1862

Lucy
Gray Irion
1859–1862

Frank Williams — m. — Elizabeth
Miller   Parthenia Irion
b.1847   1854–1937

Hattie Hayden
Miller
b.1882

Frank Miller
b.1878

Eliza Lucy Irion Neilson used familiar or shortened names for the following family members:

Neilson Family

John Abert Neilson (Lucy's husband)
  Mr N—, Neilson, Jack
Sarah Dandridge Neilson (Lucy's sister-in-law)
  Sister, Sissie
Elizabeth Symons (daughter of John's half sister, Anne Frazier Neilson Symons)
  Lizzie
Catherine Cabot Neilson Hopkins (Lucy's sister-in-law)
  Kate, Sister Kate, Cadie

The Neilson Family Tree

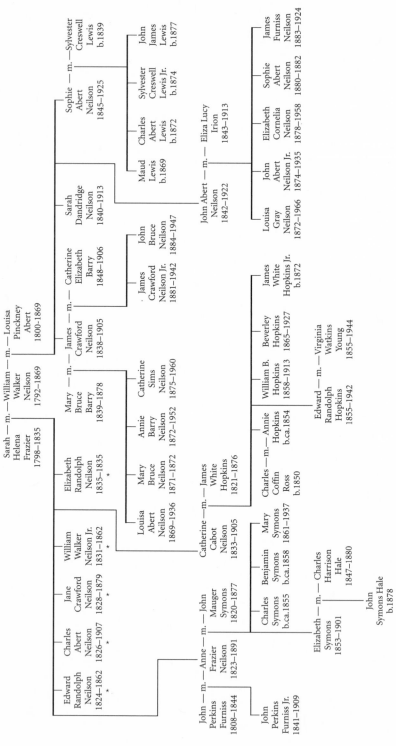

* Not mentioned in correspondence

Detailed lineage not included on this tree.

Introduction

*E*liza Lucy Irion suffered with "marriage trauma" in the weeks preceding her nuptials to John Abert Neilson. She had tried to persuade John to agree to a fall wedding, but he "would not hear to such postponement, & begged that it should be the 13th of April [1871], as that was his birthday!" Lucy reluctantly agreed. She loved John and had enjoyed their private engagement with its romantic trysts and chance encounters. But marriage threw up sobering realities for the vivacious twenty-eight-year-old bride-to-be, who had always regarded family leadership and domestic responsibility as the province of her older sisters. Trimming her lilac dress in readiness for her wedding day, Lucy struggled to untangle her feelings of "trembling" joy and nervous anticipation from her fears about "home & change." "My heart aches at the prospect of so soon separating from my home-folks," she admitted, "& yet today I told Jack I would be all ready to go with him! Strange, strange! how strong the feeling, which makes us willing to break all other bonds! Heaven wills it so."[1]

Columbus, Mississippi, had been abuzz with news of the romance long before Lucy and John's engagement was formally announced. John had spent months tilling the ground at Wildwood farm in the hope that his labors would translate into self-made manhood. He dreamed of agricultural success and earned wealth, and the day he would be ready to take Lucy as his wife. In the meantime he pleaded with Miss Irion to exercise the utmost discretion about their arrangements. "I am particularly anxious to keep this impudently-inquisitive public entirely in the dark as regards my plans & prospects for the future," John wrote Lucy on September 15, 1870. "While I dislike & condemn deception, I greatly admire those who can conceal their designs until the proper moment arrives to execute them." Lucy happily consented, hoping that by keeping "Madame Rumor" at bay, she could prolong giving up the domestic comfort of Willow Cottage. "I don't think he much fancies so long an engagement," she remarked to her sister Lizzie, "but t'will be short to me." When "Santa Claus" delivered a ring to Lucy in December 1870, she knew the game was up. "The town has been—& is, in a blaze about our affair," she admitted, "& hitherto I've been enabled to combat the reports, by wearing no shining pledge—now, however, I'll be more annoyed than ever!" She cheekily added, "There's comfort in gloves."[2]

Lucy was not the only one anxious about "home & change." The Irion family had always likened matrimony to "death & destruction," a wrenching of emotional ties that robbed the family unit of its strength and cohesion. Lucy's sisters, Lizzie and Cordele, and her sixteen-year-old niece, Bess—who had moved to Willow Cottage after the death of her mother in 1865—struggled to accept the engagement, and "a passionate fit of crying" soon gave way to waves of resentment. "[Cordele] can't bear Somebody in her sight," Lucy disclosed anxiously to Lizzie, and "says he has just come to break up our family! Vows she won't speak to him." Bess also spent many a tearful night brooding over Lucy's departure. After devoting hours to "thirteen exquisitely crocheted mats," she ungraciously threw the gift in Lucy's lap. "Here, take your mats and go along to housekeeping," she said offhandedly. While they approved of John and assembled a generous trousseau for Lucy, the Irion women concluded that the spring wedding sounded a death knell for family life at Willow Cottage.[3]

When Lucy married John in an "impressive ceremony" filled with "kissing & handshaking & nice pleasant speeches," Lizzie, Cordele, and Bess did their best to hide their sadness at the loss of one who had nurtured family ties and traditions. As the new bride caught her first glimpse of Wildwood, Lucy did her best to quell her "keen desire to fly, to get away." Lofty imaginings of her "future home" and her commitment "to make it Paradise of every measure, delightful to the mind, the ear and eye" fell hard against the practical realities of domestic life. "I was afraid of this new life," she wrote, "this new home, these new duties!" After throwing herself headlong into housekeeping, Lucy's postwar identity was shaped by her marriage to John and the challenges of Wildwood. She became queen of the "domestic ditty," relaying news about everything from whitewashing and servant arrangements to snowball cakes and the hyacinths she grew in her twelve-by-twelve-foot garden plot. In over 130 letters from April 1871 to September 1883, Lucy built her life around visions of a domestic ideal. She also watched her widowed sister, Lizzie, her single sister, Cordele, and her schoolgirl niece, Bess, search for their own ways of becoming women in the New South. When it came to turning the war-torn vestiges of antebellum femininity into a workable postwar reality, white southern women no longer looked to one ideal. Age, class, geographical location, marital status, and financial standing rendered the task of rebuilding southern womanhood a personal journey, a family endeavor, and a community effort.[4]

WAR AND WATERSHED

Women of the New South rebuilt their lives in their kitchens, garden patches, and sewing rooms, and in church halls, schoolrooms, and cemeteries by cooking, writing, and organizing. Their daily acts of determined renewal now form the canvas used by historians seeking to understand the extent to which the Civil War became a watershed for southern women. Were women able to build upon the challenges they confronted in wartime to refashion their domestic and civic contributions to the postwar world? Or did the white South's violent response to Reconstruction force women to invent new selves designed in large measure to resist change rather than embrace it?[5]

Understanding exactly *how* southern women rebuilt their lives in the post-war period has become critical to the debate about war and watershed. It is not surprising that much of this research has focused on the household as the site where greater questions about honor, liberty, and citizenship were fought. With their exclusive claims to political power in tatters, defeated Confederate soldiers redefined their masculinity and racial supremacy around domestic virtue and governance. Without slavery, marriage became the legal crucible of the postwar household and the lifeline available to white men in their struggle to regain their independence and public prowess. LeeAnn Whites asserts that women became casualties of the resurrection of virtuous masculinity. To rebuild demoralized soldiers, she argues, southern women subordinated themselves within the domestic sphere to become the last legitimate terrain of domination for their men.[6]

Laura F. Edwards suggests that a domestic ideal of southern womanhood emerged as companion to virtuous manhood, in which a white man's hard work and resourcefulness were translated into a "comforting" home life by the "creativity and love" of his wife. By attending to the needs of their husbands and children, "putting well-prepared meals on the table, banishing dirt and dust, selecting tasteful interior decorations, and maintaining a cheerful, supportive atmosphere," southern ladies reconstructed their identities as "worthy women." Furthermore they used this framework to distinguish themselves from African American and poor white women, whose economic status prevented them from attaining the exalted domestic ideal. Edwards notes that this traditional version of white womanhood was most successfully achieved through marriage, which usually facilitated the establishment of a new household and granted a woman the status of wife and mistress.[7]

Women such as Lucy Neilson may have rediscovered their sense of self in domestic bliss, but for others, the emergence of a "nondependent" ideal offered up new possibilities. Jane Turner Censer's research indicates that southern women born after 1820 embraced the ideal of the self-reliant woman who redefined her place in society not by subordinating herself to men but by expanding her contribution in both the domestic realm and the workforce. Censer argues that while older women struggled to adapt to the rigors of the postbellum world, younger southern ladies increasingly viewed education as a functional, not ornamental pursuit, praised economic independence among women, and grew skeptical of the idea that marriage "would somehow better a woman's lot in life." These outward-looking women invested the income derived from paid work into their homes and the creation of a rich cultural and intellectual life. They also threw themselves into memorializing the Confederate cause by burying the dead, building monuments, and retelling their stories of war in memoirs and fiction. Caroline E. Janney contends that women, far more than merely "purveyors of male confidence," took charge of "remaking military defeat into a political, social, and cultural victory for the white South." Building upon the war-time creation of an organized womanhood, southern women redefined their relationship to the state and, as Karen L. Cox notes, shaped debates over what would constitute a new South.[8]

Lucy Neilson's correspondence offers a new perspective on the watershed debate, suggesting that elite white womanhood remained a surprisingly fluid and negotiated territory, where submissive wives, domestic guardians, memorial crusaders, and single and self-sufficient women fashioned a new southern consciousness under a broader rubric of genteel postwar femininity. If elite white men were to succeed in clawing their way to a new southern mastery, they needed the solidarity and support of their poorer white neighbors and their women. Mississippi's Married Women's Property Act—expanded in 1867 and revised in 1871 in an effort to safeguard property in the face of rising debt—indicated just how much white men relied on women's "mutual commitment to maintain class privilege." The alliance allowed women to build upon the latitudes gained in wartime—they could be outward-looking, virtuous, and proactive in the school-room, in politics, or in memorial endeavors so long as their activities helped to redraw racial boundaries around white civic credibility, domestic authority, and political clout.[9]

At one end of femininity's continuum stood Edwards's domestic ideal, celebrating the proud cult of marriage and motherhood. At the other end stood Censer's nondependent vision of womanhood embracing paid employment, self-sufficiency, and intellectualism. Most women could not conform to one ideal but rather fashioned a blueprint for postwar womanhood around their personal circumstances—they entered paid employment to pursue the domestic ideal or threw themselves into memorializing the Confederacy, only to end up with an unanticipated measure of independence. Postwar womanhood was a complicated mix of personal choice, demographic constraints, economic and political conditions, and relationships to family, freed people, and community.

Lucy's correspondence, encompassing the life stories of her sisters and her niece, explores the reconstruction of white femininity from not just one but four different standpoints along this new southern continuum: Lucy as wife, mistress, mother, and advocate of the domestic ideal; Lizzie as independent widow of means, absentee plantation owner, and lover of gentility; Cordele as a spiritually guided, morally driven purport of single blessedness; and Bess as a young woman groomed for both usefulness and social polish. Certainly the Irion women sat at the conservative end of postwar femininity—none entered the workforce, and all ultimately rebuilt their lives within the domestic circle. Nevertheless they all looked outward to contribute to community life through politics, the church, and memorial activities. All these women moved from one ideal of womanhood to another as their personal circumstances changed, and in her letters, Lucy charted the struggles that accompanied this journey toward a new southern femininity.

Furthermore Lucy's correspondence highlights that while women may have approached postwar femininity from different standpoints, they did not confront the hard task of rebuilding on their own. Carroll Smith-Rosenberg's pioneering work on the "female world of love and ritual" emphasized the enduring bonds between southern women who "revealed their deepest feelings to one another, helped one another with the burdens of housewifery and motherhood, nursed one another's sick, and mourned for one another's dead." These established ties were also essential to the reconstruction of white southern womanhood. Lucy's correspondence reveals that women were actively involved in helping their daughters, sisters, nieces, mothers, and friends to resurrect their lives out of the vestiges of war and the heartbreak of defeat. Drawing upon the reciprocal, interdependent relationships of antebellum times, Lucy's female circle of family and friends pooled their resources and devoted themselves to the immense task of rebuilding, just as they had done in times of marriage, childbirth, child rearing, sickness, and death. Fashioning their individual stories within the collective bonds of family and community, the Irion-Neilson women met and overcame the generational challenges of postwar life together.[10]

Tennessee Born

Life furnished Lucy Irion and her family with more than a little experience in the art of rebuilding. Born on March 3, 1843, in Somerville, Tennessee, Lucy was the eighth and youngest child of McKinney F. Irion and Lucinda Gray Irion. McKinney, who was born in Wilkes County, Georgia, in 1792, grew up with plantation dreaming in his blood. After the death of his first wife he married Lucinda Gray, and by the late 1820s they headed west to join his siblings in Tennessee. The couple settled at Wood Lawn, a commodious two-story home flanked by wide beds of thyme and chamomile, a red smoke house, abundant fields, and two long rows of slave cabins. While McKinney threw himself into planting, Lucinda tended to their young family: John Lewis, James William, Elizabeth Charlotte (Lizzie), McKinney Jr., Cornelia A. Parthenia (Cordele), James William Gray (Jim), George Theodoric, and Eliza Lucy. Like most antebellum southern women, Lucinda bore

Eliza Lucy Irion Neilson. Irion Neilson Family Papers.
Courtesy of Mississippi Department of Archives and History.

children at two- to three-year intervals, and she buried two—James William and George Theodoric—before her own death in June 1846.[11]

Wood Lawn must have turned on Lucinda's know-how, for without her the fibers of family and domestic life quickly unfurled. As fifteen-year-old Lizzie struggled against the tide of domestic chaos left in her mother's wake, McKinney Irion slowly drowned his mastery in mismanagement. By 1848 "the crisis had come." "Debts became due," Lucy recalled, "& <u>home</u>, <u>servants</u>, & everything was torn from us to satisfy the demand for <u>money</u>." "Faithful & good servants" were sold on the auction block, and the inhabitants of Wood Lawn were "turned out into the world <u>homeless</u>." McKinney had failed dismally in the work of white southern masculinity. Stripped of his property and slaves and unable to extend protection to his dependents, McKinney forfeited his political credit, his social standing, and his status as master and head of household. Emasculated by his inability to govern, McKinney was also compelled to loosen his grip on even the closest of family ties. John, McKinney Jr., and Cordele were sent away to school, while Lizzie, Jim, and Lucy were ferried out to extended kin. By 1850 McKinney had scraped together enough money to rent a "small & humble cottage" in Bolivar, Tennessee, and family life reconvened under strict domestic economy. "Oh! what must have been the feelings of my sensitive & high minded Sister [Lizzie] when she came here!" Lucy remarked. "I remember seeing her eyes swollen with weeping, for a <u>long long</u> time—& how like the bright rays of Sol through a dark cloud, was her <u>smiles</u> to me, when she, poor girl! had <u>power</u> to smile."[12]

Even the recent sting of financial disgrace was not enough to prevent McKinney from making a mess of his new arrangements. Once again embarrassed in financial affairs, he turned to his sisters, Elizabeth Irion Holderness and Mary Parthenia Irion Hayden, for assistance. In an effort to minimize further damage to the family name, Mary hastily settled her brother's debts and insisted that McKinney move his family to Columbus, Mississippi, where she and Elizabeth could prevent him from further misadventure. McKinney saw no alternative but to accept, and in December 1851 Lucy and her siblings bid farewell to Tennessee. "We had built many aircastles of what we would do when we came to live with our <u>rich</u> Aunt," Lucy remarked, "but alas! like all such ethereal buildings, they tumbled & fell in <u>ruinous heaps</u>." James and Mary Hayden, who owned a patch of good land outside Columbus, may have been considered rich by Lucy's standards, but their life was built upon measured gentility, not planter opulence. Careful and set in their ways, neither took kindly to their houseguests. Sixty-three-year-old James Hayden had little patience or sympathy for the homeless brood of children, while his industrious wife sought payback for her domestic sacrifice. Cordele and Jim attended school, while Lucy was tutored at home by Lizzie, who bore the "burden of care." "Everyone had to go to some kind of work," related Lucy. "I use to think it very hard that I must sit in Aunt's room day, after day, & <u>knit</u> the negroes' socks, when the sun shone so brightly, & the birds sung so sweetly. I blamed poor Sis many times when she refused to let me play, but [she] told me I must learn to work, for I was <u>very poor</u>, & had <u>no home</u> of my own—I did not then think how <u>very much she</u> had to do."[13]

Lizzie's rigorous education in domestic economy helped her to take charge of household affairs when McKinney resolved, once again, to try his hand at farming, this time on an unimproved tract of land just outside Columbus. The Irion family's second Wood Lawn possessed none of the hallmarks of its genteel Tennessean predecessor. "Our house was . . . very small, our furniture mean & cheap," Lucy conceded, "& <u>poverty</u> stared us in the face at every turn. I fear none of us were very contented & submissive. . . . pride, that almost worst of passions, rankled in my young heart. I looked upon my lot as a very hard one." Lizzie regarded Wood Lawn as her father's last opportunity to salvage his reputation and felt the "responsibility of [her] situation" as she threw herself into "a great deal of work." "I think I am learning fast to attend to all my household affairs and I hope I do it with an eye single to my duty," she wrote on January 9, 1853. Still,

Lizzie worried that her lack of education and accomplishments would prevent her from fulfilling her "duties in the sphere in which I am placed." "The thousand and one calls on my attention and patience seem to exclude every thing like a settled plan of reading or thinking—," she wrote anxiously. "I feel that the education of my mind and heart would both be cultivated in order to do my whole duty to the family—With the help of my Heavenly [Father] I will try to do better." While McKinney worked hard at taming the fields and salvaging the vestiges of his tarnished reputation, Wood Lawn's success hinged on Lizzie's governance over family and household affairs. She proved equal to the task. By embracing domesticity "with [her] own hands," Lizzie's hard work furnished her sisters with all the ritual and preparatory rigor of a traditional southern girlhood.[14]

An Independent Education

Lizzie's education had been cut short by her father's financial mishaps, and she vowed not to let the same thing happen to her sisters. At Lizzie's insistence, Lucy enrolled at the Columbus Female Institute in 1855, and when cousin Tom Peters offered her a scholarship to attend Corona College in Corinth, she gratefully accepted. "Poor Sis Lizzie said she never never would doubt God's goodness & watchful care over us," Lucy wrote, "that all my life she had been wondering how I would be sufficiently educated to make a teacher of myself & now in His own good He had brought it about that these cousins should make this offer." Corona, which opened its doors to the South's privileged daughters in 1857, boasted a nondenominational curriculum founded on regional principles. Headed by Rev. LeRoy B. Gaston and his wife, Susan, the academy "was a large three story-brick-building—situated on a slight eminence with a beautifully arranged flower-garden in front." In 1858 Lucy was one of ninety students enrolled at Corona and one of forty boarders. Her uncle James Moore McCalla served on the academy's board of supervisors.[15]

While other students prepared for the heady thrills of society—and the more sobering world of marriage and motherhood—Lucy threw herself into the work of becoming self-sufficient. She found in Corona's stately halls a dynamic female community, where academic endeavor was nurtured by the warmth of schoolgirl camaraderie. She blossomed under the routine and stability of boarding-school life. "System was in everything!" Lucy recalled. "No hurry!—no fuss! There was a Bell for Rising; a Bell for Breakfast; a Bell for Prayers; a Bell for Study-hour; a Bell for School; a Bell for Recreation; a Bell for Supper; a Bell for Prayers (evening); & a Bell for Retiring! All we had to do was to obey the numerous Bells instantly!" Lucy and her friends regarded Susan Gaston—"a small dark lady— with brilliant black eyes, & a very jaunty little dress cap"—as the "power behind the throne!" "She was independent to a fault," declared Lucy. "Determination was manifested in everything! She knew how to manage, direct, carry on, & she did it to perfection! . . . A soiled cloth, or plate, or knife, or a <u>badly cooked meal</u> was never seen on her table!" Reverend Gaston's mild temperament balanced out his wife's strong character. "I should have loved him more—but somehow—I had'ent <u>too</u> much respect for him," Lucy confessed. "I could hook my finger in the button-hole of his coat, & get <u>any wish</u> gratified!"[16]

Susan Gaston may have ensured that the school was founded on academic rigor and system, but it was hardly a cloistered life. Corona's program of shorter lessons, recreational evenings, and abundant suppers balanced study against its social rival, keeping "spirits high, & health good." McKinney Irion Jr. urged his sister to "study very hard," "kill all your bad traits & cultivate with great attention your virtues," but Lucy measured herself against her ability to carve out female friendships and social standing in the academy. Miss Irion's "free & easy manner" "rendered [her] rather popular" among her peers, while a swag of handsome dresses helped her to infiltrate Corona's most select circles. At the suggestion of her roommates, Minnie and Agnes Vaughan, Lucy even adopted a name change. When "Agnes asked for my full name—I informed her t'was 'Eliza Lucy Irion'— 'Well said she—why not call yourself <u>Lucy</u> then, tis a sweet name'—I was willing enough—so I was everafterwards introduced as '<u>Lucy Irion</u>'!" "Many of my old Columbus friends thought it quite a <u>piece</u> of <u>affectation</u>," she added, "however, that mattered little with the girls at <u>Corona</u>!"[17]

Yet, as Lucy knew, coming of age involved more than a nice hat and a measure of schoolgirl credibility. Academic standing and spiritual conversion provided substance to the shine of young womanhood and, later, virtue to marriage and motherhood—and each required hard work, self-scrutiny, and commitment. With her heart in a "happy flutter" over thoughts of beau and romantic charm, Lucy kept her studies in check but found herself lagging on the path to spiritual enlightenment. "Every mail brought me letters from different friends containing the glad tidings that they too had united themselves to churches," she recalled. "Nearly all the girls had been blessed with assurances of their acceptance, & I was still in darkness. I thought myself forsaken." Conversion may have been a private revelation, but it was a milestone often attained at school and among friends; remaining in "darkness" was not an option in a young woman's coming-of-age story. After one failed attempt to join the church, Lucy sought guidance from her cousin and benefactor, Tom Peters. "When I told him I could not <u>pray</u>—that God would not hear me,—he so sweetly knelt with me, & bade me follow him in prayer," she wrote, "& as he spoke the blessed words, I repeated them after him— when suddenly I felt an 'ineffable, sheltering, loving Presence' about me, & I was at peace! . . . I never felt a disposition to make any demonstration,—there was a sacredness about my <u>new</u> experience, which forbade any public expression."[18]

With a renewed commitment to her church and her studies, Lucy enjoyed a life at the academy that was filled with "vivacity [that] knew no bounds." Flanked by her schoolmates, Lucy danced across Corinth's modest social stage, partaking in Saturday shopping trips, church picnics, and the Baptist fair, where she returned home with the heart of a local boy, Will Neilson, in May 1858. Just shy of eighteen, with black hair, blue eyes, and "an embryo moustache," Lucy's young suitor "would have been quite handsome—had not his nose been so long, & so crooked," she wrote. Still, his quiet attentions offered Lucy some relief from preparations for commencement season, not to mention further elevating her standing in the school community. "I was pleased, & gratified at his exclusive devotion," she disclosed, "for he openly proclaimed that Corona was naught without me, & I was very happy to receive all his love tokens—yet I would go for days without scarcely thinking of him, & the idea of a real love affair would have shocked me."[19]

Will and Lucy's gentle romance hit the hard edge of propriety in winter 1859, when Lucy received news that her suitor was dying of consumption. Unwilling to risk her reputation in a declaration of "friendly regards" to Will, Lucy conceded that she "could do nothing—but pray for him." "I was so determined not to show any feeling, or make any sign, that my conduct & actions were cold, & heartless in the extreme," she wrote. "Very often his Cousins Ann E. & Eugenia Polk, would come to see me & always spoke of Billy's illness, how rapidly he was sinking & how often he spoke of 'Lucy' in his delirium. I thought it cruel of them to watch me so intensely while they talked, & so great a restraint did I put upon myself on such occasions that my only answer would be, 'I am sorry he's so sick.'" When those at Corona received news of his death on February 1, 1860, Lucy felt "lifeless, numb, [and] cold" but "could not bear the idea of every little tattler going home, & remarking upon my sad face, & guessing how much I must have loved him." "This kind of publicity," she added, "was killing to think of." The romance, and its uncomfortably public demise, left Lucy's heart "very hard." "A woman should cherish her tender, loving emotions—& not smother them to death!" she noted upon reflection. "I did not really love Mr N— but then if I had, t'would have done me no harm."[20]

In an attempt to remove herself from the social malaise sparked by Will's death, Lucy worked hard on her studies and thoughts of self-improvement. "If I had studied all my school-life as I did this term," she later confessed, "I would now have been a wiser woman." Lucy mastered Latin and had the "unexpected honor" of being elected valedictorian. In the wake of his sister's academic success, Jim urged Lucy to abandon her teaching plans. "Pa is entirely out of debt & can make ten or twelve hundred dollars a year, & I will be getting five hundred dollars next year & out of the whole if we cannot keep one little creature from labor with her own hands I think we had better hang up," he wrote. "I have seen my Sisters cramped all my life & I am determined to do all in my power to make them comfortable if not happy," he continued. "I do not care for self for a man can battle &

grow accustomed to the rough treatment of its being but for a young girl to start out & have her young blood chilled in her veins by the rough talk of the domineering people that are in all communities is more than I can think of my sisters standing." With the necessary funds to allow her return home, Lucy had a "good, long, cry" at the thought of leaving the "dear Alma Mater" that had provided her with social credit and the tools of self-support. Still she felt hopeful of her future as a daughter-at-home whose familial devotion would create opportunities that might otherwise have been quashed by the drudgery of paid employment.[21]

Lucy returned to Columbus with a "heart overflow[ing] with thankfulness" and more than a few grand designs about her coming out. After years of scrabbling, McKinney and Lizzie had turned Wood Lawn into a working farm that shone with domestic stability. "How cozy & comfortable everything looked!" Lucy exclaimed with delight upon her return. "Everything had been newly painted for our coming, & oh! what [a] sweet, sweet place it was!" Mary Hayden's death, just days before Lucy's homecoming, again turned family life on its head. "Aunt Hayden in her will had requested Pa to exchange his place (Wood Lawn) for her place (Willow Cottage)," Lucy explained. "She had become so attached to it, she was unwilling to see it pass into other hands than ours." Willow Cottage had much to recommend it—it was a large, established farm nestled on the banks of the Luxapalila, closer to Columbus. At the right of the cottage, a grove of weeping willows encircled an artesian well, "not near so pretty as our 'silver-stream' of Wood Lawn," Lucy noted, "but still very pretty." Practical considerations and McKinney Jr.'s entreaties finally won out, and McKinney Sr. and his daughters reluctantly gave up their self-made home. "Ah! t'was with regret we left dear 'Wood Lawn,'—it had been our first home in Mississippi," wrote Lucy. "We had gone there in the woods;—& had been so glad of every little improvement, & now just as it was so sweet & comfortable, we were going to leave . . . all the 'familiar scenes' of our child-hood." Amid political meetings and secession talk, the Irion family relocated to the sprawling comfort of Willow Cottage.[22]

DAUGHTER OF THE HOME FRONT

After years of setbacks, the Irion family had some semblance of security—and then came the Civil War. Columbus occupied an interesting place in the Confederate war machine; its arsenal employed around one thousand people to produce munitions for the army, while the town served as a hospital base after battles such as Shiloh. For the most part, though, Columbus sat in a rare pocket of the Mississippi region that was neither a site of conflict nor a place of extended Union occupation. Frequent rumors about Yankee soldiers made the "people in general, & women in particular, turn lunatics" as they sent "negroes, & mules . . . into the swamps, cane-breaks & other of-out-the-way-places" and buried the "silver in particular & everything in general." After the Yankees had failed to materialize and the excitement had subsided, Columbus happily retreated from the coalface of war. At Willow Cottage, McKinney mapped out a war plan for the farm but never needed to put it into action. In the spirit of sacrificial patriotism, Lizzie, Cordele, and Lucy became Confederate daughters-at-home, widening their sphere of influence from the family to the new nation. "All social affairs were neglected, & jewelled fingers were busy 'knitting for the soldiers,'" Lucy recalled. "Sewing societies were organized, & every spare moment was spent, working for the soldiers. Our whole hearts, minds, & souls were taken up with thoughts of 'our cause'! We were all too anxious for anything but what concerned the soldiers!"[23]

Like most southern men of military age, Lucy's brothers, McKinney Jr. and Jim, enlisted in the Confederate army, McKinney Jr. as a private in Company B, Forty-third Infantry Regiment, and Jim as a private in Company K, Fourteenth Infantry Regiment Mississippi. Neither took kindly to the grimy, unrefined rigor of army life, where notions of citizenship, standing, and honor were as fiercely contested in camp as they were on the battlefield. "There is not but one or two things that I object to one of them is some of these little Leuts that never had a position in society at home should be over men that are so much their superiors in intellect capacity & standing," blustered Jim after only a brief time in camp. "I try to keep revenge out of my sinful heart but I do think if the good Lord spares me & them to live through this campaign I will give some of them a gentle flogging." A private's life, Jim concluded, was a miserable existence punctuated by orders and poor rations. "My ears are . . . constantly filled with oaths vulgar conversation & songs & the thousands disagreeable phrazes that are so much used among the soldiers," he moaned. "We have nothing but rotton shoulder meat & flour bread & I cannot eat it and our cook says he will not go any further with us & I know I will starve then for I cannot cook." A transfer to the quartermaster department saved Jim from possible "starvation." "Poor fellow!" Lucy wrote candidly. "T'was a providence too, for t'would have killed him in that barrenous climate to 'stay in camp.' We were—so happy for him!!" Perhaps the obfuscation of his status may have killed him first. Dispensing with his uniform, Jim immediately requested a fresh supply of "white shirts cravats collars &c." "I am now doing business that requires some nice clothes," he rejoiced. "I can acquire a greater knowledge of business where I now am in one month than I could in an army in five years. So you see I can save my country save my health learn business in its various forms & probably be promoted after a while."[24]

While Jim happily cloaked himself in the safety of gentlemanly service, 1862 turned out to be a mixed bag for the Confederacy and for the inhabitants of Willow Cottage. The year, Lucy recalled, "dawn[ed] upon us gloomily—the very weather seemed prophetic of the misfortunes which were to come, too quickly, to our cause!" In February, Tennessee's Fort Henry and Fort Donelson surrendered to Union troops. In April the battle of Shiloh brought the grisly aftermath of war to Columbus. "Our town was filled to overflowing with the sick & wounded," wrote Lucy. "Every public building, & even our churches, were taken as hospitals—& still there were more to be accommodated—private citizens then threw open their houses, & the poor soldiers found rest beneath their hospitable roofs." While "married, yes, single-ladies went to the hospitals to nurse," the Irion women did not join their friends and neighbors because Harriette and McKinney Jr.'s two-year-old daughter, Lucy Gray Irion, had succumbed to the measles two days before the battle. "No more was heard the patter of little feet, or sweet prattler from her baby-lips!" cried Lucy. "We missed our little one more than most families would—because we were so fond of her, & then her sweetness of disposition, bespoke so much pleasure in future intercourse with her!" In mourning, Lizzie, Cordele, and Lucy "staid at home, made clothes, & knit socks for such as would recover!"[25]

The Irion family's loss was compounded by the war that raged unmercifully beyond their household, a war that stained the streets of Columbus with the blood of its Confederate family. In the coming months New Orleans and Baton Rouge fell to Union forces, and death found its "shining mark" among Lucy's friends and neighbors. Days of "bitter sighing;—of dread suspense; of breaking hearts" were, however, made bearable by glints of social gaiety. When the Thirty-sixth Infantry Regiment Mississippi set up camp in the outlying fields at Willow Cottage, Lucy and her friends dedicated themselves to entertaining the troops. "Every body has the very nicest Lieut, or Capt. or private as their most especial attendant," cooed Lucy in a letter to Jim. "Numerous are the romantic adventures which occur." Briefly donning the garb of a daughter-at-home, Lucy received news about Maj. Gen. Earl Van Dorn's failed attempt to storm Corinth while she was attending a town party in October 1862, and immediately regretted her decision to attend. "How could we join in any festivities, when our own blood was being spilt!" she cried bitterly. "Such an overwhelming presentiment of evil possessed me that night—I could not talk the gibberish, & folly which was talked around me." Lucy's guilt was compounded by the news that McKinney Jr. had been wounded in the battle. "I was as one stupefied," she confessed. "I felt that I had been so remiss in my love, & anxiety for my dear beloved Brother! . . . Such vanity, & folly had been in my mind, & had filled the place which should have been devoted to his welfare!" Shot in the leg—"the ball had entered just below the knee"—a "pale, & haggard" McKinney Jr. returned home with doctors' assurances that his injury was "very slight, & that he would be well again soon!" He died on October 21, 1862. "We buried him & came back to our bereft home," Lucy wrote. "No family ever lost such a head!"[26]

The war continued to batter the Irion home circle. In addition to McKinney Jr., the family lost three soldier cousins in October 1862. As the year closed, Lucy's Aunt Elizabeth Holderness died, leaving her "rather old looking" two-story frame house to her adopted daughter (and McKinney Jr.'s widow), Harriette. McKinney Sr. and his daughters promptly relocated to Columbus to stay with her. There they learned of the death of Lucy's uncle James Hayden in May 1863. "There were so many <u>sorrows</u>—all in such quick succession too;—<u>so many</u> changes;—so much novelty;—<u>such entire new</u> arrangements that I was in a state of excitement all the time," Lucy recalled. "First, the old heads of the family had passed away;—new ones had taken possession;—new people were in the house;—all was <u>stir</u> & confusion! I don't now think it best for afflicted families to live as we did. <u>My</u> head was <u>completely turned</u>." After the tumult of Shiloh, though, town life "flowed on as smoothly & quietly as ever" and certainly had its advantages—French and music lessons, walks, rides, and visiting. Thanks to Harriette's blockade run to Memphis, Lucy was able to enter society alongside a "<u>brilliant</u> assembly of young ladies." "I had a nice supply of clothes altho twas war times," she bragged. "People were not so proud about wearing their sister's old clothes, & as two of my sisters were in mourning I had a nice supply & then Sis Hattie had exchanged two dresses with a lady for two splendid silks—more antique. These completed my wardrobe." "<u>Several</u> brilliant parties were given—& I attended all, & must say came off very creditable," she added. "Indeed I enjoyed them <u>very very</u> much."[27]

But with McKinney Jr. gone, Jim managing Willow Cottage, and Lizzie recovering from two hemorrhages of the lungs, Lucy remained preoccupied at best. The fear of losing her "mother-sister," she wrote, "haunted [her] day & night." "How I would <u>hate</u> anyone who would <u>hint</u> such a thing in my presence." In December 1863 the Irion family left Harriette in Columbus and returned to Willow Cottage. By the New Year, Lizzie disclosed her plans to marry her cousin Cullen Barron, who owned a lucrative plantation in the Yazoo-Mississippi Delta. Lucy admitted, "When I first took in the idea that Sis Lizzie was <u>really</u> going to be married—my heart <u>nearly broke</u>!" "I took one <u>long, convulsive cry</u>," she noted, "& then overcame <u>selfishness</u>—she had certainly devoted enough of her life to us—& why not now be willing that she should be happy?—But poor Cordele her victory was not so easily won—she cried constantly for an entire week—indeed she positively refused to be comforted!" Lizzie wed Cullen on a fine spring day in March 1864. One week later Mr. Barron was dead, and Lizzie found herself a widow with an inherited estate. "Just <u>one short week</u> found my <u>sister</u> a Bride, & a Widow!" Lucy wrote. "Her spirit was willing to fill the responsible place God had seen fit to trust to her,—but her <u>fragile frame</u> refused, & May found her again at the Cottage, & on a bed of suffering as she had been the year before!"[28]

The "<u>grim visaged War</u>" had exacted a high price from the Irion family. "Death has been such a frequent visitor in our house-hold during this terrible war," Lucy wrote, "yet we have been much blessed otherwise—Jim has been spared us—& no enemy has been here to molest us, & make us afraid;—while thousands have been thrust out from home, & shelter we have been quietly 'eating under our own <u>vine</u>, & <u>fig-tree</u>'!" Like most Confederates, the inhabitants of Willow Cottage had lost loved ones, suffered from poor crops, and tightened their domestic belts in order to survive the federal blockade. The town's political and social structures may have been hemorrhaging from within, but for the most part it did not show. Sitting on the quieter side of war, Columbus had not been ransacked, destroyed, or permanently occupied by invading troops. Some slaves had left for Union lines, but without a strong federal presence in the region, many had chosen to stay. The women of Columbus had managed plantations and households on their own—some in a "constant state of perturbation to know where the vegetables for the next dinner are coming from"—but few had been compelled to flee their homes or scratch out an unpalatable existence as refugees. While their frills and furbelows had been "turned <u>upside</u>-down, & <u>wrong</u>-<u>side</u>-<u>out-wards</u>," well-to-do young women such as Lucy had entered society in a coming out reminiscent of antebellum times.[29]

Unlike many of their southern neighbors, the Irion family greeted 1865 with many of the outer trappings of their status intact. With news of the Confederacy's defeat, Lucy vowed "to bear all with fortitude, & leave the future to God." "Therefore, altho' all is dark—yet we as a family are lively & cheerful," she added. "Even since the Surrender (5th May '65) we have had our Cottage filled with company, & laughter wild & free, has flowed as in the piping times of '60. My favorite song, & motto is <u>Just</u> let the Yankees wag as they will—Yet we'll all be happy still—Gay & happy—gay & happy—Yes we'll all be happy still."

Lucy's patriotic refrain was perhaps a half-hearted attempt to throw off the yoke of subjugation that bore down on so many of Columbus's homeward-bound soldiers. Still, Lucy had seen enough of war to know that harder times were dawning. When she woke up with a sore throat in May 1865, she was "just enough sick" to "smother the voice of duty" and pay final homage to her patchy existence as a daughter-at-home. "I think I rather enjoyed myself," she admitted. "I lay flat & [on] my back, & <u>read</u> & <u>read</u>! Bustling, meddlesome Yankee-dames would shake their pious heads over such self indulgence, & inward chuckle that the time for such was <u>nearly past</u>;— Well Dame Yankeedoodle I am quite willing that you should both shake your heads, & chuckle too—I am aware of the <u>change</u> which is about to come upon us, therefore I am the more determined to enjoy myself as much & as long as possible!!" Rebuilding, Lucy noted, would require fierce dedication to self-sufficiency and "staid steady woman-hood." "If I can't be a <u>fashionable</u> lady," she declared, "perhaps I can be a <u>useful</u> one."[30]

USEFUL LADIES

Columbus escaped the ravages of war only to be turned upside down by defeat. The town's white men returned home just in time to watch the domestic contours of their mastery flail over abandoned fields and preside at their pinching, servant-free tables. Months after war's end, Mississippi enacted the first Black Codes—restricting the rights of freed people to rent land or own firearms, requiring them to carry written evidence of employment, criminalizing vagrancy, and legalizing the apprenticeship of black children—in a desperate attempt to snuff out African American claims to citizenship. Depressed economic conditions, new sharecropping arrangements, and poor agricultural forecasts created a heady volatility that was soon expressed in campaigns of white terror against the black community.[31]

"Times are so unsettled," Lucy wrote weeks after the surrender. "The horrid 'blue coats' [are] in our midst;—in our streets, in our <u>kitchens</u> (<u>not parlors</u>); & in our <u>churches</u>!" "The gentlemen are like caged tigers—so restless, so anxious for settlement. Negroes all are more or less affected by the Yankee-fever. . . . New goods have been brought to town—but no one has any money to buy anything. Every body feels so poor!" Jim vowed to chase southern elitism to the corners of the Mississippi Delta, but his proposal to relocate the entire family to the Barron plantation was abandoned after the death of McKinney Jr.'s widow, Harriette. Instead, Jim headed northward with Lizzie, while McKinney, Lucy, and Cordele turned their attention to sorting out Harriette's estate. Just as they began to see their way clear, McKinney died suddenly in June 1866. "Oh! it does seem that our family is doomed!" cried Lucy. "How lonely, & unprotected we felt—altho' he had been so much our charge, yet he was our natural protector, & when we laid him away—we were indeed bereft!"[32]

By winter 1866 the Irion family also found themselves without a manager at Willow Cottage, and "every thing on the place" ground to "a perfect <u>stand-still</u>." Lucy and Cordele abandoned town life in a desperate attempt to stave off a wholesale crop failure. "I wish so much I had some one to tell me exactly <u>what to do</u>," Lucy whimpered. "I am so afraid something, or everything will go wrong." Juggling the family holdings had never been Lucy's responsibility; even her domestic capabilities lagged woefully behind Cordele's. Useful womanhood suddenly seemed as elusive as the fashionable ideal she had also dismissed as unattainable. "I know you & Jim will think I am a clumsy hand to attend to matters, & what would be so easy for you, is so hard for me, & I complain so much of hardship, & have so little confidence in my own judgement," she wrote to Lizzie, "but you must bear with me." When her patience wore out, Lucy pleaded with her sister for Jim's return. "If Jim can content himself on a little sandy land farm—after working that rich land,—it will be so delightful to have him live with us," she wrote. "I will be all impatient for him to come, & let us get settled, & I hope <u>never</u> to move again."[33]

Lucy was ill-equipped to manage Willow Cottage, and Jim and Lizzie knew it. By March 1867 Jim had returned to Columbus, and Lucy and Cordele busied themselves with the more genteel trappings of the domestic ideal. "We have at last our furniture at home for the hall, & parlor,—& we think Willow Cottage looks quite spruce," Lucy related to Lizzie. "We have been gardening some,—but the weather is so changeable." Jim's ability to secure "good hands for the farm" and servants for the cottage provided Lucy and Cordele with practical assistance and deep reassurance that emancipation had not obliterated all the markers of white southern womanhood. "Pheobe is just as sweet as she can be, & does 'tend to the Dairy, & cooking so nicely," Lucy noted. "Milly Hayden hops around as spry as ever, & has an eye over everything. Moll does splendidly about her dining-room—& Charles keeps me well supplied with wood; and Woos is a perfect jewel."[34]

An efficient household also dragged Jim out of the melancholy of defeat. Depression and alcoholism were rife among former soldiers, but Jim did not fall into this downward spiral. He successfully negotiated contracts with several of the family's former slaves and ultimately turned an agricultural mess into a profitable farm. With measures of hard work, domestic authority, and resourcefulness, he embraced the possibilities of virtuous manhood. Jim, Lucy declared, "is the gayest man about town. . . . He seems to be getting young again!" After treating the Irion sisters to "some sweet fresh-looking dresses, & a 'perfect-love-of-a hat,'" Jim asked Lucy to fulfill her end of the postwar bargain: transforming his economic gain into a generous home life.[35]

The domestic ideal demanded the creation of the "ineffable, sheltering presence of Home," but even the most adept mistresses could not accomplish this feat on their own. Lucy and Cordele had Pheobe to cook and Sophie to housemaid, and on some level it appeared to Lucy as if everything had changed and nothing had changed. But everything had indeed changed. Freed people were citizens with legal rights to choose where they lived, where they worked, and whom they married. Lucy wanted to believe in the enduring ties binding her family to their "faithful" former servants. At Willow Cottage many of the family's former slaves took the surnames of Irion, Barron, Holderness, or Hayden and continued to work for the family. Malinda "Woos" Barron, Moll, and Pheobe were instrumental to the operation of household affairs, and at times Lucy described their work in detail. Overwhelmingly, though, they circled through Lucy's correspondence in incidental comments, such as "all Colords send howdy," where she drew upon the rhetoric of slavery in an effort to ignore black women's newfound rights to citizenship and households of their own.[36]

Indeed, Lucy viewed her relationships with freed people through a typical lens of paternalist practicality: those who worked for the benefit of her family were regarded as trustworthy, while those who exercised their right to leave or requested higher wages or better working conditions were cast out of the paternalist fold, both figuratively and literally. When Jim was unable to reach an agreement with the freed "John Irons & family," Lucy dismissed their departure. "Jim did'ent want [them]," she stated. "They were too expensive—so they have gone up on black-Creek. Sophie has gone to town—<u>where</u> I know not." Instead she heaped praise on those who had signed contracts for another year. "Woos is just as smart as she can be cleans the house, washes & irons, & <u>milks</u> the cows," she gushed. "<u>Moll</u>, of course holds high domain in the dining-room—& big George is <u>jobber</u> generally—<u>Lena</u> of course is in the field—she is as much a part of the place as the smoke-house!" Even in the postwar world of emancipation and contracts, Lucy compared Lena to one of Willow Cottage's outbuildings, depicting her as an organic cog in the Irion agricultural enterprise and as a tool to be used in the construction of the new southern household.[37]

Yet as Lucy well knew, while slavery may have guaranteed consistency, emancipation did not. The free labor arrangement demanded that useful postwar daughters-at-home acquaint themselves with all aspects of domestic life. By winter 1867 Lucy had fulfilled her promise to Jim: after months of extensive training, she was well placed to manage Willow Cottage when Lizzie returned to her plantation. "Well, in earnest—I am astonished at my own self," she exclaimed proudly. "I never imagined I should feel <u>real pleasure</u> in house-keeping—but wonderful to relate, <u>I do</u>. I have never been late for breakfast since I assumed the responsibility of the <u>coffee</u>-pot. We arise at the heathenish hour of 5 O.clock, as often as any of the house-hold, <u>white or black</u>, can awaken, & that is <u>quite</u> often. I am very much tempted sometimes for the indulgence of a <u>little more sleep</u>, & a little longer morning nap—but then I know how important it is for a <u>house-keeper</u> to be <u>astir</u>—especially <u>these times</u>!" "Keeping-house is so very much easier to me now, that I have fully made up my mind to <u>do</u> it with all my might," she added. "Things which used to be so dreadfully hard, are now done with resolution & decision." Lucy made herself familiar with "every <u>crack</u>, & <u>corner</u> of the <u>Dairy</u>, <u>Pantry</u>, & <u>Smoke-house</u>," "accomplished a good deal in the way of sewing," tried her hand at making jellies and custard, and even "superintend[ed] the boiling of the slops for the cows." "Soon as I can have the nerve to venture amongst the horned occupants," she announced, "I am going to learn to milk—but that is in the <u>uncertain</u> future." Lucy admitted to being a "sad poultry tender" but marveled at her newfound knowledge of hog killing. "Now I know every item," she informed Lizzie. "Why I believe I could disect a hog with as much ease as Aunt Hayden ever could." Washing days were an exercise in imitation. "I try to follow directly in your foot-steps," Lucy told Cordele, "& go around suspecting every crack, & corner of concealing some soiled garment—all the handkerchiefs, towels, & collars are tied together—likewise all '<u>Mars's</u>' shirts are tied together by the tails, & away they go in the wash-tub!"[38]

Domestic devotion did not consume every minute of Lucy's day. Dividing her "time & attention equally between <u>home</u>, & <u>society</u>," Lucy enjoyed her share of visiting and parties. In January 1868 she met John Abert Neilson and "lost <u>me</u>

heart!" Neilson, a former medical student with dark hair, sharp features, and blue eyes, lived at Belmont, his family's estate about nine miles northeast of Columbus. The second son of William Walker Neilson and Louisa Pinckney Abert Neilson, John abandoned his studies in 1861 to enlist as a private in Company K, Fourteenth Infantry Regiment Mississippi. He was captured after the surrender of Fort Donelson in February 1862, and after a brief stint at Chicago's Camp Douglas, the daring Private Neilson escaped confinement by donning a smuggled federal uniform and slipping through Union lines. John returned to Mississippi to be commissioned a captain and served out the remainder of the war with his company. In 1866 he traveled to France to study medicine, later returning to Columbus to establish his own farm on a corner of the family estate. Putting aside his medical aspirations, John devoted his time to hard work and winning Lucy's heart. Their courtship was made up of quiet interludes, chance encounters, and an understanding that there would be no public declarations until John was financially fit to take Lucy as his wife. Lucy was entirely happy with the arrangement. She was content with her lot at Willow Cottage; the farm rolled along at a steady pace, and Jim's partnership in a dry goods business furnished her with the pick of calicos, tarlatans, and merinos. Home had become "so beautiful now—to my partial eyes at least." "The wide spreading—full blossoming <u>Mimosas</u>, now standing in all their glory—the green carpet of grass underneath—the beautiful little humming-birds all around the top," she sighed. "What sight can equal it!" Instead of "searching out new duties" as she suspected she should, Lucy made home pleasantries her only work.[39]

News that Lizzie was suffering with severe "inflammation of stomach & liver" while visiting relatives in northern Mississippi jolted Lucy from her comfortable domestic cocoon, and she made a dash to the Nesbitt estate in February 1870 to nurse her sister. Lizzie "laid low upon her sick-bed" for weeks; at one point "her pastor came to prepare her mind for the great change—to give her his blessing & last <u>good-bye</u>." While Lizzie bore her affliction with "great fortitude," a flustered Lucy wished "nearly every hour" for servants Woos and Moll to assist with her round-the-clock vigil. By April, Lucy became frustrated by Lizzie's slow recovery and longed to return home. "You may rest assured that we will start home just as <u>soon as possible</u>—but as to appointing the day, or even <u>the week</u>, it is <u>impossible</u>," she informed those at Willow Cottage. "You have no idea the number of changes, which Trot under-goes during one day—& how can we even <u>plan</u> upon such uncertainty?" "I try to be patient, & <u>pleasant</u>," she added, "but oh! sometimes, I am ungovernably depressed on account of Trot's health." Lizzie's condition improved enough to allow the sisters to return to Columbus in May. After a brief respite Lizzie, Lucy, and Bess prepared for a summer jaunt at Bailey Springs, a genteel resort in nearby Lauderdale County, Alabama. The news of Lucy's impending departure threw John into action; with financial independence within reach, he refused to let Lucy slip away to the springs without formalizing their relationship. He proposed on a moonlit buggy ride on July 11, 1870. "Oh! mercy, I was not very happy those <u>first days</u>," Lucy remarked. "I wished I had not been so precipitate in my decision. . . . how sincerely I wished <u>things</u> had not been settled as they were."[40]

Bailey Springs provided Lucy with the time and distance she needed to consider John's proposal. Immersing herself in the resort's quiet gentility, Lucy entered into a superficial correspondence with John that centered on Bailey's social gaiety, its comfortable rooms, "pleasant little dances," and "kind & attentive" guests. "Our room is almost always filled with company;—there is the Alley, with its <u>inviting</u> balls, to be visited every day—there are walks proposed, &, of <u>course</u>, taken—& oh! a hundred ways to steal the golden moments from our group," she related to John. "You ask how I spend my time, I would really be ashamed to write out a programme of one day's idleness—you would never have any respect for me again." As Lucy clung to the fleeting remnants of young womanhood, John couched his romantic overtures in the domestic rhetoric of virtuous manhood; hewn timber for windowsills, ploughed fields, and days "closely confined" to the office were the foundations of "a brighter & happier existence" that he was building for his "brave and devoted life-champion." When Lucy returned to Columbus in late August 1870, she "studiously" thwarted any attempts by John to broach a more serious discussion about "plans & hopes." "His <u>tenderness</u> towards me most breaks my heart!" she confessed, guiltily. "If I had a <u>whit less</u> confidence in <u>him</u> to whom I trust my future-life, I could not let matters go forward."[41]

John sensed Lucy's hesitancy. The couple's resolve to avert the "brazen stare of the world" had come at a price; swapping letters and photographs and relying on awkward, distant encounters at parties or in church were a far cry from their relaxed courtship the previous summer. With John working at Wildwood, Jim on a business trip to New York, and Lizzie and Bess visiting West Virginia's White Sulphur Springs, Lucy busied herself in the details of harvest time. "You would laugh to see me, trying to do (& <u>look</u>) like Jim—with his night-lamp, pass-book & pencil going down & weighing the cotton," she remarked to Lizzie. As Lucy managed 1,634 pounds of cotton and 196 bushels of wheat, John set aside his agricultural work to pen Miss Irion an impassioned declaration of love. "I do not claim to be different from other men—but <u>I do claim</u> to be <u>honest</u> in all of my expressions of <u>love for you</u>," he reassured her. "It is this that I wish you to remember, & always to bear in mind that the indulgence of momentary pleasure is not <u>paramount nor equal</u> to what I trust the future has in store for <u>us</u>." When Jim's dry goods partnership "burst forth most disastrously" in December 1870, John claimed his self-worth amid the "<u>shadow</u> of [familial] dishonor." "And my dear 'Jack' clung closer in the <u>storm</u>—as did his <u>family</u>—dear Miss Sallie especially—,"

Lucy noted, "& _each_ visit made him all the more _dear_, & he was all the more urgent for the _day_ to be appointed." With a symbol of her happiness—"as endless, as bright & as purely refined"—now adorning her finger, Lucy trimmed her lilac dress in anticipation of her spring wedding. Her life story would be fashioned within the collective bonds of family and community—celebrating both the traditional and nondependent ideals of womanhood—to rebuild respectability, domestic alliances, and community ties in the postwar South.[42]

NOTES

All Irion-Neilson material is located in the Irion Neilson Family Papers at the Mississippi Department of Archives and History, Jackson, Mississippi, unless otherwise stated. Please note that for consistency I refer to the 'Eliza Lucy Irion Neilson diary' throughout (a document that spans Lucy's life from adolescence to adulthood).

1. Eliza Lucy Irion Neilson diary, undated recollections, 1870. On the transition from belle to wife and mistress, see Scott, _Southern Lady_, 27–28; Fox-Genovese, _Plantation Household_, 113; Edwards, _Scarlett_, 21; and Jabour, _Scarlett's Sisters_, 189–90. On "marriage trauma," see Jabour, _Scarlett's Sisters_, 165.

2. John Abert Neilson to Eliza Lucy Irion, September 15, 1870; Eliza Lucy Irion to Elizabeth Charlotte Irion Barron, September 19, 9, 1870; Eliza Lucy Irion Neilson diary, December 1870. On engagement and the transformative effects of marriage on the family, see Jabour, _Scarlett's Sisters_, 151–80, 189–90.

3. Eliza Lucy Irion Neilson to Elizabeth Charlotte Irion Barron and Elizabeth Parthenia Irion, June 21, 1872; Eliza Lucy Irion Neilson diary, undated recollections, 1870; Eliza Lucy Irion to Elizabeth Charlotte Irion Barron and Elizabeth Parthenia Irion, August 27, 1870; Eliza Lucy Irion Neilson diary, undated recollections, 1871. On negative perceptions of marriage, see Censer, _Reconstruction_, 35.

4. Eliza Lucy Irion Neilson diary, undated recollections, 1871; Eliza Lucy Irion, "Engaged," July 11, 1870.

5. For earlier interpretations that regard the Civil War as a watershed for southern women, see Scott, _Southern Lady_; and Massey, _Bonnet Brigades_. For recent interpretations that highlight conservative models of postwar womanhood, see Rable, _Civil Wars_; Faust, _Mothers_; Whites, _Civil War_; Edwards, _Gendered Strife_; and Edwards, _Scarlett_. For recent watershed interpretations, see Censer, _Reconstruction_; Jabour, _Scarlett's Sisters_; Ott, _Confederate Daughters_; and Janney, _Burying the Dead_.

6. Rosen, _Terror_; Whites, _Civil War_, 132–59; Whites, _Gender Matters_, 19. See also Faust, _Mothers_, 253–54; Edwards, _Gendered Strife_, 6, 27; and Bercaw, _Gendered Freedoms_, 78–80.

7. Edwards, _Gendered Strife_, 107–44; Edwards, _Scarlett_, 182–85.

8. Censer, _Reconstruction_ 39; Janney, _Burying the Dead 8, 3_; Gardner, _Blood_; Jabour, _Scarlett's Sisters_, 277–83; Cox, _Dixie's Daughters_.

9. Bercaw, _Gendered Freedoms_, 137, 172.

10. Smith-Rosenberg, "Female World."

11. Eliza Lucy Irion Neilson diary, undated recollections, 1843–58. For a biographical sketch of Eliza Lucy Irion Neilson, see Lohrenz and Stamper, _Mississippi Homespun_, 28–33.

12. Eliza Lucy Irion Neilson diary, undated recollections, 1843–58. On male independence, mastery, and political credit, see Edwards, *Scarlett,* 3; and Friend and Glover, *Southern Manhood,* ix. On the development and consolidation of white men's legal and political rights, see Edwards, *People,* 220–55.

13. Eliza Lucy Irion Neilson diary, undated recollections, 1843–58.

14. Ibid.; Elizabeth Charlotte Irion diary, January 9, 1, 1853.

15. Eliza Lucy Irion Neilson diary, undated recollections, 1843–58. On women's education in the antebellum South, see Farnham, *Education;* Rable, *Civil* Wars, 17–22; Stowe, *Intimacy and Power,* 142–53; and Jabour, *Scarlett's Sisters,* 47–82.

16. Eliza Lucy Irion Neilson diary, undated recollections, 1843–58.

17. Ibid.; McKinney F. Irion Jr. to Eliza Lucy Irion, August 22, 1859.

18. Eliza Lucy Irion Neilson diary, undated recollections, 1843–58. On religious conversion, see Edwards, *Scarlett,* 19; Jabour, *Scarlett's Sisters,* 39–43; and Stephan, *Redeeming,* 168–72.

19. Eliza Lucy Irion Neilson diary, undated recollections, 1843–58.

20. Eliza Lucy Irion Neilson diary, undated recollections, 1860.

21. Ibid.; James William Gray Irion to Eliza Lucy Irion, December 14, 1859. On daughters-at-home, see Jabour, *Scarlett's Sisters,* 83–111. On coming out rituals, see Edwards, *Scarlett,* 20–21; and Roberts, *Confederate Belle,* 30–34.

22. Eliza Lucy Irion Neilson diary, undated recollections, 1860.

23. Eliza Lucy Irion Neilson diary, undated recollections, 1861, 1865. On young Confederate women, see Roberts, *Confederate Belle;* Jabour, *Scarlett's Sisters,* 239–80; and Ott, *Confederate Daughters.* On patriotic womanhood, see Faust, *Mothers;* Rable, *Civil Wars;* and Whites, *Civil War.*

24. Eliza Lucy Irion Neilson diary, undated recollections, 1861–62; James William Gray Irion to Eliza Lucy Irion, May 6, September 19, 1861; January 1, February 5, 1862. McKinney F. Irion Jr. echoed the sentiments of his brother about army life. See McKinney F. Irion Jr. to Eliza Lucy Irion, July 2, 1862.

25. Eliza Lucy Irion Neilson diary, undated recollections, 1862.

26. Ibid.; Eliza Lucy Irion to James William Gray Irion, June 26, 1862. See also July 4, August 26, 1862.

27. Eliza Lucy Irion Neilson diary, undated recollections, 1843–58, 1862–63. On coming out in wartime, see Roberts, *Confederate Belle,* 76–93.

28. Eliza Lucy Irion Neilson diary, undated recollections, 1863–64.

29. Eliza Lucy Irion Neilson diary, undated recollections, 1865; Eliza Lucy Irion to James William Gray Irion, July 15, 1862.

30. Eliza Lucy Irion Neilson diary, March 3, June 1865.

31. Foner, *Reconstruction,* 199–200; Bercaw, *Gendered Freedoms,* 81.

32. Eliza Lucy Irion Neilson diary, undated recollections, 1865–66.

33. Eliza Lucy Irion to Elizabeth Charlotte Irion Barron and James William Gray Irion, January 7, 1867.

34. Eliza Lucy Irion to Elizabeth Charlotte Irion Barron, March 1, November 23, 1867; Eliza Lucy Irion Neilson diary, undated recollections, January 1867.

35. Eliza Lucy Irion to Elizabeth Charlotte Irion Barron, May 4, 1867; Eliza Lucy Irion Neilson diary, undated recollections, 1865. On virtuous manhood, see Edwards, *Gendered Strife*, 121–29. Bercaw, *Gendered Freedoms*, argues that postwar masculinity centered on "depression, vengeance and mythmaking" (77–78).

36. Eliza Lucy Irion Neilson diary, undated recollections, 1865.

37. Eliza Lucy Irion to Cornelia A. Parthenia Irion, January 13, 1868. On the postwar household, see Glymph, *House*, 65, 137–66; Weiner, *Mistresses*, 185–233; Edwards, *Scarlett*, 171–85; and Censer, *Reconstruction*, 51–90.

38. Eliza Lucy Irion to Elizabeth Charlotte Irion Barron, November 23, December 14, 1867; Eliza Lucy Irion to Cornelia A. Parthenia Irion, December 16, 1867.

39. Eliza Lucy Irion to Cornelia A. Parthenia Irion, January 13, 1868; Eliza Lucy Irion Neilson diary, undated recollections, 1867, 1869. See also John Abert Neilson diary, 1861–62.

40. Eliza Lucy Irion Neilson diary, undated recollections, 1870; Eliza Lucy Irion to Elizabeth Parthenia Irion and Cornelia A. Parthenia Irion, March 23, 1870; Eliza Lucy Irion to Elizabeth Parthenia Irion, Cornelia A. Parthenia Irion, and James William Gray Irion, April 21, 1870; Eliza Lucy Irion to Elizabeth Parthenia Irion and Cornelia A. Parthenia Irion, April 27, 1870.

41. Eliza Lucy Irion to John Abert Neilson, July 17, 27, 23, 1870; John Abert Neilson to Eliza Lucy Irion, July 30, September 16, 1870; Sophie Abert Neilson Lewis to Eliza Lucy Irion, August 27, October 4, 1870; Eliza Lucy Irion to Elizabeth Charlotte Irion Barron and Elizabeth Parthenia Irion, August 27, 1870; Eliza Lucy Irion to Elizabeth Charlotte Irion Barron, September 19, 1870. Stephan, *Redeeming*, argues that evangelical men commonly used the "idiom of domesticity" in courtship, because of their belief in mastery and the transformative devotional powers of home (83–84).

42. John Abert Neilson to Eliza Lucy Irion, September 16, November 15, 1870; Eliza Lucy Irion to Elizabeth Charlotte Irion Barron, September 9, 1870; Eliza Lucy Irion to James William Gray Irion, September 9, 1870; Eliza Lucy Irion Neilson diary, undated recollections, 1870–71. Engagements were often kept private to protect a woman's reputation and in the postwar period until a man could achieve economic independence. See Jabour, *Scarlett's Sisters*, 151–80; and Ott, *Confederate Daughters*, 122.

One

Married and Housekeeping

APRIL–AUGUST 1871

*L*ucy and John Neilson spent their first few days of married life at Willow Cottage, went to church on Sunday, and then embarked on their homeward journey. After taking dinner with John's family at Belmont, Lucy caught her first glimpse of Wildwood in the fading spring twilight. The farm was nestled in a wooded grove on a corner of the Neilson estate, around nine miles northeast of Columbus. "What a crowd of thoughts & emotions have whirled thro' my heart & brain," Lucy remarked of her first six weeks as wife and mistress. "I have lived <u>more</u> than in any previous six <u>months</u> of my life."[1]

While John had worked hard to establish Wildwood long before his marriage to Lucy, the farm remained in its infancy. "We are living now in what will be the ell of the house when complete—tho' as it is, it looks like a finished cottage—with galleries on either side," Lucy explained to her cousin Laura Corrie Nesbitt Myers. "It is well built, with high ceiling, large windows, & <u>closets</u> every where possible. Then just by my room, two or three feet from the back gallery, is the <u>kitchen</u>!—now is'ent that nice & convenient;—you should see the <u>cute little stove</u>, & the tin ware shining on the shelves, & all sorts of indispensables of kitchen furniture, there just to hand." Lucy and John had also devised an extensive list of future renovations. "In the yard there is an office-room, which I will fit up as soon as possible, for the accommodation of gentleman-visitors," Lucy noted. "Off from the east gallery is the garden—which by the by is quite flourishing. The prospective orchard will be off from the <u>west</u> gallery—And in the <u>prospective front</u> there is a most beautiful <u>grove</u> of forest trees."

Lucy's enthusiasm for her life with John, however, was tempered by the distance that separated her from her family at Willow Cottage: her brother Jim; her sisters, Lizzie and Cordele; and her niece Bess. "I am not homesick, but <u>home-'folks'-sick</u>," she conceded. A steady stream of correspondence kept the longing at bay. Informing her family of her domestic progress, Lucy benefited from the practical assistance of female kin who recognized that the fulfillment of the domestic ideal contributed to rebuilding family reputation more generally.[2]

Eliza Lucy Irion Neilson Diary.
Irion Neilson Family Papers.
*Courtesy of Mississippi Department
of Archives and History.*

*Casually sipping lemonade with her sister-in-law Sarah Dandridge Neilson (1840–
1913), Lucy assumed the guise of domestic bliss while relying firmly on female kin to
assist her with the onerous task of setting up Wildwood. Her pleas for family to visit
were made on the basis of practical as well as emotional considerations.*

Lucy to Bess

Wildwood—
April 19th/.71.

My <u>darling</u> Bess.

Yesterday afternoon, as <u>Sister</u>, & I were on the gallery drinking lemonade,
she looked up the road, & espied some one coming, whom she thought was <u>Dr
Parhamm</u>,[3] we were both in a high state of <u>ease</u> as to <u>dress</u>, & <u>hair</u>, & I immediately took flight leaving my goblet of lemonade behind. I could'ent bear that
one of the neighbors should see "the <u>bride</u>"(?) in such a careless dress—but lo! &
behold! it was not the Dr, but Claude Blewett,[4] bringing me your <u>precious</u> letter!
He did'ent come in, but handed it to one of the servants. Little did I think that <u>he</u>,
above all boys of my acquaintance, should be the bearer of pleasant news to me!

Wildwood —

April 19th 1871.

My darling Bess.

Yesterday afternoon, as Sister, &
I were on the gallery drinking lemonade,
she looked up the road, & espied some one
coming, whom she thought was Dr Parhamer
, we were both in a high state of _ _ as
to dress, & hair, or I immediately took flight
leaving my goblet of lemonade behind — I
could not bear that one of the neighbors should
see "the bride"(?) in such a careless dress —
but lo! & behold! it was not the Dr, but
Claude Blewett, bringing me your precious
letter! He did'ent come in, but handed
it to one of the servants. Little did I think
that he, above all boys of my acquaintance,
should be the bearer of pleasant news
to me! But he brought "Miss Irion" letter
to me, & I shall ever thank him! That

Letter from Eliza Lucy Irion Neilson to her niece
Elizabeth Parthenia Irion, April 19, 1871.
Irion Neilson Family Papers.
*Courtesy of Mississippi Department
of Archives and History.*

But he brought "Miss Irons" letter to me, & I shall ever thank him! That is one of the "little deeds of kindness,"[5] of which the little hymn speaks—& if all make the recipients as happy as I, no wonder they are sung! I sat down, & devoured the contents—& laughed, & kinder half cried, & then laughed again & again, over the ludicrous pictures of grief which you drew. T'was splendidly written, & Sister enjoyed it quite as much as I—at supper when my plough-boy came home, I read it aloud to him, & you should have seen his enjoyment! I do thank you for the pleasure you gave.

I wish to answer right away, but you know I had to rub the poor weary plough-man's aching head after supper, & now today Sophie, Kate, Maud,[6] & Cynthia have been spending the day with us, & I have excused myself for a little while, just to tell you how glad I was to get your letter & that I will answer at length, whenever I can! We cannot tell yet, whether we can come down tomorrow-night to Mrs Ottley's,[7] or not—but if it rains much, perhaps we can! You all must not be disappointed if we do not come. I wish much for Trot to come on Friday—but I don't know if Mr N— can get off! You & Jim must come Sunday—whether Trot & Cordele can or not—there are not many bad places in the road—, & I wish they would venture in the carriage. I must see you all! I am not homesick, but home-"folks"-sick—I wish for you all to see how snugly we (?) are fixed! Sister is so good, so considerate, & so sisterly—Trot would love her for it! I must not stay out of company another moment. I don't pretend this is an answer to your note!—

Tell Woos[8] I am almost as anxious for her to come as any of you. Please accept our hearts warmest love. Mr N— is even more tender & loving than when I was at home. Give love to every-body who inquires for me. I wish all my friends could see my sweet new home!—Good-bye—good-bye—tell Jim I count upon him as a most frequent visitor—God bless you all—

In haste & love
Lucy—

Respects to all colored friends

NOTES

1. Eliza Lucy Irion Neilson to Laura Corrie Nesbitt Myers, May 24, 1871. Laura (b. ca. 1845) was the daughter of Demsey Nesbitt (b. ca. 1810) and Matilda Nesbitt (ca. 1807–86), wife of farmer Calvin R. Myers (ca. 1838–1914), and Lucy's cousin. Lucy often referred to her as "Nic."

2. James William Gray Irion (1838–1911); Elizabeth Charlotte Irion Barron (1831–1911); Cornelia A. Parthenia Irion (1836–1924); Elizabeth Parthenia Irion (1854–1937).

3. Dr. Robert Parham (1839–76). During the Civil War he served as an assistant surgeon in Company S, Twentieth Infantry Regiment Mississippi.

4. Claude Clarence Blewett (1853–1914), son of farmer Thomas Garton Blewett Jr. (1818–96) and Laura Emeline Martin Blewett (1825–64).

5. Julia A. Fletcher Carney, "Little Things" (1845), in Opie and Opie, eds., *Children's Verse*, 182.

6. Sophie Abert Neilson Lewis (1845–1925), wife of farmer Sylvester Creswell Lewis (b. 1839), mother of Maud Lewis (b. 1869), and sister of John Abert Neilson. At this time the Lewis family lived in Livingston, Alabama. Catherine Elizabeth Barry (1848–1906), daughter of farmer Bartley Barry (b. ca. 1811) and Mary Bruce Barry.

7. Ellen Gertrude Williams Ottley (1840–1916), wife of retired merchant John King Ottley (1814–80).

8. Malinda "Woos" Barron (b. ca. 1853), daughter of Nancy Barron (b. ca. 1830), had worked for the Irion family for several years. The freed people mentioned in Lucy's correspondence with the surname Barron came from Elizabeth Charlotte Irion Barron's plantation at Friar's Point.

ℬ

Lucy was not the only one adjusting to changed circumstances. With Lizzie visiting her sister at Wildwood, Bess declared that much was missing from the family circle. "You have been my <u>mother</u> when I had none, you have been my <u>sister</u> always, . . . my love for you is a passionate mixture of <u>child sister & friend</u>," she wrote Lucy on April 20, 1871. "What you have been to me is only a very little part of what you have been to others," she continued. "To Auntie whose impulsive fiery nature needed a help, you have been one. . . . To Uncle Jim who indulged in different moods, who was reserved & sometimes cold, sad & sometimes desponding, you have always been a golden beam of sunshine—To Aunt Neanie, whose reserved ways, diffident manners & seeming indifference have been as a cloud to her & others, you have been the ray of light which dispelled them all, & made the brightest sunshine in a shady place." In response Lucy tried to reassure Bess that the ties of marriage could never break the ties of family affection.

Lucy to Bess

<u>Wild-wood</u> (<u>oh! I forgot</u>)
~~Willow Cottage.~~
May 4th/.71.

My <u>dear,</u> <u>darling</u> Bess!

Your <u>notes</u> sent out by <u>Brother</u>[1] were received, & read with as <u>much pleasure,</u> as if I had <u>not seen you</u> in the meantime! Oh! my child how can I thank you for them—<u>especially</u> the one written <u>first</u>! I feel utterly unable to express the emotions which it aroused. Rest <u>assured tho'</u>, <u>every word</u> is weighed, & every sentiment duly appreciated. It almost scares me to feel that I am <u>loved</u> so much by one whose good will I prize so highly as yours,—because I am conscious of such <u>unworthiness</u>. How could you think that I would <u>laugh</u> at your letter, or think the sentiment therein expressed <u>foolish</u> & <u>school-girlish</u>! My dear, I never before read <u>such</u> a letter from so young a person! Laugh indeed! I found then great tears raining down my cheeks most plenteously! And now, I read & <u>re</u>-<u>read</u>, trying to <u>frame an answer</u>—but oh! I <u>cannot</u>, I cannot! You know <u>when most</u> I feel, I find <u>no</u> expression! What words can I employ whereby to convince you of my earnest love, & heartfelt thanks! Yes, my child, you have my <u>tenderest</u> love, of all others in this wide world! You are & will ever be what <u>none</u> other can be to me! I have for you a feeling which was never before awakened for any other than yourself! And can you believe, can you <u>persuade</u> yourself to fancy, even for a moment, that my interest will ever flag! Can I ever turn an indifferent <u>ear</u> to anything which concerns you! Remember I am as much yours as I <u>ever was</u>! I have no <u>jealous lord</u>[2] to guard my affections—but one whose heart turns with as much warmth & love to you as <u>mine</u> (<u>almost</u>)—so always <u>know</u> & <u>feel</u> that <u>we</u> are ever ready, & anxious to sympathize with you in <u>every</u> hope, disappointment, joy or sadness. Don't have me to reiterate—but <u>feel</u> in your eager heart that <u>we</u> are <u>friends true</u> & <u>trustworthy</u>!![3]

You compliment me highly by representing that I took the sunshine away from <u>home</u>, when I left—<u>you</u> are mistaken—<u>none</u> have <u>more</u> cheerfulness about them than you, & I am sure you'll never allow <u>any clouds</u> to shadow, or pale the sunlight of your heart, but will endeavor to make it pervade every nook & cranny of the dear old home! <u>Make all</u> feel it's glorifying influence! Such a person, as yourself, has always much <u>influence</u>, ask God to assist you in throwing it on the right side. I feel satisfied away from home, when I <u>know</u> you are there, for I feel confident that every member of the family is happier for having you with them. I could not resist the temptation of reading your letter aloud to Trot & Mr N—: I know you will forgive me, when you think what pleasure you gave them! Trot was perfectly delighted with it & says she knows <u>no</u> other girl of your age, could express themselves so well! I never saw her show as much <u>pride</u> for her child. As for your Uncle John, he <u>sat</u> in <u>tearful</u> admiration! I shall keep it in my <u>journal</u>, & whenever I wish to feel right <u>good</u>, I will read it! It does seem that the fates are against your ever getting to see <u>us</u>! Mr Neilson, has to go on horse-back on account of the water, & of course you cannot come. Lizzie Symons[4] was also disappointed in your not coming, & also in her own <u>failure</u> to get here. <u>Sister</u> came from Mr Symons this morning thro' <u>seas</u> of water! Never mind! I shall hope for <u>Sunday</u>! Then, perhaps, <u>you</u> & <u>Jim can come</u>! I cannot rest until <u>all</u> my family have been to see us in our sweet <u>Wildwood</u>! I am going to keep Trot just as long as possible, & then <u>Cordele must</u> come, & <u>stay</u> a "<u>whit</u>" with me. Oh! I have <u>lots</u>

more to say—but it is late, & Mr N— will start so soon in the morning, I cannot write then! It will be our <u>first separation for</u> so <u>long a time</u>! Ahem! Poor me!! Kiss Mrs Eager[5] for us, & tell her we wish so often for her! Tell all the friends <u>white & black</u>, to come to see us! Sister & Trot send so much love! Sister thanks you for <u>your note</u>, which she received today. Do come <u>Sunday</u> certain <u>you</u> & <u>Jim</u>! Kiss <u>Miss</u> for your own,

Aunt Ida

ℰ

After a short stay at Wildwood, Lizzie returned to Willow Cottage, leaving Lucy to contemplate her marriage, domesticity, and home life.

Lucy to Bess

Wildwood.
May 16th/.71

My dear, dear Bess,

I have seated myself for letter-writing! I have opened my poor little <u>bursting</u> port-folio, & there lie some dozen <u>unanswered</u> letters—they look up at me very reproachfully—they say "Every one of us bear loving words, written by loving hands, & dictated by loving hearts;—we came when <u>most</u> you appreciated us & yet having been gratified by the evidences we bear of <u>remembrance</u>, you make no exertion to respond, & quiet your upbraiding conscience by saying 'each of you shall have a <u>long</u> answer, when I feel in the <u>mood</u>'"!—Yes I turn them all over, look at the <u>date</u>, & then find myself astonished that <u>such</u> a time has elapsed since their reception. I can't decide, which deserves to be answered <u>first</u> so as a compromise I select <u>you</u>, my dear old Bess, because you have been so <u>very</u>, <u>very</u> kind in writing <u>us every</u> week. Rest assured this <u>attention</u> on your part is highly appreciated by your grateful <u>Uncle</u> & <u>T'Ida</u>.

For the first time since our marriage I am left alone with my <u>h-u-s-b-a-n-d</u>(!) —Sabbath evening when I left Willow Cottage I could scarcely keep the tears back—especially when my dear Trot would keep crying, every time I spoke a word! I wish she would try to tell me good-bye cheerfully—for all the time I am separated from her, I see her in tears, with the pitiful quiver of the lip as she kisses me! Then too I am constantly fearful of her health, & wonder if you would not send for me immediately if she should be taken with one of those dreadful spells. She imagines I am very independent of you all, & has once told me, that I would return to my <u>old love</u> & <u>longing</u> for you at home! Just as if I had ever <u>ceased</u> feeling it! I <u>know</u> I love Mr Neilson as earnestly, & <u>entirely</u> as ever woman loved a man—but not one shade has the <u>great</u> love cooled the warmth of the <u>old</u>-family-devotion! I wish you [and] every one to <u>know</u> & <u>feel</u> that I am unchanged[.] Indeed! if there is a change at all, I feel <u>truer</u>, <u>warmer</u>, <u>more dependent</u> than ever, <u>because</u> of my separation—I feel something akin to jealously lest the <u>keen interest</u> which we have ever felt for each other should grow dull. Let us cherish the <u>dear old love</u> with tender care, & let's luxuriate in its' <u>freedom</u> & warmth as we have ever done—giving <u>no</u> grounds for <u>doubts</u> & <u>fears</u>! We <u>know</u> each other well, & we love each other well! Let the <u>word</u> "change" never be <u>thought</u> of, in our innermost hearts much less <u>mentioned</u> as a thing possible! Each of you know that I could never be content away from home, with any less <u>perfect</u> a man, than Mr Neilson. But oh! Bess, if you knew him as I do, you could never think it strange, that I am so happy away from <u>home</u>—the <u>old</u> one. When you come, you will see <u>how many</u> "strokes of the hammer have been given for <u>Lucy</u>" to make her <u>new</u> home comfortable, & convenient. Every tender care is taken, lest the <u>old</u> home should be <u>pined</u> for! Then there is so much nobleness of purpose, earnestness of duty both to God & man. <u>Thank God</u> for the love of such a man! May you, my dear child, some day feel as I feel! And my heartfelt prayer is that your future husband may combine the qualities of mine! Don't think me <u>love-sick</u>. I am no such thing—this is the first time I have written <u>one word</u> of praise of 'John,' & it is to <u>you all</u>, & <u>no one else</u>! I did not think to express myself quite so freely—but "what is writ is writ"![1] The wonder is that 'a body' can refrain from giving some expression, when their heart is <u>so</u> very full! I don't believe I am ashamed of it either! "Miss" may think it "<u>fast doings</u>," but I have committed myself.

We got on very well last Sabbath evening—tho' the roads were quite heavy, & the carriage heavily loaded. I remind myself very much of a <u>grasping cousin</u> we once had, who loaded her wagons so full of house-hold stuffs from the old homestead, as to break them & the horses all down! One of our ponies (Josephine) was well <u>fagged</u> out when we got to Belmont, & Mr Neilson espying another of his horses roving around, caught her up in the middle of her <u>leisurely</u> preambles, & hitched her in, releasing the weary <u>Josephine</u>—(he is very <u>tender</u> of her, because of her <u>name</u>). We were too late arriving at Belmont to take tea with the good people; altho' they insisted—yet Mr N— thought we <u>best</u> go on home, & <u>see to things</u>, & I like a 'gude wife'[2] thought so too—& on we came. Found Mary & Fannie[3] had taken good care of everything. George[4] was in high spirits & stepped around & made himself both <u>at home</u> & <u>useful</u>—which you know don't <u>every time</u> happen so happily to combine! We left Sister at Belmont with expectation of going down to town the next day—I did wish she could come on & spend <u>one</u> more night with us, but was ashamed of my selfishness & said never a word! We had a cosy little tea all by ourselves—it felt right queer—& I believe I realized more fully that I was married & <u>house-keeping</u> than I ever did. Mr Neilson & I had a good long talk after supper—& <u>need</u> I add how <u>sweet</u> to me!

Monday-morning of course was busy enough—what with getting the house in order, & moving things into the <u>new</u> kitchen, & getting the <u>Col</u> under head-way with his white-washing, the morning passed quickly. But when the dinner hour with its attendant <u>excitement</u> was over, when Mr N— had gone—& Fannie & George went about their work—a feeling of loneliness crept over me—nor was it kept back by frequent peeps into Sister's room, which looked so suggestive of her, & yet was so painfully <u>empty</u>! I thought of you all at home, & felt <u>cheated</u> that <u>none</u> came with me. I had plenty of <u>work</u> which might & <u>should</u> have occupied my idle hands—but I was too unsettled to go at anything—so I <u>dallied</u> around doing nothing but looking at myself in the <u>mirror</u> (a favorite employment so <u>you</u> all say) to keep myself <u>company</u>—at this stage of indolence I, not being beautiful enough to stand in rapture gazing at my own image, like the fabled Narcissus,[5] bethought me of some <u>old</u> letters, which I had put away for some fortunate moment like the present—"<u>what</u> a <u>pleasure</u>—ah! what a pleasure"[6]—I had then in store. And so the "golden moments ran themselves in golden sands"[7] & found me pouring over <u>old letters</u>— Now can't you see me?—another <u>favorite</u> employment you will say! Yes, I <u>own up</u>! I was <u>settled</u> in employment then! But I did'ent so far forget myself as to leave the Col to his own sweet will. I had told him, he should go up to the field where Mr N— was, if he would work <u>very</u> steadily—with this promise, I <u>abandoned</u> myself to my enjoyment for awhile—then having satiated my dear love for a time, I put all to rights, & stepped out to relieve the 'Col' from duty—what was my surprise to find <u>that military officer</u> had taken the liberty of relieving himself from his post, & had gone up in the hay-loft for <u>eggs</u>! Then I subjected him to a court-marshall, & put him on <u>double</u>-duty—& had just returned to the house, when a rapid little knock was heard at the door, & <u>Sister</u> stepped in! How <u>very</u> glad I was to see her! She had been disappointed in going to town that morning—but I suppose she went this morning! I appreciated her visit highly—& walked a long way back with her—I a'most shed tears at parting with her—it may be so long before we meet again.[8] She has been a sweet friend to me—& I shall never forget her kindness during the first trying days of my house-keeping. I hope you all may have a pleasant visit from her. I shall feel very anxious to know of her plans—as she was entirely unable to form any definite idea, what course she would pursue. She will tell you how nice & white our new kitchen looks, & George is doing the office now (alias Prophet's chamber).[9] The little fellow is behaving very well indeed! Mr Neilson can scarcely keep a straight face when looking at him—he & Fannie & Jim[10] seem to be good friends. I make him sleep in the kitchen on one of Mr N—'s grey blankets & riding shawl. I have numerous jobs laid off for him to do, when thro' white-washing—but expect I'll get right restless about keeping him away from home so long. I know Jim must feel lonely without him!

Tell Trot & Sister that the rabbit, for which they so earnestly wished, has at last been caught. The small-dogs gave out excited yells, & so did George & Jim—an immediate request came from the former thro' the latter, to go for them. I, in compassion for youthful desire, gave a gracious permission, & away they went & brought back the prize sure enough. We will have him as a stew tomorrow—provided Mr N— thinks him "fitten" to eat—& provided Fannie & I can stew him "fitten" [to] bring on the table! So you see Mr Neilson & I can have a pie—with rabbit for the meat! provided it will be "fitten" to eat. Would'ent be surprised if Jim's song were not carried out to the very letter—latter clause especially. O! mercy how coarse!

I know very well I ought to be ashamed of myself to sit here & scribble, scribble, scribble, such miserable foolishness. It is a sad waste of time, & paper, & a wrong done to my other correspondents! Don't let 'Marse' know, for he is such an economist in stationary—but then this will not require a stamp. What a comfort! Tell 'Miss' I miss her all the time. I wish she had staid while here! I shall expect you & Jim or you & Mr Cox[11] on Sunday—send me word if you can or can't come. Ask Mrs' Benoit[12] & Ottley when they are coming—also Gus L[13]; I think Trot ought to come, & bring her work & the machine!

Tell every body howdy for me—all the colored friends I mean. Especially Woos & Moll.[14] They must come up. Now when & how many letters are you going to write me for this long letter—I am sure a dozen!

Dear child! I love you with all my heart, & so does John! You should see how proudly he leans back his stately head upon his beautiful "Tidy"[15]—Sister will tell you how prettily I fastened it to the chair with rose-ribbon. Best, warmest love for Mrs Eager—Mr N— says he cannot rest satisfied until she comes. Kiss all for me. Write & come soon to your loving

T'Ida.

1. Lord Byron, *Childe Harold's Pilgrimage* (1818), in McGann, ed., *Lord Byron*, vol. 2, 186.

2. Scottish prefix to a married woman's name.

3. Farm laborer Mary Neilson (b. ca. 1835) and her daughter, Fannie Neilson (b. ca. 1855).

4. George (or "Col") worked as a driver for the Irion family.

5. In Greek myth Narcissus fell in love with his own reflection.

6. John Dryden, *An Evening's Love, or the Mock-Astrologer* (1671), in Kinsley, ed., *John Dryden*, vol. 1, 125.

7. Lucy paraphrased "Every moment, lightly shaken, ran itself in golden sands" (Alfred Tennyson, "Locksley Hall," *Poems* [1842], in Ricks, ed., *Tennyson*, 184).

8. Sarah Dandridge Neilson was about to embark on a trip to the East Coast to visit relatives.

9. In the Bible, Elisha frequently passed the village of Shunem and ate bread with a woman and her husband. Regarding him as a holy man of God, the woman entreated her husband to build a resting place for Elisha's use (2 Kings, 4:8–11).

10. Probably Jim Neilson (b. ca. 1854), farm laborer.

11. Gideon Warren Cox (1835–1900), part owner of a grocery store with William A. Moore (1835–94) called Moore, Cox and Co.

12. Cornelia Williams Benoit (1832–1920), wife of merchant James W. Benoit (b. ca. 1827) and sister of Ellen Gertrude Williams Ottley.

13. Dr. Aurelius Augustin Lyon (1838–1918), son of Rev. James Adair Lyon (1814–82), who had served as the long-standing pastor of the Columbus First Presbyterian Church (1854–70), and Adelaide Eliza Deaderick Lyon (1817–1907). During the Civil War, Aurelius served as assistant surgeon of the Forty-eighth Infantry Regiment Mississippi.

14. Moll had worked as a house servant and farm laborer for the Irion family for several years.

15. A piece of needlework or crocheting used to cover the back and arms of a chair or sofa.

ℰ𝒶

After much consideration Lizzie decided that Bess should complete her education in Virginia. She would later enroll her niece at the Augusta Female Seminary, a Presbyterian school in Staunton run by Principal Mary Julia Baldwin (1829–97). As they made preparations for their departure, Lizzie urged Lucy to visit. "We will never be together again as one family," she wrote sadly on May 31, 1871. Cordele exercised less restraint. "Come, <u>Love</u>, come home to your loved ones who are going to be separated," she pleaded in a hasty postscript to Lizzie's letter.

Lucy made the trip. While Lizzie spent part of the time at Wildwood attending to domestic matters for her sister, Lucy enjoyed her sojourn at Willow Cottage, all the while missing John and her new home.

John Abert Neilson. Lillian Neilson Papers.
Courtesy of Special Collections Department,
Mitchell Memorial Library, Mississippi State University.

Lucy to John

Willow Cottage—
Friday—June 9th/.71

My <u>dear</u> Mr Neilson—

This is the first time I have written you a word since our marriage—eight weeks ago! With what different feelings do I <u>now</u> address you, than formerly. I wish I could tell you exactly <u>how</u> I do feel towards you, but that being <u>impossible</u> I shall not make an attempt, for fear of bordering on what some might term <u>love</u>-sickness!

How very <u>long</u> these days have seemed since our separation—& yet I have enjoyed each one of them, as you would like for me to do! I have not rendered myself ridiculous, or distasteful to my dear homefolk, by foolish repinings, & hopes & wishes—but oh! in the depths of my heart I have felt the secret yearning to be with you—& sometimes I would almost be overpowered by it—& <u>determine never</u> to voluntarily separate myself from you again as long as life lasts. Every morning, I would think of you as preparing—going forth to labor, at noon, as returning fatigued. But as evening came on with its long shadows, & deepening twilight, I wished most to be by you, to minister to you[r] wants, because then you were so tired from the long long day's toil. Have you wished for me too?—Saturday-evening will soon be here—I am looking forward to it's coming with <u>much more</u> eagerness than I did before our marriage! If anything should prevent our meeting!—well! I don't see how I can bear it!—I know Lizzie has been a comfort to you—bless her sweet heart—I hope she may come with you, we are all expecting her. Tell her I have bought another <u>yard</u> of material for her dress.

Good-bye to you both—Do come <u>early</u> Saturday-afternoon, for I shall be all anxiety.

Yours lovingly,
Lucy—

༄

With Lizzie and Bess en route to Virginia, Lucy attended a Masonic meeting in Caledonia and school commencement exercises in Columbus, all the while garnering support for John's campaign to become the next sheriff of Lowndes County. The office stood at the apex of local power; its promise of political credit and financial stability proved irresistible to former slaveholders looking to use the law to reestablish their racial dominance.

As a candidate's wife, Lucy had an important role to play. War had welcomed Confederate women into the political fold in several ways, and women remained critical allies in the consolidation of white postwar power. Lucy sounded her political voice and contributed to the campaign as a way to provide security to her domestic world, looking outward to preserve her inner circle and maintain class privilege.

Lucy made a hasty start to this letter during her visit to Willow Cottage and completed it upon her return to Wildwood.

Lucy to Bess

June 27th—[1871]

[. . .] So long since I began this letter—I had so desired it to have reached you before this—but "that comes of being married" I think I hear you say—& I reckon it does, for just as I got this far, <u>Mr Neilson</u> came for me to go home—this was Friday afternoon—we spent that night at home & on Saturday, we went up to <u>Caledonia</u> to a great <u>Masonic</u>-meeting! Well! if I could only find words to describe the beauty, & magnificence of the city I would, but really I was so <u>flustrated</u> (being a country-lady), & so bewildered, I don't remember <u>exactly</u> how things were located! But on entering the limits of the city, I grew a wee bit excited, & whispered to Mr Neilson, please to point out any public buildings of note which I might pass by unnoticed. He—being somewhat <u>more traveled</u> than I—was very kind, & readily consented—& begun forth-with, in a solemnly <u>deep</u>-<u>toned</u> voice, to entreat me to perceive!, & behold! & view! & observe, & demonstrate by <u>ocular</u>-<u>evidence</u> that building on the left, which was <u>Mr Robin-son's stable</u>!!!—And many more such like observations made he.

Oh! the people—from the east, & from the west & from the north & from the south came they—there were <u>five</u> or <u>six hundred</u>. <u>None knew I</u>—but oh! you know we <u>must know</u> them—we <u>must seek</u> an acquaintance, we <u>must</u> get <u>votes</u>, for do we not recollect that November is coming!! & we wish the sherriffality!! Very soon Mr Neilson met some of his friends, & then he presented his wife, & then she made herself as agreeable as possible—& asked after the health of the <u>chicken</u> & <u>children</u>, & in an off-hand natural way complimented the pretty girls, & spoke in praise of the <u>speaker</u> who addressed the masons, & was one of the citizens—& in a cute way all her own got along first rate. She was somewhat surprised tho' when she found herself at the head of the procession of ladies as they marched out to dinner—this was a little too much for her, the position was some what more conspicuous than she was willing it should be for her! However there was no help for it, & on she had to go!—In the afternoon she met some of her old school-mates of Corinth [Corona College] notoriety—Misses Booth[1]—they were immense women, & came near smothering her in their delight at once again beholding her in the flesh! She told them she wished their votes she is right sure if they have their way, she will get them. One of Mr N— friends[2] sent us word to come to his house—he could not come for us, on account of being sick—We accepted the invitation, & found the man, & his wife real nice people, & it was the anniversary of their second year of marriage, & there was a great <u>big baby tod-dling</u> around, of course! They looked as happy as larks!—While there, in came three gentlemen with a request to the hostess (Mrs McMorris) to let them have a <u>dance</u> in her house! The <u>spokesman</u> was, who do you think?—why! Mr <u>Foster Nichol</u>,[3] he is now a gay & festive[4] widower. The lady very promptly <u>refused</u> as she was a Methodist[5]—I was sorry for them, & spoke up, without any <u>election-eering</u> thought in their favor—Mr N— laughed, & said, "Yes! I know Lucy would like to stay, & join you"—but the little woman was firm, & they had to go else-where. I wished them better success—then Mr Neilson & Mr McMorris said I was <u>electioneering</u>—I protested "I had not thought—indeed! I had forgotten all about <u>votes</u>—but! but! if <u>they</u> pleased <u>not</u> to <u>forget us</u> on election-day"!

There were candidates as plentiful as black-berries—Maj Bell, Maj Eggleston, a Mr Lincoln,[6] & Mr N— all for sherriff. I saw Maj Bell & Bob Banks[7] just as we left the grounds—they were very much amused at <u>my</u> coming out, & vowed their <u>wives</u> should come next time. Said Mr N— had taught them something worth remembering. We had a good laugh! I tell them all I am running for <u>deputy</u>!—

We came home (Willow Cottage) that night, & found Miss & Jim glad to see us. Sunday was Commencement sermon. A Mr Whitfield[8] from Meridian—a Baptist—he gave us a pleasant little discourse—no attempt at anything <u>high-falutin</u>—but a good lesson drawn from the lovely character of Abigail found in 1st Sam:25th chapter.[9] Of course every body & his wife, & <u>all</u> his kinsfolk, was there. The children looked beautiful in the white frocks, & fresh ribbons. Proffessor[10] had a splendidly trained choir, & oh! the delightful music. Miss Clopton[11] of course did her part as was expected—dear little Mollie Lou, & her Father sang "Jesus lover of my soul"[12] as a duett, & joined by a full chorus—I just shut my eyes to fully enjoy it. Cousin Cornelia had Mr Neilson & myself to dine with her—we had a charming day—I never saw Mr N— so much pleased—he is a great admirer of Mrs Benoits. In the afternoon Cordele came in for us, & we went to the cemetery[13]—& then home taking Lizzie Symons with us. We did not go to hear Mr Cason[14] preach <u>the boy's</u> commencement sermon because it was so hot! Next morning by times Lizzie & I cut out a white tarleton for her, & went to work on it, & by night it was nearly complete—Miss helped us some too. So we did'ent go to hear the <u>Juniors</u> essays—how differently we would have felt if a certain tall, dark-eyed girl had'ent been in Wytheville [Virginia]! We went in to the Concert that night however, & enjoyed the music very much—but oh! the heat! I assure you, in the elegant words of Stephens "it was <u>grand</u> & <u>perspiring</u>"!![15] Lizzie went to her Aunt Kate's, & met her escort Mr Ed Sherman.[16] After the concert, we found Mrs Eagar, who was radiant in white basque, & overskirt—how handsome she looked! My poor <u>countryfied Sherriff</u> (elect) was dying of thirst, so his Cousin Laura took us over to the house, & Mrs Tarrant[17] was so polite as to treat us to <u>ice-water</u>! Sister Fisher[18] right in the midst of every thing, had to be introduced to Mr & Mrs N—, & tell them all about being so <u>intimate</u> (?) with our dear <u>nephew</u> John Furniss. I liked to have despaired of ever getting Mr N— away from her—he so polite, & she so "<u>newsy</u>." I saw so many of the girls, & of course every one was lamenting Bessie's departure. So was Mrs Tarrant—I told her what you had written me about going to Commencement, & thinking of one who so wished to be there. It pleased her very much. This morning, we went to hear the Graduates read their essays. I never saw a class acquit themselves more honorably! The[re] was a <u>big fuss</u> about the Valedictory—just as Mrs Eager predicted. The honor was to be divided between <u>three</u>—Lizzie Payne, Eliza Clopton, & Mary Lipscomb.[19] When the Cloptons came down, & found this was the state of the case, they quite resented, & protested against any such robbery of their <u>child's honors</u>—oh! I tell you, they took high grounds—& that aroused all others concerned, & it was carried before the <u>trustees</u>.[20] Pretty stiff doings I tell you!—I enclose a programme which will explain how they intended to divide the honor—but Miss Clopton utterly refused to read <u>her part</u>, & thereby brought down the condemnation of all upon her own head! How such an act of ill temper will spoil <u>everything</u>—She had acted so well her part in music—& read the French, & English essay very gracefully but then all was spoilt by her last act.

All the girls looked well—& did well—But none was so brilliant, so graceful, & so <u>capable</u> as <u>Mary Lipscomb</u>! I don't know that I ever heard a more excellent essay than hers, & then her <u>manner</u> was so lady-like, so easy, so modest, so natural. Lizzie Payne did her part <u>well</u>—& Sallie Goodwin[21] did nicely, & looked as well as <u>she could</u>—& you know 'angels could do no more'![22] There was a presentation of prizes, & bibles, & a pathetic <u>speech</u> from the Principle—in which, much to the surprise of <u>all</u>, he offered his <u>resignation</u> to the board of Trustees, & it was <u>accepted</u>! I had to quiet Lizzie Symons, for she liked to have shouted aloud. After the exercises were over, Cordele & I went over, & bid Mrs Tarrant good-bye—I was afraid I would not see her again—poor woman <u>how</u> she had <u>been</u> & <u>was</u> weeping! I wish you would write her a letter—even if it is just <u>one</u>—I think she would be pleased.—

June 29th—Here is my poor letter still unfinished—but just as I completed that last sentence we heard the sound of wheels, & on looking out espied Mrs Ottley, & her beautiful boys[23]—I was in a high state of undress—but would not loose a moment of her time—so I sat, & entertained her the entire time in my <u>gown</u> & <u>nothing more</u>. She was <u>too</u> sweet—& <u>too, too</u> loving! Asked so much about you all, & was so desirous of Trot's speedy improvement—She returned from the country with John much benefited—says however, if he should need another change, she will take him to <u>Bailey</u> [Springs, Alabama]—tho' as yet such a <u>thought</u> even, is a <u>dead</u>-secret with the <u>Col</u>. They hope not to have [to] go anywhere. All of us were invited to dine with her on yesterday—together with Mrs Benoit—We went & had a most charming day. <u>Both of my dear friends are</u> so loving to John & I.

The Commencement party came off in <u>all</u> its' grandeur. Mr Neilson, Jim, & I went together. There was a great crowd—ladies were more numerous than gentlemen—which rendered it not quite so pleasant as the one last year. There was a <u>full</u> delegation from Aberdeen <u>of course</u>—& many many faces of last year—looking just the same! So many things reminded me of that time. Mr N, & Jim had laughed at me about being a <u>wall-flower</u>, & kept asking me if I would'ent feel <u>funny</u> without <u>any</u> beau. I saw Gus Lyon a day or two before, & begged him please to go, & <u>be my beau</u>, for I would have to stick to the wall until he <u>did come</u>, for Mr N— said he was going to have a good time with the girls—"<u>his-eff</u>." But oh! much to my delight I <u>had quite</u> as many beaux as any woman in the house,

& never had a pleasanter time—indeed! Mr N— could'ent keep up with me at all. Lizzie looked beautifully, & seemed to have a gay time—she will give you full particulars, for she said she would write today. Mollie Houston,[24] Eloise Bell, & Lucy Neilson were quite as much sought as <u>ever</u>—after so long a married life too!—wonderful indeed!—Maj Bell & Eloise—Mr Neilson & myself had a great deal of fun over the coming election—I must not write a word <u>more hardly</u>! Tell dear Trot her good long letter has been received, & I will answer just as soon as possible—I could write now, but <u>feel</u> that I must answer some of the numerous letters, which have been written so long ago. Mrs Sam Harris, & Mr Wiley Williams[25] are anxious to know about Wytheville—the <u>price</u> of <u>board</u>—whether or not a family of 6 (six) could be accommodated in any private family—<u>four</u> grown—<u>two</u> children—if there is good <u>hunting</u> or <u>fishing</u>, & <u>all about everything</u>! Ask Trot please to take pains to inquire, & write <u>full</u> particulars—I wish to cultivate <u>brother</u> Williams—he likes Mr Neilson, & I hope for his support. I have a dear delightful letter from Sissie—she is still in Washington [D.C.]—her address will remain unchanged during the entire summer. Sophie was up one day last week to have some dentistry done—she was very pretty & well! Insists upon our visiting her this summer, & I hope we can. Mr N— is half sick—& so anxious to get back to his little home. He cannot tell exactly when the court will adjourn—t'was unfortunate that he had to leave the farm just at this time—tho' I am glad to have had an opportunity of attending Commencement, & festivities whilst down on <u>duty</u> business. Jim has made no change in the household as yet— we have not had time for a talk yet—I hope tho' we will tonight. I wish Cordele to go home with me, when I go. Jim went to Sue Golding's wedding[26] last night—I will write you particulars in Trot's letter.

Every-body, white & black, send more messages than I will attempt to write. I am so thankful that Dr Crockett[27] lives right near Trot—tell him please to take good care of her. Do be careful of yourself, & her too. Heaven bless you both. Your Lute.

NOTES

1. Mary Kirkpatrick Booth (ca. 1820–1907) and her daughter, teacher Elizabeth F. Booth (1842–1915).

2. Farmer James McMorris (1835–1920), his wife, Nancy Ophelia Stewart McMorris (1842–1923), and their daughter Ophelia Stewart McMorris (1870–1952). James worked as a clerk in Columbus before the Civil War and married Nancy on June 23, 1869.

3. Farmer Robert Foster Nichols (1843–96), widower of Josephine Bobo Nichols (1843–71).

4. H. S. Vandyk, "The Light Guitar" (early nineteenth-century sentimental song).

5. Many Methodists regarded dancing as a social ill, and the issue had been a point of discussion for Lucy, who loved dancing. See John Abert Neilson to Eliza Lucy Irion,

July 25, 1870; and Eliza Lucy Irion Neilson to Elizabeth Charlotte Irion Barron, February 2, 1872.

6. Merchant James B. Bell (1829–85), husband of Eloise Johnston Bell (1848–1928); possibly farmer Theodore A. Eggleston (1842–1908); deputy sheriff Cicero L. Lincoln (1844–1939).

7. Farmer Robert Webb Banks (1845–1919), husband of Alice Clay Sherrod Banks (b. ca. 1845).

8. Rev. Theodore Whitfield (1834–94).

9. In the Bible, David asked Nabal for his support in return for protection of his workers and property. Nabal refused, but his wife Abigail sent food supplies to David's men. When Abigail's actions were revealed to Nabal, he died, and David took Abigail as his wife (1 Sam. 25).

10. Alexander Poleman (1830–98), professor of music.

11. Eliza Brandon Clopton (1854–86), daughter of Aberdeen farmer William Hales Clopton (1813–79) and Cornelia William Brandon Clopton (1827–1911).

12. Charles Wesley, "Jesus, Lover of My Soul," *Hymns and Sacred Poems* (1740), in Ravitch and Ravitch, eds., *English Reader*, 101–102.

13. Friendship Cemetery. Both the Irion and Neilson family plots are located in this cemetery.

14. Rev. Jeremiah H. Cason (1832–1915), pastor of the Baptist Church of Columbus and husband of Bettie Cooper Cason (1834–1901). During the Civil War, Jeremiah served as a private in Company I, Eleventh Infantry Regiment Mississippi, and a captain in Company C, Forty-first Infantry Regiment Alabama.

15. Lucy may have been referring to a comment made by James Alfred Stevens (1840–1922), editor and proprietor of the *Columbus Index*.

16. Catherine Cabot Neilson Hopkins (1833–1905), wife of Dr. James White Hopkins (1821–76) and John Abert Neilson's half sister; Edward Randolph Sherman (1851–1927), son of merchant George W. Sherman (ca. 1816–65) and Virginia Randolph Sherman (1827–65).

17. Sarah Frances Hale Tarrant (b. ca. 1834), wife of John Frederick Tarrant (1838–74), president of the Columbus Female Institute (1869–72).

18. Possibly Elizabeth Fisher (b. ca. 1840), who lived in the Rossee household in Selma, Alabama. Dr. Henry Rossee (b. ca. 1843) may have had acquaintance with fellow Selma resident Dr. John Perkins Furniss Jr. (1841–1909), son of Dr. John Perkins Furniss (1808–44) and Anne Frazier Neilson Symons.

19. Possibly Lizzie Payne (b. ca. 1854), daughter of bookkeeper Albert Payne (b. ca. 1830) and Mary Payne (b. ca. 1832) of Mobile, Alabama; Mary Lipscomb (1855–1930), daughter of Dr. William Lowndes Lipscomb (1828–1908) and Tallulah Harris Lipscomb (1836–1913).

20. The Columbus Female Institute's board of trustees (1871) was comprised of Dr. William Washington Humphries (1806–77), retired physician and president; Stephen Albert Brown (1823–87), probate judge and secretary; and board members Amzi Ellis Love (1822–74), lawyer; John Marshall Billups (1824–1902), farmer; John C. Ramsey (b. 1820), merchant and minister; James Sykes (1810–85), farmer; Jehu Amaziah Orr (1828–1921), state delegate to the Confederate Provisional Congress (1861–62), state representative in the Confederate Congress (1864–65), and after the Civil War a state court judge (1870–76);

Dr. William Lowndes Lipscomb; L. B. Tucker; Charles F. Sherrod (1827–86), farmer; Rev. G. T. Stainback (1829–1907), principal of Franklin Academy; John Fontaine Hudson (1822–1905), merchant; and David Paxton Blair (1814–98), druggist.

21. Sallie Goodwin (1853–1941), daughter of banker Nathaniel Ely Goodwin (1812–90) and Ann Elizabeth Beeves Goodwin (1818–92).

22. Edward Young, "Night Second: On Time, Death, and Friendship," *The Complaint*, in Cornford, ed., *Night Thoughts*, 53.

23. John King Ottley Jr. (1869–1945) and Charles William Ottley (1871–1907), sons of John King Ottley and Ellen Gertrude Williams Ottley.

24. Mary Weaver (ca. 1852–85) married Aberdeen lawyer Robert E. Houston (b. 1839) on March 10, 1871.

25. Henrietta Williams Harris (1838–1907), widow of planter Samuel Dowse Harris (1834–67) and mother of Eva Harris (1866–1930) and Samuel Harris Jr. (b. ca. 1868). Henrietta lived next door to her parents, banker Wiley H. Williams (1811–79) and Mary A. E. Williams (1815–91).

26. Susan Golding (1850–1923) married Dr. John Gerdine (1840–1903).

27. Dr. Robert Crockett (b. ca. 1804).

ℱᴀ

With both of her domestic helpmates deployed to the East Coast, Lucy selfishly prized Cordele from Columbus—a temporary measure that became a permanent arrangement. At Willow Cottage a disheveled Jim struggled without the practical care and companionship of his sisters and devolved management of the farm to freed man Press Barron in order to concentrate his efforts on business endeavors.

Lucy to Lizzie

Wildwood—One year ago!![1]

July 11th/.71.

My dear! dearer!! dearest!!! Trotwood—

Last week Cordele replied to your last welcome letter, to which I added a postscript saying I would answer your letter very soon: thought then that Sunday would be a nice quiet day—& fully intended writing, but we sent George down home after some things, & Jim sent up two mules with a pressing invitation for us to come home—so on Sunday we went down tho' none of us were feeling well enough for church—yet we thought t'would'ent hurt us physically or morally to go down, & see what our old bachelor was doing for "his-eff." I hardly expected to find him at home—but lo! & behold! by the time we reached the big gate we saw the front door standing invitingly open! I thought perhaps he had given us out, & gone to town but no!—he was on the look out—tho' not in the highest-state of toilette you ever saw. indeed! he had on as <u>few</u> clothes <u>as possible</u>—came walking out <u>bare footed</u> over the <u>gravel</u> walk. I immediately asked for which of his numerous sins was he doing pennance! I never saw him as glad to see us before <u>hardly</u>!—Poor fellow. I felt like both <u>crying</u> & embracing him—(neither of which I did however, <u>resisting</u> because like a woman of tact, I know such <u>gushing</u> salutation did not meet with his <u>approval</u>—& <u>then too</u>, I am aware that my husband married me for <u>my beauty</u> & <u>for that alone</u>, & I grieve to state that <u>tears</u> are not becoming to my <u>peculiar style</u>, so for that cause I <u>bethought</u> me in time, & met him with a charming little smile, & cheerful nod—but my <u>arms</u> were very stiff & proper down at <u>my sides</u>)—he was not feeling well, & looked like I imagine Mr Paxton's saffron-bag, did![2]

We all staid at home, & had a most delightful day—every one lying at their ease—Jim & I on the bed, in the sitting room; & Mr N— on the couch; & <u>prim</u> "Miss" (the only exception), looked snug enough in her beloved rocking chair. I said none of us were feeling well—no we were not! Mr N— had a chill the afternoon before—Jim & Cordele were both as bilious as—as <u>cats</u>—& <u>I</u>, had very imprudently allowed myself to catch a sore throat by letting Mr N— pour a dipper of cold water on the back of my <u>neck & head</u> when in a high state of temperature. We thought & talked of you two so <u>constantly</u> it would [be] no wonder you should be home-sick!

Jim is so determined on having Bessie back, he even says that if Mr Tarrant does get the school for the next <u>full year</u>, he is as <u>good</u> as any they can get, & <u>Brooks</u> must come home he <u>will not</u> endure life without her! I told him I felt real <u>jealous myself</u>—that <u>I</u> used to be his pet—but <u>now oh</u>! the difference <u>t'was to me</u>!—he <u>pooh</u>-<u>poohed</u>—& looked very like he wished to say—"oh! well that is what you get for <u>being married</u>["]—but he did not say so!!!—

Martha[3] gave us a most excellent vegetable dinner—with apple dumplings for desert!—<u>Poor</u> Pheobe[4] has been <u>very sick</u> again with inflamation of the stomache—she was effected very much like <u>you</u>, so Nancy said—& you <u>know</u> how bad she must have been. <u>Dr McCabe</u>[5] had to be called in—I know it seemed strange to him not to have any white folks to give directions to. "They were gone—all gone from their cottage home."[6]—We came home in the afternoon—on the way Mr N— had another chill & was quite sick all day yesterday, & so <u>did</u> & <u>was</u> Cordele! I doctored my throat, & was ready to nurse them! Poor Miss! I fear she felt neglected, but Mr N— was very anxious I should be near him all the time—<u>man-like</u>, he was <u>very restless</u>, & <u>very</u> much <u>sicker</u> than <u>any one ever had been before</u>! To day both are better—& I had just thought of stealing time to write my letter—when Brother James came in with a <u>second</u> one from you—<u>how much we both</u> thank you—& what a <u>beautiful</u> letter we think it is—& every <u>word</u> so true as regards <u>us</u> (Ahem!) & Bess (Ahem!)! I get full of laugh [at] Mr N—, he puts on such a grave look, when <u>you</u> speak so <u>ambitiously</u> of <u>us</u>! I think he fears you may be cruelly disappointed some day. As for the sherriffalty—I much fear he will not get it—<u>Maj Bell</u> seems bound to win—<u>poor us</u>! But <u>who knows</u>! <u>Pre</u>-haps we may!—<u>Charmant</u>! [charming] Well <u>sherriffalty</u> or <u>not</u> we can do our best <u>endeavories</u> to be <u>lovely</u> private <u>characters</u>!—I am doing both myself & yourself injustice by answering your dear letter in this harum-scarum style of penmanship, & composition—but I will have some sort of an answer to send back home by Press who has just arrived bringing very much <u>longed</u>-for <u>furni</u>-ture. He brings tidings of Jim being sick—has bilious fever—poor fellow there by himself—but how can I help either he & myself—Cordele & Mr N— both in bed & he so far away! He wrote a note saying he would send for us if he needed us but I fear he will not.—What a poor little scattered family we are!—Can <u>this thing</u> so continue?

<u>Dear</u>, <u>dear</u> Trot <u>please</u>, <u>please</u> don't break my heart, by being so despondent—you are not <u>well</u>, you are not yourself!—You need to go to <u>Bailey</u>—I am in earnest about it—I do really think you will be obliged to retrace your steps, & go to dear old Bailey before you can find the relief needed. Depend upon it!—you are <u>sick</u>—& therefore your spirits are depressed. You <u>hav'ent lost me out</u> of <u>your life</u>—& you <u>have</u> a <u>home</u>—& you are <u>fully</u> competent for the life before you of guiding, & directing <u>our darling Bess</u>!—Bless her soul!—oh! how sweetly do those words of praise sink <u>into my heart</u>—then the best of <u>all</u>; that she acts from <u>right</u> motives, & right <u>principles</u>. "O! thou child of many prayers"—may she be protected by <u>divine</u> influence from <u>all</u> the quick-sands, & snares of life.[7] Keep us all humble!—

Twas very kind of you to take so much pains about finding board for <u>the Williams</u>. I shall tell Jim to show them the latter part of <u>your</u> letter, & let them read for themselves. I have much more to write—but cannot now—there are many things which claim my personal attention. You don't know how good <u>Press</u> is to <u>me</u>—he just leaves his work, & comes to bring first <u>Miss</u>, & then the wagon—Oh! every body is so good to us!—

I shall write again soon—Good-bye until then—

In love for both from us all—Cordele will write to her <u>darling</u> Bess as soon as she can <u>quit</u> being as bilious <u>as a cat</u>.—I must write to Jim—Mr Neilson thinks if he ever puts <u>pen</u> to <u>paper again</u> it will be directed to you both. Don't consider him ungrateful, or careless—he is neither. He laughed over Bess' letter to Cordele—which we saw <u>Sunday</u>—& so did <u>I</u>, at <u>different things</u> however—he had <u>no idea</u> what those hieographies were—but I <u>did</u>—& thank Miss Bess that <u>all is right</u>!! Her <u>christmas-present</u> is <u>not</u> going to be <u>forth-coming</u>! I hope she may be able to bear the disappointment. Good-bye again—God bless you <u>both</u>.

Your loving Lute

1. Lucy and John were engaged on July 11, 1870.

2. Edward George Earle Bulwer-Lytton, *The Caxtons: A Family Picture* (1849), 257.

3. Martha Barron, wife of Press Barron, had worked as a house servant for the Irion family for several years.

4. Pheobe had worked as the Irion family's cook and dairy attendant for several years.

5. Dr. Fenton Mercer McCabe (1828–88).

6. R. A. Glenn, "My Old Cottage Home," in Erbsen, ed., *Gospel Songbook*, 114.

7. Lucy paraphrased "O thou child of many prayers! / Life hath quicksands; life hath snares!" (Henry Wadsworth Longfellow, "Maidenhood," *Ballads and Other Poems* [1842], in Scudder and Monteiro, eds., *Longfellow*, 18).

ℬ

Lucy basked in the freedom afforded by Cordele's presence. With an extra pair of capable hands on call, an impromptu trip to Columbus was no longer out of the question. Punctuating frequent visits to friends and neighbors with the canning and preserve-making duties of the season, Lucy threw off the cloak of marital responsibility to embrace the social pleasures of her recent bellehood.

Lucy to Lizzie

Willow Cottage—
Sunday-afternoon.
Aug 13th/.71.

My dear, dear Trot,

Mr Neilson has written a letter, & thinks he has left quite room enough for me to add a post-script—but I feel so full of chat I'll take a <u>larger</u> sheet, altho' I may not have much time to write. All this last week we have been looking for letters from you, & not one word have we heard since "Saturday <u>was</u> a <u>week</u>." We think you may possibly have gone to the Springs, or on such jaunts as may be pleasant—tho', as for entertaining the idea of your being sick, we will not for a moment. I wrote Bess by Mr Mitchell,[1] & promised to send the desired watch, & lockets—& so gave Mr Chapman[2] orders to take the box to Mr M— as soon as the watch was finished—but he <u>forgot</u> it, & so we lost the opportunity—but <u>Mr Cox</u> said he was going by Wytheville, & would take it—& so I think perhaps the <u>belle</u> may be comforted, as the bearer is somewhat a favorite.

We have been spending the week at Willow Cottage—& a pleasant one it has been—We went into town only once—that was last Monday-morning—then we paid Cousin Cornelia a <u>nice little visit</u>, & went again to Mrs Taylors[3]—found her in bed keeping off her <u>chill</u>—her health is not good—she missed the chill however, & we had a pleasant visit—saw Lide Fitts, & Mr[s] Gregory[4] again. They both are the same good friends—I think Mrs G— does'ent care quite as much for me as formerly, for she & Jennie Worthington[5] are in one of those frantic love-fits, which are common among our women—(viz Della Billington & Fannie Clayton—Lucy Goodwin & Annie Torry—Sully Matthews & Lucy Gerdine)[6]—& are so absorbed with themselves, they hav'ent much room in their hearts, for others—tho' for my part, I am not an exacting friend, & her present interest, & good feeling satisfies me. There is no change in Lide however!—she looks & acts just like her old self. They said Tempe[7] was coming over soon—now I'd like to see old Tempe—& hear her say in her own peculiar way—"Good Lord! this, or Good Lord! that"—please don't consider me profane! "Miss" got her a new dress—as her pretty purple percale disappointed her sorely in fading so ugly—it is a light drab leno—just such as you see all over the world at any time, & on any body—She had Mrs Willeford[8] to fit a basque, which I think will be very becoming—I took a pattern, & made her a white swiss one, & am much pleased with the effect. We have been quite busy putting up peaches in cans—& making sweet-pickle—& quince-preserves, & drying peaches—& putting pickle in brine &c. It has been a busy time—but all is done now excepting drying peaches. We have a dozen big fat bottles of catsup—the richness & thickness of which would make Bess' mouth water—& hope to have more—but the five weeks of excessive drought ruined all vines almost. Our canned tomatoes & apples seem to be keeping well. Cordele is so happy—I wish you could see her—she looks better than I ever remember seeing her in the summer—jaunting around with us, & breathing the pure atmosphere of Wildwood agrees with her. She & Mr N— have so much fun! Much to our astonishment Mr Cox & Jim came back from Crumps [Tennessee] in a week's time—could'ent stand it any longer!—too lonesome! I laughed at them agreat deal. Both look better—how I do wish Jim would go with him north—that would make him all right!—

Thursday night we had quite a little happening-in-party. Beckie Barry,[9] & Lizzie Symons came to go with us to the celebration (Beck, self invited for our hack) then Mr Cox came out with Jim to spend the night—& Gus Lyon brought Mrs Gregory out to tea! T'was much like old times. Gus remarked he could hardly believe I was in any way changed, now that the inevitable John was not present. That was the only thing which marred my enjoyment—every thing was so pleasant, & Gus got so full of "who! who"—he remarked more than once—that our's was one of the happiest homes he knew anywhere. How many things make us wish for Bess—but she must not come back! Please write me a long letter all about yourselves—how your clothes do, & what you think & feel. I am quite unsettled in mind regarding Bess—& I want to hear of what you have decided upon. Mrs Ellen Ottley is just home from a visit to Mrs Gen Lee.[10] While in the prairie she went to see Mrs Eager—reports her as looking <u>fat & well</u>, & is coming next week to pay <u>her a visit</u>. Charlie Barry[11] is <u>now here</u> came home with us to dinner—but I went to sleep as usual, & left Cordele with <u>the boy to hold</u>! Good-bye—do write soon to Lute.

"Tell you!"

Good-bye to both.

Lute.

NOTES

1. Merchant David S. Mitchell (b. ca. 1834), husband of Rosalie C. King Mitchell (1848–1912).

2. H. W. Chapman (b. ca. 1835).

3. Indiana Matilda Gregory Taylor (1813–83), wife of druggist Henry S. Taylor (b. 1810).

4. Eliza Watt Fitts (1844–1930), wife of merchant William Aylett Fitts (1836–1925); Mary Cornelia Watt Gregory (1838–1918), sister of Eliza Watt Fitts and widow of Francis R. Gregory (1828–63). In 1870 Mary lived with her father, farmer Thomas Watt (b. ca. 1810), on his property near Starkville. Eliza and William Fitts lived next door.

5. Eliza Jenny Worthington (1842–1937), daughter of Henry Horace Worthington (1804–59), editor of the *Columbus Democrat,* and Frances Edward Crinchton Worthington (1805–88).

6. Mary Adella Billington Bell (ca. 1836–1908) of Starkville, wife of dry goods retailer Henry A. Bell (1829–1907); Frances R. Clayton (1840–1932), daughter of lawyer George R. Clayton (1808–67) and Ann R. Clayton (1811–57); teacher Lucy Goodwin (1848–1940), daughter of Nathaniel Ely Goodwin and Ann Elizabeth Beeves Goodwin; Annie Torry (b. ca. 1850), daughter of teacher Lucy Torry (ca. 1829–1903); Mary Sullie Matthews (ca. 1848–1906), daughter of Dr. Robert F. Matthews (1820–96) and Amanda C. Barry Matthews (1824–56); Lucy Gerdine (b. 1847), daughter of farmer William L. Crawford Gerdine (ca. 1821–78) and Lucy Hopson Lumpkin Gerdine (1823–56).

7. Tempe Fitts (b. 1847), daughter of John Henry Fitts (1804–82) and Virginia Wilmonia Aylett Fitts (1813–50) and sister of William Aylett Fitts.

8. Mary Kirk Willeford (1831–87), wife of printer Rueben Willeford (1831–87).

9. Rebecca Barry (b. ca. 1842), daughter of Bartley Barry and Mary Bruce Barry.

10. Regina Harrison Lee (1841–1903), wife of Brooksville farmer Stephen Dill Lee (1833–1908), the youngest Confederate lieutenant general.

11. Clerk Charles Barry (b. ca. 1853), son of Bartley Barry and Mary Eliza Raser Barry (b. ca. 1827).

Interlude

PROMISE OF THE SOUTH

*S*ummer sat quietly in the stoic halls of Virginia's Augusta Female Seminary. With commencement proceedings over and another cohort of graduates qualified to assume the mantle of young womanhood, Principal Mary Julia Baldwin set to work on the curriculum for the upcoming school year. The seminary, in all its Greek revival splendor, had traditionally paid homage to the genteel mountain breezes and planter ethos of the nearby springs resorts. But Reconstruction's winds of change had thrown the Staunton academy into a heady transformation. When forty-one-year-old Baldwin had taken charge of the seminary in late 1863, her chief concern had been to protect her depleted batch of boarders from the prying eyes of Yankee soldiers. In 1871 the challenge of befitting girls with a tangible set of postwar skills and polish loomed large in Baldwin's vision for southern women. Selling a solid Presbyterian education founded on elegance and self-support, Baldwin offered up hope to struggling southerners stuck in the mire of defeat—the promise that she would train a generation of young ladies who could lead their elders into a new, reinvigorated South. The cash-strapped elite and upper middle class believed her. For the 1870–71 session, the Augusta Female Seminary boasted an intake of 176 pupils from across the South and one from as far away as England.

Sixteen-year-old Bess Irion joined Augusta's small contingent of Mississippian students when her Aunt Lizzie Barron enrolled her at the school in fall 1872. A former student of the Columbus Female Institute, Bess had already received rigorous training in a standard combination of academic subjects and ornamental pursuits. While the school had been more than adequate, Lizzie was keenly aware that a Virginia education gave Bess and her family an edge in the postwar southern quest to reclaim position and gentility. The trip restored Lizzie's sense of self too. Nestled between the Blue Ridge and Appalachian Mountains, Staunton had survived the ravages of war relatively unscathed. Offering robust mountain air and pleasant social interludes, the queen city of the Shenandoah proved beneficial to Lizzie, whose health had suffered against the backdrop of postwar hardship and sapping delta summers. As Lizzie temporarily relieved herself as head of the family, her Virginia sojourn gave her a rare opportunity to throw herself into the pursuit of southern refinement. Mixing antebellum gentility with a new brand of useful, self-supporting femininity, Lizzie and Bess reinvented themselves away from the tight-knit world of Columbus and the hearthstone of Willow Cottage.

Two

Settling Family Affairs

AUGUST–NOVEMBER 1871

*T*he last parched days of summer lingered in the fields of Wildwood, and the Neilsons prepared for the first harvest season of their married life. Proud of her hogs and potatoes, her whitewashed kitchen, and her newfound domestic ways, Lucy also embraced the transitory pleasures of the belle-wife—who kept her house in order and her dance card full. "I have a great horror of growing <u>old timey</u>, & countrified," she admitted. While Lucy remained free of children, she resolved, wherever possible, to partake in the frivolity and "youthful thrills" of maidenhood.

Wildwood held less charm for Cordele, whose removal from Willow Cottage confirmed her status as helpmate to her younger, married sister. Swapping her role as the domestic head of one household for a subordinate role in another, Cordele was also deprived of her contributions to church and community affairs because of the isolation of Wildwood. As she surrendered her Sunday school class and put away her visiting clothes, Cordele's affection for Lucy and John did little to abate her growing resentment about the life of single blessedness she had left behind in Columbus.

At Willow Cottage, Jim too found that single life had "proved quite the contrary in the realization." With his sisters scattered from Mississippi to Virginia, Jim struggled to keep the farm in order without Lizzie's advice and guidance, Cordele's domestic know-how, and Lucy's social flair. As visitors to Willow Cottage dropped away, Jim grew restless and disinterested in the future of the family home.

In Virginia, Lizzie prepared Bess for her final year of study at the Augusta Female Seminary, investing in an education that would provide her niece with the independence, status, and skills to make her way in the New South. Even as she recovered her own gentility among Staunton's well-to-do, Lizzie bitterly equated the changed domestic affairs at home with her own loss of status as head of the family. Heated discussions about the settlement of the Irion estate resulted in Lizzie declaring that without Willow Cottage she had no home. As Lizzie knew, identity and familial relationships were defined by the household, and talk of breaking up the cottage and dividing its assets led them all, in their own ways, to question their sense of self without it.

♉

Lizzie used the weeks before the commencement of the school year to introduce Bess to Virginia society. Miss Irion's genteel foray at the Montgomery White Sulphur, one of the largest resorts in the South, prompted a family discussion about the propriety of their "gay & festive" niece partaking in the pleasures of society.

Lucy to Bess

Willow Cottage
Aug 28th/.71.

My dear, darling Bess

Your <u>short</u> letter, from Montgomery White, would have been answered as Cordele's letter will inform you (now en route), but for an attack of my old enemy, n-e-t-t-l-e-r-a-s-h—!! It has left me now—looking as I always do—a <u>pale</u> cream-color—with every freckle showing as plainly as possible! And you <u>both</u> can understand <u>why</u> I am particularly desirous of looking <u>rosy</u> & <u>well</u>—no mortal soul, out-side of my family, would believe the <u>truth</u>, if I <u>swore</u> to them:— so poor me! I will just have to let them have their own thoughts, & never a word say I—

Yesterday afternoon we came to Willow Cottage—on the way poor Mr Neilson was taken with a <u>chill</u>—& I tell you, he had a <u>big</u> & <u>long</u> one—fever continued all night, & rose again this morning—after he begun to take quinine—& has been at a steady heat all day—Not so hot—or is he as sick as he was before, but I do so dread these <u>frequent</u> bilious attacks—but the long hard rides which he is compelled to take on electioneering-tours are enough to make him sick <u>every week</u>—a man less <u>stout</u> could'ent stand them. We sent for Dr Matthews this morning, <u>to be sure</u> & prevent another rise of fever—but now it is late in the afternoon, & he has not yet come! How provoking these old settled <u>Doctors</u>!—I asked Mr Neilson to send for <u>Dr Lyon</u> in the beginning—& he said he <u>would</u>, & then changed for some unexpressed reason. I thought it would be a good time for us to decide upon a <u>family-physician</u>—take neither of the <u>old ones</u>—Matthews or McCabe—but compromise on Dr Lyon. When I say <u>family</u> physician, I mean for <u>Mr Neilson</u>—not <u>myself</u>. <u>I</u> don't design having an <u>use</u> for <u>any</u>!!

Well!—this is a long homily on <u>doctors</u> right in the off-start of a letter to my <u>gay</u> & <u>festive</u> neice—what cares she of <u>family-matters</u>?— But it shows the selfishness of <u>us all</u>—Mr Neilson is sick—& my heart is set on having him relieved as speedily as possible—therefore if I can't get a doctor, I must write about them!—

I have so much to say, & so many questions to ask—where to begin, & when I'll ever end, is for the <u>mysterious</u> future to unfold!—Well! I believe I begun about your letter from <u>Montgomery White</u>—& I will have my say about it now, before I stray off on some other uninteresting <u>family matter</u>—but now my dear, being a <u>woman of family</u>—the <u>responsible head</u> of a <u>family</u>—makes "a mighty differ,"[1] & you'll find it so when <u>you</u> are similarly situated—so don't be so <u>severe on me</u>— don't think I'm <u>too absorbed</u> for you'll be so too!! Think on <u>these things</u>!!—Well! as I was a-<u>going</u> on to say—your letter from Montgomery White was brought me at Wildwood by your <u>Uncle Jeemes</u>, & Mrs Eager!!—We were having an early supper in prospect of church-going when up they rode. I was in the act of pouring out your Uncle John a cup of coffee when they were announced—& down went the cup, & out rushed the dignified <u>head</u> of the family, to the gate, to greet them. I was so glad to see dear Mrs Eager! She seemed delighted at so <u>frantic</u> a reception, & before she was aware, was at Wildwood—<u>a settin</u> at the table, & a <u>drinkin</u> of coffee! How merry we all were—how we laughed, & how we talked, & how we asked questions. Then <u>your</u> letter <u>from</u> Montgomery <u>White</u> was produced, & read, & commented upon. Shall I repeat the comments?—I believe I will!—Said the <u>pert Mrs</u> John A— "Well! now <u>I</u> don't much like Bess remaining at Montgomery White without her Auntie—Mrs Prichett is as lovely a little woman as I ever knew—but she is young & gay—& so many of our Columbus-<u>acquaintances</u>, <u>not friends</u>—might remark upon her <u>unprotectedness</u> quite severely!— Then <u>Marse Jeemes</u> (with nose in air)—"<u>I</u> think Brooks is going to too many <u>fancy balls</u>—Every-body knows they are <u>rather dubious</u> kind of amusement— I don't like them!—She had better come home, I am sure I'd not let her go to <u>so many</u>"—(Chorus of laughter)—When silence again reigned—up spoke the <u>mild but earnest</u> "<u>Miss</u>"—"<u>I think so too</u>!!["] (<u>Chorus of laughter</u>). Then the silvery voiced Mrs Eager—"Well! am I permitted to express <u>my</u> opinion—am I enough in the family to be so privileged"—Whereupon all say eagerly "yes ma'm, yes m'a'm"!—then she proceeds—"I <u>feel</u> t'would be <u>best</u> for Bessie to be to her <u>Auntie</u>, as Ruth to Naomi—<u>never</u> to leave her."[2] Then the <u>quiet, but sage John</u> speaks—"My opinion is, that Sis Lizzie knows exactly <u>what</u> is <u>right</u> for Bess, & she will <u>do it</u> at <u>all</u> times, & in <u>all places</u>—besides Bess is as prudent, & as sensible as any woman in the land"!! This is a <u>quencher</u>—& all subside—Lizzie alone, having expressed no opinion—smiles approvingly!—while a pair of little brown eyes <u>peered</u> down behind the <u>coffee-pot</u> to hide a tear or two because of the kind <u>reproof</u>, & the <u>deserved</u> compliment to each of her far <u>away</u> loved ones!!—And so broke up our tea-party!

All went to church excepting Mrs Eager & I—Then what a talk we had! She told of her quiet stay with Lizzie & Gid[3]—of her <u>many</u> wonderings of the future—how she _often, often_ felt almost _cast down_—but waited to see _which way_ the _finger_ of Providence would point—then she came on a visit to Mrs Ottley—was _interviewed_ by Mr Tarrant—spoke face to face with him—told him _all_ she would require at his hands—all that she would, & _intended to do_! And ended by telling him she would board _out_ of the Institute (with Mrs Ottley) & would have her contract with him in _writing_!!—

Then I confided to her _all_ my heart's overflowing _happiness_ in my _dear precious husband_! How that I would not exchange places with any woman that _breathed_, & that how my love grew & grew each day—because each day I found him worthier to be _loved_! And so we talked—& talked—Next morning she left with Jim. I suppose she has returned to Lizzie now.

And now _today_ brings me your _Wytheville_ letter of Aug: 25th—my dear, how can I sufficiently thank you for your love & _confidence_—'tis so _inexpressibly sweet to me_! My dear child! my tears _will_ come at thought of your "_strong & strange love_." My heart _gushes_ out to you—oh! that my arms could now enfold you! Yes, darling, _always tell me all_ your feelings, hopes, wishes, or desires—_you know, you know_ how gladly I wait for every word—every whisper! Always feel that I am your _own little pet_ T'Ida. If at any time I can give a word of comfort, or advice, let me speak.

Your letter was so _sweet_ & _womanly_—a desire to open your heart, & yet, & yet a _shrinking_! How I can appreciate _it all_—& then too I think, I understand exactly how you feel towards the _person_ (shall I call him, "_Un_-beknown"?)—a feeling of _half_-awakened interest—too pleasing [to] loose, too _real_ to trifle with—& _yet_, & yet a _dream_ a _dream_ of exquisite _sweetness_! But he will not let you _dream_ any longer—is that why you are _sad_—or vexed—or call him _ugly names_?—Tis very cruel of _him_—he might leave well _enough alone_, I think! Perhaps he will come to the same _conclusion_ before he is satisfied! Don't be afraid of my thinking you too much interested—you'll get a little _heart-ache_ may-be—& feel, as your little _verse_ of _last summer_ said, "a little lonely, for _Today_"—but hearts grow light at _seventeen_ very quickly—& t'will only make you _softer, tenderer_—just what you need. Don't allow yourself to give him _any_ hope, if there is _no_ grounds—don't let your own _pleasure_ be _his grief_. He is _manly_, you say, & that is _why_ he must be treated _exactly right_. He will honor you all his days, as a true _christian_ woman!—& no higher honor can be bestowed upon any one!—If he in any way reminds you of my _dear John_, my heart _glows_ towards him. And his _hands_ are not so hard—"don't _look like it_"—ha! ha! What about his _whiskers_—are you _shocked_?—Now comes my trial of guessing. Poor me! Well! tis _one_ of the Messrs Taylor.[4] I think you evaded Lizzie by referring to _the other_—"L'other & L'otherest"[5]—I don't know _which_—but it's the one who grew angry with you about a _sett_ in the dance sometime since. You _mind_ writing me of it—don't you? I read the letter over again yesterday, & laughed over the spicy little episode. Now own up candidly &

tell me even if I did'ent guess right—I'm no part of a Yankee! Quit calling your-self foolish when you let your heart speak—it is just as it ought to be—trembling, gushing, shrinking, brave!! Are my epithets contradictory—no more than your heart at present. What a world of difference between the true confession—"poor little school-boy, don't you cry, you will get a sweetheart bye & bye."[6]—And what will you do about my poor dear sweetheart C.R.B[7]—oh! the chap should not have "writ" yet awhile! I much fear he will nip the "bud of tenderness" by too much eagerness! What did Auntie say?—What verdict went forth? I'm all anxiety, & curiosity. I was not as much surprised as you were perhaps—because I was somewhat prepared in-as-much-as Lucy Lyon[8] told me he had written a note to her asking for your address—so I was on the qui vive [alert]! You will have to be very careful in your conduct towards the ambitious youths of the country—Your Uncle John is anxious for C. B—'s future good. You remember he gave you a little lecture last Spring—very earnest was he too! There is no jesting [in] some cases—be true to yourself & your God!

Well, now about our writing & your complaining!—I protest against any of the accusations of neglect with which you charge Cordele, & myself. Poor Cordele! especially, for she has been true to write—& such nice good letters too—& both of you have so neglected her, that her feelings are hurt really. Trot has acted shamefully towards her—she told me the other day, with a pitiful tremor of the lip, that she had never had but one short letter from Sis Lizzie since she left, & that she felt forsaken! If Trot would only leave off such tender & untir-ing care of certain relatives (prospective) she would have more time, & strength to devote to home letters. I know she has forgotten half she promised me about being too dignified to do call duty to every body she met. September is coming. I remember it is a feverish month to both of you—so let me implore you, each to be careful! Now my dears, remember how far you are away from us—& don't exert yourselves unnecessarily—Trot has not been well the enduring summer, & this Fall may bring a dreadful crisis—do warn & take peculiar care of her. So many times, during these golden summer days, have dark shadows come stealth-ily athwart my beautiful horizon—yes, shadows of fear for my poor Trot. And you Bess, don't trust too much to your strength, & weigh, & rosy cheeks—leave off so much dancing—some is beneficial—too much injurious—try to get thro' the Fall strong & healthy.

How eagerly I will read the letter which Trot will send me, sometime. Is she trying to wean herself from me, that I get no good heart talks? She wrote me two letters at first—& now I am craving for another, & have been this many day!—'Surely for my waiting part, she will let me find at last'—that I have not lost her. Bess, do you practice much now?—does the new melancholy awaken the musical spirit? What new songs do you sing? Lizzie & I nearly cried over some of your old ones, which we were trying to hum! Will this summer's round of gaiety be too much for our level-headed neice—or will she apply herself to study & self-improvement, as arduously as she did last Fall? Her conduct then, was the wonder of many! Make a note of these points, & answer.

Mr Cox, & Jim both forgot the little box of jewelry which I had prepared, & so he went without it—ah! he was too eager for a northern flight—a pair of eyes (a match to his own) were watching for his coming. You understand to whom I allude—She had preceded him thither, a week or two! Forgive him!—He is in hot pursuit—I wonder what she will do! Don't you?

Night has approached—I have scribbled, scribbled! I hope what I have written may be as pleasing to you, as yours was to me. We have no news as yet from Jim. Heaven grant he may be improved by drinking that blessed water—wish Trot was there too! Mr Neilson's fever has gone off entirely, & now he is sleeping like an infant. I am giving him Quinine. Dr M— has not come yet—would'ent it be funny, if he has gone to Wildwood—I wrote him tho', that I was here, at the bridge-place—he surely understood that! Letter from Sister Sallie—made especial inquiries of you both, & sent dear love—said she had so many correspondents—she could write only at long intervals. [page torn] too, asks of you in every letter—they have all been sick.

Black people are just as loving as they can be, & send more messages than I ever could write. Woos staid with me last week, & was more like a sister, than servant. "Id"[9] was out the last time I was at home, & made me promise to write you a letter, & tell you how she did try to get to see you to say good-bye—but Mrs Hudson[10] was so sick she could not leave her,—& she just cried—Then how much obliged she was for the things you left her. I have not heard whether matters have come to a crisis with her or not. Cordele is sitting by writing to Cous Mary Nesbitt[11]—she sends a heartful of love. Parthene[12] is standing at my back,—& sends howdy. <...>

Write soon to your loving T'Ida.

NOTES

1. Robert Burns, "Address to the Unco Guid," *Poems, Chiefly in the Scottish Dialect* (1787), in Kinsley, ed., *Burns*, 38.

2. In the Bible, Naomi's sons married women named Orpah and Ruth. When Naomi's sons died, Ruth insisted on accompanying her to Bethlehem (Ruth 1).

3. Elizabeth Washburn Eager Harris (1849–1904), daughter of Charles Prince Eager and Laura Emily Wright Eager and wife of boot and shoe dealer Gideon Dowse Harris (1846–1919).

4. Probably a relative of Charlotte Taylor's (b. ca. 1818), proprietor of Kalorama, where Lizzie and Bess were boarding.

5. Lucy was perhaps paraphrasing "Each man seeks those of different quality from his own, and such as are good of their kind; that is, he seeks other men, and the *otherest*" (Ralph Waldo Emerson, "Uses of Great Men," *Representative Men* [1850], in Williams and Wilson, eds., *Emerson*, 4).

6. Probably a school rhyme.

7. Cranmer Ridley Boyce (b. 1851), a student at the University of Mississippi, son of Dr. James Monroe Boyce (1821–83) and Betsy Barker Patterson Boyce (1831–79). The Boyce family lived near Byhalia and were neighbors of Lucy's relatives the Nesbitts.

8. Lucy Deaderick Lyon (1855–1915), daughter of Rev. James Adair Lyon and Adelaide Eliza Deaderick Lyon.

9. Id may have been a former Irion family servant.

10. Mary Cornelia Hudson (1829–93), wife of John Fontaine Hudson.

11. Mary M. Nesbitt (b. ca. 1835), daughter of Demsey Nesbitt and Matilda Nesbitt.

12. Parthene was Cordele's maid before the war and at this time was employed by the family as a servant.

ào

Recounting news about crops, housework, and servants to her schoolgirl niece led Lucy to reflect upon the gulf between maidenhood and married life.

Lucy to Bess

Wildwood.
Sept 25th/.71.

My dear old Bess.

Your <u>big</u> letter of Sept 9th has lain unanswered much longer, than I thought at its' reception, it would, or <u>could</u>—but I had written you such a volume, & so many little house-hold duties <u>would</u> cry out for immediate attention, that time passed, & I just contented myself by thinking of you, & wishing so much, so <u>very</u> much to see you. I find I had counted more on the <u>usual</u> return of Fall bringing you back home than I was quite conscious of—every time I hear of any one's return, my heart gives a <u>thump</u> of expectancy—but then next moment comes the thought of a <u>whole</u> year's waiting—can it be so? Yes, it <u>must</u>, & <u>ought</u> to be just as it is.

Jim wrote me of his great disappointment in not meeting you in Wytheville— I think it put the old man out of humor, for he wrote a very crabbed letter, & seemed impressed with the idea that you had gone to Norfolk [Virginia] (350 miles) just on a two weeks visit, & would return to <u>Wytheville</u>. He said he had written for you both to come along home, settle down & quit <u>spending money</u>. Poor fellow!—the bachelor life, which he thought so charming in the distance,

Augusta Female Seminary, Staunton, Virginia.
Courtesy of Mary Baldwin College Archives, Mary Baldwin College.

has proved quite the contrary in the realization—he will never be satisfied with the family scattered like they are. I think it absurd in his wishing your return, when every arrangement has been made, for your stay! I am <u>killing</u> my own joy when I advise your stay, for of course my life is necessarily more quiet than formerly, & I have a great horror of growing <u>old timey</u>, & countrified, & if our <u>grand</u> & <u>inspiring Sister</u>; & <u>gay</u> & <u>popular neice</u> should return, why! I would know as much of the world as when I was in it—besides the dear dear delight of having the <u>home</u>-<u>feeling</u> renewed! But oh! I know I must not be <u>selfish</u>—& when I am so happily situated in my little home with such a <u>husband</u>, & <u>such</u> a sister, I feel it almost a sin to allow my heart to <u>yearn</u> for my distant loved-ones, when the separation is beneficial to them. But sometimes the feeling is so <u>strong</u> I cannot resist indulging in wishes of return—& find myself feeling glad, if something should make you change your plans. I had such a sweet, <u>natural</u> dream of Trot the other night—so glad were we to be once more together—I was sorry to be awakened even by the accustomed matutinal caress from my good man.

Mr Neilson went to town the other day, & brought such a package of letters home, we felt like we had seen our friends. For <u>Cordele</u> one from each of you; for himself, one from <u>Sissie</u>, one from Jim, & that precious letter which <u>Trot</u> wrote him—& for myself, one from Jim, one from <u>Corrie</u>, & one from <u>Madie</u>.[1] Now you can imagine little <u>Wildwood</u> was in a state of <u>pleased</u> & <u>social</u> excitement. When people live as far as we do in the country, hearing from the Post, is quite an event. But I don't suppose I have lived out here quite long enough—nor have I for a <u>moment</u> felt the <u>ennui</u> which a residence in the country (of <u>long</u> duration & monotony) induces, to <u>fully appreciate all</u> such thrilling episodes—however getting letters with me is always a pleasure—, & I shall dread the day, when I can no longer feel a thrill of delight, when these dear messengers, from distant friends, arrive.

Your letter descriptive of your departure from <u>Wythe</u> & arrival at Norfolk was exceedingly agreeable. I love to hear of your <u>making friends</u>, where-ever you go. I knew you would find <u>our</u> dear Miss Anna,[2] just the same sweet loving friend—her <u>note</u> did so touch me. I'll answer, & enclose in this letter. Sister Lizzie's description of her sight-seeing was much appreciated—it sounded so like her old self. I wish she would write <u>oftener</u>—it is no excuse that <u>you</u> write, or that <u>she</u> has such an <u>extensive</u> correspondence—aye! the difference is to us! At last decided upon Staunton—<u>so glad</u>. I feel somehow a <u>home</u>-feeling for that place! For no other reason, than that I've heard so long of the good <u>Presbyterian</u> school. Ha! ha!!

How gratifying to know you feel the importance of the opening of school-duties. Dear Bess! you <u>must</u> exert yourself—how high a standard we all have raised for you! We cannot help it <u>either</u>, for we know your ability.

I hope you have received a letter from Mr Neilson—he addressed it to Wytheville—before knowing of your departure. I think it one of the best letters, I ever read—& oh! so much like Brother Mc's[3] own peculiar style, I could not keep from crying over it. So often am I reminded of your dear Father—it <u>frightens</u> me!—

We look for Jim the last of this week—how glad we shall be to see the old fellow—I hope he has enjoyed his holiday, for tis is the first he has had since he was twenty-one. Mr Neilson thinks he will go to Crawford this week—if so, we will go to Willow Cottage—

Town still quite dull—new goods are coming in, & people are returning from their jaunts, but trade is not very brisk as yet.—

Cordele was down at home Saturday, found all well, but Woos—thought she had a chill. Press is pushing with his cotton. Even to Pheobe, & <u>Woos</u> & <u>Lide</u> in the field. The weather is charming for gathering crops. Mr Neilson will make very little cotton—but plenty of <u>corn</u>, wheat, peas, hogs, & potatoes. <u>Homely</u> subjects for a young lady—but knowing my practical <u>neice</u> so well, I venture to mention such things.

Cordele thinks Woos is going to marry this Fall—tho' this is quite under the ruse, in-as-much-as she has never mentioned the subject to us—tho' from certain signs "Miss" is sure <u>matrimony</u> is brewing. I shall be sorry for her to marry <u>John</u> Abrams[4]—but suppose it's not as <u>I</u> wish. We think also that <u>Yan-daloo</u>, & <u>her man</u> are making preparations for the consummation of their <u>pro-longed</u> affair. <. . .>

My letter from Madie was so delightful—t'was written before Gus went, & she gave me a full description of how she was situated. I am almost tempted to enclose the letter for you two, to read. Of course she is all enthusiasm over her <u>new</u> home. And I am acquainted with the position of every article of furniture in her house—for Gus <u>drew</u> a <u>diagram</u> of the whole! Dear old Gus!—what a pleas-ant visit I had from him. Madie is almost crazy to know "how goes the <u>world</u> with <u>me</u>" (Comprehenez-vous?) [Do you understand?]—so she enclosed a <u>note</u> of <u>inquiry</u>. How I laughed over it—<u>so much</u> like her! Says she is as yet <u>free</u> as a bird(?) Willie <u>Odeneal</u>[5] is now on a visit to her. I went to see Will, & sent ever so much word to Madie on that very subject—Gus wanted to tell me that there was nothing the matter—for he dwelt on "<u>how</u> little changed Sis was." Dear mercy! how I write! Lulie Harrison Fort[6] would suit <u>you</u>, Bess—she has sent for her Mother <u>already</u>—& her mother has gone with a trunk filled with ready-made clothing for the <u>Unbeknown</u>! So <u>reports</u>, <u>Callie</u>.[7] La! how much I could tell you, if I could only see you. Your christmas-present is still further off than ever—ahem! Oh! no! I must quit gossiping, & go, & make up some light-biscuit for supper! Cousin Cornelia sent me a new receipt—which is delightful, & so easy, & I succeed admirably. Mr Neilson is so gratified, & I am so proud! I am learning cookery right fast, considering I'm such a Mrs Wragge.[8] Good-bye till after sup-per—wish you & Trot & Miss Anna were here to help eat the nice biscuit, & I'd let Trot drink as much coffee as she wished.

Well! supper's over—& as the biscuit, batter-cakes, coffee, & butter-milk were each in their turn <u>praised</u> & enjoyed by <u>our</u> man, <u>Miss & I</u> feel the complacency of gratified cooks; & I leave <u>my throne</u> (Mr N—'s <u>lap</u>) & resume my writing with a determination of "not writing much more to Bess—altho' I've such a <u>world</u> of talk for her."—

The glaring sunlight has gone, & in its' stead the soft, soothing rays of the calm moon flood the earth—& "of what shall I say it reminds me"? Why! of the <u>youthful thrills</u>, which it ever awakened in my heart in the tender years of <u>first maidenhood</u>! Years fraught with <u>tumultuous</u> feelings! <u>Now</u> in my maturity, I look back & <u>smile</u>—not in scorn, nor derision,—but in <u>sympathy</u> with the old feel-ings, & whenever I see a <u>girl</u> passing thro' a similar experience, I feel a drawing towards her. You understand, of course, to what subject I am approaching—ah! gently—the affaires d'cour [love affair] of a tender maiden should be broached very <u>techingly</u>—well! now my dear, how <u>du</u> you feel towards the <u>soft</u>-handed, <u>hard</u>-headed, knight of Wytheville! "<u>Better</u> I thank you"?[9]—is there no news from that portion of the <u>globe</u>? Keep me posted & send his photograph if you can get one, without exciting a <u>hope</u> in his heart. (The above style is borrowed from Maidee (Mrs. Cannon)[10] Jno. A.) <u>Story</u>!—every <u>word</u> original—<u>like</u>-<u>wise</u> <u>style</u>!—

Corrie wrote that Auntie & Uncle Tom[11] had gone to see Cous Bob Hunts' family[12] this summer & brought back one of the daughters—<u>De</u>—a very pretty girl—Your friend Mr C.R.B—was quite <u>attentive</u>, & sent all sorts nice things to her during her stay. So you see you have a <u>rival</u>. He is a born flirt, I believe—but don't do anything to wound him. I laughed over your feelings expended on Mr Cox's devoted head. I am anxious to see him again.

How do you feel since you got into the <u>papers</u>?[13]—Surely every paper in the South will copy that <u>neat</u>, & <u>appropriate</u> complimentary notice of the departure of the charming young lady from Columbus Miss! <u>Ah</u>! <u>me</u>—<u>so sweet</u>. No wonder you like <u>Wytheville</u>—aught to hear your Uncle Jeemes' opinion of the <u>same</u>. Don't you think it funny for Mrs Weaver[14] & Jim to go <u>galavanting</u> around the country together?—

Our new <u>trial</u> preacher is expected now in a short time—Mr <u>Wharry</u> at last. We, of course, are on the tip-toe of expectancy. The ladies have renovated the Parsonage, & they say it is nice & comfortable now—but nothing is done to the church. We shall be very glad to go again to the dear old place of worship—But how many familiar, & dear faces we will miss. The <u>Steers</u> family[15] have <u>sold</u> out <u>everything</u>, & are going to Shrevesport [Louisiana] to live—how much we will miss them in our community. Saunders Billups[16] has bought their lot—& he & Wilda are going to house-keeping right away. Maj Henry Whitfield[17] had rented the place, & Miss <u>Laura</u> was again in <u>town</u>—much to her delight I suppose! Now they will go to the <u>hotel</u>![18]

Now I must stop sure enough—with asking you <u>please</u> to write every <u>particular</u> of your <u>new</u> life—of all your surroundings—not forgetting a description of any <u>new clothes</u> which you may have <u>purchased</u> & <u>had made</u>. You astonish me by saying <u>turbans</u> are worn—I thought every thing would be wide brim. But dear me! I am a season behind hand, for I've seen nothing new at all, since the last Spring's opening. Tell dear old Trot how much I would like a talk with her—next best thing is to write. I owe <u>eight</u> more letters <u>this</u> minute, & ought to be ashamed to consume so much time with one. Kiss Trot & Miss Anna for us all. Cordele is much better in health than she was last week—she hopes to escape the entire <u>Fall</u> without sickness. Mr Neilson was again threatened with chills—but I hope will miss them.

We spent the day at Sister Anne's last week—Such a delightful day too!—Liz told me of your letter—but said I must <u>not read</u> it. She looked as pretty as <u>her</u> <u>picture</u> that day. She & Pattie Mills[19] were to have come up here Saturday—but did not. Oh! Beckie Barry has at last paid me a visit—a nice sweet visit too—I enjoyed it so much. She told us something so funny—said when <u>Pattie</u> was out at their house, she fell in love with <u>Charlie</u>–& oh! <u>such airs</u> & <u>graces</u> to captivate him!

He was much flattered at first—but she <u>staid</u> so long—he got <u>tired</u>. Now what do you think of that "<u>affaire d'cour</u>" [love affair]. I want to have one good laugh with <u>Liz</u> about it. They were rather looking for <u>Nephew</u> John Furniss at Millwood[20]—I hope he will come—Sunday was his birthday!—Sister Mary, Brother James, & the babies[21] spent the day with us yesterday! All so pleasant. Lou is so pretty & bad!—Letters from Sissie report her still in Washington—she has been sick—but is now well, & enjoying herself. Sophie reports more sickness—Mr Lewis has had his <u>fourth</u> bilious attack. "I will not say good-evening"—for fear I'll write all night if I do!—Write soon to your own T'Ida. Heaven bless you both!

[John Abert Neilson added the following postscript]
Don't you believe half of what is herein writ! I tell you what she is getting too much for me. She took my pants from me long ago—I am going electioneering tomorrow.
Love to Sis Lizzie & large share for yr-self.

Yr. uncle
John

Notes

1. Mary Adair Lyon Childress (1849–1928), daughter of Rev. James Adair Lyon and Adelaide Eliza Deaderick Lyon and wife of lawyer John Whitsitt Childress Jr. (1845–1908).

2. Anna Leigh Short (1832–1916), widow of planter Thomas H. Short (b. ca. 1799).

3. Lawyer McKinney F. Irion Jr. (1833–62), Elizabeth Parthenia Irion's father and Lucy's brother.

4. Farmer John Abrams (b. ca. 1850).

5. Willie Blanch Odeneal (b. 1847), daughter of farmer Ebenezer Patrick Odeneal (1804–77) and Rosamond Dearing Odeneal (1801–76).

6. Louisiana Victoria Harrison Fort (1851–1939), daughter of lawyer Isham Harrison Jr. (1824–64) and Julia Randolph Whitfield Harrison (1828–1905) and wife of Robert Wallace Fort (1848–78). She was expecting her first child, Robert Wallace Fort Jr. (1871–1934).

7. Caroline Dyer Harrison (1845–1924) was Louisiana Victoria Harrison Fort's sister.

8. Mrs. Wragge was a fictional character in Wilkie Collins, *No Name* (1862), whose head began buzzing at the thought of making her husband an omelet.

9. Lucy paraphrased "Much better, I thank you, Dr. John" (Charlotte Brontë, *Villette* [1853], ed. Lilly, 247).

10. Susan Cannon, *Maidee, the Alchemist, or, Turning All to Gold* (1871).

11. Byhalia farmer Thomas Nesbitt (b. ca. 1808) and his wife, Malinda Nesbitt (b. ca. 1804).

12. Farmer Robert Hunt (b. ca. 1807), his wife Lucinda Hunt (b. ca. 1825), and their daughter Adelia A. Hunt (1853–1934).

13. Southern newspapers printed columns on visitors to the most popular springs resorts.

14. Ellen Weaver (1823–95), wife of commission merchant William B. Weaver (1818–78).

15. Cotton broker Schuyler Bliss Steers (1832–89) and his wife Kate Clarke Steers (1836–88).

16. J. Saunders Billups (1849–1919) and his wife Wilde Sykes Billups (1852–99).

17. Lawyer Henry Buchanan Whitfield (1835–82), husband of Laura Young Whitfield (1839–77), was mayor of Columbus in 1871.

18. The Gilmer hotel was named after John Gilmer (1792–1860), the largest original stockholder of the hotel company. Opened in 1858, the Gilmer was converted to a military hospital during the Civil War. Andrew W. King (1816–93) was proprietor of the hotel in 1871.

19. Martha "Pattie" Barry Mills (1851–78), daughter of lawyer Willard Curtis Mills (1816–77) and Cyrenthia E. Hunt Mills (1825–82).

20. Millwood (or Corner Cottage) was built in 1837 by Dr. Aurelius N. Jones (1807–54) and Cornelia A. Gibson Jones (1818–56). The Symons family probably named the house after John Mauger Symons, who was a sawmill owner.

21. Louisa Abert Neilson (1869–1936) and Mary Bruce Neilson (1871–72), daughters of James Crawford Neilson and Mary Bruce Barry Neilson.

૪ð

With Cordele and Woos at her side, Lucy impressed John's kin with a good dinner and a liberal dose of vivacity. Mrs. Neilson delighted in the admiration shown her by John's cousin, cotton broker George William Abert (1829–1912). The social interlude provided happy relief from more pressing concerns, including John's flagging support in the campaign for sheriff and the fear that next year's wages could not be met by farm income alone.

Lucy to Bess

Wildwood.
Oct 17th /.71.

My dear, dear Bess.

Imagine a nice cozy fire, a bright lamp, a cheerful looking room, with <u>two</u> women as occupants—very dissimilar in appearance are these <u>two</u>—one large & dark (—not to say with the <u>odious</u> Rochester "big, & brown & buxom"[1]—) the other, fair, (& oh! <u>misery</u>) <u>Dutchy</u> in form. These two <u>mysterious</u> persons are <u>sisters</u>—& love each other very much. They are alone tonight, but there's a '<u>vacant chair</u>'[2] across the hearth, sitting <u>expectant</u>—the usual occupant is off on a visit to a sick neighbor. The <u>mysterious</u> sisters try to find congenial employment during the absence of the <u>usual</u> occupant—so one sews <u>industriously</u> on a new <u>striped</u>

calico-dress—whilst the other brings out her old Port-folio, & from its swollen, &—alas! bursted sides extracts a letter overwhich she pours with intense interest, & then makes ready pen, ink, & paper for the purpose of answering!—And would you believe it, that mysterious person "stands before you"[3] in the form of myself. Yes, actually I must throw off the impenetrable mask, & confess myself.

Your dear letter of the 7th was so joyfully received, & devoured on sight. All of us do so thank you for it. I dreamed the night before it's arrival, that I received a letter so large, from you, that it "had obliged" to be folded in a package like a newspaper. It was sweet, & kind of you to take so much pains to tell us all the particulars, which so interested us. It takes time & thought, as well as inclination, to write such satisfactory letters, as yours, & you deserve thanks. Of course, every thing connected with you both is of the last importance to us. If you only knew how much you were in our thoughts.

Trot's letters to Jim are very sweet & we take them to ourselves as much as we can! The last, relating the beautiful acts of kindness shown by those comparative strangers—thrilled me with a gladsome feeling that there were such, such noble specimens of the human race. How delightful to have actual evidence of such disinterested kindness. Thank those friends for us all. Jim took Mr Stevens address, & said he would certainly write him—of course he was touched to the very heart. But 'John' did'ent seem to think it at all remarkable that every body should'ent pull out their purses to you! That letter was brought out by a hack-full of city-relatives! To wit—Mrs Bradford, Miss Maria Barry, & little Maria, Miss Jennie Abert, & Cousin George![4] They came, & spent the day. We had sufficient warning of their coming, & were fully prepared. We had the tables set in Cordele's room—& everything in order. Woos was up too, & did so well. Had us a good dinner—Chicken-Pie—& smothered chicken, salad, beans, tomatoes, "lima-beans"—potatoe compote,—dried fruit, baked-apples—crackers, pickles, jellies &c for first course—then sweet-meat custard, & a most delightful Queen-Pudding for second, & coffee for third! All seemed to enjoy it—indeed! I've heard of it since!—The friends were so pleasant—so chatty—so full of bouancy! Mrs Bradford is a delightful companion—& my dear Cousin George was almost affectionate to his Cousin Lucy—almost petted her! Ha! Mr Neilson says "he is charmed with you Lucy—he admires you—I can see it in his manner."—But the sensible(?) Lucy thinks it is because she is now Mrs John A—, & he is amusing himself with her "just for today"! He has been out of society so long, & the said Lucy is rather fresh therefrom, & he likes her chatter! She rallied him upon the cut of his new style coat—the color of his gloves, &c &c—all of which talk rather amuses him being so unaccustomed to that style. I've a good laugh on Miss for he has expressed a desire to have "Polly"[5] to keep him company in his room. Says every body goes to bed so early, & he has no one to talk to!—Gay companion Polly would be at night—a poor substitute! Mrs Bradford & Tommie[6] went to

Bailey late in the season—She was delighted with the effects of the water. Says she saw Mrs Farrar[7] at Tuscumbia [Alabama], & she asked affectionately for Trot. Tommie was taken very ill with Typhoid Pneumonia, & came home, & was considered dangerous for sometime—he is up now, but Sister Mary saw him the other day, & she says he looks wretchedly. Annie[8] was up at Pontotoc on a visit to some relatives—she hurried home on her brother's account—& brought a young gentleman cousin with her, Henry Bradford![9] When she found Tom so much better—then she went to enjoying her cousin—took him to see the girls, or had them to see him. Lizzie was there at last accounts having a delightful time. Annie saw Susie Duke[10] in P—, & oh! she sent so much word to you & Trot! Jack sent word that he & his sweetheart were going to be married sometime this month. Sent particular word to Miss Bessie! I fear this will be a sad month to you—for My dear, I must prepare you—Mr John D & Alice[11] are to be married on the 24th! Don't allow the shock to be too much for you! It is all important that you should keep up appearances anyhow! Bet Humphries Franklin[12] is now with her Aunt India[13]—as she came thro' Nashville [Tennessee], she saw D. Cahal[14]—& when D. found out that she knew us all—she liked to have kissed her. <...> Your friend, Charles Barry is now in at Mitchell & Hardy's[15]—there's joy! I have heard of no new developments in his love-affair!—

Old Esquire Donnell[16] is dead—I believe he was one of our oldest citizens—much respected. The town is remarkably healthy, & has been all fall & summer.

We were glad to hear of your purchases—do send us samples of your dresses, if convenient. I know your cloak must be beautiful—is it white or black—& what is the shape! I am so glad you both got your things in Norfolk. Tell Trot please not to grieve over her money any more—just give it up—Nobody blames her—& all are sorry for her. I think with Mrs Partington[17] that she must have had a "fellow-feeling &c &c" you know the rest—that is the only way I can account for the loss. I think you have just cause of complaint against your dear Guardian, & what you said "corroborated with my taste" exactly. Jim opened your letter, & had full benefit before I saw it—said if he had known how many secrets there was between us—he would not have read it. I could'ent keep from blushing—to think he had read some parts. He came out Sunday, & spent a sweet day with us—t'was such a day as he & you came up last Spring—how I did wish you could have been with him again. He was so cheerful—, & after dinner, & a good cup of coffee—he & John were so bad we women could scarcely remain in their presence. He was out in a big rain going back—hope he will not be sick.

How pleasant your school must be—which class did you enter?—As your French teacher[18] is so charment [charming], I hope you will like the language more, & learn to speak & read it fluently. Do try—please Bess! [I] hope your vocal teacher[19] will be agreeable—I was in hopes t'was a man instead of woman. Do your best tho', & I know you'll succeed. Now Bess, I am going to give you a piece of advice—which I know you'll not relish very much—but I won't with-hold on that account. I act towards you, as I hope you will always towards me—in all earnestness. I do think you should cease corresponding with the Wytheville-friend—like-wise C.R.B. Dont think I am over particular—you well know I am not—but if its no! with one it ought to be no! emphatically—no communication at all—any, will compromise you. Just let him write on if he wishes. I know he will tire after awhile. As for the other—he talks of receiving your letters—our relatives say they hear of you thro' him. Suppose you drop him too! Plenty of time my dear!—Cordele had a long letter from Cousin Mary Nesbitt—she spoke of looking for Trot to spend the winter with them—what could she have meant?

I really do not know whether Woos is going to marry or not—she vows she is not. She will not acknowledge to any preparations—says "Miss Neely gave a false alarm." I often wonder what is to become of her next year—I well know she will never consent to come up here, so far from that beloved church, & we of course cannot give wages to a servant ten miles off. Besides she is a more expensive one, than we can afford. In a month we shall know for certain who will be sheriff—the Radical nominee Lewis[20]—every body thinks. The negroes are a unite, & they are four to one in this county. Mr Neilson will not be disappointed, for he has never been very sanguine—still he would be very glad of the office. T'would make the coming years look less gloomy financially—But there is always work for willing hands, & if Providence sees fit that the coming years shall be years of struggle—why! we are prepared for them, & only ask His help. I am a rich woman, so long as I have the love & confidence of such a man. How full this great love makes my life. I would be an ingrate indeed, to be discontent with my lot.—

The fall weather setting in reminded "Miss" that she needed some additions to her wardrobe,—so the last time we were down at home,—we went in to town, & purchased two pretty, bright calico for her, & a bonnet, & hat for each of us. Oh! don't understand that we each went to the unheard-of expense of getting both a bonnet & hat—I mean she got a white velvet bonnet white plume, & red flower—& I got a black velvet hat—trimmed in white & black—mine is high crown with a turned up brim—not quite a turban—I will need no hack hat. They are neither very expensive for this market—$5—each. We took our own money—determining not to trouble the gentlemen. Cordele will not get a nice dress until after christmas. We can then tell how the cotton will turn out.

Don't think strangely of Sissie's not writing to you—she has so many relatives & friends—she wrote one or two letters around, & then stopped—because the number was too burdensome. In every letter to us she makes particular inquiries of you both. I know there is no lack of interest. Do pray write to Mrs Eager as often as you can & don't dilate too much upon your love for Miss Baldwin—there's a strange look in the glorious black eyes, when [with] the thought of any one else occupying her place. You know of course, that she, & Mr T— had a fuss—&

Above and facing: Dress, hat, and shoes. Irion Neilson Collection.
Courtesy of Collection of the Museum of Mississippi History,
Mississippi Department of Archives and History.

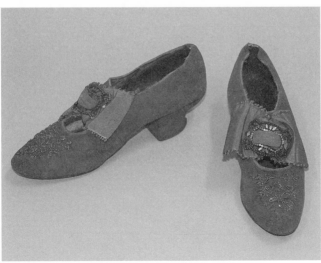

she then accepted a place with Mr Stainback in the public school—she boards at Mrs Ottley's.

I did'ent enclose a stamp, & a little piece of pink paper that I know of—just happened to be in the envelope I suppose. What <u>paper</u> do you have reference to—when you ask me Jim's opinion—the <u>Wytheville</u> one? I've never heard him say.—

Cordele is anxious to know if <u>Willie Allen</u>[21] goes to Miss Baldwin—& if you have seen or heard anything from Gen <u>Liley</u>[22] since your arrival. I believe I have answered all your questions. My dear John will write as soon as he can—but it takes him <u>forever</u> to get up an inclination—& <u>longer</u> to <u>execute</u>! Don't call your letter "<u>no count</u>"—it was sweet, & loving, & <u>true</u> & womanly, & that made it more appreciated, than if all the flowers of Rhetoric had adorned it's pages. Ah! the "house-dog bays a deep-mouthed welcome home"[23] John's coming—Good-night!

—Wednesday-night—I must just add a little more to what I wrote last night to thank <u>Trot</u> for the <u>precious</u> letter I received from her today—your little note too was truly acceptable—& contained what I most wished to hear—i.e. you intended throwing off the knight of the <u>summer</u>! You are a sensible girl—above your years. Don't get the photograph either. I do wish to see it—but would <u>not</u> have <u>you</u> committed. <u>That</u> darling letter from Trot, is what I've so <u>hungered</u> for! Cordele & I enjoyed it as a feast <u>savoring</u> of <u>old time-style</u>. Yes, it was exactly what we both wished. I will write again as soon as I can. I've been with you all day!—Ah! the plans Miss & I do lay for you both when you are home again. With love from us all. Your own T'Ida.

NOTES

1. Lucy paraphrased "big, brown, buxom" (Charlotte Brontë, *Jane Eyre* [1847], ed. Leavis, 248).

2. Henry J. Washburn and George F. Root, "The Vacant Chair" (1861), in Crawford, ed., *Civil War Songbook*, 117–20.

3. Acts 4:10.

4. Juliette Bradford (1826–91), widow of planter John D. Bradford (1809–60); Maria Barry (b. ca. 1840), an occupant of George William Abert's household; Maria Barry Abert (b. ca. 1862), daughter of George William Abert and Martha Pattie V. Barry Abert (1832–66); Jane E. Abert (ca. 1843–87), daughter of Charles H. Abert (1795–1867) and Jane C. Abert (1805–60) and sister of George William Abert; George William Abert, who during the Civil War served as colonel of Company K, Fourteenth Infantry Regiment Mississippi.

5. In 1869 Mary C. Marshall Jones (1847–76) had asked the Irion family to care for her parrot named Polly.

6. Thomas B. Bradford (1849–91), son of John D. Bradford and Juliette Bradford.

7. Lucy and Lizzie met Mrs. Farrar during their visit to Bailey Springs in 1870.

8. Annie Bradford (b. 1853), daughter of John D. Bradford and Juliette Bradford.

9. Henry Bradford (b. 1851), son of Judge William Daugherty Bradford (b. 1818) and Rosalie Spotswood Dandridge Bradford (ca. 1825–98).

10. Lizzie and Bess had traveled with "Capt. Duke & Sister" to White Sulphur Springs, West Virginia, in 1870 (Eliza Lucy Irion to James William Gray Irion, August 29, 1870).

11. John D. Young (1848–90) married Alice Baskerville (1850–1928) on October 24, 1871.

12. Bettie Pegram Humphries Franklin (b. 1845), wife of farmer James Franklin (1840–91).

13. Indiana Matilda Gregory Taylor was the sister of Bettie's mother, Martha Elizabeth Gregory Humphries (1817–45).

14. Teacher Dee Cahal (ca. 1850–1909) of Lebanon, Tennessee.

15. Merchants David S. Mitchell and N. H. Hardy (b. ca. 1818).

16. Grocer and former mayor of Columbus Levi Donnell (1801–71).

17. Mrs. Partington was the central character in Benjamin Penhallow Shillaber, *Life and Sayings of Mrs. Partington* (1854), *Partingtonian Patchwork* (1873), and *Ike and His Friends* (1879).

18. Mad. Marandaz was the resident French governess and teacher of Spanish, and N. Lucy Tate (b. ca. 1851) was assistant in English and French.

19. John Lewis Brown (1815–81), Anna Mary Morton Brown Fultz (1840–1923), and Tacie Daniel were teachers of vocal music.

20. Ohio-born Hiram W. Lewis (1843–1912) became sheriff (1872–75).

21. Willie Allen was a student of the Augusta Female Seminary. Her father was Maj. William W. Allen of Liverpool, England, who, according to school records, lived in Alabama in 1874–75.

22. Perhaps Lucy was referring to farmer John Lilley (b. ca. 1842), who in 1870 lived in Augusta County, Virginia. During the Civil War, Lilley had enlisted as a first lieutenant in Company H, Fifty-second Infantry Regiment Virginia, and he was promoted to full lieutenant colonel in 1864. Lucy met him in June 1869.

23. Lucy paraphrased "Tis sweet to hear the watch-dog's honest bark / Bay deep-mouth'd welcome as we draw near home" (Lord Byron, *Don Juan* [1819–24], in McGann, ed., *Lord Byron*, vol. 5, 47).

৪৯

As the winter approached, family affairs centered on discussions about the fate of Willow Cottage. With Jim unsupportive of a "full & explicit" arrangement between family members and John unwilling to accept anything less, Lucy wrote to Lizzie in Virginia in an attempt to encourage a settlement. With the homestead in limbo, Cordele was forced to the sad realization that she would remain indefinitely at Wildwood.

Lucy to Lizzie

Wildwood.

Oct 24th/.71.

My precious Trotwood.

In my last to Bess—I announced that my heart's desire & prayer had been answered in the arrival of your letter—& now, I seat myself to respond & thank you again, & again for the life-like 'feast of reason & <u>flow</u> of <u>soul</u>.'[1] 'Tis just such a pleasure as I knew, the (to me) <u>very</u> tardy spirit would moved you to confer, & therefore I grew impatient of its' bestowal. I know you consider me very exacting, & so perhaps, I am—but when you remember how I am your <u>own</u>, <u>own</u> child, that you 'raised by hand,'[2] you should be a little compassionate, & in your heart forgive. I did do my best to love your letters to Jim as if they were <u>my own</u>, <u>own</u>—but the sweet <u>possessive</u> feeling would not hover over them, & of consequence I went on waiting, & wishing for <u>mine</u>. So <u>at last</u> it <u>did</u> come, & oh! if you could have seen <u>my</u> sincere joy, you would feel repaid for the trouble the writing cost. Of course Trot, I don't feel that <u>utter</u> dependence upon your love & presence, which used of old to make me so <u>desolate</u> when separated from you—but you have <u>next</u> to the <u>first</u> place in my heart, & how closely our lives have been interwoven you <u>best</u> know—so when I <u>miss</u> so dear a part of my <u>inner</u>-self, how can I keep from <u>pining</u>. Four months since you & Bess left!—<u>four years</u> almost, in feeling!—Cordele, & I think, & talk, & plan for you every day. We have quiet, sweet days, & altho so far off from our former associates we never feel lonely—we have not felt the monotony of country-life yet, which seems so to ennui others, much more self-sufficient than we. I look forward with a little dread for Cordele during the coming wintry days, when frequent communication will be impossible—then too, she is contemplating a <u>formal</u> surrender of her S.School-class, when next she sees Judge Goodwin. She <u>feels</u> she cannot do justice to him, to herself, or the children, when obliged by circumstances to be so irregular. I do feel <u>so sorry</u> for the sacrifice of <u>pleasure</u> & <u>pride</u> which this costs her—but she looks upon it as a duty, & very sweetly submits. Last Sabbath Mr Neilson took us down especially for church—we went late Saturday evening, & returned the next evening—Cordele said as she walked among her flowers that beautiful Sabbath-morning before <u>sun-rise</u>, she almost <u>shouted</u>, so full of gratitude was her heart. I laughingly told her, she was equal to <u>Nancy</u>—shouting at that <u>unheard-of-hour</u>—but I was <u>touched</u>, altho' I jested. Every body was so glad to see her at S.School—& her little boys were more than ever affectionate—then, Mr Cason gave us so stirring a sermon—altogether she thought she had never enjoyed a day more. It is beautiful to see how she & Mr N— love each other—it does my heart good. What would <u>she</u>, or <u>I</u> do if <u>he</u> was <u>quere</u> or <u>curous</u> towards my sister in his own home? Thank Heaven for such a husband!!!

Jim was out at home with us too, & such a sweet reunion it was—we sat up till almost twelve—& that is very wonderful for us "chickens I tell you." Jim improves in health constantly—& in spirits too—he is now enjoying a charming flirtation with the widow H—"not the one so noted in history—but &c &c"[3] you can apply the latter clause.

The time is approaching for a business settlement, & I confess to a considerable dread—for you know how opposed Jim is to anything like a full & explicit statement of affairs. How much that disposition to avoid a thorough examination has already cost him![4] He must of course take the initiative, for Mr N— cannot. Mr N— will never enter upon any business arrangement in the world unless, everything is as plain as can be. I am so afraid Jim will think him over-particular—but you know Trot now is a time for division—& he must have a full understanding of what portion is mine before he can undertake the cultivation of the farm—he must lay his plans—he must make an estimate of the costs & profits. You know how generous & free Jim is—he just says "yes, take the place, & go on with it—do with it as you please"—but you know that's not the right way—we have always had things in common—but now, we must come to a settlement on the major points, of course minor points are unimportant. I find myself wishing for your clear head, & active measures—but I am right glad you are away, & not have all the disagreeable things in the family to perform. I do not know whether it will be necessary to have any legal proceedings, or not. Jim said he would inquire. If you should mention this to Jim—please don't let him know I said anything to you on the subject—& be sure not to be too urgent for active measures for it is full two months before the time!—

Write me what Gov Alcorn[5] says of your business-affairs—what of the pending Allen-suit? I feel right anxious on several points, on which we used to talk—you know one debt especially, I was always on thorns about—is it settled?—If these questions seem impertinent, don't answer.

We were disappointed in not having our friends Mesdames Benoit & Ottley to spend the day with us—they promised on Sunday—but early this morning a "blinding mist (fog) came up & hid the land," & never, of course, came they.[6] But I cannot blame Miss Ellen, for her little Charlie has come near having Pneumonia since her return from St Louis [Missouri], & she did right not to expose him to the dampness. I paid her a little visit Sunday, before church time—she was anxious to have us take dinner with her—but I left Mr N— at home taking Quinine, as t'was his fourteenth chill day—& could not stay. She is just as sweet as she can be. And asked so much of you, I just told her I would read your letter, when she came, & then she could understand exactly how, you were surrounded. She is prettier than she ever was, & has fallen off twenty pounds—has gone back to her girl-ish-figure—& you know how glad she is. She enjoyed going to St Louis, & especially while she was so slender—Col McLaran & Charlie Williams[7] both <u>commented</u> & <u>complimented</u>. Says she is going to write to you. Mrs Eager is just as <u>happy</u> as she can be—only wants <u>you</u> & <u>Bess</u> as roommates now to complete her enjoyment. <u>Gid</u> has sold his plantation, & is coming to <u>town</u> to live. Don't know whether to house-keep or not! <u>Bad</u> move <u>I think</u>.

Everybody is back now from their summer's jaunts;—& looking quite fresh & gay in their new <u>health</u>, <u>flesh</u>, & <u>clothes</u>. It looked quite like old times in our S.School—but, <u>oh</u>! no preacher yet. Some blame Judge Goodwin for Mr Wharry's non-arrival—they say he wrote, <u>unauthorized</u>, to Mr Wharry not <u>to start</u> until he had <u>secured</u> the money for his expenses—thereby intimating that the <u>church</u> was not to be relied upon for an <u>hundred</u> dollars even—so of course the new man thought if it was so doubtful about $100—where would his salary of $2,000 come from? And so & so—we are <u>flat</u> again—no stir; <u>no prospect</u> of any life. Gus Lyon went around, & <u>without</u> the <u>slightest</u> difficulty collected all moneys for necessary expenditures—that was one favorable <u>symptom</u>—but the Judge <u>wet</u>-<u>blanketed</u> that by writing as he did. I think <u>our</u> people <u>talk</u> too much, & <u>act</u> & <u>pray</u> too little—they all get together & say—"oh! our poor church—& oh! <u>this</u> & oh! <u>that</u>"—but <u>never</u> a move do they make."—

This <u>month</u> is so replete with events, & memories, <u>for us</u>. On the <u>fourteenth</u> twelve years ago, our little Lucy Gray[8] was born—what a great girl she would have been by this time, if she had lived—would, perhaps, have been with you & Bess at Staunton. "Where hast thou been these years, beloved?—what hast thou seen?—what visions fair, where thou hast been?"[9] How good the Father was to take our poor little sensitive baby. I know she would have been a great & <u>exquisite</u> joy to us, & especially to <u>you</u>—but think how safely folded from all troubles! Then comes the sad sad anniversary of our sainted Brother's death—the 21st;— <u>nine</u> years have passed, & brought with them <u>healing</u> for your poor <u>broken heart</u>! Blessed <u>healer</u>, <u>Time</u>! I can never, never forget your <u>agony</u> of look & <u>tone</u> all those dark <u>first</u> days. Would to God—I may never again witness such. But you can never suffer so any more in this life.

—Then comes apace the 30th—a <u>bright</u> day always with us, for it brought the <u>first</u> child, the <u>first</u> grand-child, & the <u>first dear precious</u> Neice to a <u>proud</u> family! She has ever been a joy, & we look forward to the <u>future</u> with glad expectant hearts—for "the star-light of love glimmers bright" in its' distant sky, & "the <u>whispers</u> of Fancy are sweet."[10]—Yes, we all look upon her entrance into <u>womanhood</u> with the greatest love & pride—& oh! that her adoring be not merely "the adorning of plaiting the hair, & wearing of gold or of putting on of apparel— But let it be the hidden man of the <u>heart</u>—even the ornament of a meek & quiet spirit, which is in the sight of God of <u>great</u> price"![11] What a <u>lovely</u> descriptive character Peter has <u>drawn</u> for our example! We wish her natural gifts <u>all</u> cultivated—her opportunities <u>all</u> improved—we wish her accomplished, polished, prepared to take her <u>proper</u> position in society—also gay & pleasure-loving to some extent—but oh! the first, the greatest desire & prayer of all our hearts', is, for a meek & quiet spirit! Our dear child!

—O! Trot your letter—your precious letter—so filled with a spirit of gratitude to your Father for allowing your 'lines to fall in such pleasant places'![12] Tis a sermon—every word of it breathes a prayer. Such a life of ease & refinement suits your finer nature—expands your hitherto starved inner self, & qualifies you for glorifying with the sun-shine of your own nature, the shady sides of all hearts. You wished for the pen of an Eliott[13] wherewith to sketch the different characters of your house-hold—allow me to express my decided preference for your own. It suits me best. I'm much obliged to George for the pleasure she has given me—but you have given me more.

What a pleasant household you must have—& the two most prominent characters, Mrs Stark,[14] & Miss Baldwin must be perpetual feasts to your soul. I know all those with whom you associate now—& am much obliged for the introduction. You do right to consider your health first of all, & I am glad you have ample opportunity of caring for it. That is an excellent arrangement of the house, to systematizing your time—for boarders are so apt to grow into "gadders & gossips"[15]—they have to have a good deal of determination not to be. But Trot I find a little smile lurking around the corners of my mouth at your trying to be systematic—regularly so, I mean! When could you ever have a set time for anything save sleeping & eating—not even your devotions had any formality of time or place. But you must stick to your promise about writing to us—we shall expect, & look, & get mad if we don't receive. How glad I am that Bess, is thrown with so exalted a person as Miss Baldwin—t'will do her good. I am in love with her from very description. That was a compliment indeed, which she paid you—quite deserved I think—but I am glad she has the wit to appreciate you.

I hear of no very interesting gentlemen friends or acquaintances—are there any of suitable age or capacity in your circle? I know your admiration of the sterner sex, & imagine an acquaintance or two, if for nothing else than to keep you posted on the "great questions of the day"[16]—the "Situation" &c &c—would be quite agreeable. How I wish I could hear you talk, talk talk!—

The latest excitement in our social life, is that Mrs Dug Randall (neè Emmaline Baldwin)[17] has given birth to twin-girls! Both are dead however, & the mother was very, very ill at the time! Mrs Ottley thinks it was like an indiscreet girl of sixteen at this state of affairs, to have twins! Ha! ha!—

Poor Yandaloo was very ill all last week with congestion of the bowels—she requested the prayers of the S.School on Sunday—we went to see her after church, & found her somewhat better. I think she will get well. How pitiful her large brown eyes looked into mine! I wished I could stay, & nurse her!—

Wednesday—We have just returned from spending a pleasant day with Sister Mary. It was the anniversary of her marriage-day.[18] Five years ago she was a bride!—She had <u>Gen</u> & <u>Mrs Blewett</u>[19] to dine as well—all was so pleasant. Plenty of <u>babies</u> & <u>nurses</u> & all that kind of <u>bother</u>—but for all that, every body enjoyed themselves, & the babies did remarkably well! Cordele received your letter. Jim sent it up yesterday by Brother James. She was delighted, & feels a swelling of the heart to think no Virginia quilt could <u>out look</u> her's. She will write next week, or the latter part of this. We should keep up a <u>regular</u> line of letters. If you have money to spare, I wish you would have some <u>good</u> pictures of yourself & Bess taken, & send us a <u>few</u>! Remember I have <u>none</u> of you. Bess has received my long letter by this time—& I expect has an answer on the way. I will not again write such a long letter—it is not <u>right</u>! Mr Neilson has read what I said on <u>business</u>— he thinks tho' a settlement should take place in <u>Nov</u>—so he can know what to <u>do</u>.

There has been some political excitement in town—one white man killed at <u>Artesia</u> by [an] infuriated mob of negroes—the leaders were arrested, & brought to Columbus—negroes threatened to burn the town—guards out all night. All quiet now. I am scared about <u>election</u> times.

All friends send love to you both. Write soon, to your affectionate Lute.

Heaven protect you, & send you safely to us.

Notes

1. Lucy paraphrased "The Feast of Reason and the Flow of soul" (Alexander Pope, "The First Satire of the Second Book of Horace Imitated: To Mr. Fortescue," *Satires, Epistles, and Odes of Horace Imitated* [1737], in Davis, ed., *Pope*, 344).

2. Dickens, *Great Expectations,* ed. Cardwell, 8.

3. Lucy first mentioned Jim's romance with "P.H." in a letter dated March 17, 1870, and urged him to "content" himself with other ladies. "I haven't much fancy for you marrying a widow!" she remarked. By "the one so noted in history," Lucy was probably referring to Queen Henrietta Maria (1609–69), wife of Charles I (1600–49), King of England, Scotland, and Ireland (1625–49).

4. In 1868 Jim had opened a dry goods business with merchant William Campbell (b. ca. 1837). The business failed in 1871.

5. James Lusk Alcorn (1816–94), governor of Mississippi (1870–71). Alcorn was born in Illinois and commenced practicing law in Mississippi in 1844. He served as a member of the Mississippi House of Representatives (1846, 1856, and 1857) and Senate (1848–54). Alcorn had provided Lucy's sister, Elizabeth Charlotte Irion Barron, with legal representation for several years. "He is a very entertaining man," Lucy remarked in her diary in July 1869. "How I wish he was not such a Radical of such deep dye, so black!"

6. Lucy paraphrased "The rolling mist came down and hid the land: / And never home came she" (Charles Kingsley, "The Sands of Dee," *Anton Locke* [1850], in Rhys, ed., *Kingsley,* 158).

7. Merchant Charles McLaran (1808–91) was a planter in Columbus before the Civil War and founder of the Columbus First National Bank (1847). He received great notoriety for building Riverview, a Greek revival mansion constructed between 1847 and 1853. After the Civil War he moved to St. Louis, Missouri, with his wife, Ann Maria Jennings McLaran (1831–1919), and family. Charles Williams (1836–1903) was Charles McLaran's nephew and employee.

8. Lucy Gray Irion (1859–62), daughter of McKinney F. Irion Jr. and Harriette Hayden Irion Hogan (1837–65).

9. Lucy paraphrased "Where hast thou been this year beloved, / What hast thou seen? / What visions fair, what glorious life / Where thou hast been" (Harriet Beecher Stowe, "Only a Year" [ca. 1850], Harriet Beecher Stowe Papers).

10. Lucy paraphrased "And the starlight of love glimmered bright at the end / And the whispers of fancy were sweet" ("Passing under the Rod" [folk song], in Vance, ed., *Ozark Folksongs*, 89).

11. 1 Pet. 3:3–4.

12. Ps. 16:6.

13. George Eliot was the pseudonym of English novelist Mary Ann Evans (1819–80).

14. Mrs. Stark was probably a boarder of Charlotte Taylor.

15. Jane West, *Letters to a Young Lady; In Which the Duties and Character of Women are Considered, Chiefly with a Reference to Prevailing Opinions* (1806), 347.

16. Prussian statesman Otto Von Bismarck (1815–98), who used it in a speech on September 30, 1862; see Feuchtwanger, *Bismarck*, 84.

17. Emmaline C. Baldwin Randle (ca. 1838–1921), daughter of Daniel Baldwin (ca. 1787–1865) and Emmaline C. Chester Baldwin (ca. 1806–79) and wife of dry goods merchant Frederic Douglas Randle (b. 1833).

18. Mary Bruce Barry Neilson married James Crawford Neilson on October 24, 1866.

19. Thomas Garton Blewett Jr. and Mary Jane Witherspoon Blewett (1835–76).

৪৯

Lucy's desire to settle family matters at Willow Cottage offended Lizzie, who regarded any division of the homestead as spelling an end to her role as head of the family. While John viewed the estate in economic terms, the Irion siblings fiercely debated the meaning of home and their changing place in family relations.

Lucy to Bess

Wildwood
Nov 10th/.71.

My dear dear Bess,

Yours of Oct 29th, also Nov 5th, are before me, & with right good will I set about answering both. You think, perhaps, I have been rather "<u>deliberly</u>" (as

George says) about replying to the <u>first</u>—but then I had reasons for delay; <u>now</u> however I no sooner "<u>juster behold</u>" your <u>last</u> (& <u>contents</u>) than I <u>fly</u> to pen, ink, & paper!!—Shall I right here comment thereupon, or shall I linger with a fond delay, like a <u>coy</u> maiden, over the subject <u>nearest</u> my heart, & leave it until the latter portion of my letter? Well! I believe I decide to play the rôlê of the aforesaid <u>coy</u> maid, & discuss <u>everything</u> else first!

Your opening burlesque upon the popularity of a certain Mrs Barron of your house, was duly appreciated by all of us, & <u>Mr Cox</u> too—for I may at once acknowledge to have read it, together with other extracts from your letter, aloud to him! Now don't look any more shocked than you can possibly help—don't put on any more <u>horrified airs</u> than you can get along <u>well</u> with—for I well remember <u>young ladies</u> are given to <u>such</u> like when <u>most</u> they feel complimented!

You well know I would not read aloud anything to our fastidious friend, which I did not consider <u>spicy</u>—so bow your head as <u>gracefully</u> as you can, & whisper in a high-bred tone—"Thank you."—Seriously tho' you would not <u>care</u> at all; if you could have seen how <u>proud</u> & <u>amused</u> your old <u>Uncle Jeemes</u> looked, & how <u>gratified Mr Cox</u> appeared. This same gentleman is just lying in wait for your entrê [entrance] into society to have a <u>rare</u> feast of amusement! Don't allow <u>expectations</u> to be aroused in your young mind—nor do you allow yourself to grow <u>suspicious</u>—ahem!—he will be just enough in <u>earnest</u> to make your time pass agreeably, but no more—only that, & <u>nothing more</u>. So you may enjoy him, for you well understand that <u>sort</u> of thing! We had a most delightful visit from Jim & Mr Cox on Sunday. They seemed to enjoy themselves, & I am sure we did. We had the table set in Cordele's room, & so there was no <u>fuss</u> or stir about din-ner. Jim compliments me by saying I set a better table than <u>anybody</u>!—he means <u>anybody he</u> knows—& that is narrowing the compliment down to <u>one</u> table (<u>Mrs Shattuck's</u>)[1]—but you know when we get a pleasant speech made us, we should not <u>analyze</u> it too strictly. These little visits of Jim's are so sweet, but so <u>fleet-ing</u>—the shortening days, make each one more so! We go down to Willow Cot-tage every two or three weeks—the negroes seem glad to see us. Mr Neilson says he does'ent exactly know what to do with the place—he asks Cordele, & I, what <u>we</u> think, & we say "do as you please"—he then goes to Jim, & he gives the <u>same</u> response—so <u>he</u> thinks, if Press would take the place, procure labor, & <u>take</u> the <u>mules</u>—we furnish the <u>land</u> & what farming utensils are on the place, & <u>nothing</u> more. Then we should be entitled to a <u>third</u> (⅓) of the crop, without <u>any risk</u>. He puts as low a price on the mules as he can—so the negroes can <u>buy</u> them if they choose. He feels unwilling to risk them entirely with negroes, therefore considers it <u>safest</u> to <u>sell</u>—as we are so far away. All this, of course, is unsettled as yet—but if left with Mr N— that is the best plan, "<u>in his opinion</u>." The house will still be in readiness for any of the family at any time—the garden, <u>fruits</u> &c &c will be put under Press' especial care, & <u>he</u> made responsible! Mr N— will assist in planning the crop, & <u>supervising</u> generally! Tho' if Jim concludes upon <u>any other</u> plan, it will be all right with Mr N—; <u>any arrangement</u> Trot or Jim think best, we are all willing to accede to. Mr N— has merely spoken of this plan because Jim wished him to take charge of things—said it <u>worried</u> him to have the care of the place, <u>now</u> situated as he was. Tho' according to "<u>my</u> way of <u>thinking</u>," he will <u>miss</u> the <u>care</u>, & feel somewhat at a loss. He is so very much attached to the place; it will cost him an effort to give it up—& if he could make it pleasant, & <u>profitable</u> to himself, I wish he could, & would keep it. I know it has been a darling wish of the family to have <u>us move</u> down, & reopen our little home—it would be pleasant too but I don't think it will ever be, & so we must not dwell upon it, as possible. This is Mr N— own little farm, & altho' it seems small, & you may think him <u>wasting</u> his <u>time</u> & <u>energies</u> upon it, yet it is <u>his</u>, & <u>he loves</u> it, & would have to be <u>very</u> sure of a good living elsewhere, before he could be persuaded to leave it. Of course, <u>I</u> feel an attachment to Wildwood—very peculiar! Very tender!

Nov 15th/.71.
So long a time has elapsed since I begun my letter, I consider it necessary to apologize! And I have been <u>pained</u> by having several opportunities of sending it to the Post too—but it was not finished, & so it had to wait. I <u>will</u> finish my <u>ditty</u> now, tho' I know of no one going to town for days. I have not postponed writing <u>willfully</u> either, but by force.

    <u>Yesterday</u>, Cordele received <u>Trot's</u> letter of Nov 7th. How well that woman writes, when her health is good!—what a source of pleasure, & instruction [in] her letters! I enjoyed her last immensely—tho' <u>two</u> things rather <u>marred</u> my enjoyment—one was, <u>that</u> my last letter to her was <u>not</u> answered, & the other, that there was a half <u>reproachful</u> tone, in her wailings over having "<u>no home</u>"! Now I may be a little too sensitive on this subject, because I have thought a <u>great</u> <u>deal</u> on it, & wished I could have things ordered to suit <u>all around</u>, & as it seems a continuation of my <u>other pages</u>, I'll linger awhile longer <u>thereupon</u>!

    This is the way, I feel about <u>Willow Cottage</u>. If the other members of the family wish to retain it as a <u>home</u>-stead, why! <u>should</u> it not be? You all seem to feel that Mr Neilson & I willfully <u>break up the family</u> & home—when I think we are as innocent of such an act, as two poor people can be. It cuts me to the heart to hear all of you, continually saying you have "<u>no</u> home"—you have <u>just</u> the same one awaiting you on your return, that you have had for years. It stands just as you left it—if you were to return tomorrow, or today, you would find a <u>sweet</u> reception, for Woos keeps it ever the same. I am always thinking, & planning of how I will go down next Fall, & have everything in <u>expectation</u> of your return. Why you all should talk <u>then</u> of being homeless, quite astonishes me. If you are, it is your <u>own fault</u>—<u>my share</u> of the property will be a mere <u>trifle</u> to <u>you</u>, if you wish to retain it as a homestead!—so now please don't make me feel like a "<u>condemned</u>

criminal" (as Cordele would say) any more—for I never think of anything else, than that the little home will be <u>reopened</u> if it is the wish of the family, & I sincerely hope it may be. But you all may conclude that it is too inconvenient, or too expensive, or some other reason, for not keeping it—then will it be <u>our</u> fault? We have been too happy, too united to forget the past, & none will grieve over the <u>final</u> breaking-up more <u>than I</u>—I have never considered <u>this</u> separation as any other than temporal, for Trot is the <u>head</u>, & of course <u>she makes</u> the family. How I wish we could all have a talk. I hope nothing I have said sounds snappish or illtempered, for <u>indeed</u>! I do not feel the slightest so—but things look so different <u>written</u>. When will the time come for your <u>return</u>! O! Bess I feel as impatient for your school days to be over, as you possibly can! I am right ashamed of myself—but I know then you can be <u>more</u> with me, & my dear Trot will come <u>home</u> to her child—I am <u>tired</u> of doing without her—am I not selfish? But I wish her to come, & <u>settle down</u>, & "let me feel that I have not lost my"[2] Mother-Sister! Oh! that both of you could "put your arms about my neck" as I dreamed you did last night! <u>Your sweetness</u>, your loveliness of character has been so brought out, in "the <u>subjects</u>" of our last letters. And your <u>declaration</u> that you will do <u>right</u>, for the sake of <u>right</u>—& not merely because <u>I</u> wish you;—<u>warms</u> my heart & fills it with joyful thanksgiving! My dear child! <u>Your promise</u>, I feel to be as <u>true</u>, & inviolable as any ever made under Heaven! I <u>know</u> when you give your <u>word</u>, it is given in sincerity—& whatever sacrifice of feeling it may cost, it is kept!—How <u>precious</u> to us all, is that feeling of <u>trust</u>. Thank God!—I could'ent help reading <u>all</u> of your last to Mr N—, & Cordele—I mean the <u>long</u> letter. It was so <u>noble</u>, so true—so <u>struggling</u>. I appreciated <u>every</u> feeling, & loved you all the more for the hardship! My voice was so broken with sobs as I read the last pathetic & <u>glowing</u> lines, I could scarcely read audibly, & when I was thro', & looked up my dear John was sitting by, with tears of love, & sympathy all glistening on his cheeks. How much he loves, & with what interest he looks upon you. La! I do so often think of <u>you</u>, when he is so <u>lovely</u>, & <u>sweet</u> & <u>funny</u>, for I know you would almost take a <u>fit</u> <u>over him</u>!—

We went over to see Sister Anne Sunday—had a delightful visit of course. Lizzie was just as bright, & pretty as a bird! She has been in town for several weeks, & had <u>so much</u> nice attention from both <u>ladies</u> & <u>gentlemen</u>. If you could only see her <u>take off</u> a <u>green</u> fellow, who fell in love with her, you would <u>exhaust</u> yourself!—<u>as I did</u>! And then I showed her <u>the picture</u>! Now I have come to the <u>most important</u> point in my letter. What shall I say of it? Well! I must say, when I compare it with <u>faces</u> of our circle—the <u>majestic</u> Lyon's—the <u>Adonis Lee's</u>—the <u>classic Cox'</u>—I think it sinks into the <u>decided plebeian</u>! I was prepared for his being ugly—but a kind of <u>aristocratic</u> ugly—an intelligent, intellectual, <u>ugly</u>— but not a <u>common fat</u> ugly!—I believe you are hoaxing us!—<u>surely this man</u> is not the one! Jim said he looked common, but I thought it was because he was over particular about your beaux. Do write, & tell me that this fat man's smile never caused you emotion of any sort. I return the picture—send the right one next time.

Cordele says answer her letter when you can—she will write to Trot as soon as her eye gets better, it is sore now. She will go to town next week to attend Conference. Don't you know that will delight her? We were very much obliged to you for sending the samples—we enjoyed looking at them, & now can dress you up whenever, & however we please. Mr Neilson sends a heartful of love to both. Heaven bless you. Write whenever you can to your loving T'Ida.

NOTES

1. Melissa Elizabeth Curtiss Shattuck (1841–1929), wife of merchant George F. Shattuck (1833–1905).
2. Edward George Earle Bulwer-Lytton, *My Novel* (1850–53), vol. 3, 304.

ℬ

Cracks began to appear in the domestic arrangements at Wildwood. While Lucy informed Lizzie that Cordele had made every effort to be cheerful, family matters remained unresolved and uncomfortable. John's refusal to relocate to Willow Cottage had ruffled more than a few feathers. Lizzie abandoned her financial claim to the property and with it her emotional claim as its head. Cordele grew resentful and unhappy, and, in more frequent moments of anger, she declared that Wildwood was nothing more than a "fly in the precious ointment."

Lucy to Lizzie

Wildwood.
Nov 28th/.71.

This is just such a November-day as you read of, in which doleful things happen! The wind is certainly grieving most piteously over some misfortune, some great world-sorrow, for its' sobs are heart-breaking! Then occasionally it relieves its' mourning, by blinding sheets of misty tears(?)—however, you nor I, are rarely affected by weather—if you were only sitting by this cosy little fire with me, instead of being snugly housed at Mrs Taylor's—why! I'd be as happy as woman well could be in this world! I am all alone this afternoon—Cordele is at Mrs Ottley's, & Mr Neilson, of course, out attending his farm & mill duties.

Cordele wrote you that he had a mill on his place—but I do not think she was quite explicit in explaining the whys, & wherefores—One of his neighbors has a saw-mill, & being obliged to move on account of scarcity of suitable sawing timber—proposed to Mr N— to put it on his land—Mr N— to furnish & haul the logs, & he to saw them, & then divide lumber. This was an excellent plan for Mr N—, for he has much valuable timber, & he hopes to realize some money, without much risk or expense! So now we have the busy saw in hearing distance, & the whistle blows quite like the cars!

I know 'Miss' will be delighted, when she returns—she will feel like she is nearer the world! You would 'most break your heart crying to see what a brave struggle she is making to be content out here—to be bright, & cheerful with the long long winter in view; the long long muddy miles which lie between her & Willow Cottage, church, & S.school! But she does her whole duty, & is so sweet, so helpful, so submissive, but oh! when an opportunity does come for going home—how her eyes do dance, how joyously excited she becomes; & what thankfulness of heart is expressed in every tone & look! It had been a month since we had been in town to church, so Mr Neilson said we could go down on last Saturday, & leave 'Miss' to attend Conference. Ah! if you could have seen her!—& heard her plans, her anticipations! T'was beautiful to see one made so happy by so small a service. If we could live at the Cottage & keep Pheobe, Woos, George, Parthene, Edward, Lide, Johnie, Fred, Jack & Margaret[1] about the house 'as of yore,' I think 'Miss' would be too happy for earth!—She loves Mr Neilson dearly, & would do anything for him—but this Wildwood is the 'fly in the precious ointment'—it is too far—too everything, in short. But she has the good sense & taste never to so express herself, unless I urge her.

This is a digression however—Saturday evening came at last, & off we started to Willow Cottage via town! Having arrived, without let or hindrance, drew up in front of Bhlum & Chapsky's,[2] & called for Mr Irion. That gentleman soon showed us his benign smile, & after very brotherly salutes, informed us that Willie Odeneal, & Gus Lyon, himself & Tempe Fitts were coming out to tea & stay all night! Well, did you ever hear of such a thing, & we campers too! We told him to come along—we had ham, coffee, & bread enough. We went on out, & made suitable preparations, & here they came! What a genuine old time frolic it was!—everybody so glad to see everybody, & every thing just as free & easy as could be! Gus Lyon of course in his glory! Willie had more than she could tell (in the parlor) about Madie, & oh! as much fun as we had in a promenade on the gallery! Such a lovely, balmy moonlight night it was! After our promenade Gus said he wished to have a private talk, & promenade with Mrs Neilson too, so out we went, & had a secret pow-wow! (Woos was on the look-out, & afterwards got after me sharply for doing just "zactly-like" I was a young lady promenading with a young gentleman, taking his arm, cutting the other young ladies out, & never mind, she heard what we said too, & was determined to tell Mr Neilson!)—Then Tempe & I had a chat too. Neither of the young ladies would acknowledge to having anything <u>serious</u> on hand. All asked of you & Bess, & wished for you to complete the circle! Now I know you must be somewhat curious to know where we put them all to sleep—for you remember we are minus <u>two</u> beds at home Jim having one in town, & I one here. Well! we took the bed off the trundle, & put it on the parlor-floor for Jim & Gus—then the couch for John—then Cordele & Tempe slept on the feather bed in the sitting-room, & Willie & I on the mattress on the floor! 'Twas a blessing it was a <u>warm</u> night. All, next morning returned to town—& attended church, & Jim came back home with us to dinner, & he & Cordele went in the buggy to town, & Mr Neilson & I came on home. How delightful to have such <u>reunion</u> of friends. <u>Jim</u>, poor fellow, was <u>charmed</u>, & says when <u>certain</u> parties come from Va [Virginia] (<u>M.P.F</u>) he wishes us to have another <u>camp</u>. I told him Cordele & I were at his <u>service</u>. I hope he will have it Christmas. The <u>servants</u> were all delighted, with having company once more. Like old times.

I am beginning another sheet altho' I know I ought not!—you don't write me <u>long</u> letters—they all somehow seem <u>cut off</u> too suddenly. I think you start out with the intention of writing long ones—but someone calls your attention, & off you go. Now, you will think me cross & exacting & <u>jealous</u>—yes, I am I suppose! You don't give me enough of your <u>time</u>, & <u>attention</u> you know you don't. I have been right blue about it, & could'ent help feeling that you were being weaned from me. Why! don't you write <u>talking home-self-talking</u> letters—I am glad to hear about the strangers but I wish for <u>yourself</u>. I said Sunday when I read your last letter, "I wish Trot would write more"—Jim said—"Well! I tell you she has nothing much to write about—every body strangers"—"Yes she has, Trot has plenty in her <u>head</u> & <u>heart</u>, which she knows I wish to hear." All of them laughed & said <u>I</u> was <u>spoilt</u>!—Cordele & I too have sometimes doubted if you & Bess <u>read</u> our letters, for there are many things we ask, you never design to notice—Please <u>read</u> once any how! I wrote Bess a long letter—most of it business, & now I will continue the subject a little longer in yours.—

Do you think you act quite right in giving up your claim to your share of the home-property! Have you weighed the matter well? Can you <u>afford</u> to give a "<u>quit</u> claim"?—Is your <u>living</u> secure enough for such a step? I know you explained to me how you had paid off a debt of your estate with some notes of Pa's estate amounting to some $2500. I don't feel right on the subject somehow. I am afraid you will have reason to <u>regret</u> some day. I thought when last we talked the matter over, you had determined not to give a <u>quit-claim</u>—until your own affairs were more settled. Now, my dear, don't be <u>too</u> generous—we are much more able to struggle than you are. Suppose the Allen suit should succeed—what would you do? What does the hard-head-long-sighted <u>Gov</u> say? I do hope he may <u>settle</u> that <u>one claim</u> of yours any how, & let your poor mind be at rest on that point. <u>Somehow</u> I am growing somewhat morbid on the subject of <u>debt</u>—& am <u>impatient</u>

that all my <u>loved</u> ones should be freed from the galling load. There is that <u>bill</u> of Dr <u>Boyce</u>, & also Dr <u>Vaughan</u>[3] yet unsettled. I told Jim, I thought he ought to sell your horse <u>Stewart</u>, & give you the money;—the horse is of no use except to Dr Shattuck[4]—of course Jim would be deprived of many a pleasant <u>ride</u>—but he can always get a <u>mule</u> & the old buggy from home. I don't like for you to be <u>worried</u> with these debts—which ought to have been paid long ago! If I am <u>too</u> officious, please, tell me to <u>hush</u>-<u>up</u>! Press has <u>eighteen</u> bales of cotton ready for market, & hopes to get <u>five</u> more—so I hope Jim will soon return you your money, which was such a god-send to him this year. I hope the farm will pay expenses. Write me fully on business. Mr Neilson's farm will pay expenses—but nothing more. He owes some money to Sister Sallie, also to another party—not much—but I beg him to dispose of his lots in Okolona, & pay up <u>every dollar</u>—& then we'll begin square with the world—& hope to continue so! I am going to be as economical as I can, without being penurious—& I know he has energy & strength, & with God's blessing we will make a living, & something to spare, even if <u>we</u> did'ent get the Sheriffalty. It was no disappointment to either of us, for we knew <u>long</u> ago, the thing was <u>simply impossible</u>—& so we had not founded <u>one</u> hope thereupon. Ah! Trot you are so <u>ambitious</u>, so eager for the <u>main chance</u>! Strange you should always be surrounded by <u>those</u> who had little of your spirit. What would you not undertake to accomplish? What stop, what bound would there be to your energy if you had your husband to <u>lean upon</u>—I should rather say, <u>strengthen</u>! For there is <u>power</u> in your very presence—but <u>some</u> never feel it—or if they do—it irritates! Oh! if you were here—how we could talk—there are so many points I would like to hear your opinion of. Many things which interest me <u>now</u>, which never did before. I feel it a cross to be separated so long from you—& yet how selfish of me! I try not to become <u>contracted</u>, & narrow in my thoughts & feelings—yet I need you, to expand my ideas, I <u>feel it</u>—therefore you should write me often, write me long & write me freely—I am your child!

I wish you did have some <u>real man of the</u> times as an acquaintance—don't understand that I wish you to find a husband, I <u>do not</u>. But then I know you <u>so well</u>, & know your <u>need</u>, & appreciation! The other day Mr Neilson & I were speaking of <u>Landrum</u>[5]—I asked if he was not rather too "<u>gassy</u>," for any avail. Mr Neilson said he thought he was decidedly so—I replied that "Trot had watched his political course, & was much disgusted"—Mr N— looked up in surprise, & said "Sis Lizzie?"—"Yes"—said I—"she is the greatest politician in the country next to Maj Worthington."[6] There was shown a <u>bran</u> new phase of your character to him. He says—"tell Sis Lizzie I am not neglecting my oldest Sister in thought & feeling—but am so busy making a living for her <u>youngest</u> sister, & <u>prospective neice</u>! "<u>Tot</u>-<u>Neanie</u>" Now there's impudence for you! He is so bad! More anon!

Was'ent Bess' picture good? I hope to get your's tomorrow, (which is <u>mine</u>) Don't let the child work any more for me please—<u>command</u> her not to!—I enjoyed the reading of the description of Weyer's Cave [Virginia]—& thank you.

Now answer this letter before you <u>forget</u> all about what is in it—not that it is so interesting, but it is my <u>preach</u>, & you must listen, tho' it be poor! I hope I have a long letter from Bess in the Post. Mr Neilson goes down tomorrow with cotton, I shall be all day alone. Wish I had a bran new novel—Have you read Charles Reade's last "<u>Terrible temptation</u>"[7]—they say it is <u>terribly dirty</u>—not fit for eyes polite. Tell what you <u>are reading</u>. Good-bye—God bless you both my dear darlings. Write whenever you can to your loving Lute.

NOTES

1. Edward, Johnie, Jack, and Margaret had worked for the Irion family for several years. Johnie (b. ca. 1859) was the son of Nancy Barron.

2. Dry goods merchants Jacob Bluhm (1837–1903), husband of Eva Bluhm (ca. 1842–73), and M. Chapsky (b. ca. 1854).

3. Dr. Bolivar A. Vaughan (1827–97), husband of Martha Wade Vaughan (1833–1905).

4. Dr. Joseph W. M. Shattuck (1829–1904), husband of Ellen E. Shattuck (1833–1907).

5. John Morgan Landrum (1815–61), U.S. representative from Louisiana (1859–61).

6. Henry C. Worthington (b. ca. 1835), son of Henry Horace Worthington and Frances Edward Crinchton Worthington and editor of the *Columbus Democrat*.

7. Charles Reade's *A Terrible Temptation* (1871) included sensational plots about one woman taking another woman's child as her own, confinement of the sane in lunatic asylums, and the mistresses of London society men.

Three

Farm Business

December 1871–March 1872

*L*ucy entered the holiday season with a degree of domestic uncertainty hang-ing over her head. With the future of Willow Cottage unresolved, she threw her-self into hog killing and what she described as the most "trying time with most house-<u>keepers</u>." Cleaning of house, yard, office, and kitchen in preparation for the coming festivities left Lucy feeling exhausted, and all the more grateful for her sister's willingness to take hold of domestic affairs. Cordele directed activities in the dairy yard and kitchen, and the women of Wildwood spent December bak-ing Augusta cakes and making pies. For Christmas dinner they roasted a rooster and made an old-fashioned boiled custard to mark the occasion.

While the holidays passed pleasantly, farm business and ways and means of making a living preoccupied the Neilson family as 1871 drew to a close. John devoted much of his time to sawmilling in the hope that he could raise enough money to secure the labor needed to manage the crops at Wildwood. At Willow Cottage a bountiful crop harvest was tempered by Press Barron's unwillingness to sign a contract to manage the farm in 1872. Unable to afford the wages of some of her family's former slaves or successfully coax others away from town life in Columbus, Lucy accepted her role in the farming economy and wrote prosy let-ters to her sister and niece in Virginia—"all about garden & chickens—just all married people think about."

Yet garden plots and chickens were not the only things on Lucy's mind. As she remodeled Lizzie's old dark calico dresses instead of making new ones, Lucy declared that she was not economizing but rather suspected that other signifi-cant changes were afoot—namely pregnancy. "You know things do happen <u>most years</u>, & <u>who knows</u>?" she gingerly confessed. Yearning for Lizzie's counsel, Lucy admitted that while Cordele's domestic prowess had its benefits, she was sorely lacking in sisterly support. Cordele, however, equated Lucy's prospects with an end to her own plans for a summer jaunt in northern Mississippi, placing yet another wedge between her and her life of single blessedness.

Lucy's anxiety and failed attempts to appease Cordele's resentment were compounded by the miles that separated her from Lizzie and Bess. While proud of Lizzie's commitment to Bess, Lucy wondered how she would summon the courage to bring a new life into the world without the steady arm of the head of the family.

ༀ

Lucy was forced to make an embarrassing apology to Bess after being informed that the picture of her niece's "common" beau was not a prank but of a legitimate suitor.

Lucy to Lizzie and Bess

Wildwood.
Dec 4th /.71.

My <u>darling</u> Trot & Bess—

I must write you a partner-ship letter this afternoon for I feel so like chatting to both, & Bess must just excuse me this time, & Trot, will like it all the same—won't she? Well! in the first place, I wrote Tròt, a long letter last week, & received by return messenger <u>two</u> letters, one from each of you—that dear letter from you Trot, in which you so sweetly <u>explained how</u> you felt, & <u>why</u>, about our little home. I do know you can beat the world in <u>loving explanations</u>, & can with your inimitiable sweetness set all to rights, & make all <u>glow</u> with love & good-feeling. That was <u>just the</u> letter I <u>craved</u>, I hungered for, & oh! how like a sweet morsel have I rolled it under my tongue ever since. That was what I call <u>heart</u> talk—& I defy the <u>coldest</u> not to be warmed by its genial tone. You surely possess a charm in making yourself <u>felt</u>. I thank you for that letter, & like the renowned "O.T.," I <u>want more</u>![1]

Then in the second place, I read with pleasure Bessie's "dear little bit" written Nov 24th at 12 o'clock (<u>p.m</u>). in this you Bess, acknowledged the receipt of my "charming adorable letter," but said you were not <u>answering</u> it—only <u>talking</u> some first—which talk, I must say entertained <u>us</u> highly, & made us laugh; especially the latter part where you complained most lugubriously of your delayed christmas-present. And you <u>paid</u> me off by not sending your picture—well, but then I can <u>view</u> Cordele's to death, & then you sent me that nice <u>edging</u> for my pillow-cases—I must confess, to <u>a liking</u> of <u>such pay</u> as that—tho' I do hope you have one of those <u>pretty</u> pictures in reserve for me, & only just trying to tease awhile—now hav'ent you?—that's a dear? Send it along by next mail—"<u>will</u>-<u>do</u>"?

Then as my good man & I were "a <u>sittin</u>" by the fire one cold winter's night, there comes a '<u>voice</u>' from without, saying "Halloa"!—then my good man arises, & walks out to see <u>whose</u> 'voice' it was, when it turns out to be one of our tenants who had been to town, & brought a letter that "<u>Mr Irons</u> had sent to Miss Lucy"! Oh! I of course "all a <u>flutter</u>" until I possessed myself of the dear missive, & whose chirography should I recognize, but Bess' again. On breaking the seal, out came a picture of my darling old Trot! Oh! how life-like it is! How fat—how healthy looking—how handsome, & oh! such a sweet expression of eyes & mouth! My precious Trot! How gladly, how proudly, how thankfully I gaze upon your reflection! To think it is you, grown so stout, so well! I take out the little Photograph taken long ago, & compare!—there I see a pale,—no not pale—but delicately fair face—inexpressibly sad in its' quietude—with little curls clustering so prettily around—surely a poetic picture—& one I love—but it fills the heart, & eyes while you look upon it, for it has a tired look—a wistful look—but this last, has the look which makes you glad!—all the softness, all the fullness of perfect maturity! A look of one who has fought well's life battle & come off more than conqueror! Ah! my dear, I don't know that this almost glimpse of your-own-self has made me any the more patient of our separation! Then that sweet letter—so like your own, own tongue could talk, & the frequent dreams I have had of seeing, hearing, feeling you, makes me a'most as "Trot-sick" as I used to be! Tho' I can never feel the utter void of heart which used to overwhelm me during your frequent absences—because of my great, my satisfied love for the sweetest man in the world. Tis useless to thank you for the picture, for you know already how grateful I am.

Now Miss Bess I am going to scold you a little—what a complaining letter you did write, after that long one of mine, which you said yourself you had not answered; & then Cordele wrote you (or Trot) a long letter, & I added a note in that—& so you have no "reason to complain" old lady. Remember we live a good long way from the Post, & communication is getting less, & less frequent as the winter advances—for the roads are bad already! Don't get impatient, & accuse us of neglect, for you don't know how such accusations wound the spirits that love you! Certainly if you could know how constantly our thoughts were with you, you would not consider us careless.—

You spoke of not being well. I hope you were only unwell—& nothing more? Take great care of yourself in that severe climate—both of you! I was grieved to hear of you having colds—now, pray be more particular than ever you were before—for I fear colds for both. Bess you spoke of Mrs Taylor's have knit you some shoes—what kind. I say over-nets for your boots in walking to school— such as people north have—but Mr Neilson thinks they are bed-room slippers. So you see, we discuss you both in every little particular, altho' so far away! So which of our suppositions is correct? Ha! ha! Do tell!

Poor me! I resolve & re-resolve not to write you all such long letters, for I consume all my time, & every body else is neglected. But I think of so many little things, which I wish to say, & am silly enough to write. Cordele is still in town, attending Conference. We were to have gone down for her yesterday, but really the weather was too bad! I tell you, it seems a <u>long</u>, <u>long</u> time since the old lady left me—what I am to do next Spring when she goes to Auntie's I know not! I would'ent be selfish enough to keep her tho'. Last week was the trying time with most <u>house-keepers</u>—viz—<u>hog</u>-<u>killing</u>! Poor me! I did hope Cordele would be with me—<u>but she was'ent</u>. And, of course, I just had to go <u>ahead</u> & do my best— which was any body-else's very worst. I had'ent much <u>lard</u> anyhow, & let half of it get <u>scorched</u>! But I tell <u>Mary</u> & <u>Mr Neilson</u> t'was their fault, for I kept racing around after them to <u>come</u> & <u>see</u> & they would'ent! We've had a <u>heap</u> of fun over it—but then that don't help my lard! Well! I'll know better next time. I am thro with every thing now—except <u>souse</u>. I've put up quite a nice supply of sausage in skins for Spring. La! I am changed about many little things—I quite surprise myself—for instance, in early rising—stirring around these cold mornings, & start things to going. Cordele says marriage does bring changes more ways than one! Ha! Ha!

I know you both would laugh to see me sitting up in dresses made of <u>your</u> old ones—the dark calicos which you left. I thought I would wear them awhile & then make <u>quilts</u> of them. Yes actually thinking of making <u>quilts</u> for <u>you</u> to go to house-keeping with! Don't think I am going to the extreme of economy. I am not—only I wished to wait awhile before getting new home dresses—for you know things do happen <u>most years</u>, & <u>who knows</u>? I am not trying to excite your curiosity or expectations <u>unduly</u>—but I can't tell yet how the world goes! Oh! but I hope, I pray—<u>not till Trot comes</u>! We have many a sly laugh tho'—about "<u>Jim Abert</u>," "Tot Neanie," & "little <u>Brooks</u>"! If you were at home I would'ent <u>care</u>— but oh! I would need you <u>both</u>, in such a long & trying ordeal! Yes, I know "<u>Aunt Mary</u>" would be of the greatest assistance <u>mentally</u>, & <u>heartily</u>, if not physically! Poor little Mrs Ransom,[2] she has my sympathy!—I must stop now, & attend to supper. How I wish you were here to sit down with us.

—We do have such pleasant evenings—such delightful fires—such a comfortable room, & bright lamp—then after some love-making after the separation of the day—we go to work—Mr Neilson reads aloud, & I knit or sew! We are now reading a very interesting, as well as instructive, book—"Queens of Society"[3]— of both English & French courts. I like the book much, & shall desire Bess to read it, when she returns—the copy we have belongs to Mrs Ottley. Such a book gives you much information, <u>without</u> much reading—therefore well suited to <u>young</u> ladies—who have a desire to know, at least a smattering of history, & hav'ent time or inclination for much research. What are you reading Trot?—<u>People</u>!—I expect you are "summat" tired of <u>paper books</u>, & prefer <u>human</u>-books—is it not true? I fear from what Bess says, you are rather <u>bored</u> by the foolish jealousies of the ladies of the house—well! now don't allow yourself to be!—I hope, Bess, you passed a better examination in your "<u>hardest</u>, <u>meanest</u> book that ever was seen read or studied"—How far off is the Seminary from Mrs Taylor's—not far I hope. We have been having very severe weather, & we thought what must it be with you! Ah! the old allusion of your's, Bess, to the "pig-tails" & "cow-tails" brought back a scene in our home, which was too humorous to be soon forgotten! How we laughed over the various degrees of intelligence you would have to impart when you returned, of the different members of your house-hold. I am highly complimented by your having to sing at two Soirees. Pray tell me who attends.

Oh! Bess I beg ten thousand pardons about your sweetheart's picture—I should not have expressed myself so freely—but I don't think I can retract. I know it is hard for you to give up corresponding with C.R.B—. I think it unwise in your ever allowing a correspondence until after school days. It is awkward to discontinue when once begun—& there is always danger of hurting a friend's feelings. Be very careful therefore!

Mr Neilson will go down tomorrow for Cordele. I am so glad. Hope she will bring letters from you both! I don't know when I'll go down—I hope before Christmas anyhow—for I wish Phebe to bake me a nice lady cake. I want a little something nice if I am away up in the Wildwoods. Lizzie & Ben Symons[4] were over Sunday—Liz just as sweet as ever, & so glad to get here—but could not spend the week, for she had some sewing, which she wished to finish before the holidays—says she don't expect to have a speck of fun—the town is too dull for endurance, so she is coming to see us. I told her well—but not to come if there were any possibility of a frolic in town—my house must be a dernier resort (with Jim's emphasis & construction)! <. . .>

—Do write soon. Mr N— joins me in love & prayers for you both.

Your own Lute.

NOTES

1. Lucy paraphrased "Please sir, I want some more" (Dickens, *Oliver Twist* [1838], ed. Tillotson, 12).

2. Mary Fontaine Alexander Ranson (1845–85), wife of Staunton lawyer Thomas Davis Ranson (1843–1918). At this time Mary was pregnant with Charlotte Alexander Ranson (1872–1950).

3. Grace Wharton and Phillip Wharton, *The Queens of Society* (1861).

4. Benjamin Symons (b. ca. 1858), son of John Mauger Symons and Anne Frazier Neilson Symons.

$\mathcal{G}\mathfrak{d}$

The arrival of a gift from Bess made Lucy reflect on her relationship with Bess's mother, Harriette Hayden Irion Hogan. "None ever grieved more sincerely, than, I for an own sister!" Lucy noted in her diary after Harriette's death in December 1865.

Writing from Willow Cottage while John visited Okolona on business, Lucy updated her niece on the crops, the household, and a good serve of town gossip—including her decision to accompany John to the Methodist church to hear Bishop Hubbard Kavanaugh speak. While Lucy horrified her Presbyterian congregants, the episode revealed more about her companionate marriage, which allowed her to assert publicly her right to make the choice about which sermon to attend.

Lucy to Bess

Willow Cottage.
Dec 11th/.71.

My dear, <u>darling</u> Bess—

You just <u>must not work</u> any more for me! I tell you I am <u>speechless</u> on the subject of this last beautiful present—the <u>Tidy</u>! My dear child, it certainly is the <u>very prettiest</u> piece of crocheting I ever saw! But you really must consider your <u>own</u> pleasure a little, & not consume all your spare moments on me! Now I am in earnest & most positively decline any more work from your willing hands, <u>until</u> you have more leisure. Perhaps in the future I'll grow selfish & never be satisfied—so you had better stop while you have any chance, for the way I am petted <u>now</u> by my entire family, & circle of friends I'll be the most abominably <u>selfish</u>, <u>spoilt</u> woman in the world! How beautiful my <u>Tidy</u> is!—How my little home is ornamented by specimens of your handiwork! I am grateful! I am appreciative! I wonder what makes people <u>all so good</u>, so sweet, so loving, so willing to work for me! I am sure I do not deserve so much from their hands. And none are more so, than you my <u>dear</u> Bess! Well! I've nothing to render in return but a heart <u>overflowing</u>, & <u>ever</u> flowing with deepest, purest love! Accept that my child, for it is yours I assure you.

As you grow <u>older</u> you take the place in my heart left vacant by your poor Mother—she was the idol of my child's-heart—& the dear friend of my older years. You seem so much like her. I find myself confounding you in my heart, as <u>one</u> & the same. And we loved each other on thro' all ills, & loved on till she died! Nothing separated us in heart—tho' so much was done by other parties to destroy our precious friendship! Thus I hope it may be with us—<u>let nothing</u> ever come between us! We belong to each other, & let's ever hold our friendship too high, too sacred to allow any change! My dear the time seems long & dreary to await your coming. But oh! we must not be too impatient. I know your time is usefully employed therefore it does <u>not</u> hang heavily on your hands. I am

Columbus, as seen from the Tombigbee River in the late
nineteenth century. T. C. Wier Family Papers.
Courtesy of Special Collections Department,
Mitchell Memorial Library, Mississippi State University.

ashamed of my impatience—but I cannot grow accustomed to the absence of my
dear "<u>darlings</u>" away off in Virginia. I try to reason with myself, & think on all
the blessings by which I am surrounded, & then despise myself for ingratitude to
my good Father!—But I believe I wish for you to witness my happiness, & rejoice
with me!—

You see I am now at Willow Cottage—we came down yesterday (Sunday-
morning) to hear our <u>trial</u> preacher <u>Mr Boud</u>[1] (of Galatin Tenn[essee]), & Bishop
Kavanaugh[2] (of the Methodist-church). When we got to S.School I horrified
many of our <u>blue-stockings</u> by an announcement that I was quite in a quandary
to know which to hear! I <u>went</u> with Mr Neilson, & I know there was many a
pious-head shaken on <u>my</u> declusion. But my <u>husband</u> was quite determined (in
a <u>very quiet</u> way) that I should go. And I was glad I did go—besides gratifying
him, I heard the <u>best</u> sermon I have heard, since Dr Styles'[3] heavenly visit. "<u>Miss</u>"
was not as much horrified at me as I thought she would be—but she marched
<u>straight</u> up stairs, & took her seat in our pew—Jim did not sit with her—but <u>Col
Abert did</u>!—We all came home to dinner Jim with us—& such a sweet little easy
time we had! After supper we went to church to hear Mr Boud. I suppose I am
quite too hard to please—but I do not think he has <u>polish</u> enough for our people.
Tho I suppose I should look to the <u>higher</u> virtues, & he seems to be possessed
with <u>earnestness</u>, & <u>sincerity</u>! He will remain until Sabbath, & administer the
sacrament! Those who have met him in the social circle are much pleased.

Mr Neilson staid at Col Aberts' last night, & took the morning train for Okolona! He hoped to transact his business there today, & return on tonight's train—we are to go to town to meet him in the morning, & then off for Wildwood. The negroes have made a good crop on this place, & most of them have plenty of money—consequently they are in a good humor with themselves, & the world! I think Press will keep the place—tho, of course, he refrains from a decided answer until New Year. They have all worked well, & I am glad they are rewarded. Nancy & Woos will have $235.00 coming to them. They have saved every cent of their wages. That is doing well for them. I don't know what Woos intends to do next year—she does'ent know either—but I don't expect she will marry—altho "Miss" is constantly on the qui-vive!—[alert]

Your friend Sallie Goodwin has gone to Cincinnati to make Lizzie a visit—now don't you know she will enjoy the new of city-life!—It is reported that Lucy Jep Harris will marry soon, a Mr Duncan[4] from Memphis [Tennessee]—the "leader of the Son" there. They say he is quite a beau Brummel.[5]

We received cards to De Jones'[6] wedding—which comes off tomorrow (12th)—she marries a Mr Tomlinson—a man six years younger than herself. An only son, & rich! But he must be just a student at College—ah! I fear for her happiness! I am going to write to her as soon as I finish this letter. Dear girl!—Mamie married a merchant in New Orleans—named Campbell—a widower with one child![7]—Well! I am glad the girls will have protectors. Mr Neilson laughs at me for being so relieved that they have some one to take care of them. Yes, I am, for they had been so long homeless. I love those girls, & shall always feel the greatest interest in them.

—Jim said you ran a risk of a $3–0 fine in marking the Tidy—"papers"—when the fringe was all hanging out—You should have marked it "thread" or something of that sort. Jim came back home with us last night from church—he is more than ever infatuated with his Goddess P.H!—she must have been exceedingly kind to him on a last visit, for he is now ready for anything!—Really it is right touching his devotion—I don't know what he & Va will do!—Both are such flirts!

Saturday night the Swiss Bell-Ringers[8] will be in town, & P.H will go with him. I know he longs for the time to come. His great desire to have you at home is almost unspeakable—Last night coming along he said so earnestly "I do wish Brooks was at home. I am 'most froze' to see her"!—He looks so well now, & his side-whiskers, which give him quite a distinqué [highbred] air!

—George came from town, & brought me Trot's good long letter of the 6th—& also some reports of yours. The letter was most acceptable with only one item which caused a qualm of uneasiness, & that was a return of the old enemy headache! She wrote of everyone's kindness—but especially of your sweetness, & thoughtfulness. Bless you! Your reports are sweet to my eyes, for so well do they show <u>duty nobly done</u>! Thats right, <u>my dear Bess</u>! I wrote you & Trot a long letter in co-partnership <u>last</u> week, which I hope you got. I will write to Trot again soon. In regard to my <u>health</u> (?). I am still in doubt whether I am <u>delicate</u> or not! Ahem! Can't tell yet. <u>Such things</u> take their time—so the wise ones say.—I'll keep you informed.

The negroes make such a fuss over your <u>pictures</u>—they look & look, & <u>comment</u> to their hearts' content—& that <u>Tidy</u>—they "<u>do</u> think Miss Bessie is mighty smart." <u>Moll</u> of course is all <u>a wonder</u>!—I must not write more—I must say something to <u>De</u>! Cordele joins me in love, & wishes for your health & happiness. Write soon to your loving T'Ida.

Martha is in the room now, & is laughing at "<u>Mimmie</u>" being so fat—she can't help looking at <u>her so hard</u>! Mrs Eager does look so <u>stylish</u> this winter—<u>two</u> beautiful <u>dresses</u>. A drab, & black Alpacca!—Good-bye old <u>girl</u>. I <u>do</u> thank you <u>for the Tidy</u>. Write when you can to us all—In love T'Ida.

NOTES

1. Rev. Henry B. Boude (1833–1913) assumed the pastorate of the Columbus First Presbyterian Church in early 1872.

2. Rev. Hubbard Hinde Kavanaugh (1802–84), bishop of the Methodist Episcopal Church.

3. Rev. Joseph Clay Stiles (1795–1875), prominent Presbyterian minister and author, who had visited Columbus in early 1871 and married John and Lucy.

4. Lucy Jeptha Harris (1845–1902) married lawyer Robert Perry Duncan (1838–91) on February 6, 1872.

5. George Bryan Brummell (1778–1840), a wealthy Englishman known for his fine clothes.

6. Cordelia E. Jones (1846–ca. 1912), daughter of Dr. Aurelius N. Jones and Cornelia A. Gibson Jones and wife of salesman William H. Tomlinson (ca. 1848–ca. 1895). Cordelia Jones spent her childhood in Columbus, but after the death of her parents she moved to New Orleans with her sister, Mary C. Marshall Jones.

7. Mary C. Marshall Jones married E. F. Campbell.

8. Lancashire handbell ringers.

※

Christmas gave every southern wife an opportunity to celebrate their status with tidy homes, bountiful fare, clean children, and stylish entertaining. Conceding that she was not an "over-neat housekeeper," Lucy still joined her neighbors and friends in the rush and bustle of the holidays. As she and Cordele decorated Wildwood with evergreens, John returned from deer hunting to pen a greeting to his sister-in-law Lizzie. "For a Xmas turkey—we had a big <u>rooster</u> which was just as *good & even better than a turkey,"* he remarked, *"for it furnished opportunity to exercise imagination, & that's good you know, then if it had been a real turkey, why there would not have been room in the stove to have cooked it." "So you see my little wife & I, are learning to adapt ourselves to circumstances,"* he added.

Learning to adapt was not limited to domestic affairs. With her pregnancy all but confirmed, Lucy struggled with thoughts of her own mortality. As invitations made their way to Wildwood, she was also forced to acknowledge that marriage and motherhood placed her a world away from the bellehood she had enjoyed only a year earlier. As she debated whether it was appropriate to attend a New Year's celebration or dance at the Masonic ball, Lucy tried to convince herself that the social restrictions placed on married life offered her protection, even if she was compelled to leave the frivolities of the season to her unmarried peers.

Lucy to Lizzie

Wildwood—
Dec. 28th/.71

My dear, dear Trotwood,

Your letter, written sometime since, has lain unanswered much longer than I intended—& indeed! I do not know, exactly, <u>why</u> I did'ent have my usual weekly (?) answer, in readiness to mail on Sunday, when we went down to church, excepting that I had a <u>general</u> "cleaning up" of house, office, kitchen, & yard for the <u>coming</u> festivities of christmas, & really felt <u>too tired</u>, & <u>domestic</u> for any other employment. You know how <u>such</u> duties do occupy ones time—& must be attended, however little inclined one may feel—but I must say when <u>time</u> & <u>help</u> are given, I generally feel like going right to work. I am not one of these over-neat housekeepers—neither am I much of a <u>rusher</u>, when emergencies come;—but I just go along, & try to keep things in some order, & allow no <u>corners</u> to drop, if possible. I have Fannie at my beck & call now that the busy season is over—& she is as good a girl as I know of anywhere. She has learned to cook real well, & is very little trouble. I hope to retain her next year—I've heard nothing of her going away—but there's no telling.

We have breakfast every morning before <u>sun-rise</u>, & that is doing well, I think these "<u>soon</u>-coming-mornings." We made suitable preparations for christmas. Pheobe made me a large cake—I prepared mince-meat for pies (<u>new</u> recipe)—& Cordele & I make some delightful <u>Augusta-cakes</u> (with raisins)—Then in lieu of a dignified <u>Turkey</u>, we had a <u>big rooster</u>—& just called it a "Turkey" thro' courtesy. Of course we had our <u>stand-by boiled custard</u>—altho' so unfashionable—yet so <u>very home like</u>. We had a pleasant little <u>dinner</u>, our first Christmas at Wildwood, & Bro James & Sister Mary were so pleasant too. We thought of our absent ones, & altho we knew they were faring sumptuously on a Virginia-dinner—yet we knew they would have enjoyed home more. I don't suppose Jim can get out at all during the holidays. He is leading such a busy life now, & seems to enjoy it. Looks very well in health.

We expect to go down tomorrow, & attend a grand <u>Masonic</u> ball given at the Gilmer. It will be <u>the</u> occasion of the holidays. Of course I am <u>glad</u> to go—I like such <u>places</u> now even more than before marriage—because I feel so <u>free</u> & <u>pro-tected</u>. Willie Odeneal is very anxious that we should attend a <u>leap-year-party</u> at her house on New Year's night—but I don't know whether we will go or not. I would not take <u>much part</u>, only look on, & enjoy the others. Don't understand that I am trying to be <u>settled</u>—but I don't think it would be <u>just</u> quite <u>dignified</u> enough for a married woman. I wish Mr Neilson to go, for I know he would enjoy himself, & he would be so <u>popular</u> with the girls. We have no other invitations, that we <u>know of</u>—except to dine with Sister Mary. You must tell us of your enjoyments during the holidays—& of Bess. Santa Claus brought me nothing but <u>candies</u> & <u>fruits</u>, yes & a nice <u>cheese</u>,—Mr Neilson asked what I wished, & I told him, I was like the negroes, I wanted "<u>something to eat</u>"—& nothing more. Tell Bess her <u>usual</u> box of candies from Mr Cox came to us this time. Yes, he gave it to "John Neilson & his <u>babies</u>." What do you think of such <u>impudence</u>! Ever so many of the outrageous men had a big laugh over it at the store, & then told Mr Neilson not to tell <u>me</u>. Scamps!

Your letter, dear Trot, made me weep as I have not for months—so tender, so loving! Then you had had one of those dreadful headaches, & that made me sorry. I do thank all of the kind inmates of Kalorama for their attentions. Your letter was like a <u>soul</u>-satisfying draught from some delightful fountain—it met my every craving, my every need. I have read it so often, & thanked you for it. When I attempted to read it aloud to Mr Neilson, I <u>broke</u> down utterly, & he too was much touched. But Trot, you must not feel any uneasiness about <u>me</u>. I am as <u>robust</u> as ever you saw me—& only a little <u>disturbed</u> at times (?) And oh! such love, such tenderness, such devotion as my dear husband lavishes upon me, would quite convince you of my being well attended. But still when trouble does come, I know <u>no</u> one on earth will take your place! All that is in the future, & may not <u>come at all</u>, for who knows?—time will have to <u>develope</u> (?) affairs, before we can be certain of anything—so let us not anticipate an evil until it is inevitable! Cordele is more <u>distressed</u> than I am almost—she is one of Job's comforters,[1] I tell you,—I tell her she ought to be ashamed to treat me so. She is really hurt with <u>you</u> for not writing oftener to her—"shore nuff" <u>martyr now</u>. She has been in better spirits ever since you touched upon her <u>martyrdom</u> in living up here, & has been more resigned! Do write to her, for she is a sweet sister to me, & we have good loving times together.

Bess' reports were <u>splendid</u>. I shall enlarge upon them in my next to her. I received her <u>sweet</u> letter the other day, & will answer just as soon as I get back from town. May the new year bring us happiness as the <u>old one has</u>. This <u>last</u> has certainly brought <u>me</u> a <u>full</u> life. God bless my dear dear Sister & Neice. Write both of you as often as you can & we will do the same. Cordele sends best love to both. Good-bye. Lute.

NOTES

1. Job 16:2.

ঞ্চ

The Masonic ball, held at the Gilmer Hotel on December 29, 1871, was attended by "<u>Jews</u> & Gentiles." While Columbus residents accepted the presence of Jewish men in business, they barely tolerated their participation in society. Reflecting on the night's proceedings, Lucy was quick to scoff at the "handsome" Jewish women, and she was relieved that she had been spared the embarrassment of having to dance with Jim's new boss, merchant Jacob Bluhm. Bereft of the frills and furbelows that had once defined their place in society, Columbus's "gentiles" affirmed their status by excluding Jews from their homes and shifting the boundaries governing respectability and refinement.

Gentility may have been contested on the ballroom floor, but it was made at home. Contentious discussions about farm contracts continued: while Moll was now able to demand what she believed to be a suitable wage for her labor and others could choose to stay or go, Lucy tried to convince herself that her family would ultimately decide "what to do" with particular laborers or servants. Nancy's decision to "<u>play lady</u>" was perhaps the most disconcerting for Lucy, whose claim to white southern femininity rested firmly on both mastering the domestic ideal and discrediting the right of free black women to do the same.

Lucy to Bess

Wildwood.

Dec 30th/.71.

I think, my dear Bess, your letter of Dec 16th is the very sweetest, most <u>home-like</u> letter, you've written since your departure. Others have been more brilliant, witty, & comprehendsive, but this suited us all, in-as-much-as it was so like a "little social chat with Bess." We all enjoyed it together (as I read aloud), & with one accord pronounced favorably upon its' merits. Well! well! now that the holidays are over, we shall expect an account, in detail, of your proceedings—how often, how longingly have we thought of our absent ones! We know you have thought of us too. I wrote to Trot of our "<u>gay</u> & festive" time up to the <u>Ball</u>. We attended,

& oh! the folks—the crowds—of all sizes, shapes & ages. Jews & Gentiles. It was a "Masonic Ball"—but extended outside of the lodge, as well. I tell you it was a mixed crowd! Why! the Jews looked like they would take the house! Some beautiful Jewesses, & dressed so handsomely! How they could dance too! All the fancy dances! And with Gentile-men too!!! Dick Hudson[1] had a good time! I could but think of a Dr-friend of ours! Ha! Ha!—I wish you could have "juster behold" Mr Bhlum—why! he just beat "Clay Long"[2] at the fancy dances. He & some Jewesses were just flying down the floor, when I gave Jim one look—he laughed out-right! Then I asked him what on earth he was going to do with his "Boss."—

There was such a crowd, & so many young ladies, Mrs Jno A. grew faint-hearted about having any beaux for dancing—the first sett had almost formed before a soul even looked as if they even like to dance—but oh! just in time, came Dr Maxwell,[3] & was'ent she glad! Then others of all sizes & ages came, & Mrs Jno A— danced every sett but two! I did not dance with any of the Jews either, altho' Gen Blewett declared he saw me waltzing with Hushman[4] (that little dwarf one). If Mr Bhlum had asked me tho', I should most certainly have danced with "Boss."

It was such a big occasion that even Clough Beard[5] was out, & looked more seraphic than ever, & came over, & took a seat by me, & had a nice sweet talk— "all about Bess." Then Dr Emmet Lanier[6] came with more smiles, more bows than usual—& asked in a very professional manner after my health!

Mollie Matthews is one of the reigning belles this season—a rival beauty with Sue Billups.[7] They are opposite styles you know. Mollie has a young lady-friend (Miss Spence)[8] visiting her at present. She is from Murfreesboro Tenn, & says Madie Childress is the most popular woman in the town. The Bradford girls have a cousin, "Anne Bradford,"[9] visiting them too. I saw her at the ball—she is not pretty—but is graceful & vivacious. Jim took "Columbus Annie" to the ball. Lizzie Symons did not go. I was so mad with her—she was here yesterday, & I gave her a blessing—she was sorry, after it was too late—but she did'ent think her Pa cared for her to go. Sister Annie was as mad as I was! I am determined she shall go to the "Leap-year-party" on New Year's night at Willie Odeneal's—so have made arrangements to take her with us! "Little Tempe" was down in time for the holidays—Clough took her to the Ball! Are you jealous? I saw Mr Lewis Green[10] there too—(the great Mathematician) I could not help thinking of what you wrote me of Lucy! Well! I am wonder stricken! If ever I lay eyes on Gus or Theod'e[11] I shall ask them about such behavior on their parents' part! They would most certainly take me to task about you, & I shall return the officious-ness! Saw Mrs Hardy[12] at the Ball too—she asked so much of you both, & sent so many messages. The principle feature in the supper was oysters. How I enjoyed them! We had supper in Restaurant style—seated at tables. That was nice.

Lizzie says she has written to you at great length sometime since, & hopes you have received it. She confesses to having treated you in an un-christian manner, about writing. I hope she may improve with the New Year. Her new cousins have come—Ella Workman & her brother Charlie.[13] She is a little thing—right pretty too—about 19 years old— <...>

What you say of your determination to do your duty regardless of inclination, makes me honor you. Yes, you are in the right path, & you surely feel the reward. The reports, which Trot forwarded, do you great credit—& all of you [us] were proud when we read them. And how you must be studying to have mastered 2,000 pages in 50 days—what was the Book? I do love to hear the particulars of your life. I feel interested to know when you take a new piece of music, & what it is. It is only thro' you, that my musical knowledge comes. I am glad you are protected from the weather too by having thick shoes—how did you ever get them broken!—Write me if you had a dance Christmas, & when "Tom" & his friend come—tell me what they are like! I laughed at what you said of Staunton being so dull, for I thought it must be. I try not to be uneasy about you or Trot either—but last night I had such a miserable dream of poor Trot's being so ill, & I had neglected her. What a keen pang of remorse rent my heart, & what relief was the awakening! How does Trot get on without her dear friend Mrs Stark. I know you have something funny to tell about her departure. What a picture you brought before our mind's eye,[14] when you spoke of going around feeding all those grown-up folks, out of a bowl! Oh! Bess, I know you were then in your glory—Dear child, how long seems the time when we shall be amused at your pranks, & tricks. I feel almost jealous that some other people, beside ourselves, have you all to themselves. Never mind tho'—we will wait—& then what a joy-ful reunion! Sometimes I cannot help having despondent thoughts, & fears for the future—I feel like there is such an untried ordeal awaiting me! I cannot be any more out-spoken, than, I have been as regards my health. We think there is trouble brewing—tho' there may not be. I am almost reconciled, when I see the joy, keen & exquisite, which the thought causes to spring in my husband's heart.

I was surprised sometime ago by a visit from Mrs Regina Lee. She was visit-ing Mrs Blewett, & they all came over. Miss Regina was so very pleasant. Said she had heard from Ellen Ottley how cosily, we were fixed up, & she determined to come & see for herself. Oh! she had so much to say about you both. I showed the photographs, & she thought you had not only improved in looks, but clothes. She sent so many messages—which I have forgotten. I showed the sett of matts you crocheted, & also my beautiful tidy—she liked to have taken a fit over the tidy, & wished one just like it, of course. She asked if I remembered "an imaginary picture I used to draw of myself living away up in the country with a house full of logs." Oh! mercy! I was horrified at her having heard of that ridiculous non-sense—& told her she had entirely too good a memory! Never mind you & Trot told on me that summer at Iuka!

Your <u>sweet dear</u> Uncle John has just come in, I ask him for a message for you—he says—"Tell Bess, I think she might write me <u>ten</u> letters, one every week—then I'd answer <u>all</u> in one; & then she could start on another number <u>ten</u>, & so <u>continue</u>." There's his message just as he worded it—so contemplate the impudence at your leisure. Cordele wrote a letter of thanks for her edging—& says she is now waiting patiently, for the spirit to move you or Trot.

We were rather surprised not to get a letter from either of you the last day we were in town—perhaps tho' you were absorbed in Xmas. I have granted my maid permission to go to a fair tonight—so I will have to get supper, with the assistance of George & Edward. We are going to keep Ed next year up here. We are quite undecided what to do with Moll. Woos, we know not what we will do. She has been sick for <u>two</u> weeks, & looks a perfect sight. Press has rented the place, & is getting in hands rapidly. His brothers <u>Tom</u>, & <u>Bob</u>[15] will both live with him. Also Booker & Beckie[16] again. <u>Nancy</u> will <u>play lady</u>, & have her two sons Gentry & Johnie in the crop. Nobody wants <u>Moll</u>—she is such a price! I thought of asking Pheobe to come, & live with me, but I suppose I might as well petition the <u>bridge</u> to come.

We are going down tomorrow, & Monday Mr Neilson & Press will settle all things, ready for the year. Do write Bess whenever you can—but don't <u>force yourself</u>, when you feel tired. Your Uncle Jim said you wrote him a <u>mean</u> little letter in answer to his long one—& I told him well! I knew you had just exhausted yourself on a <u>good</u>, <u>long</u>, <u>sweet</u> letter to me. So don't write when you are so weary. God-bless you both. Kiss each other for Aunt Ida.

Notes

1. Richard Fontaine Hudson (ca. 1849–91), dry goods clerk.

2. Henry Clay Long (1845–1916), dry goods clerk.

3. Dr. Pinkney J. Maxwell (1834–93).

4. Joseph Hirshman (1840–99), merchant.

5. William Clough Beard (1849–1924), dry goods merchant.

6. Dr. Emmett Sykes Lanier (1844–95), husband of Sue Turner Sale Lanier (1855–81). During the Civil War he enlisted as a private in Company B, Forty-third Infantry Regiment Mississippi.

7. Sue Billups (1851–1930), daughter of John Marshall Billups and Sarah M. Billups (ca. 1827–64).

8. Florence Spence (b. ca. 1854), daughter of store owner John Cedric Spence (1809–90) and Elizabeth Spence (ca. 1813–84) of Murfreesboro, Tennessee.

9. Anna Bradford (b. ca. 1848), daughter of Judge William Daugherty Bradford and Rosalie Spotswood Dandridge Bradford.

10. Lewis Green Jr. (b. ca. 1855), son of farmer Lewis Green (b. ca. 1815) and Zanetta Green (b. ca. 1826).

11. Judge Theodoric Cecil Lyon (1839–84), son of Rev. James Adair Lyon and Adelaide Eliza Deaderick Lyon.

12. Maria Clifford Hardy (1840–78), wife of Dr. Cornelius Hardy (1827–1908).

13. Possibly Ella Workman (1852–1925) and Charles Edward Workman (b. 1855), the children of bank cashier William H. R. Workman (1825–89) and Maria Warner Minor Workman (b. 1827) of Camden, South Carolina.

14. Lucy paraphrased "In my mind's eye, Horatio" (Shakespeare, *Hamlet*, ed. Thompson and Taylor, 181).

15. Tom Barron and his wife, Tilde Barron, had worked for the Irion family for several years. Farm laborer Robert Barron was the husband of Lidia Barron.

16. Farm laborers Booker and Rebecca Hariston.

༄

Away from the social whirlwind of Columbus, Lucy and John turned their attention to farm finances. The sawmill generated some profits, but the size and location of Wildwood made the prospect of working for the Neilsons an unattractive one for most freed people. After the war, many African Americans had abandoned planta-tion life for town work. Those who stayed on the land largely opted for sharecropping or renting, a tenuous system that at best provided families with the opportunity to live and farm together. While white farmers became deft at exploiting the arrange-ment, it was still a far more attractive option than the modest wages offered by farmers like John.

Lucy to Bess

Wildwood 19th Jan/.72.

Well! dear Bess, it is just such a day as one likes to write letters—at least letters of the heart, & not of <u>duty</u>—dark, dreary, & wretchedly gloomy out of doors, makes a bright hearth all the more enjoyable; & then thought is busy with things & people at a distance, as well as at home,—need I add that Staunton is the abiding place of my heart & mind much of the time?—

Last night such a vivid dream of yourself & Trot "visited my <u>pillow</u>." I feel the emotion yet, caused by the imaginary sight of you! I thought Trot & I were walk-ing along, I had my hand in her arm, & said, "O! Trot, I have <u>dreamed</u> so much of seeing you, I must give you a little <u>pinch</u> to see if it is <u>really you this time</u>, & no dream"—with that I caught hold of her arm, & found it real flesh & blood—a <u>great deal of it too</u>—so nice, & round, & fat. <u>You</u> were <u>sick</u>—the travel & your <u>usual</u> appetite on the road, had <u>disordered</u> both <u>stomache</u> & <u>liver</u>, consequently you were pale & gaunt. I felt <u>real</u> mad to think all your <u>Virginia</u>-<u>roses</u> had fled before we got a sight of them. But still you were not too sick to be full of spirit, & talked away of your <u>dresses</u> & petty things quite volubly.—Now was'ent this too natural to be <u>only</u> a dream—was'ent there too much of <u>real</u> feeling? How lost I felt when I awoke, & found you just as far off, as ever.—Cordele & I talk so much of you, it is no wonder that my dreams are much the same.

We have a very pleasant home-life—altho' you would perhaps think it lonely. I don't believe any of us suffer from that feeling. Cordele does beautifully—she is just as bright, & cheerful as she can be—& is a never-ending source of home-pleasure to my dear John. Her quiet, <u>orderly</u> ways, & constant little attentions suit him, & make his heart ever warm towards her. She has taken the <u>Dairy</u>-department entirely off my hands, & also keeps eyes & ears open to all <u>cackling hens</u>, & makes Edward, & George hunt eggs—& oh! the nice ones we do get. I have even had enough to send to market twice—& sent on for "Blackwood's Magazine" with the proceeds—See how thrifty I am growing. I shall enjoy those <u>eggs</u> all year, for you know that is a choice <u>journal</u>. You'd be surprised to see how well our <u>new cook Mary Rice</u> (alias Moll) does—she also washes & irons very well, <u>thus far</u>! I did so <u>dread</u> having her for a dependence—but if she will only continue, as she has begun, I shall <u>thank</u> her <u>all my life</u>. When we came back home from town last time—after having attended the Leap-year-party, & been so gay—altho' I knew that Mary & Fannie, & Uncle Sambo would all be gone, by the time we came back—yet, when we came, & found our little Home so deserted—the cows lowing at the gate—the dogs nearly starved—the cats run away—the <u>calves</u> eating up the <u>door</u>-<u>mat</u>—I confess to a sinking of the heart, I never felt before, & shall I make a clean breast of it, & tell you that I had <u>two</u>, <u>big sobbing cries</u>, before I became quite reconciled.

Mr Neilson has no one <u>at all</u> to help him in the farm excepting <u>George</u> & <u>Edward</u>. This is the <u>distressing</u> part to me. I was so in hopes he would not have to work so hard this year—& now the prospect is, that he will have more than ever. The saw-mill is doing well, & that will bring in some profits—then too he is getting more tenants to settle on his place, & <u>clear</u> land—so that <u>in time</u> the farm will be profitable for the most of it is <u>good</u> soil—but as yet it is <u>wildwoods</u>. Negroes have such a disposition to <u>rent</u> land, & work to themselves that it is right difficult for the white-people to obtain labor—& for <u>wages</u>, they will hardly hire at all—they wish <u>part of the crop</u>, & this is why Mr Neilson has so much difficulty—his farm is too small to go on shares. I hope it will all come right, & I try not to be too impatient for Mr Neilson to be relieved. He is so well & stout, & so delights in work, that I would not care, if the <u>hot</u> weather would not come & make him sick. I'm much afraid you & Trot will think I'm growing very contracted, & that my whole mind is centred on my home-life, & "<u>ways</u> & <u>means</u>" of making a living—but I talk to you as if you were here, & believe me, I do not inflict others with <u>like ditties</u>. I wish you to know every thing which concerns us both good & bad—as we wish to know of you. But when I sit down & write great <u>home</u>-<u>ditties</u>, & then neither of you make the slightest allusion to any of the items, I feel a little ashamed, & think you must feel bored. Your lives are so free & generous, ours must seem so narrow—so stinted!—But we do live very "comfortably together"[1] any how—not-with-standing we are "ten miles from a lemon."[2] But when you both come, our lives will undoubtedly be enlarged, for both are women to be felt, & wished for—therefore God speed the coming!—I sometime think no other home is brighter, or lovelier than ours—we do not "pine for what is not"[3]—we have so much real love for each other, that we ever find it enables us to make "a fire in the kitchen"[4] without any diminution.

We were quite disappointed that Jim did not come last Sunday—he promised, & I know something unusual must have happened to prevent his doing so—tho' there's been no communication with town this week, & we are still in ignorance of the cause of his detention. I have not seen the old fellow since New Year's night—& it seems a long, long time. Willie Odeneal was coming too—but was just recovering from a spell of sickness—she has never been to see me yet—I am quite anxious to have her come. She is one of the truest friends I ever had. As for our other friends Mesdames Ottley, Eager, Benoit &c &c, I havent seen in so long, I have no news at all to write of them.—

Sullie Matthews has some friends staying with her now—cousins from Huntsville [Alabama]—she gave them a party last week. I do not know whether it was a large company or not—but I know she slighted country-friends. Cousin Robert ought to be ashamed to treat his relatives so—never mind! he shan't come to our next wedding in the family—shall he?—

There was a "Hop" in town last week too—which Lizzie Symons attended, & enjoyed. Cordele & I took Edward & the wagon, & went over to Sister Annie's last week—the reason we took the wagon, was because I wished to return a couch, which Sister A— had loaned me last summer, & I knew she must need it soon, since she had the "Workmans" with her. They were all so glad to see us, & were so pleasant, & have such a good cook, who gave us such a good dinner—we enjoyed ourselves very much. They promised to come to see us this week, & I have looked every day—but still they come not.—

Sister Mary has moved into her new house. It is very snug, & convenient—she is rejoicing in the feeling of ownership—which I don't wonder at—they have been married five years, & have just moved into their own home. Both of her children have whooping-cough—poor thing! I pity her—we spent yesterday afternoon with her—she is just as sweet to me as she can be. Cordele will spend several days with her next week. We've had recent letters from both Sister Sallie, & Sophie—they both make inquiries of you. Sister Sallie is still in Washington, or rather has return[ed] there, after a visit to Phil[adelphia] & Baltimore [Maryland]. Sophie announced the fact that they had made up their minds to leave Gainesville [Alabama]—to settle they know not where, as yet—but neither of them had any health there, & t'was useless to stay longer.

Cordele will go in town in February to take care of Mrs Merritt[5]—during her husbands absence—I am glad for her that she is going—but sorry for myself. She wishes to go to town tomorrow to get a new dress, have it cut & fitted, so we can make it in time for her to wear while on her visit. We think of getting a light drab, & trim it with <u>brown</u>—as those two colors seem much combined this season.

We went to walk Sunday-evening, & missed two beaux of Cordele's—Dr Lea & Mr <u>Gabe</u> Vaughn[6]—we were so sorry—but they left word they would come again next Sunday. We laugh at "Miss" so much about old bow-legged Gabe. We have <u>Polly</u> up here now—Cordele is going to send Manie word to take him—for she will go to North Miss in the spring &, I'm very sure I do not care for his presence—he is too much trouble. Poor Poll! I get right sorry to think how tired everybody is of him.

Poor Yandaloo Frazee[7] is not well yet—She has been sick since September— she wrote Cordele the other day, that she had only left her room once in all that time. She is all "shaven & shorn"[8] of her beautiful hair too—poor girl! Her case is much like Trot's—she is <u>hungry</u> all the time now—& only irish potatoes, & light bread to eat.—I received a letter from Eva Hillyer[9] the other day—asking your <u>address</u>—said when she returned to Geo[rgia] she found your letter awaiting her—it had been written some <u>two months</u> then, & since they had been so unsettled that she had had no opportunity of before writing for your address. They live now near Atlanta.—I never hear from <u>Madie</u> now—nor Lide[10]—nor <u>Corrie</u>, nor any of my correspondents scarcely—it is not my fault either, for I have answered all their letters.

Your letter of the 8th Jan, was much appreciated—I am glad you took the pains to tell me of your school-life—of course <u>everything</u> interests me, that in the least concerns you—I think of you so many times pouring over your studies. Tell me how the dreadful examinations were gone thro' with—I hope you were successful. Your French is very important—& oh! how I do long to hear "sweet notes from a contralto voice"—& to see "laughing, loving eyes."[11] Your poor Piano down at home is more <u>tin-panny</u> than ever—I'm afraid it will be ruined there without being used. We all laughed over your <u>stabs</u> at the Episcopal-school[12]—of course we know Miss Baldwin's is in every respect superior—but did you beat them in the <u>bill of fare</u> on Christmas-day? There's certainly was very elegant (<u>on paper</u>.) It does me good to hear you praise Miss Baldwin—because I think it is so elevating for a girl to love such women, as she. [...]

Mr Neilson is perfectly incorrigible as to writing—I feel right sorry for him when he is obliged to write a letter—but he loves you very dearly, & is as interested as if you were his own flesh & blood. <u>Judge Simms</u>[13] & <u>Jim</u> both urge him to take your <u>guardian-ship</u>—but I am afraid—aint you?

My letter is as long as your's because I write so closely—forgive me if I have been too prolix, & prosy. I will not say another word about Trot's writing—she can do as she thinks <u>christian</u> in the matter.

Give my love to her however, & tell her her loss will always be a sweet regret. In the dim past, I remember how delightful to me was our communion. Moll says tell "Miss Bessie, I have an <u>engagement ring</u>—she must <u>look out</u>." Send her some message. Write & God bless you

T'Ida

NOTES

1. This phrase appeared in several literary works including Alcott, *Little Women* (1868), ed. Showalter, 318.

2. "My living in Yorkshire was so far out of the way, that it was actually twelve miles from a lemon" (Sydney Smith, *Lady Holland's Memoir* [1855] in Bell, ed., *Sydney Smith*, 13).

3. Percy Bysshe Shelley, "To a Skylark" (1820), in Hutchinson, ed., *Percy Bysshe Shelley*, 596.

4. English nursery rhyme.

5. Henrietta Isabella Hargrove Merritt (ca. 1843–ca. 1897), wife of merchant Henry S. Merritt (ca. 1835–ca. 1890).

6. Dr. R. K. Lea (b. ca. 1834), dentist; farmer Gabriel Vaughn (1812–88).

7. Yandaloo Frazee (1848–90), daughter of tailor George Frazee (1815–72) and Mary Jane Blair Frazee (1820–57).

8. "The House That Jack Built" (Mother Goose nursery rhyme).

9. Eva Walton Hillyer (ca. 1846–1927), daughter of politician and lawyer Junius Hillyer (1807–86) and Jane S. Watkins Hillyer (1807–80). Junius was a representative from Georgia (1851–55) and solicitor of the U.S. Treasury (1857–61).

10. Eliza Williams McCarthy (1845–1925), daughter of Isaac Williams (1793–1869) and Eliza L. Williams (1808–65) and wife of druggist Maurice McCarthy (ca. 1820–93). Eliza was Lucy's closest adolescent friend.

11. Eliza paraphrased "Rich notes from a contralto voice / Loving, laughing eyes" (Moineau, "Song," *Dublin University Magazine: A Literary and Political Journal* [October 1867] vol. LXX, 465).

12. Stuart Hall, Staunton, Virginia.

13. Lawyer William Henry Sims (1837–1920), later lieutenant governor of Mississippi (1876–82), was the husband of Elizabeth Louisa Upson Sims (1837–1913).

ᔕ

Lucy continued to watch for signs of pregnancy. Her menstrual cycle had stopped in October 1871, and yet she remained in doubt about her physical state and ambivalent about motherhood.

Anxious and unsettled, Lucy suffered through a visit by two Methodist ministers who engaged her in a lengthy debate about the ills of dancing. Infuriated by their comments, Lucy resented their presence and the fact that she and John remained spiritually separated by the Presbyterian/Methodist denominational divide.

Lucy to Lizzie

Wildwood—
Feb: 2nd/.72.

My darling Trotwood—

Are you alarmed at this <u>mammoth sheet</u> of paper?; & do your <u>eyes hurt</u>, in anticipation of the task of perusing its' many lines? Well! I don't wonder if either of the two feelings should fill your breast—but this I will promise,—<u>not</u> to write any more than I can <u>possibly</u> help, & to write it "<u>werry loud</u>,"[1] so that your poor eyes won't suffer any more than absolutely necessary!—I could find no other paper about the house, & so was obliged to content myself with some of Mr Neilson's <u>account</u>-book; for I could not postpone answering that <u>precious</u> letter of your's, so much wished for, & so eagerly <u>devoured</u>!

I can't, somehow, make you understand how very essential some sort of communication with you, is to my <u>well</u>-<u>being</u>—I can't absolutely say, "<u>happiness</u>"— for so long as there is no estrangement in hearts (only in <u>pens</u>) between us, & I know that you are well & pleasantly situated—& I, myself, so well & pleasantly situated, I cannot be sentimental enough to grow <u>unhappy</u> over the non-arrival of letters. You know I am <u>severely practical</u>, or else <u>what</u> a charming opening for <u>morbid</u> feelings! Why what a world of <u>feeling</u>, I could <u>undergo</u>, that Mrs Burne, Mrs Haliniski[2] (?), Mrs Ransom & <u>Co</u> should so cheat you out of your <u>time</u>, that your own child should <u>grow</u> neglected & apparently forgotten! No better field for bitter herbs could be found, think you?—But, instead, thinks I to myself,— "I wish Trot could find just one little spare corner of <u>time every</u> week for a little home-writing—it seems to me but right that she should—she is our head, our Mother—one in whom we have ever confided our every feeling, good, bad, or indifferent—we are great grown folks now—but still the old feeling returns, & we feel a <u>wee bit neglected</u> & <u>hurt</u>, if we do not receive <u>some</u> attention from the sweet old ["]source of all our childish pleasures & comforts."—Now, I think I am right <u>mild</u> in my thoughts to <u>myself</u> about my <u>dear</u>, Trot. And when I read of how fully your time is taken up, I do confess to a feeling of <u>jealousy</u>—not that I doubt your <u>love</u>—but I am jealous of <u>your rights</u>! I know so exactly how <u>any one</u> can monopolize you, who wishes. This I do not <u>like</u>—you may well say it is not dignified—it is not doing yourself justice—I feel like I ought to be there to protect you. You never could do that little service for yourself?—could you?—Don't get out of patience—I know tho' how sweet to every one is some <u>privacy</u>—& from your account you have none! I can <u>quarrel</u> about this <u>inconsideration</u> of your devoted(?) friends—but when I read that you have been <u>worried</u> in mind & heart, <u>then</u> I have the minor points without thought, & all my wish is to know <u>what</u> worried my own old darling! I think you did not treat me with your <u>usual</u> freedom of confidence, or else you would have given me a hint, or clue anyhow— I am not <u>obliged</u> to tell my husband other peoples' thoughts & feelings, if I do tell all my own—so if you ever feel like having a little "pen & ink" confab all to ourselves, why just mark "private," & it shall be <u>strictly</u> so. I don't like the <u>tone</u> of your last letter—it smacks smartly of a tired-world-weariness, which is so unlike my fresh, bright, enthusiastic, world-<u>embracing</u> Trot. Look here, old Lady, what's the matter?—did it just happen that you were a "little weary just <u>today</u>," or does something abide with you, which causes you to chafe under its wearisome stay? Tell me candidly—I'm none the less your-other-self than formerly! It was so according to your old custom to awaken in the morning, & think of some comforting promise of Our Father's. When any of your old <u>peculiar</u> ways are brought to mind, I feel a keenness of impatience at our long separation which is almost unbearable—I try to check such feelings, but fear I fail lamentably. And then <u>you</u> feel a homesickness which only augments mine—I am like Bess, I am beginning to count how long she will have to remain in school—then I'll begin counting how long before your return. I know it is best for you to remain in that climate, as long as possible, & reproach myself for being so selfishly impatient. Your disease is one of such strong hold, you cannot hope to feel entirely relieved for years. Don't over-tax your strength, & I confess to a <u>fear</u> of too close con- finement to that <u>sewing</u>-machine. My dear, now you <u>must not</u>! Remember your health is paramount to every other consideration. I know Mrs Ransom is obliged to you for such aid, for it must be a world of trouble to make a wardrobe of such dimensions. You ask, if you will not have to make similar ones this Spring?— well, all I know is, that since the <u>19th Oct</u>—there has been no "<u>visitors</u> from the country"—comprenez-vous [do you understand]?"—there are other accompa- nying circumstances, which make a body feel strange—but <u>said</u> to be <u>natural</u> enough. Now of all this "your finger on your lips I <u>prithee</u>,"[3] for no one save Mr N— & Cordele know anything of it. I will keep you advised of any further <u>developement</u>, in time for the necessary <u>outfit</u>—if anything does "<u>come of it</u>," I shall be much obliged to any one, who is good enough to assist me. Sometimes I'm quite in doubt tho', for I've never had the numerous <u>qualms</u>, which some describe—& then there's no difference in my appearance. I can't help being a little lowspirited at times, & my <u>tears</u> lie <u>very shallow</u>. I get so mad with myself for this weakness—but I can't help it—& then after a <u>little shower</u>, the sun shine is brighter. This is my only evidence of <u>nervousness</u>—for you know, I was never before very tear-ready! I'm afraid I'm somewhat <u>rebellious</u>. I did not desire any change for a long time—the future looks <u>hard</u>. But then you know "we women cannot choose out lots"[4]—& it is all right, that we cannot. I know what your sentiments are on this subject, & they are good, & noble, & truly christian. I hope I may feel better, & not bring down a curse upon myself & my husband by rebellious repinings.

Sunday-morning—Feb [4th]—Here I am all alone—Cordele, Mr Neilson, Mr Ramsey, Mr <u>Massengale</u>[5] (two Methodist-preachers) have gone to church, & left me here waiting for <u>Jim</u>, who promised to come up today. I will employ the time in finishing my prosy letter. Last night the two preachers staid with us—& gave me a prolonged lecture on <u>dancing</u>—tell Bess she ought to have been here to have shared the <u>scourging</u>—you know Mr Ramsey was never any favorite of ours—He used always to abuse our church, & seemed to really <u>hate</u> Mr Lyon. I was determined if I went to church today not to <u>commune</u> with them—for they plainly intimated that they wished no <u>dancer</u> to meet with them around the Lord's table—but I did'ent go—& I try not to have any <u>very</u> bad feelings—tho' I can't thank them for separating me from my husband. Until I feel right, I shall never commune at this church, I shall wait, & go to my own—if I ever have another opportunity.

Time passes, & still Jim does not come, I fear he will not—& how disappointed I will be, for I have treasured this expected meeting, & all alone too. I wish to hear him talk, & he can never do so freely before others. As to his leaving Columbus I cry out in my selfishness "<u>No, No</u>"—& not yet can I say anything else. It is a month since I saw him—& how keenly my heart yearns towards him.—

We have been quite anxious this week about Sophie's little Maud—but yesterday a note came, relieving our anxiety—she was at death's door for days. Sophie had no hope of her recovery—had Typhoid-fever!—They are very undecided where they will locate—but have determined to leave Gainesville—we hope she may come up here right away & stay, until they can settle upon some plan. Sister Sallie is in Washington with her Aunt Ellen Abert[6]—she is of the greatest comfort to the old lady, & does'ent speak of returning home until next Fall;— tho' she may change her plans <u>any time</u>.—Sister Mary has been uneasy about her children this week—they both have whooping-cough so badly. Cordele went, & spent some time with her to help with them. I have not seen or heard from any of Sister Annie's family since our trip in the wagon.—

Cards came last night for Lucy Jep Harris' marriage. She marries a Mr Duncan from Memphis, on <u>Tuesday</u> at the Methodist-church. We are only invited to the church—but I'm much obliged to them for remembering us at all. Julia Powell has married a Mr Barron[7]—a nephew of <u>Mrs</u> Powell's—& <u>teaching</u> school out at Artesia! I don't know whether they will live out there or not. No other news about the town, I believe. I enclose a scrap of Mr Neilson's sentiments politically! I never saw any one, more delighted than Moll was over your little letter—I am glad you wrote—she does very well yet—first-rate cook! Tell Bess I was much disappointed in not getting a letter from her yesterday—what's the matter with her? All would send love. God bless you both—your Lute.

Notes

1. Dickens, *The Posthumous Papers of the Pickwick Club* (1836–37), ed. Patten, 290.
2. Mrs. Burne and Mrs. Haliniski were boarders at Kalorama.
3. Shakespeare, *Othello*, ed. Honigmann, 174.
4. Edward Robert (Owen Meredith) Bulwer-Lytton, "Changes," *Clytemnestra, The Earl's Return, The Artist, and Other Poems* (1855), 337.
5. Rev. T. Y. Ramsey (b. ca. 1818), former pastor (1869–70) and presiding elder (1868, 1870–74) of the Columbus First Methodist Church; Rev. Leroy Massengale (b. ca. 1807), Methodist preacher from Macon, Georgia.
6. Ellen Matlack Stretch Abert (1792–1872), widow of John James Abert (1788–1863), who served as head of the U.S. Army's Corps of Topographical Engineers for thirty-two years and was responsible for facilitating and surveying the region west of the Mississippi River. Ellen's grandfather was Timothy Matlack (1736–1829), scrivener of the Declaration of Independence and founder of the Society for Free Quakers.
7. Julia Augusta Powell (1849–1903), daughter of farmer Richard D. Powell (1799–1875) and Emma Jane Hardy Powell (1815–ca. 1898), married teacher James McCaden Barrow (1841–1904). James was the son of Emma's sister Virginia Katherine Hardy Barrow (b. 1813) and William Johnson Barrow (1809–95).

A picture of Bess's new beau received approval from the family circle and prompted Lucy to indulge in another lecture to her niece about the dangers of romancing.

Winter's isolation had not taken the shine off Lucy's domestic life at Wildwood. "I wish you could see John and Lute you would think they had been married about a week instead of ten months, the way they do affectionate," Cordele remarked in a letter to Bess on February 7, 1872; "have broken the rocking chair down, now they have to sit in an old fashion split-bottom-one that can't break: beautiful doings, I tell you."

As she prepared her garden plot for spring, Lucy noted that John's inability to secure farmhands had been partly relieved by her sending Moll out to the fields when necessary. Lucy hoped the measure would also reaffirm her authority and quash any ideas that Moll may have had about her right to dictate her own wages, duties, or hours of employment.

Lucy to Bess

Wildwood.
Feb: 16th/.72

My dear Bess,

This is one of the times, that I am going <u>to try</u> to write you a <u>short</u> letter—for I hav'ent done such a thing since you left last summer. But I have such a way of <u>stringing</u> out little home items which are nothing in themselves; & my <u>journey-ings</u> have not been very extensive this year (a visit to Sister Annie being the longest), therefore I have nothing <u>foreign</u> to dilate upon, so I have made up my mind to be very concise in this letter anyhow—& tell you in the briefest manner how glad I was to get your letter of 5th, & how very glad I was to see "<u>Miller</u>"[1] with my own eyes, & how splendid I think <u>he is</u>, & how much strength of character his face indicates—especially his fine eyes, firmly set mouth, & massive <u>chin</u>! He's none of the stupid <u>fat</u>, ease-loving-sort—do excuse me, for referring to a former picture—but remember I am of the <u>fat</u> kind myself, & am perhaps a little fastidious. I know I should like "Miller"—he looks the real high-born Virginia-gentleman—of course he is of the <u>F.F.V</u>—'s?—ahem!—But you must have a <u>care</u>, & not <u>entrap</u> & be <u>entrapped too seriously</u>. You are such an inborn <u>flirt</u>. I believe you are incapable of real <u>platonic</u> affection—the only one you ever had, was when a child, & as you grew to woman-hood, it was rather a <u>bore</u> than otherwise, & you so willingly gave it up. Of course I speak of Mr W.A.C[2]—. I don't think you should encourage that <u>flirting</u> inclination—it might bring <u>great pain</u> to some true heart—which might be a grief to <u>you</u>, in after life.

—Oh! what a long homily I've unwittingly gone off into—I begin to have my fears as to the conciseness of this letter—But one word more, don't think I'm <u>too hard</u> on you, & don't imagine I do not sufficiently sympathize with you—then I am greatly obliged to you for <u>feeling obliged</u> to <u>tell</u> & <u>show</u> me <u>everything</u>, & you will always know I am a most gratified recipient—therefore I thank you for sending the picture, & return it without further delay—for I am uncertain if I will see Lizzie for months—the roads are getting so bad, there's little communication between our homes. We are going on in the even tenor of our way—since the cold weather broke Mr Neilson has been going [doing] some farm work—the <u>mill</u> too requires a good deal of his attention—that will be very profitable, I hope—the wagons are constantly passing hauling away lumber, & make things look quite busy. I <u>lend</u> Moll to Mr Neilson as much as possible, & she is <u>so delighted</u> going to the field—I am glad of it—for I did'ent want her to be putting on airs about <u>change</u> of work. Mr Neilson is quite pleased with her, he says she <u>rushes</u> right a head.

You would laugh at my <u>flower-garden</u>—now it does'ent pretend to be but <u>one bed</u>—12x12 ft long—still that is quite enough for a beginning—& I am not much given to garden-work as Trot can testify!— The sweet little white hyacinths are blooming away with all their might as if doing their best to make surroundings look less wild, & uncultivated. The roses too, I think will live, & violets are blessing us with a bloom now & then. I am anxious to go down home for some grape-vines, garden-herbs, & apple & peach scions. I can better enter into Trot's great desire for trees & shrubs, than ever before. I think such things will do well here—the soil is fine. Raspberries I must have too—I shall not attempt strawberries yet awhile anyhow—they need so much attention. But our poor garden has'ent a paling yet. We expect a carpenter in about ten days to begin work, & Mr Neilson has most excellent material to make a fence of. Not an Irish-potatoe have we in the ground—nor even an onion—I read "Keeler"[3] most desperately—but will have to make up my mind for a late garden—the ground is too wet, even if we had a fence. The chickens seem not to have found my flowers, or if so they are too heathenish to know what dainty bits they would afford. I bless their ignorance, or good-nature. We have some little chicks hatching off today—I hope we may raise them. If you were here how you would delight in the eggs—what cakes, what good-things you could make without any ado for material. The boys (George & Ed) bring in a dozen (average) every day. Oh! Mercy what a funny letter for a young lady—all about garden & chickens—just all married people think about—I always vowed I'd never be so prosy—but how can I help it?—

February is over half gone—you have now only four & a half months to go to school—I am almost as bad as you were about counting the months, weeks, & days before my marriage. But then you can't come home—can you?—Ah! cruel Fate!—Sometimes I am wicked enough to wish to pass the intervening time unconsciously—especially, if what I anticipate is to be endured! O! Bess!—

Cordele wrote Trot on last Monday—& I received one from her by return "male"—How gratifying to get letters regularly from her—you know she has a way, all her own, which makes people wish to keep in hearing of her. I will answer her letter by next opportunity—I think my domestic-ditties had better been reserved for her letter—but what is writ is writ, & you'll be equally as much interested as I, in such things, in a very little while—especially if you decide to take the Dr of the "crimson-locks"—for he lives in the country & is a farmer. Cordele is so funny about your letters—she says she will never mention another home-item, if you don't take more notice, & comment on them. Says she told you before christmas about receiving a sett of furs, & you have never said one word about them—all "Bess thinks about is Miller & Fliller, & Ransom, & Yansom & all these folks that nobody knows or cares about"—I tell you this as a little hint—for oh! she does look forward to your letters with such acute pleasure, & when you write as if you never had even read her letters, she feels disappointed. I tell her you are hurried when you write, & have no time to hunt up old letters, & notice items—but she thinks you might remember from the last reading. I tell you, when you get thro' school I'm not going to be content with such hurried letters either—Cordele says your head must be decorated with beaux (bows) all the time—but you had better "hush, my dear, sit still, & study for a while yet, & then you can go."[4] Oh! the ditties she has in store for you. She really pines for some of those long old-fashioned-chats you & she used to have!—I hope she can go to "North Miss" this Spring, & then she can get another budget of narratives. It is very unselfish of me being willing for her to go—for what will I do so far separated from all my family!—if I did not have just such a husband, I could not bear the idea. But, oh! Bess, such ever watchfulness, & care is so blessed; & I hope I do fully appreciate him in all his many virtues. When so blessed, I am afraid to murmur at anything!

Encourage Trot in well-doing—I know you will write whenever you can. Excuse the utter dullness of this letter, (long in spite of all my resolutions to the contrary)—but really I have no communication with our friends in town, & have nothing to tell of them—Jim writes us nice newsy notes occasionally, which charm us—& we have our letters, & papers, & magazines to keep us from stagnating. I do not feel oppressed by the isolation tho'—since all is blessed by Our Father with good health. Praise his holy name for that. Write soon to T'Ida.

Give our hearts full of love to Trot—reserving an equal amount for yourself! Kiss Miller for us, & tell him we do like him very much. I think he was very smart learning how to crochet. I expect his Grand-ma was quite pleased with her present. Good-bye, dear,—Don't forget your higher duties while so absorbed with those of earth. God bless you both.

NOTES

1. Mr. Miller does not appear to be connected to Frank Williams Miller (b. 1847) of Mobile, Alabama, Elizabeth Parthenia Irion's future husband.
2. William A. Campbell.
3. Oscar T. Keeler, *Keeler's Mississippi Almanac*.
4. Lucy paraphrased "Hush my dear, lie still and slumber" (Isaac Watts, *Divine and Moral Songs* [1715]); see 1866 edition, 111–12.

ℬ

Mary Bruce, the infant daughter of John's brother, James Crawford Neilson, and Mary Bruce Barry Neilson, died in late February 1872. "Our dear, darling little Manie breathed her last," wrote James in his diary. "Although I know that she is far better off . . . my heart bleeds for the dear child."

Death was an inextricable part of childbirth and child rearing in the South. In 1860 over 20 percent of all deaths occurred among infants and over 43 percent among

James Crawford Neilson.
Lillian Neilson Papers.
*Courtesy of Special
Collections Department,
Mitchell Memorial Library,
Mississippi State University.*

*children under five years of age. The loss, so close to home, came just days after Lucy
had informed Mary of her own pregnancy.*[1]

Lucy to Lizzie

Wildwood.
Feb 23rd/.72.

My darling Trot—
    Your letter of the 6th has lain unanswered longer than I wished, but I have
been hindered by the sickness of poor little Mary Bruce, Sister Mary's baby,—
She has had whooping-cough for six weeks then was teething, & <u>pneumonia</u> set
in, which was too much, & the little thing <u>died</u> yesterday-afternoon about 4 ½
o'clock. She suffered so much, it was good to see her relieved—but poor <u>parents</u>!
Sister Mary's submission is beautiful—not <u>one</u> word of repining even, much less
of rebellion, & little Manie was so peculiarly <u>her's</u>, for she was shy of most others, but clung to "Mama." In a few days she would have been a year old—had the
same birthday as mine—tho' she was so strong & active she had walked before

she was ten months. Beckie Barry has been with Sister Mary for two weeks, help-ing with the children—the baby was so much better last Saturday, Beck came home with us, & staid until the next evening—but on Monday-night she had a relapse, & was violently ill then till death. Poor little <u>wistful</u>, <u>pleading eyes</u>, I can see them now, as they looked into mine. How bright & <u>satisfied</u> they must look now!

Lou has almost recovered from the cough—but has had two chills this week; the one this morning was quite severe. Mr Neilson went down last night after supper, to town, for the coffin—& they took the remains to our cemetery in town this noon—Cordele & Beck accompanied them, but I did'ent—Mr Neil-son, & I came on home, leaving Sister Anne with Sister Mary & Lou—I feel little in a writing-mood, but I'll have an opportunity to the Post tomorrow, & like to have a letter ready once a week any how. We have been almost two weeks without hearing from you, & I was really right uneasy, & of course I dreamed of <u>your</u> being on the <u>verge</u> of <u>death</u>, & that someone had sent me a diagram of the internal workings of your stomach & liver, during your illness. You know you used so many times to wish you could see <u>your liver</u>!—Last night however, Jim sent out a letter from Bess to him, one from <u>you</u> to him, & one from Bess to Cordele—Altho none were for me—yet I was so glad to hear you were both well. Ah! that <u>old</u> pain in your side—when will it ever be entirely cured? It is like a <u>thorn</u> in <u>my</u> flesh[2]—& like one in your side I expect. This season of the year makes me uneasy about you <u>liver</u>-folks—please take <u>all</u> the care & precau-tions! Cordele had a touch of bilious colic the other day—but it passed off, & did'ent put her to bed. That is rather remarkable, & I <u>tease</u> her by telling her, it was because she was up in this <u>healthy country</u>. She will not acknowledge there is any good in this <u>Nazareth</u>![3]—She is going home with Beck for a visit—next week I suppose. I hope she may have <u>invitations</u>, & make a long visit in town—she has been right low-spirited since her disappointment in visiting Mrs Merritt.—

The weather has been fine, & spring-like for some days—& I feel quite impa-tient for my garden to begin—Mr Neilson is doing what he can in his crop—but is "<u>hip</u>-a-<u>hop</u>"[4]—now with some <u>boils</u> on his ankle—these make him very restless, for he wishes to <u>work</u>, <u>work hard</u>—but is hindered by them. Jim is just "<u>taking on</u>" with the "<u>widow</u> H"—I told him I was going to report to <u>Va</u>-<u>head</u>-<u>quarters</u>—but he begged I should'ent. He writes a note, by every opportunity—so sweet in him. I was so much interested in <u>your</u> sleigh-ride, & the description of the old church was delightful. I enjoyed what you said of the <u>Virginians</u>—for I know you can't help laughing at them—I am sure I <u>should</u>. I am glad you send Bessie's reports, for all of us feel so interested. Bless <u>her heart</u>—tell her I wrote her as prosy a letter as this last week—but she <u>must</u> answer anyhow. I think you owe me another letter, or rather you must have written before my last reached you, for it contained some items, which I think you would have commented on—I can't tell you how I yearn for you these days—I feel if "Trot was only here I could bear anything"—Cordele is too sympathetic—every shade on my face, is doubly reflected on hers. She grieves over the coming events. I asked her the other day, please to quit dilating on the ills to come. I am frightened any how. Please, dear Trot, write me as often as you can, for I need your strong counsel now. My husband is all he can be—but I am selfish in my great desire for you. Excuse this letter. Write me freely & I'll do the same with you. I have had my first talks with Sisters Anne, & Mary—they are both just as sweet as they can be. May God help us all—

In love Lute.

NOTES

1. James Crawford Neilson diary, February 24, 1872, Lillian Neilson Papers; McMillan, *Motherhood*, 167.
2. 2 Cor. 12:7.
3. John 1:46.
4. "Irish Barber" in Henry, ed., *Folk-Songs*, 409.

ॐ

In late February the weather improved enough for the Neilsons to make a long-over-due trip to Columbus. In a letter to Bess, Lucy relayed news about Willow Cottage, passing over the revelation that Tilde Barron, an Irion family servant, had given birth to a daughter named Anarchy. Instead of dwelling on the changes wrought by emancipation, Lucy did her best to focus on what she regarded as the long-standing ties of mutual obligation and affection between African Americans and whites.

Lucy to Bess

Wildwood.
March 4th/.72

My precious, old Bess.

Your last letter was so delightful, & I find myself answering it tonight, altho' I am "so tired & so sleepy"—yet I must not allow another opportunity escape, of posting you some kind of an answer. I laughed heartily at your pretending such violent interest in everything in my last homely letter. [Thank] you, dear girl, for being so pleasant, & polite—if you were here, I know you would feel as much interest as a practical woman could in our every little improvement—but then away off hearing of things makes quite a difference. I indulge myself in egotism to my heart's content in writing to you both, & you encourage the hideous practice—which you should'ent.

We went down home a week ago, & spent the night & day—our first visit since new year—the negroes all were delighted to see us, & did'ent try to hide their feelings. I think they had been somewhat hurt at our long absence—aint they strange creatures? I received your letter while there, & read it aloud—Nan sat half-crying & half-laughing & half-shouting all the time. Pheobe cooked for us as usual & Parthene slept in the house as usual—Woos, of course, was not up to all her former duties—tho' she was perfectly willing, & would have done anything we wished. I had a yoke-neck dress to cut & fit for Aunt Pheobe—& a big chat with every one, Bettie (Holderness), Bob's wife,[1] in the midst. Poor Booker has been very sick with Pneumonia—but he is better. I hope well now, & has professed religion, & Nancy is just shouting over him at every breath—Beckie was as good a wife while he was sick, as she is poor, when well! 'Tilda's little baby is mighty pretty, & plump—her name is Anniekie (I don't know how to spell it). Of course all the women "got after me" on a certain subject, & I was much petted thereupon! I got a nice lot of Rasp-berries—& all kind of garden herbs—Catnip, calamus &c. Mr Neilson also put out apples, peach, pear & damson—we have already two fig-bushes living—I put up my best wishes for each twig which went into the ground—also brought two Scoupenong-vines from home—I hope in time to feast you on all kinds of fruit. Come & see & taste—won't you?

We went by town Monday, & called at Mrs Ottley's to leave Cordele to pay a visit. T'was at noon, & Mrs Eager was there—I was so glad to get a sight of their dear faces once again—they were glad to see us too, & scolded us good for burying ourselves so long in the (dreadful) country! I declare, they talk as if I had as much leisure time, & as few duties as Lucy Irion had!—& "kinder" talk as if I rather overdid the matter in staying so much with my husband (?). They made me promise to come next week, & stay several days, & Cordele kindly offered to take care of my home, & good-man, while I went. I will be pleased to go, & know I shall enjoy seeing all my friends very much. It is very loving, & sweet in Miss Ellen to be so determined not to give up my society altogether—I appreciate her interest more than I can express, & I know you & Trot will too. They had no news to tell us—all the town very quiet;—the Col is now in New York. I was in hopes Cordele would have pleasant weather for her visit, so she could go the rounds, & bring home ditties by the bagful—but lo! & behold cold, cloudy days first, & the sleet, & snow—I told Miss Ellen that "Miss" had a nice new dress, & to make her put it on, whenever occasion demanded. Gus, & Theodoric Lyon were going to take tea there that evening—so there were beaux right off. Miss Ellen told me to make haste, & come while Col was away, & we three widows (two grass) would have a gay time. Ahem!

I know you wonder what I will <u>wear</u>—I hope I can alter my light-silk, so as to squeeze into it on dress-occasions—then my black-silk with long full over-skirt & sacque—& my <u>rose</u>-morning-dress—see now, I shall do very well! I must call on Lucy Harris Duncan—& Regina Lee anyhow, if no more fashionable visits—I hope no body will tease me! I try to be sensible!—

Went to spend yesterday (Sunday) with Sister Mary—while Mr Neilson went down with brother James to town to carry <u>Beck</u> home. We had a quiet, peaceful, pleasant day—T'was little Manie's & <u>my birthday</u>—did you think of me? Sister Mary is grieving with a <u>godly</u> sorrow for her little one—just so <u>resigned</u>. She hopes to come & see us this week, & on Saturday to go to her Father's. Sister Annie came over in the afternoon, & had much to say of your last letter to Liz, & the beautiful present she had received from you—she says your <u>proposed</u> Summer's tour, has nearly <u>crazed</u> Liz—but poor thing! I bet, she does'ent get out of Columbus—for that <u>Cousin</u> is in the way of every enjoyment. Sophie has written her a very pressing invitation to come & pay her a visit—but it is doubtful whether she goes or not. She & Ella are going to town this week to visit Pattie Mills—then to <u>Aunt Cadie's</u>, & then to Mr <u>Barry's</u>—quite a round of <u>gayeties</u> (?) During this week Cordele will be with Beck Barry—Sunday we will probably go down for her. They hope the new preacher, Mr Boude, will be here by that time.—

In one of your letters to Jim you asked if I had ever received your <u>large</u> picture—why, my <u>darling</u>, long ago, & wrote you about it, & am just waiting to present myself with a pretty frame for it—I wish it right before my eyes <u>all</u> the time, I do love it.—

Bess, I did'ent mean to complain of <u>your letters</u> to me—for don't I know exactly how you are situated, & don't I thank you for every <u>line</u> you steal the time to write—but I was merely giving you a little hint about '<u>Miss</u>,' & her peculiarities—I laughed till I <u>hurt</u>, over your message about the <u>furs</u>—come at last!— Cordele just can't get along without your sympathy, & interest being excited in everything which concerns her.—She vows she will <u>not go</u> to North Miss, & <u>leave me</u>—she says it will be <u>unsisterly</u>. I tell her that <u>Woos</u> can come, & take care of me—but she says she will <u>not</u> hear of going—perhaps after all is over, she will go, & return in the Fall when <u>you all do</u>! <u>Wonder</u> what Trot <u>thinks</u> of her determination. How many many times do I wonder "what Trot <u>would</u> think"—on almost every subject which occupies my brain. Jim very sweetly came to see me while I was at Mrs Ottley's—he did not come out home that night before because he & Mr Lee[2] had gone to see Lizzie Symons.—I tell you he is taking on with his "<u>Wid</u>" <u>shamefully</u>. I don't know what he can mean—the whole town is talking of their <u>marriage</u>—Bah!—I think he is compromising his dignity, <u>myself</u>—you know I am <u>great</u> for people sustaining their dignity of position & character! He was to have come out to see us yesterday—but for the <u>bad</u> weather, & roads—& <u>bring</u>

her!—I know she will criticize everything about my home with great <u>severity</u>, but I am quite willing.—

I am right <u>mad</u> to hear of both of you having <u>colds</u>—I'm afraid you are not sufficiently careful. I wrote Trot a <u>mean</u> letter last week, & I think Mr Neilson must have carried it around in his pocket a week before he mailed it—I hope she will write as soon as she feels able. I do think Miss Marshall's[3] picture beautiful, & shall keep it to ornament my Album, with your permission. I hope Mrs Taylor can get a suitable house, & that your pleasant household may not be broken up. Miss Baldwin must be an <u>angel</u>, sure enough!—

The recipe for Oyster-pie made me very <u>hungry</u>—I shall keep it, & use it, when an opportunity offers. I have no picture of your Uncle John save one which was taken <u>after</u> a <u>Parisian-wine-party</u>—I <u>won't</u> send it, for 'tis too <u>squint</u>-eyed. My poor man had to go to bed alone for here I sit, & <u>scribble</u> nonsense—My letter does not <u>expand</u> itself over as much space as yours—but remember I <u>inter-line</u>—which makes mine as long as yours. Mr Neilson does enjoy your letters, & is waiting for you to send him one—also <u>Trot</u>—but he is very lenient towards correspondents. He would send love but is fast asleep—Kiss each other for us. God bless you—

Your T'Ida.

NOTES

1. Bettie and Bob Holderness were probably former slaves of Col. McKinney Holderness (1782–1850) and Elizabeth Holderness (1784–1862), Lucy's uncle and aunt.

2. Grocer William Hollinshead Lee (1841–1910).

3. Probably Ella Marshall (b. ca. 1856) of Bennettsville, South Carolina, who was a student enrolled in the Augusta Female Seminary at this time.

※

At the behest of her Columbus friends, Lucy left Cordele in charge of household matters at Wildwood to make a visit to town. While enjoying the company of friends, Lucy penned a lovesick letter to John on March 13, 1871, the anniversary of their eleventh month of marriage. "It seems I never saw <u>days</u> pass <u>so slowly</u>—tho' friends are so kind—yet for all that, there is one little sequestered spot, which holds the <u>one</u> object of my devoted heart," she wrote John. "I try not to be foolish—but oh! I do miss those dear sheltering arms—so strong, so loving & so tender. I am glad to be able to visit my friends—& I am much obliged to you for being so unselfish— but I don't feel as if I ever wish to come away again without you." Once settled back at her writing desk at Wildwood, Lucy recounted her week to Lizzie and Bess.

Lucy to Lizzie and Bess

Wildwood.

March 20th/.72

My dear, dear Trot & Bess—

I am home again after a visit of a week in town with our friends—while there, I received a letter from you, Trot, written on the 6th—then one from you, Bess, dated the 10th—then on Saturday, a joint letter to Mr Neilson & myself from Trot—these dear letters made my visit all the more enjoyable—& as I have the same things to tell each of you, I thought it would not be amiss to write to <u>both</u> at the same time. You don't care—do you Bess?—I rarely do such a way, because I know your preference.

Last Saturday was a week Mr Neilson & I, with our two wait-men George & Ed (they are <u>so bad</u>, we are afraid to leave them at home) went to town—& were gladly welcomed by our friends Meses Ottley & Eagar. We took dinner with they [them], but went out to Willow Cottage that afternoon to spend the night, as Jim was coming, & <u>also</u> Gus Lyon & Willie Odeneal. We had a delightful time— the men were so bad tho' we could hardly keep from driving them out—but you both know how "dear, delightful & <u>charming</u>"[1] they <u>can</u> be—so we <u>had</u> to endure them. These little <u>reunions</u> at the <u>camp</u> are very pleasant—they are a little <u>flustrating</u> at first, when we have to go out, & be in such a <u>hurry</u> about getting things in <u>ship-shape</u> by the time the guests arrive—but after all, they are meet- ings we can n'er forget. The two old bachelors, Jim & Gus, do so <u>thoroughly</u> enjoy them—they never appear to such social advantage—as for <u>my John</u>, he's always <u>affable</u>—(<u>bless his heart</u>!) I had to pretend to be very <u>cold</u>, & sit up with my velvet sacque on all the time. I came near melting—but it is the most <u>becoming</u> wrap I have, & so I had to <u>swelter</u> for sake of appearance—I could not bear the idea of any <u>change</u> being perceptible by "<u>optics keen</u>"[2]—<u>doctors</u> are so <u>knowing</u>. I thought Willie would hurt herself laughing! She is so sweet to me, & is <u>rejoiced</u> at the <u>prospect</u>! Cordele had a chance of coming over from Mr Barry's, & I was <u>so glad</u>, for she's house-keeper there—& then I had not seen the old lady for two weeks— [page missing]

Captain was very glad to see me, & not <u>saucy</u> one bit. The children all (Percy McLaran, Ed Prowell, Mary Prowell & <u>Lou Ellen</u>[3]) were delighted to have me, & behaved so sweetly. Cousin Cornelia reminds me of the <u>little</u> woman who lived in the shoe, with all those youngsters. Oh! we talked so much of you both— every body is nearly <u>thread-bare</u> (<u>in feelings</u>) at your prolonged stay. Wednesday- morning I went by to see Sister Kate, sat awhile with her, & my <u>lovely</u> nephew Jim White[4]—then went on, & met Miss Ellen coming for me—as we had planned to go out to Willow Cottage to get some flowers—while there who should come over, but all the crowd [of] girls from Mr Barry's. We had a merry time, & then returned to town in time for dinner—after which, I went [to] Cousin Jennie's, & found that my coming was made quite an occasion. Cousin George was there to meet me—also Mrs Lee & Sullie Matthews were invited down to sit with us—they came in due time, also Sister Kate Hopkins. We had a merry time of it—& then lo! a table of nice refreshments—(sardines, pickles, crackers, cake, Charlotte Ruse, wine &c)—Sullie declared it was a party, a genuine party, & my party too. Then came music from Sullie & Cous Jennie, & little Maria danced beautifully for us. I never saw Miss Maria in such spirits—& I thought she would eat me up. I was quite popular, "to hear me tell it"—as Tempe Fitts would say—but it is the truth, it seemed everybody was good, & sweet, & kind. I rushed back as soon as I could leave my party to Miss Ellen's, for Willie Odeneal had left word she was coming round to see me—but it was so late, she had gone home—after coming twice, & Miss Jane once—I was so sorry, & Miss Ellen was right provoked, until I explained of the "gay & festive scene," which awaited me, such as a party, with plenty of "champagne, waltzing & style"—country folks head was quite turned! After tea, Jim came round for me to go to the Concert (the Arion Band[5] have formed themselves into a troupe of minstrels, & have been entertaining the town with a series of concerts, & this was one)—as we were in search for a good seat, Willie Odeneal beckoned to us, & we found delightful seats with her, & her escort Mr John Hudson[6]—After awhile Willie leaned over, & said—"oh! I forgot I was mad with you, & was'ent going to speak to you"—then I explained my conduct, & she very sweetly accepted my explanation. Then Jim looked back across the other aisle, & said—"Why, yonder's "Steam-boat" (Gus Lyon) going out"—I said—"I bet he saw this crowd, & is coming round here"—when sure enough—here he came, & asked if he could get a seat—I told him Willie was door-keeper to our box—she admitted him, & there we were with Charlie McCauley screwed up in the corner. We had a good time. The performance was very entertaining—in-as-much as I am not much travelled, & never saw professional minstrels—then our crowd were so congenial. All my acquaintance around were nodding, & smiling me welcome—I half suspect I looked so pleased, they could'ent help smiling at my backwood's freshness. For I assure you I had none of the blasé ennui [dis-interest] about me. Thursday, I spent with Miss Ellen. Mit Williams[7] called in the morning, & Lizzie Eager Harris in the afternoon—late that afternoon Willie Odeneal came again, & took me home with her. All the family were so pleasant, & I do think Mr & Mrs O— are the friendliest old friends I ever had. Of course, they had many questions to ask of you both—Willie had a visitor, & we excused her, but Lurene[8] was in one of her brightest moods, & of course we all were entertained. They were all right mad with me for not spending the next day with them—but I could not.

Willie went with me—we called to see Mrs Taylor & Bet—Mrs Taylor could'ent see us tho', for she was going to have company, & her cook was sick &c &c. Bet was quite bright, & entertaining. Then we went round to see Yandaloo for awhile—she is quite well now, & rejoicing in being able to <u>eat</u> as much as she pleases of '<u>most</u> every thing—she was going out in the prairie to spend several weeks, for a change—I wish I could have her with me some—but I <u>can't</u>. I think she feels a little hurt about it too—but I cannot help it. Willie & I then journeyed to Dr Shattuck's, & called for all the ladies. <u>Mrs Dr</u> had called on me, & I had missed her. In came Lizzie Eager Harris with little Laura[9] in her arms—my first sight of her—& <u>she is a beauty</u>! Mrs Merritt just as merry as a lark—she is so relieved to be rid of house-keeping, & with her <u>beloved Shattucks</u>! Poor <u>Miss Liss</u> had a head-ache, & could'ent see us—Mrs Lee[10] was as bright as a button—all in a high <u>giggle at me</u>. I was <u>so teased</u>! Mrs Dr Shattuck is so kind & loving to <u>Jim</u>—he sits right next her at the table by the <u>coffee-pot</u>—they all pet him, & Mrs Lee is his (<u>old</u>) <u>sweetheart</u>. I thanked them for their kindness to him.

Willie went to dinner with me at Miss Ellen's, & in the afternoon <u>Sullie</u> called, also Sister <u>Kate</u>—they staid until late, & then Willie, & I rushed down to her home, for her to change her dress, for Jim was coming after tea to take us to see the <u>children-dance</u>—for you must know Prof Cleaveland has another <u>full</u> school, & it is now quite an attraction—they were to have a Soireè that evening. We went, & enjoyed the sight very much. Miss Ellen & I went together, & Jim & Willie. Cousin George came & sat by me, & was quite devoted all evening. Little Maria, & Virgie Ayers[11] were the prettiest dancers in the hall. Virgie & Sam Cleveland danced the Highland-fling to perfection! I sat near Laura Whitfield, & she was <u>too funny</u>. Gave me a great <u>ditty</u> on the preservation of <u>my form</u>, if I should ever have any <u>babies</u> (?). Willie <u>staid</u> all night <u>with me</u>—

Next day twas Saturday, & I was sure of seeing my dear husband—I was sitting down mending poor Jim's <u>neglected wardrobe</u>, when Mrs Eager said, "I see somebody"—, & there he was! Oh! did'ent we have a good, <u>little</u>, <u>joyous</u> meeting all to ourselves in the parlor! I could scarcely keep from crying, I was so very glad to be with him again. Willie soon after took her leave. She hopes to get to see me sometime this spring—Gus Lyon will bring her—Jim can't now, as we have his horse Stewart. It begun to rain, <u>to rain</u>—but we were bound to go home.

Mr Neilson came back to dinner, & as soon as we could, we started home. I thanked my dear friends for their <u>great</u> kindness, & love. I had thoroughly enjoyed my visit, but now I was willing & ready to go back with my John to our little nook in the wildwoods. How precious is that <u>home-feeling</u>—is it not! The rain poured on us all the way—but we were snugly protected by our hack, & got here all safe. Then I found I had a beautiful garden all paled in—the carpenter had worked steadily, & finished it all nice, & pretty. We are to have a new plank fence around the entire yard—& have already a "petition" fence running from the Office to the well—thereby dividing the back & front yards—surroundings will look so snug in a little while. Then we will have a new smoke-house too. Now will we not be improved by the time you return? I feel we are settled for life—Cordele can't enjoy the improvements for she feels the same. Cordele had not come in from Mr Barry's, & so we had to leave her down there—but Monday morning Jim got a spring-wagon, & sent her home—<u>he</u> is so afraid Mr Neilson will be inconvenienced—& does every thing in his power to help us along. Cordele had a delightful time—, & has come back quite cheerful. She was gone three weeks—I am glad we are all back at home once more. I love my home, & am astonished anyone could think it lonely. What a little [word missing] I have written, & not an item in your precious letters have I noticed—But the joke about Mr Crawford,[12] I read aloud at Miss Ellen's, & everybody roared, & the <u>Col</u> laughed till the tears ran down his cheeks—Even Johnie tried to see the <u>point</u>, & laugh too. Bess, your letters are real comforts to me—you are much more <u>motherly</u> than Trot—I envy Mrs Ransom all the sweet attention she gets from Trot—how I would glory in her sweet <u>petting</u>. Everybody pets me—white & black—but I want <u>you</u> & Trot! I am <u>too</u> selfish! I am foolish too at times, & feel like tearing Trot away from all those <u>new</u> folks, & leaving her to myself. Good-bye for this time, I have much more to write but not now—God bless you both, & send you to me—Lovingly Lute. [. . .]

NOTES

1. Rosina Bulwerh-Lytton, *The Peer's Daughters: A Novel* (1850), 73.

2. Lucy paraphrased "But optics sharp it needs, I ween, / To see what is not to be seen" (John Trumbull, *M'Fingal* [1775–82]); see *The Southern Literary Messenger* [April 1841], vol. VII, 321.

3. Percy Blewett McLaran (1860–1934), daughter of Cornelia Williams Benoit's uncle Charles McLaran and Ann Maria Jennings McLaran; Edward M. Prowell (b. ca. 1859) and Mary Martha Prowell (1860–1943), the children of farmer James Walker Prowell (1817–98) and Mary Madry Prowell (ca. 1838–64); Lou Ellen Benoit (1862–1937), daughter of James W. Benoit and Cornelia Williams Benoit.

4. James White Hopkins Jr. (b. 1872), son of Catherine Cabot Neilson Hopkins and Dr. James White Hopkins.

5. Community band.

6. John Hudson (b. ca. 1853), son of Mary Cornelia Hudson and John Fontaine Hudson.

7. Mary Agnes Williams (1844–1911), daughter of Wiley H. Williams and Mary A. E. Williams.

8. Teacher Loraine S. Street (ca. 1843–1912).

9. Laura Harris (b. 1872), daughter of Gideon Dowse Harris and Elizabeth Washburn Eager Harris.

10. Elvira Anne Lee (1818–81), mother of James William Gray Irion's friend William Hollinshead Lee.

11. Virginia P. Ayres (1861–1943), daughter of bookkeeper L. Q. C. Ayres (b. ca. 1830) and Virginia P. Ayres (ca. 1837–96).

12. Lucy may have been referring to merchant W. F. Crawford (b. ca. 1830), next door neighbor of the Odeneal family and living in the neighborhood of the Ottley family.

Interlude

HEART OF THE HEARTH

*S*pring arrived in Columbus carrying winter's last blanket of snow. As its white veil soaked into the fields, James Crawford Neilson's tenants worked hard at getting the cotton rebedded and the corn crop under way. By mid-April 1872 ninety acres were planted, but Neilson had hoped for more. Joe Trull, who had been contracted to work the "mound field" was "dreadfully behind" in his planting, and a shortfall on just one of Neilson's four tenant contracts promised to eat away at the profits he would reap from his half share of the harvest. Trull's "slow hand," however, turned out to be the least of Neilson's worries. Within weeks the spring rains dried up, the ground hardened, and the cotton crop came up badly. "Looks puny," Neilson remarked in his diary. Times were tough, but the eldest-born son sat assuredly at the center of his father's financial legacy. Shortfalls or poor crops were a frustrating setback to Neilson, not a descent into the uncertain world of smaller farming operations such as that of his brother, John. Tilling the ground himself on a corner of the family estate, John believed that hard work and tenacity would set him on the path to self-made manhood. Wildwood had none of the material comforts of Belmont, and there was only enough land to hire laborers to assist with the crop. His farm was a legacy of a different sort, built from the ground up.[1]

Lucy Irion knew what she was getting into when she fell in love with the younger Neilson son. "Poor young fellows" such as John, she noted, were often passed over by "dove-eyed-darlings," who accepted the proposal of "the first old, broken down man (whose purse is long enough)" in an effort to stave off the "struggling days of first married-life." Lucy was no such woman. When she took John's hand in marriage, she agreed to work alongside him to make a home out of their "little Pens in the wilderness." Like James's wife, Mary, Lucy spent her days preserving, mending and sewing, baking snowball cakes and pies, roasting turkeys, entertaining guests, managing servants, and tending the vegetable plot. Yet her vision of womanhood was not an incarnation of the antebellum southern lady or the sacrificial postwar housewife who rebuilt her family through service and submission. Like John's self-made manhood, Lucy's postwar identity grew out of a desire for familial autonomy and financial independence, a self-made gentility that rested on the strength of hard work, not the laurels of times passed. While her neighbors clung to the vestiges of antebellum domesticity, Lucy invested in a companionate marriage, an agricultural partnership, and the scrimping modesty of a new southern ethos.[2]

NOTES

1. James Crawford Neilson diary, April 15, 30, May 6, 1972, Lillian Neilson Papers.
2. Eliza Lucy Irion to Laura Corrie Nesbitt, March 17, 1869.

Four

The Burdens of Womanhood

APRIL–SEPTEMBER 1872

*S*pring 1872 heralded a time of new beginnings for the Irion women. At Wildwood, Lucy dispensed with oblique references to "Tot Neanie" and the expanding state of her wardrobe and instead searched for practical and spiritual guidance from Lizzie. More than marriage or housekeeping, impending motherhood resolved Lucy's internal conflict about her place within her family and her community. As she prepared to give birth, she also prepared to die. With Lizzie and Bess in Virginia, Lucy used her writing to reassure her kin, and herself, that she was ready for the "coming trouble."

At the Augusta Female Seminary, Bess made final preparations for school commencement proceedings. The first member of the Irion family to graduate after the Civil War, Bess represented her family's investment in a new brand of southern womanhood, one that valued intellectual achievement both as a hallmark of gentility and as a tool of self-sufficiency. Lucy and Cordele packed up their baubles and finery to send to their niece, aware that a successful season in Virginia bode well for the family's standing more generally.

In Mississippi, Cordele struggled to reconcile her antebellum visions of single blessedness with a postwar existence that smacked of familial dependence. After wallowing in pity and resentment for several months, Cordele now faced the prospect of either redefining her sense of self or alienating her loved ones completely. An altercation with Lucy and a firm word from Lizzie made Cordele rethink her position. Abandoning her role as a peripheral helpmate to her sister, Cordele used Lucy's advancing pregnancy and an unexpected change in servants to reposition herself at the center of domestic life at Wildwood.

Lizzie found herself at the vortex of this familial whirlwind, compelled once again to act as a "mother-sister" and guide each of her loved ones through contrasting rites of passage. Still, she did not do this alone. In the postwar South, it took the devotion of a family and a community to educate a young lady or prepare a wife for motherhood. Lucy benefited from the prenatal advice of her sisters-in-law, the baby clothes and tokens made by family and friends, and the domestic support provided by Cordele. Bess relied on Lizzie's parental support and the material contributions made by Lucy and Cordele. Rebuilding white southern womanhood was a collective endeavor, in which the exchange of time and resources reaffirmed relationships, respectability, and community.

♁

With her pregnancy confirmed, Lucy entered into a series of frank discussions with Lizzie and Bess about her preparations for the birth. Urging Lizzie not to return from Virginia, Lucy tried to reassure herself that the assistance of other family and friends would be enough to see her through childbirth.

Lucy to Lizzie and Bess

Wildwood.
April 1st/.72.

My dear, dear Trot & Bess—

I write a joint letter again—or rather it is the continuation of the other <u>volume</u>, I sent week before last—a kind of sequel! I have received no answer yet—but feel confident there is one, from <u>you</u>, Bess, on the way—I think Trot ought to write to me as often as she can, for I may never see her again, & then won't she feel <u>sorry</u>? Please don't think I jest too lightly on so serious a subject, for indeed! sometimes such a <u>fear</u> comes over me, of dying before I ever see you two again, that I am real childish. Tho' I would not have you think I am inclined to melancholy, for I am not—I am <u>very well</u>,—consequently am rarely low-spirited. There are few women blessed as I have been all <u>the</u> time—no trouble of any kind scarcely. If Bess were here, she'd have very little <u>doctoring</u> to do—but how I would love her <u>cudling</u>, & petting, & deep & lively interest in everything! Bless your dear heart, how I do love you!—& how my eyes do always overflow with tears at the thought of your sweet love & interest—so like your dear Mother would have felt. The more one has, the more they wish—all my life, I've been petted by out-side friends, as well as family—I thought after a month or two of married-life—my friends would little bit slacken in their sweet ways—but not so—It is almost a year now (—in a few days the 13th will roll around!—) & not one has seemed to loose interest—& <u>pet</u> me <u>now</u> more than ever. Still I long for Trot & Bess!—their <u>big</u> niches in my daily life are vacant, & I'm ever mindful of it too. Yes, both of you have your peculiar way of petting me—Bess <u>so sweet</u> & <u>funny</u>, Trot so <u>good</u>, & <u>strong</u> & <u>trustworthy</u>! I feel there is a great gulf between us thro' which I have to pass—& pass alone—no! not '<u>alone</u>,' I should not write the word—when each daughter of Eve, has such special promises made her[1]—sure promises too, which will <u>never</u> fail! I am physically a great coward—never before in my life, did I look forward to any suffering as <u>inevitable</u>—, & therefore I grow very faint-hearted at times—for the '<u>flesh</u> is <u>so weak</u>'—tho' most of the time the '<u>spirit</u> is strong, & trusting'[2]—Mr Neilson is such a "tower of strength"[3] to me—but poor Cordele has never a comforting word—I am stronger than she! I find tho' as each day brings the trying time nearer, I feel less <u>actual fear</u>—more trust—more faith <u>that</u> '<u>all will be right</u>'—'all will be <u>well</u>.'[4] I know each of you will pray for me!

That little sentence in your letter Trot—viz "I could not be willing to leave you in your coming trouble—that would draw me from one end of the world to the other"—is truly pathetic in the exquisite tenderness!—Tho' as for you coming to me at such a <u>season</u> would be actually tempting Providence—no, I must do <u>without</u> you! I would be miserable at the thought of you running such a risk. No, you could not <u>venture</u> home at that time—no! no!—emphatically no!—My tears flow as [if] I were signing my own death-warrant—forbidding your presence, when that presence at <u>such</u> a time would be, next my husband's, the <u>most</u> precious! But Trot, you must not think such a thing possible—I do not—& you'll not hear a word of <u>pining</u> from me any more—I am just indulging myself in this letter—as I do sometimes in a good <u>cry</u>, & feel all the better. One thing tho' you must <u>write</u> to me—write <u>heart</u>-<u>letters</u> too—lock all those <u>intruding</u> people out of your room, & write as you know I would love. I almost <u>hate</u> those people when they interrupt your sweet talks to me.—

Miss Ellen is just <u>too</u> loving, & sympathetic, & is so willing to advise me on the practical subject, of <u>buying</u> & <u>making</u>. Mrs Eager treats me as if I were a new-born-babe so tender, so affectionate—she offered to come & be with me, to take <u>your</u> place—now was'ent that just like her? But I refused upon the spot—for every vacation, she has some <u>lovely</u> occupation which prevents her resting as she ought. She is coming tho' to pay us a long visit, before the time—how glad I will be to have her. She has also offered to do any little shopping I wish done. Cousin Cornelia is <u>all interest</u>, & tells me to call on her for anything, & everything!

Sister Annie will be <u>right here</u>—also Sister Mary. You both would love them all <u>more</u> than ever for their exceeding kindness—they seem to be doubly tender because "your Sis Lizzie can't be with you." Sister Mary is a <u>sister</u> indeed!—she advises me in <u>everything</u>—tells me things that no body else thinks of—& has furnished me with little patterns of all things needful—& made me an exact list of such materials as I would need, & the <u>number</u> of <u>yards</u>. These little things are such helps to "<u>poor Mrs Wragge</u>"—why! the art, & science of <u>cooking</u> is nothing to this last mystery. I have made <u>nothing</u> yet—I feel so loth to begin. I wish I had

Bess to stir me up! I believe Cordele has hemmed one ruffle. How we did laugh over Bess "needing edges, & socks & sacques" in July, when she should be a young lady! O! Bess!

Now I believe I have told you everything except of the <u>doctors</u>, & <u>nurses</u> (<u>black</u>)—I am in favor of our beloved Dr McCabe—but Mr Neilson, & Mesdames Ottley, & Benoit are strong for <u>Dr Matthews</u>. Oh! horrors, I take the blues, when I think of doctors!—<u>Woos</u> will be on hand, & <u>Martha</u> says she is <u>bound</u> to come too—Aunt <u>Hetty</u>[5] the old family-nurse of the Neilson's must thro' courtesy be sent for!—so you see I have written <u>everything</u>. This entire sheet is devoted to <u>myself</u>—but I will not apologize for I must tell you both all things, & I believe you wish to hear too. Lizzie Symons is going to embroider a flannel-skirt. I am glad of any help-tho' I don't say so to any one but home-folks. I know Willie Odeneal will make a pretty sacque or something for <u>her baby</u>! I had such a dear letter from Madie Lyon—I will enclose it for you to read—tho' you must send it back for I have not answered it. It speaks for itself. De Jones <u>Tomlinson</u> also wrote me long letter—she is much in love with her husband.

What do you think of "<u>Hannah</u>"?[6] We have read it with much pleasure—I confess to feeling a little weary of so much <u>child</u>-talk. Then some of the sentiments were as sweet as ever Miss Mulock wrote. [. . .] Write whenever you can. I write such long letters, I can't find time to write oftener than I do. Kisses for you both.

Notes

1. 1 Tim. 2:15.

2. Lucy paraphrased "Watch and pray, that ye enter not into temptation: the spirit indeed is willing, but the flesh is weak" (Matt. 26:41).

3. Book of Common Prayer (1549); see 2001 edition, 129.

4. Lucy paraphrased "All will be well now! All will be right!" (Richardson, *Clarissa Harlowe* [1747–48], ed. Ross, 294).

5. Hetty (d. 1873) was a Neilson family servant who, according to James Crawford Neilson, "nursed all of father's children and attended on my wife at the birth of our three children" (James Crawford Neilson diary, January 1, 1873, Lillian Neilson Papers).

6. Dinah Maria Craik (often credited as Miss Mulock), *Hannah* (1871).

ℐᴓ

With Jim's removal to Aberdeen for work, Lucy continued to beg Lizzie not to leave Bess in Virginia and return to attend the birth, declaring that her niece's coming out far outweighed any practical or emotional concerns she had about her impending confinement.

Lucy to Lizzie

Wildwood—
April 11th/.72

My dear, dear Trotwood.

Your letter of the 3rd was received only yesterday—it had perhaps lain in the office some days but we had no communication with town. I answer, as you requested, immediately, & let me assure you, in all honesty & candor. It was like a "gale from the olden times" for you to begin your letter by asking for a <u>confidential talk</u>! How I settled myself for it, feeling glad of being once more summoned by you for the dear delights of <u>private confabs</u>! So I shall now proceed to answer, right away, all your questions & then to other things.—

First, as to Cordele going to 'North Miss,' I think is not even a desire of hers now. She was right disappointed at first, & <u>duty</u> was hard for her to make up her mind to perform—but she struggled all by herself, for of course I did not say a word to influence her to fore-go the pleasure of a visit, on my account—but I was very much gratified when she expressed herself as determined to stay with me, for oh! such a desolate feeling came over me when I thought of having no "kith or kin" to appeal to, in time of trouble. You know that no one could take the place of a sister, (an own blood sister)—in whom you could confide & call upon for <u>any</u> service. We, as a family, have always been so entirely <u>one</u>, that we <u>could</u> feel no kind of reserve to each other—& how thankful I am too. As to her being <u>restless</u>—<u>that</u> she has been—distressingly so at times—one day tho', when she was somewhat cross, & gloomy & disposed to consider herself a martyr—I burst out crying & told her, "I wish she would go to North Miss—& not have to stay with me at all; but that I was as helpless as my unborn child, & felt entirely dependent upon her—that everybody was sorry for me except herself & was more tender than she!"—I never saw any one so taken aback in my life, she asked my pardon so sweetly, & looked so thoroughly contrite, I felt provoked with myself for giving away to such bitter expressions, for she had not intended to hurt my feelings, & was not aware that her selfish repinings stabbed me to the heart. It "woke her up" tho', & from that day, that hour, that minute she has been the sweetest tenderest, most <u>help-ful</u> sister in the world. It touches me to the heart, & Mr Neilson looks on in wonder, tho' he does not know the <u>cause</u> of the change. She helps me in everything, housekeeping, gardening, & sewing—besides keeping a <u>critical out look</u> upon things which always <u>did</u> & <u>will</u> bore me to "<u>see after</u>"—such, for instance, as keeping Moll up to her <u>washing</u> duties, & <u>putting away</u> things after she is done; as for <u>ironing</u>, it is such a delight for her to render actual assistance every week, I just let her have her own choice—it does'ent matter much if Moll does'ent know much more at the end of the year than she did at the beginning, for I don't think it will be long before she marries, & then I <u>know</u> she will bid farewell to <u>whitefolks</u> forever, for she never has considered herself quite free, nor do I <u>allow</u> her to be too big a woman around me. We laugh a great deal about our <u>boarder</u> doing all sorts of work—but the truth is, I like to speak before "<u>the family</u>" of Cordele's <u>paying board</u>, tho' Mr Neilson will see at the end of the year, that it is not so large as Jim would allow. Now, dear Trot, make yourself <u>quite</u> easy on Cordele's account—she says she would'ent have you come back here at that season, for any consideration—she is perfectly satisfied, & <u>anxious</u> to stay now. I suppose you have received my last letter, in which I forbade your coming in as strong terms as I could, & I repeat now, that you <u>must</u> & <u>shall not</u> think of such a risk. I really would prefer your being away, for I would be so anxious about you. I speak in all honesty & sincerity. No, you stay with dear Bess, & keep her with you just as you are—her schooldays are nearly over, & she will so much need you this summer, as her first season in society. Oh! guard her with all your watchful, tender care—even should I not live thro' the coming trouble, you will have done your <u>best</u> duty to stay with her—she needs you more than I, for there are so <u>many</u> "snares & quicksands" for such a girl as she, & no one could be as jealously guarded as you. Mr Neilson says my decision is just as it should be—he trembles at the idea of Bess being left <u>away out in the world</u> (& in <u>such</u> a world as he knows it to be) without you. I never saw a man so utterly <u>domesticated</u>, in another family as he is in mine—he seems really to take more intense interest in our affairs, because his family are more independent of each other in thought, feeling, and especially <u>acting</u>. Now he feels as much care of Bess as Jim does, & is more impressed by the responsibility, because he is more cautious, more thoughtful than Jim. Now, woman like, I will make a sudden bounce from the <u>high moral</u> obligation, we each owe the other, to prating of <u>fashion & dress</u>. I wish to send Bess my lilac silk for an <u>evening</u> dress for the summer. I think it will look very sweetly as a dress for the Ball-room. I fear it is too soiled for any <u>day</u> wear—but there is two yards left for any change the waist may require, & she could piece under the overskirt if it is not long enough—then that sett of jewelery which I have so long worn, & enjoyed could be put in nice order for her, & sent at the same time—then she is welcome to my <u>lace point</u>, if she wishes a <u>white</u> one for change, for I presume the one you spoke of getting her is black. Mine is not fine, but will look pretty for evening entertainments. Let me know how soon she will wish these things, & I will express them to her—give me particular directions as to the address. I wish I was with you to help plan her summer-out-fit, I know you dread the worry.

I am glad you wrote me so freely of your business-affairs—I like to know all about every thing which concerns you. If you wish more money, perhaps Mr Neilson could dispose of your horse "<u>Stewart</u>," & your cow "<u>Jane</u>." I spoke to

Jim in the Fall about selling the horse, but he would not do it—he is now up here, & working makes him look thin, tho' I am glad Mr Neilson has him, for he is so careful of all stock. Horses are very poor sale in our country, <u>mules</u> are preferred—tho' perhaps in the Fall, a better price could be had—the cow has no calf, nor does she look as if she would soon—we had her driven up here, but of course she <u>won't</u> stay—tho' we hope Press will take good care of her down at home.—

I hav'ent fully realized that poor Jim is sure enough gone—have heard nothing from him yet—was much disappointed in not getting a letter yesterday—I have written to him tho—& hope he will answer soon—I feel anxious to know how he is pleased with his new abode. Don't feel so miserable about <u>his affair</u>—I was sorry to tell you, but thought it best. We hope <u>everything</u> from <u>separation</u>.

Your letter to Cordele was better than any sermon I ever read. My dear Sister, you are surely blessed with the gift of aptly expressing your ideas—& then such comfort you do impart. Mr Neilson was much moved by your religious sentiments, & says you should write oftener—it does us all good. Now would it be too much of a tax upon your time & inclination for you to write to one of us every <u>two</u> weeks—that's the plan Cordele & I have adopted, she writes one week to you, I, the next to Bess, & vice-versa. Now you & Bess could also do that way, without burdening yourselves. I think your letter will be very beneficial to Cordele, & I <u>know</u> it has had a good effect upon me—bless your warm heart!

Do you know I have felt a wee speck hurt, that you have made so few <u>inquiries</u> as to my plans & arrangements. I did not for a moment doubt your interest, but I thought you would feel anxious to know every thing—so in my last letter, I sat down & gave you a full <u>ditty</u>, <u>unsolicited</u>. I know I am spoilt to <u>death</u>—but I can't help it where you are concerned.

"<u>Tot</u>-<u>Nenie</u>" is flourishing!—quite lively indeed!—keeps one constantly reminded of her presence (?). Sends love to "Aunt Tot" & "<u>Aunt</u> Bess" (never do, for so old a lady as Bess, to be only <u>cousin</u>, she is <u>Aunt</u> too)—says tell you both not to hurt yourselves working for her—"<u>Auntie</u>" can make two pretty dresses for her share—not at all expensive, but pretty—plenty of time also, for they will not be needed until the <u>Fall</u>, as the little lady will not be "<u>going out</u>" <u>much</u> until then. "Aunt Bess" must not take time from out-door exercise, to be working all sorts of things—wait until after school, for until then, every spare moment should be spent in helping "<u>Auntie</u>" with her own pretty things, which she will so much need in the summer, when she is a young lady. "Aunt Nenie" is now sewing away for dear life on a gown—she's so kind! (Is all this <u>indelicate</u>, I hope not, it is only for you & Bess).—

Spring is "trembling in the valleys" [1] with us now—the great honest "Dogwood" eyes are glaring thro' the woods in every direction—"I need not so [say] of whom they remind me"—this afternoon we had a real thunder-storm, which betokens a change of seasons—everything is very late. None of the farmers <u>up here</u> are planting cotton yet—tho' I expect Press is nearly done. We hav'ent been down home in sometime, will go as soon as possible. Cordele sends very best love, & says she would have written to Bess, but had no paper. I return Tom Taylor's[2] picture—when it was received, I exclaimed, "<u>why</u> there's <u>Miller</u> again"— "No" said Cordele "it is not Miller." Then said Mr Neilson "It <u>must</u> be <u>Fliller</u>." The boys are exceedingly alike—tho' they are kinsmen, I suppose—both are handsome & brave looking—real "Lord's of Creation."[3] Give my love to all those people, who are so kind & loving to you, my dear old Darling—but they deserve no credit for loving & being kind to <u>you</u>. I repent of what I said in my last, about <u>hating</u> them. I was only <u>worried</u> with them then! Mr Neilson sends oceans of love—he is busy all the time, & is accomplishing his aims gradually—such energy!

Tell Bess I have received <u>no</u> letter from her in answer to either of my <u>two</u> last letters—she said in Cordele's last that she had written—but I fear I have lost it. I hate losing it—& hope it may come yet. Good-bye my dear, good-bye! Kiss each other for me, & always plead for me at the Great Throne.

Your loving
Lute.

Moll & the boys send best <u>howdy</u>.

NOTES

1. Edward Robert Bulwer-Lytton, "Associations," *Clytemnestra, The Earl's Return, The Artist, and Other Poems* (1855), 262.

2. Thomas Tailor (b. ca. 1854), a boarder at Kalorama.

3. Lucy paraphrased "About the lords o' the creation" (Robert Burns, "The Twa Dogs: A Tale" [1786], in Kinsley, ed., *Burns*, 111).

℘ව

Lucy became increasingly frustrated by Moll's attitude toward her work. Emancipation had rendered the post of the all-purpose servant an unenviable one, and African American women often demanded the right to specialize; if they were cooks, for example, they wished to be employed as cooks only. Moll may have been rebelling against her varied roles on the farm, but Lucy could not fathom her displeasure and labeled her indolent.

Lucy to Bess

Wildwood.
April 21st/.72

My darling old Bess,

I have only time to write a few lines before bed-time, while your Uncle John is printing a few words to Jim, (I've finished a four page letter to him), & now turn to have a few words with you, just while I'm waiting on the printer. My dear, old John! O! Bess, I could right now, fly off at a tangent of praise & deep, deep love for him, which would completely tire you—so I won't—Good-night!—

April 26th—Several days have passed since I scribbled the above nonsense—I have had no opportunity of resuming a similar strain since then—but this bright Spring-morning I lay aside every other employment, & indulge in the great pleasure of communing with you. I am aware that model-house-wives would be shocked at the unreasonableness of my indulgence, but I am not one of the "moddles"—nor do I care to be, where every better feeling of one's nature has to be made subservient to the regular rules of house-keeping. I think the house was made for the woman, & not the woman for the house. Tho I would not have you think I have seated myself to write, utterly regardless of all morning duties, for such is not the case—every thing about my little home is in order—Moll thro with the kitchen, & with Cordele's over-sight is busy with pots, & wash-boards, & soap-suds—all by seven o'clock. My dear John, & the boys have long since been to business—& we had company to spend the night—the Methodist-preacher—he too has gone on his early way rejoicing. So you see we are industrious country-folk—such a good healthy place, everybody feels good, & lively, & sprightly in the mornings! Thats what Mr Neilson tells Cordele.

[. . .] I know your new silks must look pretty, & stylish. Write me every little thing concerning yourself, or clothes, or duties, or any thing. But now you must not burden yourself with letter-writing—your time is too fully occupied—I would not try to write to any one, save your family, & only notes then—I know how busy the last days of school are—you hardly have time to breathe. We will excuse you—altho' we will miss your letters sadly—yet we are not unreasonable. Trot must write.

You speak as if you thought your letters were too numerous, & too lengthy to be much appreciated—you were never more mistaken—all as [of] us dearly love them—but we must now wait until after Commencement. How my heart sympathises with you, & how much I think of your approaching entrance upon Life, as a grown young woman. God keep you, my darling, from every sin & folly! My heart is full of prayer for you, & of hope, & of bright expectations. [. . .]

Dick Hudson has at last won his prize—<u>he</u> & <u>Sue</u> Billups were married last week,—have gone on a Northern tour. I feel right glad for Dick, for he was so much in earnest, & fought so bravely for her.

I have strung out my letter very tiresomely—but I love to take my time, & write leisurely. Cordele will go home tomorrow, also to town—I would like to go once more—but don't expect I can. Cordele will get her some dresses, & a nice hat—she dreads the responsibility, of course—I can't help laughing at her.—She is so improved in spirits, & interests herself in everything. How good to have her feeling better.

She & I have made a <u>dozen</u> garments—but will have to leave off next week, & work on other things. I hope to get most of my sewing done before warm weather—for I know I will be <u>no</u> earthly account. Oh! for a <u>good</u> servant—but Moll is not much help—she is tired of both house & field work. I would not be surprised if I sent her back home—if Press will take her—I don't know what I shall do—but don't think I can stand her.

—Excuse <u>house-keeping ditty</u>!—Good-bye. Our best love to you both. Cordele wrote last week, & will write again next. Heaven help you, & send you safely home. Your loving T'Ida.

ℐᏁ

Lucy pondered her own mortality as she sewed baby clothes instead of the wedding garb she had prepared a year earlier. The time, she noted, lent itself to a renewal of faith and preparation for any emergency. Moments of contemplation and spiritual submission were slotted in around domestic duties and preparations for Bess's coming out.

Lucy to Lizzie

Wildwood—
May 9th/.72.

My darling Trotwood—

Two of your charming letters, & a <u>note</u>, now lie before me, & most gladly do I seat myself to reply—altho' I much fear drowsy slumber will overcome me, before I'm half thro' with what I would like to write—for when I start a letter to you or Bess—it seems that I can <u>never</u> get thro'. I have postponed answering your letter of April 13th so long that, it will appear rather out of date now—but do let me <u>thank</u> you any how, for it is so delightful I read it every now, & then!—no one can excel you in doing the graceful, polite & <u>pleasing</u>; to say nothing of the <u>heart</u>

which always glows thro' everything you do, say, or write—thats the charm you feel yourself, & impress others in proportion.

The dear old 13th!—How glad will I feel all my life long, that things <u>went</u> on just as they did on that eventful day. What a new life I entered upon, & how every one (both white & black) gave me "<u>God speed</u>" in word & deed! Your letter was a <u>reflex</u> of the day, I shall treasure it peculiarly. Trot I wish I could make you fully understand how thoroughly happy & <u>heart-content</u> I am with my <u>husband</u>! He certainly is that "all to me for which my soul did pine"[1]—& I feel with—

> "Each throb of my heart
> A <u>wish</u> to bless—
> With my life's <u>best worth</u>
> The heart & the hearth
> Of John, my John"![2]

I always had a horror of marrying a man possessed of <u>littleness</u>—It seemed nothing so disgusted me, nothing so made my heart sick, as the idea of being united for life with a man <u>capable</u> of <u>littleness</u>— Well! how God has protected me in this peculiarity—my husband is so noble, so large, so expanded—so far above anything verging on littleness—that I, <u>like you</u>, a worshipper of <u>man</u>-hood, as represented in <u>him</u>.—Oh! Trot for a good, long talk.

Your last letter has touched me particularly. Your reference to my frequent allusions to death, does move my heart to its profoundest depths, for I know if I should be called hence, a life long shadow would fall across your path, which no earthly brightness could illumine—but then to hear of the <u>sweet submission</u>, & the <u>entire giving-up</u> into our Father's hands, of all things, makes me feel so happy! There is a spirituality about your expressions recently, which I never before felt—you surely walk very near the throne! "<u>Teach</u> me half the happiness, that thy heart doth know"!—[3]

But Trot, I can't feel now while I am in <u>perfect</u> health, with everything around me to make life dear & desirable, a willingness to <u>die</u>! I can't realize how much greater happiness awaits God's chosen beyond the dark gulf! Perhaps if I was in great peril, all these earthly ties, would be snapped asunder, & their utter insignificance would impress me, when brought in contrast with the awful presence of my Creator—perhaps too a feeling of <u>utter dependence</u> will come the little prayer "<u>Lord help</u>" be my <u>only</u> thought & wish! I try to prepare my mind & especially my <u>heart</u> for any emergency. Your good talks in <u>all</u> your recent letters has strengthened me, & while my hands are busy with household-duties, or sewing on the <u>wee wee</u> garments, my mind, & heart are pondering all you have said. You have been so good about writing too. Don't burden yourself with the thought of <u>duty</u>-letters—but oh! write often. I know how busy you are now, & will be until after Commencement—but write <u>short</u> letters any how—Bess misunderstood me, I did not mean she did not write every week—but merely suggested that until after Commencement, she should write every other week—this was in consideration of her poor burdened heart & mind for the present!—

Now about the dress which I propose sending Bess—do pray, you speak as hesitatingly about taking it, as if it was some valuable estate! My only fear is that it is not nice enough for her—but if she can have it turned, & altered, perhaps it will make her a pretty evening dress for a change (—she should have as many as possible)—then next winter she can have it died some bright color (crimson or corn) for an underskirt! If you think it best to have it died right now, before altering it—all right! The dress is hers—as to her feeling any hesitency in accepting it—I am not afraid but I will get value received in the numerous presents from her to "me & mine"[4]—now does this make either of you feel better! Don't be so powerful particular with me. I & my family are as they always were to each other. I don't know when we will send the box—but just as soon as possible, & with all the articles desired carefully looked up, & sent enclosed.

I received Bess' long letter of April 29th—will answer next time. Bless her life! We think of her nearly every hour in the day, & pray for her too! She seems so fully to appreciate your exertions in her behalf—I love her for that! I hope so much rush, & stir, & mental excitement will not make her sick—make her stop all unnecessary correspondence, & reading until after Commencement—let her rest mentally, & physically all she can! I am very proud of her having so much to do at the Concert. How I wish I could be there to see & hear her! God grant her success—but not for vain glory!

—Cordele & I have been very busy this week with her Spring-wardrobe. We have nearly completed three Polanaise for her—, & they all look beautiful to my backwood's eye! I would so like to hear what Mrs Eagar, or Miss Ellen think of them. One is a Calico—the second a striped black & white Grenadine—the third a Bishop's lawn. She will wear the two last with a plain black Grenadine—the two suits are very stylish, & becoming. Mrs Jackson[5] cut, & fitted a Polanaise-pattern for her, which is a perfect success, & has given me no trouble at all. Her hat is elegant & stylish without being especially becoming—but then I'm behind the times. It seems so strange for me not to be making pretty things for myself. Ah! well!—

We've had company recently—Dr Furniss has been up, & as he & Mr Neilson are like brothers—I tried how nice a dinner I could have when he, Mr Symons, Sister Anne, Lizzie, & Minnie[6] came last Sunday to dine with us. You know we are our own cooks now—on Saturday Cordele & I made some transparent-custards, a nice, rich black-berry roll, & some tea cakes—also had a nice fat Guinea killed, which my cook Parthene picked, & I dressed, & parboiled ready for stuffing, & baking next day. Then next morning we were up with the lark, & had breakfast, & the house put in perfect order in a little time—then Cordele set the table in her room, <u>beautifully</u>, with everything in readiness, while I went to the kitchen, & got everything ready for the stove. Then Sister Mary, Brother James, & Kate came by, & stopped for a visit on the way to church—After awhile the others came—there was great <u>howdying</u>, & kissing, & talking until church time, when all went except Sister Anne Minnie & <u>I</u>—of this I was glad, for I was bound to go to the kitchen to see after every thing! <u>George</u> is a <u>first rate</u> cook, & he did stand by me manfully, & Parthene did all in her power, so I got along without the slightest trouble, & every thing was done, & in readiness—& I had time to bathe my face, & cool off before they came back from church—then I went to the kitchen, & served up the dinner, while Cordele staid in the drawing-room, & received it—there was broiled ham, lettuce, peas, Irish potatoes, baked rice, dried peaches, pig-hash, baked fowl—, & the nicest biscuit (baked just to a beautiful brown) for the first course, & the desert above mentioned with wine & wine-sauce! They all seemed to enjoy my dinner very much & Mr Symons would'ent believe, when they told I cooked it myself! I can <u>roast</u> a <u>pig</u> too! We have had two recently, & I was successful both times. I am right proud of learning how to cook.—

All are ready for bed & I must stop. Good-bye—do go to General Assembly, & enjoy it. All send love, & say write. God bless you both.

Lute

<...> Yes Cordele received Mrs Taylor's picture—we think her <u>splendid</u>. I enclose a letter from "Hogan"[7]—which I took the liberty of reading—

NOTES

1. Edgar Allan Poe, "To One in Paradise" (1834), in Quinn, ed., *Edgar Allan Poe*, vol. 1, 49.

2. Mrs. Gideon Townsend, "John," in Tardy, ed., *Southland Writers*, 386–87.

3. Lucy paraphrased "In times of happiness or woe, / When joy or ill the heart doth know" (Rev. D. C. Eddy, "A Time for All Things," in Ferguson and Percival, eds., *The Oasis*, 229–30).

4. Alfred Tennyson, *In Memoriam A.H.H.* (1850), in Ricks, ed., *Tennyson*, 463.

5. Dressmaker M. Jackson (b. ca. 1834).

6. Mary Symons (1861–1937), daughter of John Mauger Symons and Anne Frazier Neilson Symons.

7. John T. Hogan, Elizabeth Parthenia Irion's stepfather. Harriette Hayden Irion Hogan had married John in 1864.

The uneasy arrangements between Lucy and Moll finally came to a head. Lucy dismissed Moll and hired Cordele's former nurse, Parthene, as her replacement. The events bolstered Lucy, who claimed white, house-proud competence and compared it with what she described as Moll's sloppy domestic ineptitude.

Like many women of her generation, Lucy was willing to undertake some of the housework herself, while hiring out the more onerous duties to freed women. Growing domestic confidence, Lucy realized, was an admirable skill to nurture, but she also wanted the freedom to devote her time to the household tasks that would enhance her status and not commit her to endless days of drudgery.

Parthene's employment at Wildwood also provided Cordele with a more central role in household affairs. Abandoning her position as a helpmate to her sister, Cordele was now imbued with a new sense of purpose.

Lucy to Bess

Wildwood.

May 20th/.72

Dear old Bess! your <u>three</u> letters of dates April 29th—May 8th; & 15th are before me, & I <u>will begin</u> to answer tonight, tho' when <u>ended</u> I'll say not. But my heart is so full towards you, my thoughts so constantly with you, that I turn from every "cumbering care," & "steal awhile"[1] to tell you how much you are to me. How is it possible tho, to put in words the <u>deepest</u> emotions of one's heart? Your letters do so breathe of love & truth & gratitude I feel as if I'd had <u>spiritual</u> communion with you whenever they are read! I do thank you for them, & their frequent coming only makes me more anxious for others. I am <u>awful</u> to my other correspondents—there are some letters lying in my port-folio <u>unanswered</u> since <u>January</u>, & <u>Madie's</u> even still looks up at me reprovingly—but I can't help it—I am a busy little woman these days—there is house-keeping, & sewing, & company to be entertained, & oh! when I have an opportunity for writing, my pen instinctively goes scribling to you, or Trot, or Jim—my three loved & absent ones. I am <u>busy</u> but I am so happy in my home!—& right here, I know you will excuse a little <u>domestic-ditty</u> for I wish you & Trot to understand exactly how I am situated, & <u>feel</u>, as regards a cook. I do not wish you to feel that I am <u>burdened</u> with household cares, at this <u>particular time</u>, for I know it would annoy you both.—

I stood Moll just as long as I could—I had made up my mind to all sorts of "<u>slap-dash</u>" work, & <u>untidiness</u>, & <u>indolence</u>, but when she "capped the climax" with <u>impudence</u>, I very quietly told Mr Neilson we would send her home. She vented her spleen to <u>Cordele</u>—I heard not a word—I never saw "Miss" so aroused in my life—she came in the house as white as a sheet. I said not a word to Moll—next morning tho' Mr Neilson told her to pack up bag & baggage, & get ready to go home—she was very much surprised, & seemed loth to go—cried when she bade me good-bye!—The only reason I hesitated about sending her away was because I knew after awhile all the house-hold duties would fall upon Cordele—<u>now</u> I am perfectly able, & really think the exercise beneficial—when I consulted with Cordele, & told her <u>why</u> I hated to dismiss Moll, she <u>begged</u> me not to keep her a moment on her account for she had all along dreaded the summer with such a servant to worry over. Martha is such a pleasant negro these days—she talks & does exactly right about these children—Cordele went down, & told her all about Moll's behavior, & asked if she would not send Parthene to help me, she very willingly assented, & now our little maid is always at hand to do any thing we wish—I had to overlook everything, that Moll did anyhow, & oh! you can't conceive of what an annoyance she was! It is so strange to me how so much good training as <u>Trot</u> gave that negro should be so utterly lost. I was not cross to her—All say I am less irritable than any woman, they ever saw, in my condition. My health is so good I have no excuse, & I make every effort to behave as well as I can <u>now</u>, for you know "pretty is, as pretty <u>does</u>"—that's my only hope of being called <u>pretty</u> these days—I don't believe one word Charles Lamb says about that proverb being a fallacy![2]

Well! I must say "<u>good-night</u>"—Mr Neilson is almost nodding over the <u>bible</u>, waiting to have prayers—Several days have passed since writing the above, but before leaving the interesting (?) subject under discussion I have a few more remarks to make, & then to more <u>pleasing</u> things.—

You have no idea the change in my feelings since this time last year as regards <u>servants</u>—<u>then</u> I felt as helpless & dependent as a babe, <u>now</u> I am <u>independent</u>, provided my health does not fail—I know the long hot summer is before me, & that I will not be able to attend to duties as I now am—but then Woos has promised to come & stay awhile, & if she disappoints me, I <u>can</u> get <u>others</u>—of course I prefer Woos to anyone—there are two very good cooks living on this place, & I am sure of either one or other when needed. I can always get help whenever I wish, for rough work such as Parthene cannot do. Our washing is done out by one of the Neilson family servants—a <u>very</u> reliable woman, who comes for, & brings it back—furnishes soap, & charges only $3.00 per month—we consider ourselves fortunate in securing her services. Trot must not think hard of the people down at Willow Farm—for we have asked none of them to come—& would not be willing to pay them such wages as they have been accustomed to receive, if they did come—so thats the way matters stand with us. I know from experience, how you both feel—we have accustomed ourselves to a houseful & yardful of servants, of all sizes ages, & descriptions—but it was folly as Trot said then, & now I know what a <u>heavy</u> burden we bore financially, & all because we did not make up our minds <u>to do</u> ourselves—but then we always had so much awful sickness—did'ent we?

The <u>only</u> source of trouble I had <u>was Moll</u>, & now she is gone, we get along as smoothly as any family you ever saw—Mr Neilson & <u>Ed</u> are our <u>milk</u>-<u>maids</u>—it was very awkward at first for Mr Neilson to <u>milk</u>—but he is so evenly balanced a character, whatever he esteems his duty, he goes at, & soon becomes interested in. Cordele never was <u>happier</u>—she has her beloved Parthene by her side from morning till night, & even at night for the child sleeps in the room with her. Such times they two have over <u>washing</u> the chaps clothes, & hunting nice good <u>stove wood</u>, & hen's nests—I look on in great amusement. Parthene is very handy in the kitchen, & I think will be a good cook when grown—I have already drilled her in <u>my ways</u>, & she is obedient, & I have very little to do. But Bess I do wish you could see what nice <u>light biscuit</u> I can make. I am as proud as a pea-cock. I am astonished at myself taking <u>such real</u> delight in things, which used to seem so <u>hard</u> & such <u>repulsive drudgery</u>! Don't I sympathize with Lizzie Symons, she feels just as I did!—but I hope she may <u>make</u> herself more accomplished in kitchen lore than I was, for it is so good, to feel that you can set your husband down to a well prepared meal—matters not, if it is <u>plain</u>—I'll teach <u>you</u> all I know—but I have learned very little in the <u>cake</u>, & custard-line—when you come, we will experiment together. Oh! how many plans have I not made in connection with you my dear, dear girl!

I try to reason with myself, & prepare for your being a young lady in society, & that my home is so remote, there will be very little to attract a <u>gay</u> member—& then it would be wrong for you to <u>exclude</u> yourself from society—there you will properly belong—but oh! I feel inspite of all, that you are mine—<u>neice</u>, <u>child</u>, <u>sister</u>, <u>friend</u>!

Only a few more weeks, & then your school-days are forever ended—unless <u>you</u> prefer they should not be!—what say you?—Ah! Our hearts are with you in the coming Commencement exercises—would that our <u>bodies</u> could be also! I am proud to think you are put forward in the Concert—it is a distinguished compliment to be considered competent in so large a Seminary as that. I don't think you feel at all puffed up, & oh! that you may keep humble, & very near the <u>Throne</u>!—I wish particularly that <u>Jim</u> could go on. I know what a dear delight it would be to his loving heart, to see his "<u>Darling</u>" come off with credit.

You astonish me by mentioning numerous books, which you have read—how could you possibly find time? I like for you to tell me all these items—I am glad you have a taste for literature, & <u>you</u> have a good person to direct your course, for I consider Trot's taste very pure.

I think now, we can get the things, & send the <u>box on Saturday 25th</u>—but don't be disappointed if it does not come at the right time for we may not succeed in our intentions. I received your letter containing the <u>directions</u>, & am very much obliged—I do not think it <u>awful</u> in you at all—it was good & thoughtful, &

I do appreciate it. I have been using the preparation of alum, & <u>borax</u>, & whiskey for some weeks, <u>Sisters Annie</u>, & Mary <u>put me</u> on it, or rather <u>it on me</u>! As for <u>exercise</u>, & <u>two visits per diem</u> to a <u>necessary</u> friend, I think I may. I am a <u>moddle</u> of promptness. There never was a <u>healthier</u> woman, & oh! how thankful my dear husband is, & how tenderly he watches over me, & how anxiously he looks forward to the, <u>final</u>.—Cordele is so good, &, so <u>true</u>—in not a <u>single thing</u> does she <u>fail</u>! She had such a splendid time in town—how she glories in the precious remembrance. Everybody was so sweet, & good & loving, & so attentive too. It made me love my friends more than ever! We have made several attempts to have Mrs Eagar with us—but have failed. I hope she may come next week.—

Your wish as regards Lizzie Symons joining the church, is fulfilled—she came forward at our last Communion, & oh! how my heart <u>rejoiced</u>! She & Willie Odeneal have been so deeply concerned for more than a year—how good the Lord is!—

I hope you have not been too much of a "horphan" since Trot left—I know you a[re] petted to death by those good people in the house & Seminary—I don't blame them either, for you have such good, honest, warm-hearted ways, which will always win friends. Dear Miss Baldwin—how glad I am, that Providence guided your wandering, & undecided steps to Staunton—for to know <u>her</u> is worth all the glitter, & show of every school in the North. She certainly is a most remarkable woman—& deserves the success which attends her every undertaking, from the management of her school, to the charming, & delightful Pic-Nic at the Springs!—How instructive & <u>expanding</u> to the mind are all such advantages, which you as a school enjoy—the grandest, & noblest of both physical, & moral nature!—I shall look forward to a good letter from Trot, telling of her visit to Richmond, & all she saw, & heard! Can't we all <u>talk forever</u>, when we next meet? Cordele received a letter from Jim. <. . .>

You ask of Dr L—'s state of mind & heart towards his lady-love—well! poor man, I am sorry for him, for he is utterly blinded, & morbid on the subject—I fear I haven't enough patience with that sort of feeling—for we, as a family, are <u>free</u> from morbidness if nothing else.—

I am glad you sent the <u>chaps</u> such <u>thrilling</u> messages—they of course have much to say in return, Parthene especially.

Mr Neilson, & Cordele both unite to warmest love, & wishes for your health, & success! Cordele wrote you a long letter—<u>make</u> Trot write—I know <u>you</u> will, if you have a moment of time. God bless you!—T'Ida.

NOTES

1. Lucy paraphrased "I love to steal awhile away / From every cumbering care" (Phoebe Hinsdale Brown, "Private Devotion" [1818], in Lounsbury, ed., *American Verse*, item 4).

2. Charles Lamb, "Popular Fallacies—Handsome Is That Handsome Does," *The Last Essays of Elia* (1833), in Bate, ed., *Elia*, 294–96.

ℬ

At the end of an uncomfortable June day, a heavily pregnant Lucy wrote to Lizzie and Bess demanding the latest news on commencement proceedings.

Lucy to Lizzie and Bess

Wildwood—June 21st/.72

My dear Trot, & Bess,

It seems such an age since I heard from either of you, I must have a little chat this evening altho' I've nothing of interest to say, & the weather is so warm I can scarcely leave off fanning to use the pen.

My dear old Trot, you've been off on a trip of which I am waiting to hear a detailed account—& Bess, you will surely send me a volume, for what have you not to tell now since becoming "<u>Miss Irion</u>" sure enough. I will not congratulate you tho' until your letter comes, then I can do so formally. I received your note announcing the safe arrival of the box. I hope you had time to have the dress altered, so as to be of use. You were not explicit enough in announcing the <u>exact time</u> of Commencement, & it was upon us before we were aware. I did'ent dream of its being until the last of June. I hope so much excitement, & exercise has made neither of you sick. You Bess said in your last that Trot was not quite well, I have thought often of her, & wondered if she could stand so much fatigue without being real sick. There must be letters awaiting us in town from each of you, Mr Neilson will go tomorrow, & then I'll be satisfied—tho' I must write this stupid little letter, & let it go along to keep you from being anxious about me. My health continues most excellent, & spirits most bouyant. My sewing is nearly all done—the little wardrobe is not expensive—but plenty good for one of the "<u>boys</u>." Cordele is broiding a flannel skirt, & Lizzie Symons has one to embroider. Kate Barry is over-casting a Piquet-wrapper with <u>Turkey</u>-<u>red</u>, & I have another to border with a gay little stripe of the same material. As I finish each little garment, & fold it up, I think of you both. I know Trot would not be half satisfied with quality or quantity, or <u>making</u>—but then she must not be so ambitious until we see, what is the result. In your last letter Bess you expressed surprise that I should feel well enough to write—la! if you could see how active I am, you would cease to wonder. I have left off none of my duties as yet, & do every thing I ever did—except draw water at the well, & lift out our dining-table—but I went blackberrying one afternoon last week, & climbed a ten rail fence <u>twice</u>. It is no use in a strong healthy woman giving up so soon. I am just as careful as I can be, for I would'ent hurt myself or prospects for the world—but then, when I feel every bit as well as I ever did, I can't play invalid. Dr Matthews told Mr Neilson to tell me I was doing exactly right. I had a letter from Sister Sallie telling of being with Trot, I almost cried of envy—& there poor Trot crying over me in La Fayette Square [Washington D.C.] just as if she were at home—bless her heart! I feel that I must see you both now that school is out. What are your plans, tell me everything! Ah! Bess I can imagine how you luxuriate in your freedom—don't you sympathize with your color'd friends more than ever?

Jim's visit did us a world of good. He was the best old fellow in the world, & was so highly amiable he did not even show ennui of the country! I can't say what he felt, but he was polite enough to conceal any such feeling. I don't think he can stand being separated from you all much longer, I declare it is wonderful that man's love of home & home-surroundings. He wants "Brooks so bad he is most froze"—he said a dozen times—then once he said "Now our next trouble in the family is Brooks marrying"!—I burst out laughing—"most families regard matrimony as a blessing, but not so with our's—they talk as if it was death & destruction" said I— <...>

[Pheobe's visit coincided] just at the time of Jim's—all happened by chance too. She was so good, & careful of me, & just took entire charge of the kitchen, & cooked so good & homelike—Jim enjoyed everything, & would say "Well! don't Pheobe beat the world on fried chicken"—then of course we had that old joke about "cooking the best fried chicken of any nigger ever we tasted"—Trot would have disapproved—don't blame her either—it is time for us to be more dignified.

We are in a high state of torn-up-ed-ness—as we are having our house painted. Croli Whitfield[1] is doing it, & we are very much pleased—tho' it has taken him an age—this is now the fifth week, since he began—he has lost two weeks from sickness of self, & family. I feel right impatient at the delay, for who knows what might happen any day or night—& the bigger [the mess] the surer to come!

I am positively ashamed of my egotism. My darling ones please excuse— but this may be my last chance for sometime, & I improve the opportunity—but every one of my letters are so long, & all about self, and surroundings!—

I received such a sweet letter from Corrie Myers—she begun by announcing, that she was sitting by the crib of her little daughter![2] There Bess, I know you are glad to hear of a girl-baby in the family anyhow. She seemed to have gotten along remarkably well, & had come from her new home to her Ma's when the baby was not quite three weeks old! Cousin Mary was with her, & Cousin Lizzie called out for Cous Sue,[3] & that compelled Cous Mary to return to Aunt Mattie—& Corrie said it was either to stay by herself, or run the risk of going home, & she ran the risk, & it did not hurt her at all! She sent me a lock of her baby's hair— black as mid-night, & as soft as silk—she did not tell it's name tho'—Cous Lizzie has another <u>boy</u>! Three for her—good luck. Jim told me that <u>Sue Golding Ger-dine</u>[4] was in the <u>fashionable</u>-way too! Mrs Weaver told <u>him</u>!—

Good-bye, my dears—write soon. Mr Neilson would send his love if he were <u>near</u> enough, but he is out at work. May Heaven protect us all. Your loving

Lute.

Be sure to give any <u>change</u> of <u>address</u>!

NOTES

1. Croly Whitfield (b. ca. 1810), farmer.
2. Lucy Myers (1872–1927), daughter of Calvin Myers and Laura Corrie Nesbitt Myers.
3. Elizabeth Nesbitt Eddins (1835–1908), wife of De Soto County farmer Oliver Frank-lin Eddins (1834–1903). The couple married in 1865 and by 1872 had three boys: Thomas Eddins (ca. 1868–ca. 1940); Benjamin Eddins (1871–1950); and William Demsey Eddins (1872–1939). Susan Nesbitt Berry (b. ca. 1835) also lived in De Soto County.
4. Susan Golding Gerdine gave birth to Thomas Golding Gerdine (b. 1872).

ℱꝺ

News of Bess's success at commencement proceedings thrilled the inhabitants of Wildwood and prompted John Neilson, an infrequent correspondent, to pen a note of congratulations. "You have come up to the full measure of my expectation," he wrote Bess on June 23, 1872, "which causes me a double joy—one for myself & Lute, and the other for the sake of Sis Lizzie who has no doubt been made to feel amply repaid for the care and anxiety she has bestowed upon you. Now isn't this the sweet-est feeling in the world!?" The time and resources invested in Bess had produced dividends: academic achievement at a top Virginia school reaffirmed family honor and gentility and provided Bess with the necessary qualifications to compete in the heady social season that lay before her. Lucy expressed her pride in a postscript to John's letter.

Lucy to Bess

[Wildwood, June 23, 1872]

My Darling Bess—

How can I tell what I feel or what is in my heart! If you could have seen me this morning while reading your letter, you would have thought some dreadful <u>calamite</u> had befallen you, so freely did my tears flow—but oh! thank God you were not the cause of sorrowful tears, but <u>thankful</u> ones, & I was happy that they flowed. My dear dear child, how vividly you drew the picture of the scene; we were there actually in feeling, & saw & heard all. My excitement was extreme, & as you carried us on, on, I sobbed aloud, I could'ent help it! The audience assembling, the lights, the music, the grand opening Chorus, the performance of the difficult instrumental piece, the feelings which arose in your mind, & heart as the time neared for your trial, all were so well described, & so fitly expressed, we were made to feel as you felt, & hear & see as you did! Then could'ent I see you as you approached the Piano, following your teacher?—could'ent I sympathise with your every emotion—then oh! you begin on, on, on, till you are thro', & in the little Music-room crying on Miss Daniels' shoulder! I too am crying, & if I had been in Trot's place, should have disgraced myself! Then the medal was conferred upon you so unexpectedly—how glad, how thankful, how proud I am! Then Trot says you behaved so modestly thro' it all—oh! that was like an humble christian girl, should have done! I do congratulate you, I do with all an overflowing heart!—You say so truly that it will ever be a time of sweet remembrance, & so it will, for it will bring to mind, duty nobly performed & rewarded!

I read your letter aloud to Mr Neilson, & Bro James, & Cordele, I tell you, there was not a "dry eye in the house," all were so effected, & did'ent care if they showed their feelings!—I have just written you & Trot a long letter, & must not write any more at present, tho' the temptation is strong. Cordele will write this time too—we are a happy thankful family this night! Thank God! We hope, we rejoice in the right way! Cordele will write regularly, if I cannot—but I think you both are a little too hasty as to my sickness, I do not anticipate any thing of the kind for a month or six weeks yet. I will write again very soon. I expect Mesdame Ottley & Benoit to spend tomorrow with me.

Good-bye my poor tired child, do rest yourself well. In love, & pride your own T'Ida.

As she set her house in order, Lucy felt bewildered by Lizzie's decision to embark on a northern tour. Unsettled and alone, she penned a letter to Bess to convince herself that all would be right in the coming weeks.

Lucy to Bess

Wildwood—
July 10th/.72

My dear old Bess—

I sit me down to write you a few (?) lines—now you need'ent to laugh for I'm determined this shall not be one of my "linked trifles long drawn out"[1]—for once, I am going to write you a short letter. Cordele received your letter written just before your visit to Lexington [Virginia]—& since then we've heard nothing; we hope for a letter tomorrow, but shall not set our hearts too much upon its' coming, for we know you have been off a frolicing, & we ought not to be selfish enough to desire so much of your time. I feel so dependent on you tho' as a regular correspondent, for poor Trot so belongs to the public, we have learned to wait the pleasure of her master to allow her a little time for us, private individuals.

I am glad she had an opportunity of going on her Northern tour—but I must confess to a sinking of the heart, when I thought of the increased distance, which separated me from her, just at this particular juncture of affairs—Virginia seems comparatively near, & I wish to hear she is back again. Of course she will write us of some of the wonders, she has seen—but oh! the nice talks, when the blessed time of reunion comes! I wonder many many times, if I will be here to welcome you!—I can't feel otherwise, than that all will be right, & I'll have a little-wee-bit-of a stranger to welcome you too! La! Bess, it seems strange to me even yet, that I have prospects of a child of my own—altho' for so many months past, I have been talking, thinking, writing, & working for it, & almost it alone—yet I'm slow to feel the great "Mother-love," which must be so tender, & which others feel long before the child is born. Such a poor heart-broken letter I had from Madie Childress, the other day—She feels the loss of her baby very acutely—I am so sorry for her!—[2]

I am very well yet—beginning to feel fatigue very sensibly tho', if I take a little too much exercise. My work is done, & now I'll set my house in order—& hope to get everything settled comfortably, so that things may go smoothly for Cordele & Woos.

My darling old husband is having a part of the back gallery enclosed & extended for a dining-room! Now don't you know he is the best man in this world to his poor unworthy wife? I fear I love him too, too dearly!—Our house is all nicely painted, & we feel very clean, & sweet!—

I wish Cordele to go on a little visit to Sister Annie, & then she will retire to the gayety of home-life for awhile. The weather has been very warm with us for the last two weeks—we have a very clever woman in the kitchen now—she lives on the place, & comes from home every morning. Pheobe will come back to me again soon—so don't be anxious on my account. I am well taken care of, you may be sure.—

Dear Sister Annie, & Lizzie came over to see us this afternoon—so bright, so cheerful—their little visit did me good. Liz looked so pretty, & stylish. She will not go North this summer either—I think you took a very sensible view of a tour, & hope nothing may prevent you & Liz going together next Summer. Would'ent that be so very nice?—Or have you other company engaged?

I shan't ask you to excuse the egotism of this letter—but hope you'll send me one in return just as full of <u>yourself</u>! How does young-lady-hood feel? I am so proud of your success at the Commencement. I have to check myself about talking too much on the pleasing subject. You wrote so modestly to Mrs Eager of it too!—She showed me the letter. She has been staying this two week with Sister Mary. Has only given me one day & night—<u>so sweet tho</u>'!

Uncle John & Cordele join in love to you both. God bless you!—T'Ida.

NOTES

1. Lucy paraphrased "Of linked sweetness long drawn out" (John Milton, *L'Allegro,* in Orgel and Goldberg, eds., *John Milton,* 25).

2. Mary Adair Lyon Childress gave birth to a stillborn baby girl.

ℬ

A letter from Lizzie offering to return home reassured Lucy of her sister's love and support. Suspecting that she would give birth in a matter of days, Lucy informed Lizzie that the spiritual and practical preparations she had made over the last several months were now complete.

Lucy to Lizzie

Wildwood.

July 15th/.72—

My precious Trotwood—

Your letter announcing your arrival at Staunton was most joyfully received, & now I have only time to write a short note in return for Mr Neilson is on the eve of departure for town, & I don't wish an opportunity to escape. What makes you tantalize me so by begging to come to me, when you must know how <u>dreadful hard</u> it is for me to say "<u>No</u>." But I have said "No," & I must continue saying it— for I would not feel right to allow you to risk so much. We must just place it all in the hands of Our Father, & <u>He</u> will take all care! What a sweet promise & invitation we have thro' Peter, to cast all our care upon <u>Him</u>, for <u>He careth for us</u>![1] Even if things should go <u>ill</u> with me—it will be our misfortune to be separated; but not our fault. I feel hopeful—I can't do otherwise when my health is so good—If I have a <u>long</u> illness then I know you must come—but think of Mary Lyon lying in almost a dying condition for three days & three nights—her babe taken at last with instruments—& then to be up & at the table in <u>ten</u> days. Of course I look forward with dread—but I pray to be mercifully sustained either living or dying. Don't feel <u>too</u> anxious on my account. We will write by every opportunity, & you <u>must</u> write oftener—I can't help feeling a little <u>forsaken</u>, when you write so seldom, & are so far off. Even tho' <u>all</u> the world should write, I yet pine for your letters.—

I know you must have had a delightful visit North—but Cordele & I both felt a little <u>scared</u> for you to be such a distance—we would wish you back in Virginia, as tho' that was <u>no</u> distance. I told Cordele I knew you were thinking of me & would have <u>great scared feelings</u> come over you, matters not <u>where</u> you were, or by <u>whom</u>, or <u>what</u> surrounded! I knew you would oftentimes feel like sleeping in your <u>wrapper</u> for fear of something happening! Ha! ha!

I wrote to Bess last week. I hope she enjoyed her visit to Lexington. I know she will write as soon as practicable. You would love <u>all</u> these dear friends & relatives who are so kind, & tender of me—Sisters Anne & Mary seem to feel <u>all</u> the responsibility, & pet me most delightfully. I have a nice little dining-room now—my <u>darling husband</u> has everything he can done for my comfort & pleasure! I hope to set my house in perfect order—so poor Cordele will have as little trouble as possible—she is so dear to me—but <u>oh</u>! how she dreads the next weeks—she is going down home this morning to make some <u>final</u> arrangements, & I hope will bring Pheobe, or Woos, or some of our old set home with her—we must have some one all the time now—Mrs Eagar <u>won't</u> stay any with us, because we have no regular cook—she has left Sister Mary's now for town—she is <u>all</u> concern for me! There never was a woman so sweetly cared for—<u>thank God</u>! Cordele will write next week, or the last of this! Don't be uneasy if our letters are not prompt, for if any thing happens that is <u>not good</u>, you will hear soon enough.

I enclose a card for <u>Bess</u>—it is pleasant to be remembered!

We hear from Jim often—do write to him—he complains of you—He is so <u>solicitous</u> for me—it makes me <u>cry</u>!—

Mr Neilson sends best love! Oh! may the good Lord keep us all safely. Your own loving child—Lute.

NOTE

1. 1 Pet. 5:7.

℘ঌ

Lucy gave birth at Wildwood, drawing upon the skills and support of her sisters-in-law, two freed women attendants, and a male doctor. On July 24, 1872, Lucy and John became the proud parents of Louisa Gray Neilson (1872–1966).

Lucy to Lizzie and Bess

Wildwood—
July 26th/.72—

My dear darling Trot & Bess—

Here I lie flat on my back, but so bright & happy & thankful a <u>Mother</u> as ever was blest with a little daughter—Oh, it makes such a new strange thrill of pleasure come into my heart as I look upon the little helpless darling lying by my side—It makes me <u>cry</u> too, with over-much feeling when I wonder what you two would say of her! I will not dwell upon the time of sorrow—when joy came so sweetly in the morning!—but oh, if you could see what a nice plump little thing she is, & how expressly like her proud "<u>Papa</u>," you would not wonder that my heart was so open to receive her. Her <u>hands</u> even are so exactly like his, that he can't help laughing at them himself—head covered with brown hair like his—& mouth, & eyes like his also—<u>ears</u> I am glad to say are <u>small</u>. She is beautifully formed, & so strong—so vigorous! Of course Mr Neilson & I were disappointed in her sex—but we vowed to the Lord to be satisfied, if it came all right, & so we try to be. She weighed <u>eight pounds</u>, I never thought to have such a nice fine looking child—I thought t'would be little, & poor & <u>weason</u>-looking.

I wrote to Bess Monday-evening when the <u>premonitory</u> pangs were upon me—I was not sure, but I shrewdly suspected that my time had come, & so it had—from Monday-noon until Wednesday-morning <u>5/4 o'clock</u> I was sick—but not until after supper Tuesday-night did things get serious & from 12 o'clock until <u>five</u> it was <u>terrific</u>! Dr Matthews was so tender, so kind & oh! Sisters <u>Anne</u> & <u>Mary</u> did stand up to me as <u>heroines</u>. I shall never forget their great love, their great help—also Aunt <u>Hetty</u> & <u>Jane</u> (two <u>coloreds</u>)—Aunt Pheobe did not <u>dare</u> come nigh—scared to death! Poor Cordele staid in the next room, & cried the <u>live</u>-<u>long</u> night—she did very well tho', & did not take to the woods as she threatened beforehand. Now she is so devoted to "Tot-Neanie"—we can't make her let her lie on the bed a moment—of course she will be spoilt to death! The <u>nourishment</u> has not come yet—am expecting it today—will be so glad, for she is like both "<u>Pa</u> & <u>Ma</u>" very healthy, & very hungry! Sister Anne is still with me—bless her <u>dear</u> heart—Sister Mary will return when she goes home—Pheobe will go home Saturday, & Woos will come up.—

I am so well, & so grateful to my Heavenly-Father—every body is so good to me! Mr Neilson went to town yesterday, & <u>all</u> the young-men sent me some message. Jim will come next week, I reckon. Sister Mary wrote you a little note the other morning—I suppose you have received it by this time. I received Trot's letter of 22nd yesterday—Tot-Neanie was just <u>three</u> day's behind, her <u>birth</u>-<u>day</u>! <u>Parthene</u> is delighted at the prospect of being nurse. Good-bye Darlings, I am so tired now, & Sister Anne says stop! All send love—I know you will write as soon as possible. Praise & thank the Lord with us, for oh! I was wonderfully sustained—no terrible <u>fright</u> was allowed to overcome me, & I was perfectly myself. Tell Mrs Taylor about the baby. The Lord bless us all. Tot-Neanie sends a kiss—

Lovingly

Lucy

୫๑

As family and friends gathered to assist with the baby, Lucy admitted to feeling disgruntled by the absence of Melinda "Woos" Barron, a long-standing Irion family servant, who had promised to visit Wildwood after the birth. Lucy described Woos's nonappearance as outrageous and was unable to accept that the family's former slave had a life and responsibilities independent of their own.

Lucy to Lizzie and Bess

Wildwood—

Aug 2nd/72

My dear Trot & Bess—

This is my second letter to you since the baby was born—I have not heard from you, but know there must be letters for me. I will write a short letter now so you will not be uneasy about me. There has not a thing gone wrong with me so far—this is the <u>ninth</u>-day, & I am sitting up some—I have nursed baby twice while sitting up, & she does not feel so very heavy. I do wish you could see how fast she grows—so fat & <u>smart</u>. We think of course there <u>never never</u> was such a child!

Jim wrote me such a sweet loving letter, & wished to come to see "our baby" right away—but I wrote him to come next Wednesday, & then I'd be up, & baby would be two weeks old—I did hate post-poning a single day, but thought it would be more prudent. Sister Anne staid with me until last Saturday, & dear Sister Mary has been here ever since—just left home & husband, & came to me. I can never thank her sufficiently, & will so gladly do all in my power to help her, if ever opportunity presents. Pheobe went down home last Saturday, & Woos was to have returned, but "<u>big George</u>"[1] had just arrived from Tenn, & of course she broke her engagement made months ago. Sent word she would be sure to come Monday, now it is Friday, & not a word have I heard from her. Cordele can't believe she has wantonly broken her promise, but thinks she has some good excuse—still she ought to have sent me word, & besides they <u>all</u> promised I should not be left without help in any time of need, & if <u>Jane</u> had not kindly come to the rescue, I don't know what we should have done. If Woos fails me this time without a legitimate excuse, I <u>never</u> will have anything more to do with her—nor do I wish my family. It is outrageous to be treated in such bad faith.

—Now comes the important part of my letter—this is—<u>a great decision</u> must be made! A <u>name</u> for the baby! No one will take the great responsibility, & yet <u>all</u> wish to be heard. Mr Neilson says the <u>Virginia</u>-folks must have <u>their say</u>— so we all await <u>your voice</u>. Well! my name for her is "<u>Elizabeth Cornelia</u>"—& called "<u>Bessie</u>" for short—so all <u>my</u> family <u>will be included</u>. Ha! ha!—but Cordele declares any such naming will compliment no one—so she suggests a combination of the two grand-mothers names[2]—"<u>Louisa</u> Gray"—& called "<u>Lou-Gray</u>." Sister Anne says she thinks it ought to be "<u>Lizzie Barron</u>," & nothing else—Mr Neilson says "wait, & hear what Sis Lizzie says."—I don't know what <u>Jim</u> will like—& so it stands—every body having a different name, tho' "Tot-Neanie" still holds sway.

Sister Mary sends her very best love, & says Baby & I have both been good. I am tired now—All send love, & baby sends kisses—God-bless you

Lovingly Lute—

I received Bessie's letter of the 26th, & was glad to hear from you. Do write often even if I don't answer every one—I'll have lots more to do when I get well, than I did before—we are trying every where to get <u>help</u>—but hav'ent succeeded yet. I'll just have to trust to Providence—oh! how I do long to see your dear dear faces.

NOTES

1. George Halbert had worked for the Irion family in the late 1860s.

2. John Abert Neilson's mother, Louisa Pinckney Abert Neilson (1800–69), and Lucy's mother, Lucinda Gray Irion (1801–46).

ℰ

As Lucy continued to discuss names for the baby with Lizzie, she also noted an improvement in Cordele's manner. The baby and an increased domestic load had given Cordele a greater sense of vocational purpose, one of the linchpins of single blessedness.

Lucy to Lizzie and Bess

[pages missing]

I was right low-spirited when Sister Mary left—& would have relieved myself with a good cry, if I could have done so on the sly! Oh! she is so <u>very</u> good to me. Yesterday she went down to church—(it was Communion at our church), & brought baby a present of a beautiful white sacque from Cousin Jennie Abert! I was so much surprised & gratified. Ella Workman also sent her some lovely têteing for a skirt! So you see how popular our Daughter is already! I think it will be plenty of time, for you to bring your contributions—if I should need them tho'—I will let you send them. We laughed, & said our child was going to be a charity-child, & we are much pleased with the number of contributions already received.

Bess, I know you will not object to my sending to Mrs Field[1] for your crib—or would it be better for you to write to her first, & then let me send—I will not need it for some time. I believe your Mother only lent it to her! I think I have answered all your questions about baby—she is so sweet & good—sleeps all the time.

And now about the name. I suppose you have my letter by this time on that subject—it was a right sweet little co-incident, that Trot wished to name the child, & Mr Neilson unwilling that any one else should! He wishes a compromise however, & while his heart is all aglow with gratification at your selecting his beloved Mother's name—yet he would like to substitute "Gray" instead of "Abert"—so as to combine both family-names, & at the same time to distinguish her from Brother James' "Louisa Abert"! Our families are so much together—it will be hard to distinguish between so many Lous & Lucys!

My heart still clings to "Tot-Neanie"—so many of my friends just say, of course her name will be "Lizzie"—& I wish it could be—but I reckon I must yield this time, & wait! I wish you could have seen Mr Neilson's face this morning when I read your wish to call the child for his Mother—he was holding the little thing, & oh! how joyfully he hugged her, & what a beautiful smile illuminated his face! And so shall her name be writ "Louisa Gray"—or "Louisa Abert"—just as you decide! Why did you say you had no right to name her—Trot, don't you ever say you have no right to do any thing with me or mine! It riles me to have you speak so! Cordele is so good to me—& and so devoted to baby—we have to scold her down-right about spoiling her. I have given baby to her, & oh! how her heart is bound up in her already. It [is] right for you to make up your mind to love her soberly, & with reason.

Oh! for your return my dear wanderers! I am more impatient than you can possibly be—knowing so well, what a treasure I have to show you! I reckon by the middle of Oct you can come—Jim says by the first—but I don't. Jim will stay sometime—he has gone to town today, & will bring Mrs Eagar back with him—sometime this week—

Mrs Lyon is in town, & sent me word she was coming to see me—I'll be so glad to see her. The new preacher & wife[2] are coming to spend several days at Sister Mary's, & are coming to call on us. All my neighbors have been to call on baby—Gen & Mrs Blewett, & both children included![3]—Not a word from Woos yet—nor any of them. <u>Jane</u> still faithful to her post. Cordele & she are making apple-jelly this afternoon—it is <u>beautiful too</u>! They put up ten jars of apples (air-tight) this morning. What would I do without my good Sister?

Sophie Abert coming this Fall too! You will all be here tho', & I'll feel that I have <u>towers</u> of strength! I can't begin to tell how much Mr Neilson does love Baby, so I'll not attempt. Good-bye my own precious Trot & Bess—may God unite us all again in one family-circle—Lute—

NOTES

1. Emily Field (b. ca. 1825), widow of Judge Joseph W. Field (ca. 1800–69).
2. Rev. Henry B. Boude and Eleanor Chambers Boude (1834–98).
3. Claude Clarence Blewett and Thomas Garton Blewett (1871–1936).

ℒↄ

After a month of deliberation, Lucy and John named their daughter Louisa Gray. Lizzie and Bess made preparations to leave Virginia to visit relatives in northern Mississippi before returning to Columbus.

Lucy to Lizzie and Bess

Wildwood.

Aug 30th/.72.

My darling Trot & Bess—

I hope you did not feel any uneasiness on account of the absence of our <u>weekly</u> (?) letter—I feared you might, & yet it was almost unavoidable, tho' nothing was the matter, save <u>want</u> of <u>time</u>! Does that sound a <u>lame</u> excuse for people living so quiet as we? But I tell you, it has not been so quiet for the last five weeks—there's been constant <u>goings</u> & comings & stoppings too. The annual "big-meeting" came off at our church near-by, & Mr Neilson & Cordele went regularly, night & day, for a week—this threw me much alone, but with constant care of the baby—so I found no time for writing—tho' I wished much I could for I always seize the pen with avidity when a letter is to be written to either of you.

Your letters of the 11th & 14th were gladly received, & read with apprecia-tion—Trot has found her pen moves more freely since my trial is over & oh! such dear letters she sends me—how fondly do I pour over them. Of you Bess, I never had cause of complaint, for you were so prompt to write even when so busy with school-duties. I bless you both for the good your letters have done me. By this time you must be in Wytheville, & have bade adieu to Staunton & all its' tearful admirers! We laugh at the folks "toading-on" (as Jim says) over you—I don't wonder, for they are all so stiff & formal among themselves, they need the social, genial-French-element of both your natures to warm them up, & show them how to enjoy life! I am sorry for them—but oh! when I think of you being even just a mile nearer us my heart leaps for joy! O! that the autumnal-breezes may blow up early this season, & may the snipping crispy frost fall lavishly o'er hill & dale scattering all miasma to the winds! Jim prolonged his visit, & came again to see us—he is so sweet & loving—& I will be glad for him, even more than myself, when you come home—he will urge your return, I fear, earlier than you should come, because of his impatience to have you with him. He needs you both. <. . .> He complains that you & Trot have ceased to write to him—Why? Don't let Staunton get more letters than Columbus or Aberdeen! Poor Jim was so loth to return to that hateful Aberdeen—I won't say to him "I told you so"—but I did my best to dissuade him from leaving Columbus, & his established business name & influence, for an old-fog-gy place, bitterly prejudiced—& then I don't like the fickleness of the man for whom he is working! I think he is thoroughly disgusted with the move, & will return to his old place in January. He is offered a good salary, & everything held out to induce his return. He says after you stay home a month he is bound to have you with him in Aberdeen—I feel quite a horror of anything separating us so soon after our reunion—but for his dear sake I suppose you will have to go! He is distressed at not getting you board at his beloved Shattuck's—but there's no room suitable. I am sorry too, for it is so very pleasant there, & Bess would have such a nice (?) time—then their house is central. Mrs Ottley does'ent wish boarders—she had a long talk with me, when out here—She did'ent mention your names in connection, & indeed! I had forgotten about your old promise—but I know now, that was her object—she's very cute! I admire her tact! Jim said he mentioned in her presence, his anxiety about board, & she said never a word! I told him not to say another word on the subject. Jim said he would try Mrs Armstrong[1] when he went back—but I hav'ent heard from him since. We wish a central position for the elegant ladies from Virginia! Oh! that I had a big house a big fortune, & a central position. It makes me cry to think of us all not living together. Every-body is just waiting your return to devour you both. I fear I shall pine for you away off here in Wildwood! I feel some pangs of jealousy already. But won't you please be good enough to stay some with us?—promise you will. It seems our family have the very warmest, & truest of friends—we are not forgotten, altho' separated from them by time & distance. My friends have shown me every attention. Dear Mrs Lyon came to see me, & oh! how I did enjoy her visit—she seemed pleased too—& praised the baby to my heart's content. You would have laughed at Dr Gus—he would go to the bed, & look, & look at her so funny—finally he took her in his arms as carefully, &

tenderly as an old nurse. Said it made him sad to see all his old friends married & with babies—felt like all his generation had passed away & left him alone. He promises to <u>bring</u> Willie Odeneal out very soon—she has recently returned from Tuscaloosa [Alabama]. She has sent me many messages about baby, & is <u>enraged</u> that her name is not "<u>Lizzie Barron</u>" (as it should be).

Mr Neilson & Cordele have decided with your permission to call her "Louisa Gray" "<u>Lou-Gray</u>" for short. I don't think Mr Neilson would like to <u>Frenchafize</u> his Mother's name by calling it Louise, & besides we are almost obliged to call her by a double name—outsiders would never distinguish the two <u>Louisas</u>. If baby had been less a Neilson, & more an Irion, I would have asserted my rights, & called her Tot-Neanie—but as yet there has been found no trace of resemblance to her Mother or family—which is a constant source of regret with <u>Cordele</u>! She is so pretty (to <u>us</u>) & <u>fat</u>, & <u>good</u>! We took her to spend the day with Sister Mary last Wednesday—then five weeks old. She has received <u>forty</u>-calls in a month— very popular, considering she lives ten miles from a lemon—is she not?—Mrs Barry <u>even</u> has been to see her—first visit. And Cousin Jennie Abert has spent nearly a week with us—don't you know the world is coming to an end? Cousin Jennie wishes you could <u>board</u> with them—(<u>ah</u>!)

It will not be long now before you are with our relatives in North Miss, & will see the <u>new babies</u> there before you do mine. I've had two letters from Corrie since the birth of her's—she is a happy Mother—but I fail to picture her in mind as a Mother. They are awaiting your arrival with pleased expectancy. Cous Mary wrote to Cordele too, & told us a secret—which she has probably communicated to you as well—Cous <u>Sue</u> & <u>Simms</u> are to be married soon.[2] Won't it be a right strange co-incident Trot, that you should happen to be there just at the time of both her marriages—bless her dear heart. I hope she will be happy. I know <u>he</u> will be. Poor little Bobbie[3]—Cous Mary grieves over him! If you have not heard this piece of news—don't mention it in your letters for we were requested not to write of it. While on the matrimonial subject—Mr Neilson heard of his old sweetheart "Kitty's" intended marriage with a gentleman named Merriweather from Kentucky. I have been trying to console him ever since.

—Bess, you probably know more of Lizzie Symons' movements than I—as she has not written to me. She did not go to White Sulphur as I heard, but to <u>Mont Vale</u> [Springs, Tennessee], & thence to Washington—Phil &c &c. Cousin George said she was very much admired where-ever she went—as I knew she would be!—she has improved so much. I am very proud of our two Neices Lizzie & Bessie—but Trot what are we to do with them both about their <u>penmanship</u>— was there ever just such awful writing as they send to people! I am in <u>despair</u> on <u>their</u> account. All the family & <u>intimates</u> are after "Liz." We all laughed at what

Bess said of the <u>dear fourth</u> being her child—why! bless me! how many <u>do</u> you expect me to have. But I want you to love Lou-Gray, & quit talking like you had no part or lot in her! As to the presents you will bring her—I have no thought or desire for anything that is not your handiwork. I always expected that such was to be. I must not write longer. Baby sends lots of wide-mouth kisses to both <u>Aunties</u>. Write us very soon. Cordele & Mr Neilson unite in love. In haste

Lute.

Woos <u>did</u> come up at last & staid two weeks—she thought her <u>excuses good</u> & Jim & Mr Neilson told me to pass it off—but I did give her a plain talk once, in a kind manner. She was just as good to me & baby <u>as she could be</u>.

Among the visitors whom baby has received was Mrs Lucy Sturdivant Barry & her little girl[4]—she returned her bridal call after her child was a year & half old! Ha!

NOTES

1. Pamela Armstrong (1816–89), widow of John Armstrong (1794–1844).

2. Susan Nesbitt Berry married farmer Sims E. Chalmers (ca. 1833–1902) on September 27, 1872. Her first marriage, to Augustus D. Berry (1833–65), had taken place on December 19, 1854.

3. Robert D. Berry (ca. 1858–1938), son of Augustus D. Berry and Susan Nesbitt Berry Chalmers.

4. Lucy Sturdivant Barry (b. 1832) and farmer William Robert Barry (1830–1909) married in 1869 and were the parents of Lucy (b. 1871).

❦

After being invited to name the baby, Lizzie felt miffed that Lucy and John had not followed her suggestion. Lucy tried to appease Lizzie while diverting the conversation to her sister's return to Columbus.

As she adapted to a new routine, Lucy still made time to assist John with Grange matters. Established in 1867, the Order of Husbandry, most commonly referred to as the Grange, was a fraternal organization championing the moral and economic interests of elite white American agriculturalists against merchants and railroad men. Consisting mostly of former planters, the Grange established educational programs for its members and strategized on ways to gain the upper hand in tenant relations. The Grange movement made its way to Mississippi in 1872, and John, Lucy, and several other farming families in Columbus enthusiastically joined its ranks.

Lucy to Lizzie

Wildwood—
Sept 5th/.72.

My darling Trotwood—

Your letter of the 31st from Wytheville, was received, most gladly, last night—it had been so long since any intelligence of the welfare of either of you had come, we felt rather anxious—lest even Virginia-climate had failed to keep off August-sickness. I addressed my last letter to Wytheville, which I presume has reached you by this time, & you are no longer concerned about us.

We all keep well, & if you could see the baby you would never dream of her being only six weeks old—so large, & "shore nuff" baby look & weight. Cordele remarked today, she did hope nothing would happen to her before you & Bess came. I am right much exercised in mind about your hurt feelings in regard to her name. Not for the world, my own old-darling, would I, or any of us, wound you—we thought it was a matter of indifference to you whether the middle name was Gray or Abert—indeed! you said we could do as we pleased—that your preference was "Abert"—but would give your gracious permission for us to substitute the "Gray" if we choose—your "werry words Pip"[1]—don't you mind! So I was quite taken by surprise on reading the post-script to your last letter to find that you really had your heart set on "Abert"—then oh! poor me! I remembered what I had written about the "Louisa" being changed to "Louise" too—& "thinks I to myself "what will Trot say now"—I do think, upon reflection, we have treated you rather queerly, after having formally referred the naming to you, the distinguished "head of the family,"—then to go to changing, & substituting, & finding fault! Do excuse us! You remember those little verses of yours—you gave me for my Scrap-book long ago?—telling all the world so sweetly that "more offend from want of thought, than from any want of feeling"![2]—For myself I have no part in the naming—I am like your Virginia-friends, she is "little Trot" with me—but she is so much a Neilson, you would'ent think her any kin to me. Mr Neilson & Cordele say they will leave the settling of the name until you come.

—It is gratifying in the extreme to have such friends as you made in Virginia—I said we laughed at you all—but you well know I am touched to the heart by such love & kindness as was shown you both. Tho' I can't say I am much surprised—I tell you, two such women, as yourself & Bess, make any house attractive, & no wonder the house-hold grieved over your departure—oh! I fear I'm too impatient, too eager for your coming—I would be stricken sorely if anything should happen either to you or any of us. Tell us in your next exactly when you will leave Wytheville for De Soto. Do take good care of yourselves & don't get sick & loose all your health before you get home after, so long an absence. Oh! when

I think of having <u>good,</u> <u>strong,</u> <u>loving Trot</u> to look up to, & lean lovingly upon, I am ready to cry like a tired child—& yet I don't feel oppressed by care—I'm as happy as the day is long with my dear husband, sister, baby & home—but every child feels <u>petted</u> when restored to its' Mother after having been separated. What a blessed re-union I anticipate—God grant no ill may befall any of us—& that we may all realize the pleasure we so joyfully anticipate. And how proud we shall be of Bess—how much talk we will have!—I must not write more—I must help Mr Neilson with some <u>Grange</u>-business. Hoping to hear from you right soon, & thanking you for all the nice letters you send me; & wishing you to <u>urge</u> Bess to write I remain your loving child Lute.

Of course Cordele and Mr N— & baby send love of the warmest, & most absorbing kind. Tell Bess Sister Annie said she saw Adair Lyon[3] when here—& he is <u>killingly handsome</u>[.] Give her <u>warning</u> to keep her heart!—And <u>Cran</u> I must hear from him when you see him. We miss Bess' letters—

NOTES

1. Pip is a character in Charles Dickens, *Great Expectations* (1861).
2. Charles Swain, "Want of Thought," *English Melodies* (1849), 292.
3. James Adair Lyon Jr. (1852–1915), son of Rev. James Adair Lyon and Adelaide Eliza Deaderick Lyon.

Raising a Family

NOVEMBER 1872–SEPTEMBER 1873

*L*izzie and Bess returned to Columbus to enjoy the slow, autumnal days and the simple pleasures of country life. Lucy lavished so much attention on her sister and niece that she abandoned even the most basic household duties in favor of long talks and catching up. The result, Lucy feared, may have given Lizzie and Bess the impression that she was sorely lacking in domestic skills. "I hope when next they come to be able to do better," she resolved. Willow Cottage had been leased, and Lucy realized that familial respectability rested on her ability to create an orderly and hospitable life at Wildwood.

While Lizzie and Bess's arrival had thrown Lucy's routine into disarray, all agreed that domestic relations at Wildwood were more settled than they had been for some time. Cordele was central to this order, as were the freed women who worked as nurses and servants or were hired to undertake more labor-intensive tasks such as washing. After refashioning single blessedness to suit her own circumstances, Cordele felt more than a little apprehensive about abandoning her post for a stint with relatives in northern Mississippi. Yet she was also aware of the importance of extended visits, which affirmed bonds between extended kin. Lucy's belief that her childbearing years would limit her ability to travel meant that the role of family representative fell to Cordele.

For Lizzie and Bess, Columbus and northern Mississippi seemed a far cry from Virginia's social stage. While Lucy was suitably impressed by her niece's gracious manners and social finesse, she believed that family and community ties took precedence over high society on the Eastern Seaboard. Home life, she noted, had taken a backseat during Bess's education and needed redressing in a place filled with loved ones, old friends, and community. Lizzie remained unconvinced that "coming out" in sleepy Columbus would maximize Bess's prospects, and so she whisked her niece off to Virginia at the first available opportunity.

With Lizzie and Bess at Wildwood, Lucy admitted to having shamefully neglected her correspondence with Jim.

The decision to send Moll back to Willow Cottage created an impasse in contractual negotiations between John and Press. Lucy urged Jim to step in and smooth things over; if Press left, it was likely that several other contracts would be in jeopardy, along with the Irion family's reputation in the African American community.

Lucy to Jim

Wildwood.
Nov 12th/.72

My dear Jim—

I feel quite rebuked for allowing so long a time to elapse since receiving your last pleasant letter—indeed its' very coming rebuked me, for I had missed sending you a letter <u>that</u> week for the first time since you left Columbus. Yes, I confess I was selfish in my unbounded delight in once more having Trot & Bess with me—I did <u>nothing</u> (<u>literally</u>), but talk to, & listen at <u>them</u>—I neglected all household duties, & upon my word, forgot all I had learned about <u>cooking</u>—which circumstance was unfortunate; for you know, <u>no</u> family, however blest with christian fortitude, can be happy when fed with indigestible food! I hope when next they come to be able to do better. Well! now is'ent it delightful, to have them back again? And ar'ent you proud of your well-bred neice. Does'ent she make an elegant appearance, & ar'ent her company-manners dignified, & pleasant! And oh! her <u>voice</u>! I tell you I was <u>thrilled</u>! Make haste every one of you, & come home!

Dear old Trot—so unchanged—so loving—so <u>interested</u> (tho' she tries not to be) in all which concerns us—her children. I feel rich in having such a member belonging to <u>my</u> family. Mr Neilson is just beginning to know her, & is perfectly charmed—

We have been on another visit down at home—went on last Saturday—spent the night, & went to hear Dr Lyon preach on Sunday—took dinner with Cousin Cornelia, & home again that afternoon. T'was quite a <u>surprise trip</u> in-as-much as I had considered myself as having gone into winter-quarters—but quite agreeable—t'was so very like old times to see Mr Lyon in his old pulpit, & hear his sermon—rich in instruction—delivered in his peculiar style which, always suited me. Then our friends were all so <u>very</u> cordial. Saw <u>Mr Cox</u>—of course had many little pleasantries with him—tho' he looks not a bit like a <u>groom</u>—quite <u>Fatherly</u> & settled[1]—he says tell Bess he's just as ready & willing <u>now,</u> as before marriage to bring her _out_—& indeed! he had told his _wife_ (actually said, "_wife_" without a blush) that he must reserve the privilege of flirting a little with Miss Bessie—so she must clear up her _brows_ & not be angry with him. Just as we were leaving the store—he called to me, & asked "if Jim Irion would return to Columbus this winter"—I answered _emphatically_ in the affirmative—was I right—& I wonder _why_ he was so anxious to know.—

I think our going to Willow Cottage had a good effect on _Press_—for he & Mr Neilson had misunderstood each other, & Press was _quite_ determined to leave the place—_now_, I think he will probably _stay_—or at any rate he does'ent think Mr Neilson meant to cheat him. Mr N— has a most _unfortunate manner_ with negroes, & I _know_ he was entirely too stern with Press. _Moll_ is not _worth_ the displeasure of so good a tenant as he, & _I_ told him that I knew _you_ would be satisfied with whatever wages he thought _she_ deserved. Mr Neilson thought she ought to have $5 per month—as he understood _you_ considered her worth _last_ year—but she has _lost_ so much time, & been so disagreeable _all round_, I think a _bare_ support is all she need expect—Mr Neilson thought any reasonable deduction for lost time should be made—but you & Press must settle it—Mr Neilson wishes to have nothing _more_ to _do with it_.

Write soon to

Your loving

Lucy—

NOTE

1. Gideon Warren Cox married Elizabeth Augusta Murdock Sykes (1841–1921) on October 3, 1872. Elizabeth's first husband, Dr. William E. Sykes (1835–64), served as a first lieutenant and adjunct in the Forty-third Infantry Regiment Mississippi and died in the battle of Decatur. Elizabeth and William had two children, James Murdock Sykes (1861–91) and Willie Edmund Sykes (1863–1938).

✿

_As summer scorched the fields of Wildwood, Lizzie and Bess returned to Virginia and Cordele made her highly anticipated visit to northern Mississippi. The trip that Cordele had been loath to give up just a year earlier had lost its appeal in the wake of her reclaimed domestic role and her attachment to her baby niece. Lucy missed her sister personally and practically. "We all, (both white & black) are _lost_ without our 'Lieutenant,' our 'stand-by'—our 'regulator'!" Lucy wrote Cordele on June 2, 1873. "I've been trying _hard_ to attend to all the little things which you kept up, but _sadly_ have I failed."_

Lucy to Cordele

Wildwood.
June 13th/.73.

My dear Cordele—

Three of your letters have been received, & I with great pleasure proceed to answer them. I wrote you before any came & hope you have my letter by this time—Your first was a long time coming. Jim got his & sent it out to me that was the first I heard from you.

I was so sorry to hear you had been sick, I hope by this time you are well & cheerful—do try to be cheerful, & don't allow yourself to be so homesick. I never, in my life, read such a letter as your last—I am afraid you are real impolite to our dear kind relatives. I don't mean to scold, but you know what an extremist you are in every thing—last year you were miserable because you could not go, this year you are miserable because you did go! Just think how ridiculous in a woman of your "sability" to be so childish. Govern yourself, & make out your visit—after all the expense of preparing & going I wish you to derive the benefit of both social & physical enjoyment. I do not wish you to return in August—I consider it dangerous. Every-one prophesizes a sickly season with us on account of so much rain, & I'm glad you are away. I will keep my word & send for you, if we get sick either Mr Neilson, babe, or myself. When Sarah[1] is sick, I can get Aunt Ann to help me—I don't reckon Sarah will wish to go out of service for long—I'll take her back as soon as she is able to come, if she wishes. If she don't, I can get other help I know. Now please, my dear, just enjoy yourself, & make others enjoy themselves by your presence, & don't borrow trouble on our account, & don't allow your love for the baby (for that is the secret of all your discontent) mar every other pleasure.

I get along very well—I've become accustomed to nursing now, & I don't feel tired at all. Baby is right bad sometimes (actually gets into tantrums), & I have to "pink-pank"—but then she is so sweet, & loving & has more little lovely ways. I forgive her for being bad! She climbs about now considerably—but won't "lovey," or try to walk. She & the kittens are good friends—they are not so afraid of her, & such pretty plays they do have around her, & she laughs so merrily—but when she gets hold of them, I tell you, she gives them tight squeezes—then she will hug them up, sway to & fro, & look up for me to sing "by oh! baby."[2]—she does dolly so too. She has had two big bumps this week—climbing around. I know you think it careless in me to let her fall—but if I help her all the time she never will learn to walk. Do tell me about little Lucy—I do love that child, & wish to see her most, next to our Aunts & Uncle. I do wish I could go to see them—they must not think I am indifferent—please make them understand that. But they know newly married folks ought to stay at home, & make every thing stir, so they can get a good start in life. I am not ambitious of great wealth, but wish a comfortable support for our family.

You don't know how Mr Neilson enjoys your <u>homesickness</u>—he laughs until he nearly cries—says "he told you so"! He gave you a <u>month</u> to get tired, & lo! & behold you've been gone only <u>two</u> weeks! He sends you more saucy messages than I will write—Says "look <u>sharp</u> some old <u>Caboose</u> will catch you, & make you stay away from home <u>all</u> the time"! He will write sometime, tho' I don't pretend to say <u>when</u>! I had a letter from Trot last night from Oxford—she wrote so lovingly, & asked particularly when I had heard from you—told me to enclose her some of your letters, to let her see what you had to say for yourself. I suppose they are in Va now—enjoying their friends—God grant them health, & happiness. I had a note from Willie Odeneal last night too—she will be married on the 3rd July—"at some <u>romantic</u> hour between <u>mid-night</u> & <u>sun-rise</u>"—& leave on the train to meet Maj & Mrs Norman Jones[3] at Humbolt [Tennessee], go on to St Louis—from thence a tour thro' the north. She invited <u>us</u> to come, & <u>stay</u> all night so as to be certain to witness the ceremony—said she would feel hurt if we did not come. Dear girl! I do love her, & do hate for her to leave Columbus. I spent one day last week with Sister Mary—met Mrs Vaughan & "<u>Sister</u> Reeves"[4] there—I have been looking for them over this week to spend a day with me— expect may-be they'll come today. I <u>do</u> like "Sister Reeves" very much—she is <u>plain</u>—but has <u>good sound</u> sense, & pleasant manners. The day I spent with Sister Mary who should come driving up but Mrs <u>Knapp</u> & <u>Mollie</u>.[5] They came to see me—found me away from home, & <u>followed</u> on! I do know we have the luck of missing those people. They were very pleasant—asked a great deal about you. I am going over in that neighborhood just as soon as I can "<u>suade</u>" Mr Neilson to take me—he is nearly thro' ploughing, & his crop is as clean as the floor any how—every body else run over by the grass—his corn is beautiful—too much rain tho' for cotton. Our garden looks well—except cabbage—I don't know what is the matter with them—no more flowers seeds have come up—or if they have the grass will not let them grow. I take care of the box plants—the fish geranium will <u>not</u> bloom. Cousin Mary <u>must</u> come home with you in the <u>fall</u>, a visit will do her good. I certainly appreciate her love for me, & return it <u>tenfold</u>! I am so sorry about the fruit all being destroyed. Sister Annie & Mr Symons came over the other day for potatoe-slips—& took dinner with us—I enjoyed their visit so much. Sister Annie brought one of Lizzie's letters to read to me—she is dreadfully <u>homesick</u>, & begs to come back—Charlie[6] will stay six weeks or two months.

I hear the wagon coming, & I must close. Baby sends her little heart full of love to <u>you</u> & all the kin—especially little Lucy—

Our love to <u>all</u>.

Write soon, & I will do the same—Your loving
Lute.

Sarah says you need not laugh at her about getting homesick <u>while in town</u>! She & all Colords send howdy, & say "Come along home."

NOTES

1. Sarah had worked for the Irion family for several years.

2. Perhaps Lucy was paraphrasing a slave song, "By Oh Baby Go Sleepy!" in Clarke, *Dwelling Place*, 158.

3. Willie Blanch Odeneal's sister Theordoria Odeneal Jones (b. 1841) and her husband Norman C. Jones. Willie married William H. Perkins (d. 1918).

4. Sarah Evalina Perkins Vaughn (1825–91), wife of farmer George Wilber Vaughn (1822–94); Lucy referred to George as "Capt V." Mahala Reeves (b. ca. 1819) was the wife of Rev. Walton J. Reeves (b. ca. 1819). James Crawford Neilson noted that Reverend Reeves's family remained in Guntown, and he visited them twice a month (James Crawford Neilson diary, January 19, 1873, Lillian Neilson Papers).

5. Mary Jane Glover Knapp (b. ca. 1828), widow of jeweler Isaac M. Knapp (1812–70) and mother of Mary A. Knapp (b. ca. 1854).

6. Charles Symons (b. ca. 1855), son of John Mauger Symons and Anne Frazier Neilson Symons.

෪

Lucy was quick to confess that domestic matters ran more smoothly with Cordele at the helm. Managing the baby while taking care of the household was certainly a balancing act that left little time or energy for other pursuits. "Our daughter as you may remember is none lighter for two weeks steady growing, & being possessed of Neilson energy & Irion-exuberance of spirit, makes the office of nurse by no means a sinecure," she remarked on June 14, 1873. "At first I was awful tired at night—both <u>mentally</u> & physically—But now I've grown quite accustomed to the labor, & don't feel the fatigue. It is troublesome to follow around after the little creatures, & constantly have them in mind—but we would not have our child less active, or less sprightly for any thing."

Lucy to Cordele

Wildwood—
June 17th/.73.

My dear Cordele—

I have written you two long letters which I hope you have received, & have answered. I have three letters from you, & I expect there is another awaiting me in town. We had thought of going down early this week to spend the night with the

Barry's—go by Willow Cottage—then thro' town & home again next evening—but you know how slow we are, & how long we have to talk of doing things before they are done. I don't know when we will go—it rains every day—not a plow can run—still Mr Neilson cannot not get off—I've taken an inward vow not to say another word on the subject. Just stay at home forever.

I hope you have entirely recovered by this time, & are happy & cheerful—please don't get mad at my last letter—I did not mean to be cross—but I was sorry you were allowing yourself to get in such a melancholy frame of mind—for I know so well, how very miserable you can get over nothing! We are all well, & getting along peacefully, & quietly. One day is so much like another I really lose count—the calendar alas! stands still, & so does the watch, most of the time. I do try to remember to water the flowers & attend the chickens. Oh! if you could only behold our flower-bed—just so over-run with grass, even the roses can't bloom—I look on in sad-eyed wonder at the m[a]gical growth of spontaneous nature. The vegetables are doing well—they were well worked before all this rain, & so the grass is not bad with them. Squashes, beets, beans, potatoes, lettuce, & onions make the table look (& taste) so nice—I think of you whenever we sit down to the table. The chickens have quit dying, I am happy to say. Very few lay now—but numbers go around clucking & sitting on nothing. Henry[1] said he found another duck-nest today under the far-crib—yesterday he found a hen's nest behind the smoke-house (?) with eight eggs—I don't think I'll set any more hens—too late—dont you think? These rainy days are trying on the washing—Sarah does her very best, & I don't complain—altho' I know things would be managed better, if you were at the head. She takes lots of pains with T'weet-hearts little clothes, & enough of them she has every week. Babe is well altho' cutting more teeth—I discovered another new upper one this morning—not the eye-tooth, that has'ent come yet—but the one next. I never heard of a child having as little trouble—thank Heaven!

We ask her all the time where you are—today she looked all around, then pursed up her little mouth, as if going to cry—I don't know whether she understood me or not. I am getting all my sewing done slowly but surely—I will be entirely done by hot weather, & will have only the mending to attend to each week. Every day I thank you all for helping me so much before you left. Babe will not try to walk a bit more than when you were here. I exercise her some every day—I think she is so heavy on her feet that is why she is so averse to walking. You must tell me ever so much about little Lucy—how large she is, & how many teeth has she—I suppose she is running everywhere now. If I don't talk enough about Lou Gray to suit you (?) just let me know. She still is thrilled with delight when seeing the chickens fed, & watches every evening on the gallery for the "moo-cows"—I think about you then particularly, & kiss her for you every time she says "moo." She gets very lonely especially in the long afternoons—sometimes I let <u>little Jane</u> & Sarah-Ann come up on the back gallery & play—but then they are so <u>dirty</u> & don't play with her very well—so I conclude it is best to amuse her myself—& put up sewing, or book, & devote my time to her. I went to church Sunday—left her with Sarah—she was just as good as could be, & did'ent care about my return at all. It was the first time—she has ever been left just with servants. "Bro Reeves" preached a much better sermon than I expected to hear—was rather long tho', & I got a little impatient, <u>thinking</u> of <u>T'weet-heart</u>. I expected Sister Mary, of course, to come to our house the <u>third</u> Sunday—but she chose to go to see Sister Annie, & Bro James came on to church, & then dined with us. You know Sister Mary declared she would not go to hear Mr Reeves rant anymore. I wish to go to town on Commencement Sunday—but la! me—I don't know. I'll have the baby's picture taken as soon as I can, & please <u>make</u> Corrie send me one of Lucy's. Ask Nic if she has entirely cut my acquaintance, & determined never to write again? Tell dear old Auntie, I think of her every day & wish she could see, & know my husband & baby. I wish she could see our home, & surroundings—does she love me these days—And has Uncle Tom given up the idea of coming to see us? Dear Uncle how I do love him, & sweetly remember all his kindness to us. Does Aunt Mattie break any?—is she sweet & cheerful as ever. My dearest love & a <u>hug</u> for her. Tell Susie I just know she beats everybody house-keeping—I can see her going around so quietly, & doing things so nicely. Do tell me about <u>Bobbie</u>—not one word have you said about him—And <u>Dan</u> & <u>Bun</u>[2] what are they up to these <u>rainy</u> days. I wish I could see Cousin Lizzie's her fine boys—& Cousin Watt—has he changed any—I want to know about "<u>Cousin</u>" <u>Sims</u> & <u>Calvin</u> too. Tell Cousin Mary to make you read this letter <u>over</u> when you answer it, & take <u>due</u> notice of <u>all</u> my inquiries.

I don't know when Lizzie Symons will come home—before long I hope, for she has promised me a visit.

Good-bye dear—Baby would send love & messages, but is asleep—& Mr Neilson has gone over to Capt— V's to have some work done—so he can't send any "<u>sauce</u>" this time.

Write whenever you can. God bless you. Sarah sends Howdy!

Your loving Lute.

I enclose a picture which Willie Odeneal sent out—<u>Your</u> self & myself teaching "<u>little Tot</u>" to walk. Please preserve it.

Notes

1. Henry had worked for the Irion family for several years.
2. Carpenter Robert D. Nesbitt (b. ca. 1848) and farmer James A. Nesbitt (b. ca. 1850), sons of Demsey Nesbitt and Matilda Nesbitt.

Columbus, *Columbus Dispatch Pictorial and
Industrial Edition*, 1905. Newspaper collection.
*Courtesy of Special Collections Department, Mitchell Memorial Library,
Mississippi State University. Used with permission of the Commercial Dispatch.*

ℰ

Lucy and Lou-Gray visited Columbus to attend the marriage of family friend Willie Odeneal to William H. Perkins. With Willow Cottage rented out to the Edwards family, Lucy made Cornelia Williams Benoit's home headquarters and devoted the rest of her visit to showing off the baby to family and friends, relishing the ways in which motherhood had also strengthened community ties.

Lucy to Cordele

Wildwood.
July 14th/.73.

My dear dear Cordele—

It has been sometime since I wrote you, but you <u>know</u> my silence was not from negilence or want of affection. Every day I have wished to write but something would interfere. Since my return from town I have been happy in having

Mrs Eager with me. She certainly is one of the most desirable persons to have in the house. So sweet, so loving, so entertaining, & helpful in every way that she can be. It does not pester her at all to have baby <u>always</u> around. I feared it might. Babe loves her, but she is getting right spoilt about her poor <u>Ma-ma</u>. No wonder, any other child would be unendurable, so constantly with their mother. I suppose by this time you have received her picture—has she changed any? Don't you think it good? I do. She was quite <u>sober</u>, indeed! almost scared at being left alone on the little divan—you know what a cautious thing she is, & she feared falling. She was playing with her <u>diaper-pin</u>, but I see the artist has painted it over. Did you laugh or cry when you first saw it—I expect you did a little of both. Oh! I had such a delightful visit in town. My friends were so kind! I made Mrs Benoit's head-quarters—it seems so natural to go there <u>first</u>! We went down Friday-afternoon, & spent a pleasant night with the Barry's—they were very glad to see us, & not at all frustrated by being taken by surprise—but Beck was not at home—up at William's, of <u>course</u>, nursing sick <u>babies</u>! She wrote me a note afterwards, & said she almost cried from disappointment when she found that the long promised visit had been paid in her absence. Saturday we went by Willow Cottage, & looked after things there—all seemed to be getting on well, & very good care was taken of everything. I like those <u>Edwards</u>,[1] & think they <u>try</u> to do right by us. We spent about an hour there—got some nice peaches, & went on to town—first thing had Babe's picture taken—it was pouring down rain too—, & then went to Cousin Cornelia's. She gave us such a cordial welcome. Mr Neilson came back home that night by himself—no good Cordele to keep house for him this time during my absence. Sunday-morning it poured down rain so we could neither go to SSchool or church—I was very much disappointed—but Jim came down & spent the morning which was <u>all</u> I saw of him. He does not look well—tho' he has not been sick at all. Sunday-night we went to church & heard a <u>good</u>, <u>impressive</u>, sermon from Mr. Boude. Monday-morning I went down bright & early to see <u>Willie</u> Odeneal. She was <u>calm</u> apparently, but I thought very much excited. Florry Pugh, Annie Dearing,[2] & Mr & Mrs John O— were there. Willie begged me to come back next day, bring baby, & spend the day, which I did, & had a nice time—all were so sweet to <u>Babe</u>, & she was as sweet as a <u>pie</u> to them. I concluded not to spend the night of the marriage there, as there were so many—but to stay with Mrs Ottley as she had invited me. Monday night I went with Cousin Cornelia to the Commencement-party at the Gilmer. Had a delightful time looking on—did not dance tho'—too old & settled now. Tuesday-night we went to the Institute to some charades which the school-girls got up—<u>Jim</u> acted Mr <u>Clodhopper</u> to perfection! Wednesday I returned some calls—Mrs Evans'[3] first—saw <u>Anna</u>—home on a visit—did not see her <u>lovely</u> husband tho', wish I could. She & <u>all</u> asked of you & wondered how you ever left <u>baby</u>. Then went to Mrs Cox's—of course she made a big fuss over <u>baby</u>—indeed! she was very pleasant. Then to Sister Kate's—where I met Lizzie Symons just returned from Hot Springs [Arkansas]. Left Charlie there. To the Hotel to see those folks. Went to Mrs Fields, & just caught a glimpse of <u>Anna Short</u>. Mr Neilson came, & we spent the night at Mrs Ottley's. Next morning at <u>three</u> we went down to the <u>mar-riage</u>. All were in readiness by <u>four</u> & they were married. Willie did not look at all frightened, & Mr Perkins was as happy as the <u>lark</u> which we read of in verse as being up ready to meet the sun.[4] (I am really ashamed to send this letter—but oh! babe is so <u>bad</u>—just <u>frolicing</u> around scaring me to death crawling off the gallery.)

Tuesday-morning.
Babe was so full of fun yesterday-evening I just had to put up my writing, & take a play with her—now my morning duties are all done, & she asleep I'll resume the thread of my discourse. I stopped right in the midst of the marriage ceremony Mr & Mrs Perkins would not like standing so long on the floor—would they?—

Well! Mr Boude was short, & concise in the ceremony, & <u>soon</u> they were wed, & we all crowded around, & the usual handshaking, & kissing, & wishing <u>good things</u> took place—just then the <u>whistle</u> of the train gave an impatient snort, & threw all the party into commotion. Soon the bridal party drove off at a good round trot, & all looked gay & happy! Willie received a great many handsome presents. Four silver baskets, an elegant silver-ice-pitcher; a large <u>silver</u> waiter & goblets; a splendid silver cup; a fruit knife; a pair of pickle-stands, a beauti-ful berry-spoon; a pair of napkin rings; a <u>watch</u> & <u>chain</u>; a book, & lovely <u>vases</u> & stand—& I gave her as a little token of remembrance & wish that she should use it in my favor—a box of French-writing paper marked with "P"—& a pearl & gold pen. Her clothes were perfectly beautiful—both <u>top</u> & under-wear—I helped to pack her trunk. And so she is now Mrs Perkins & is off for the summer. I expect her poor Father & Mother feel her loss very deeply—they neither could bear to speak of her going away, & yet they are delighted with their new son. Thursday morning George brought down the hack for us, & we with Mrs Eager started home about <u>eleven</u> o'clock—oh! it was hot—it was burning, & no dinner when we got here—but we put on a bold front, & stood it all without complaint. I forgot to tell you that Wednesday-evening late, I heard <u>Manie (Jones) Campbell</u> was in town stopping at Mr Wiley Williams—of course I flew to see her, & found her just the same sweet Manie—no change at all except she looks thiner. Her husband is <u>so nice</u>. I quite fell in love with him. While in town I received a box by express from <u>De</u> Jones Tomlinson containing two pairs of <u>exquisitely</u> made diaper-drawers, & a lovely sacque for Baby! Now don't you know babe is the luckiest little girl in the world. I wrote a note of thanks, & enclosed baby's picture.

Friday the 4th we were invited to a grand Pic-nic at <u>Cox's</u> Mill[5]—given by Capt. Benoit, <u>Col Ottley</u> & <u>Club</u>. They call themselves the Modoc-club![6] We retraced our steps of the day before & altho' it was warm, we felt fully repaid—for it was a <u>grand</u> affair—Every-body was out. The elite, bon-ton, & tip-top were flourishing. The whole affair was a <u>burlesque</u> upon the late <u>Modoc</u> war, & on the <u>glorious fourth</u>!

They (the club) were dressed in full Indian-uniform—<u>war-dress</u>—all complete! There was music, dancing—& oh! the delightful <u>social</u> intercourse & then the <u>dinner</u>—I never saw a better or greater variety! And <u>ice</u>-<u>cream</u> for the whole crowd—(about <u>400</u> people)—& ice lemonade, & every thing so <u>orderly</u>—no <u>drinking</u> any thing stronger than <u>beer</u>!

Saturday we were glad enough to rest, & Sunday Bro James & family came down & spent the day—the gentlemen went to church, but we ladies staid at home, & <u>talked</u> & <u>nursed babies</u>. You never saw any child grow, & fatten as little Annie.[7] She is almost as tall as Lou-Gray, & fully as fat. She almost crawls—but has no teeth yet.

Last week we spent quietly, & I fully enjoyed Mrs Eager's good company. <u>Sunday</u> we all went to Sister Mary's & spent a pleasant day— In the afternoon up drove Lizzie Symons, Pattie Mills, Minnie & Ben—had been to <u>see</u> us. We had a merry time, & when they started back, they begged so hard for Mrs Eager I had to let her go with them. We expect to go over to Sister Annie's tomorrow & bring her back. Mr Boude will hold a protracted meeting up at Unity-church[8] this week— beginning Thursday—we hope to attend.—I know you are having a good time with our relatives—I so often think of them in their pleasant homes. I much fear I will have very little <u>preserving</u> & canning done before your return—even blackberries are <u>scarce</u>. Mr Neilson has'ent taken time to send for fruit. Mr Edwards said we might have some from Willow Cottage. I've made nothing, but a little apple-jelly—My vines for <u>pickles</u> are not doing well, & the garden is a sight! Mr Neilson hopes to get to work in it this week. The box-plants are doing finely— Mrs E— has taken them under her especial charge, & trains the vines, & waters them every evening. Baby can walk a few steps alone—& can go everywhere by holding on to one hand—she has promised to walk nicely by the <u>24th</u>. I wish to make her a birthday-cake! Mr N— is not very well today.

Robert & Aunt Ann too are sick—first sickness we have had. It is healthy throughout the country. Our best love to <u>all</u>. I do love them all. What does Uncle Tom say of his little <u>bald</u>-<u>headed</u> neice? I do wish he could see her—& will be so glad when he comes—wish t'was the <u>Fair</u> & Assembly <u>both</u> he was coming to attend. Write soon to your loving Lute.

NOTES

1. Possibly Thomas J. Edwards (b. ca. 1840) and Fannie W. Edwards (b. ca. 1846).

2. Florence Pugh (b. ca. 1841), daughter of Joseph J. Pugh (ca. 1807–55) and Louisa Ann G. Perkins Pugh (b. ca. 1821); Anna Dearing (b. ca. 1853), daughter of James Hunter

Dearing (ca. 1823–64) and Martha Ann Hendricks Dearing (b. ca. 1829) and cousin of Willie Blanch Odeneal Perkins.

3. Hannah Stanton Evans (1811–1907), widow of lawyer Richard Evans (1802–70). Hannah's daughter Hannah Stanton Evans Brown (1846–1923) was married to Walter Augustus Brown (1832–1908) and lived in Meridian.

4. George MacDonald, "Sir Lark and King Sun: A Parable," *Adela Cathcart* (1864), vol. 3, 66.

5. Mill owners H. E. Cox (b. ca. 1822) and his wife E. E. Cox (b. ca. 1821).

6. The U.S. Army sought to remove the Modoc people from their homelands in California to the Klamath Reservation in Oregon, resulting in a series of battles between 1872–73.

7. Annie Barry Neilson (1872–1952), daughter of James Crawford Neilson and Mary Bruce Barry Neilson.

8. Unity Presbyterian Church was located in Caledonia.

✺

Lou-Gray's first birthday was celebrated among family and friends, and Lucy wrote Cordele of all the particulars, along with a full update on household affairs. Lucy also inquired about the health of Cousin Corrie's husband, Calvin Myers, who was gravely ill. "The doctor fears he is going into a <u>rapid decline</u>—" Lucy informed Bess on July 27, 1873. "He has a bad cough & pain in his side—blisters have been applied, with <u>some</u> relief."

Lucy to Cordele

Wildwood—
July 27th/.73.

My dear 'Miss'—

It is Sunday-afternoon all of us have napped, & now as Mr Neilson has taken Lou-Gray out for a ride, I'll commence a letter to you—tho' don't know when I shall finish—I received your nice long letter of the 14th & thank you for it. I wrote you last Monday, & every week since you've been gone except when Mr N— wrote. I don't know what has become of the letters—the idea of you not hearing from us in <u>three</u> weeks. Hav'ent you received the baby's picture yet? Trot & Bess have received their's, & written back how much they like it—so have Sissie, & Sophie. All think it very good. It makes me feel glad to hear how well you are, & grow so <u>fat</u>. You were poorer when you left than I ever saw you. The trip will do you good in every way. We <u>do wish</u> to see you very much—but don't want you to return until you[r] visit is over. I wish Trot & Bess to come home too when you do—I don't think there'll be the slightest danger, & then at the <u>Fair</u> they'll see every body & every thing worth seeing. Time passes right slowly with us—it seems a long while before you come. We all keep well, & every thing goes on smoothly. Sarah still keeps at her post, & has not said a <u>word</u> to me yet. <u>George</u> plays nurse when I go away from home.—

Thursday was Baby's birth-day—we had a nice good dinner—Ham, a brace of roast fowls, a corn pudding, a chicken-pie, tomatoes, stewed & raw,—onions— okra, lima beans—potatoes—&c &c—for desert a nice cake & apple-float. Jim & <u>Gus Lyon</u> came out the night before—& Sister Mary, Bro James, Lou & Annie came & dined—but no one came from Sister Annie's at all—we were much disappointed—especially the <u>two</u> beaux, for they expected a nice time with Lizzie. I heard that Minnie was sick—but thought Lizzie would come any how. I dressed Baby in that beautiful little dress which Bess gave her—a lovely <u>blue</u> sash that Mrs Eager sent, & looped her sleeves with some sweet little pins which <u>Jim</u> brought her—they have "Baby" enameled on them. Oh! I wished for <u>all</u> who loved her, but especially for <u>you</u>—she did look & behave so sweetly. I wished to have her sit at table but had no suitable chair, so she went to the <u>kitchen</u> as usual. Sarah complained bitterly that "Miss Lucy did'ent give Babe one bite of her birthday cake or pie or any thing but what she has every day—<u>taters</u> & <u>milk</u>"!—All passed off well, & all seemed to enjoy themselves. I fear tho' the gentlemen were a little bit bored with so many <u>babies</u>! They started home early, but we heard afterwards they broke down on the road. Gen Blewett said he saw them with a <u>whole</u> tree dragging under the buggy. I had no private talk with Jim at all. He said he had intended taking a week's holiday, & spending it with us—but poor Mrs Bhlum has been <u>crazy</u> for weeks (since her child was born), & Mr B— is confined to her room all the time, & if she does not get better, Jim will have to go on North. I am sorry for the Bhlums—but a trip would do Jim a world of good, & then he would feel in <u>right element</u> again. He looks well, & had some good laughs while out here—some saucy talking amongst the men, I tell you!

Gus was in <u>his glory</u>—till <u>other</u> company came, & then he looked rather restless. Aunt Ann helped Sarah about dinner & <u>breakfast</u> both, & I tell you everything was <u>good</u>. Jim seemed to enjoy it all. I am having <u>nice</u> flour now, & light-biscuit, bread & cake do splendidly. What do you think—I could not get a black-berry for <u>Jam</u>! There were very few, & then everybody was so busy, they would not get me any! How I shall keep house without <u>Jam</u>, I don't know—what will I do for Queen's Pudding, & <u>roll</u>! I will have to make up in <u>Marmalade</u>—but I'd put off making that as late as possible—had I not? I've canned some peaches—but did not have enough to fill more than half our jars. I've <u>eaten</u> up nearly all the <u>jelly</u> I put up already—not <u>I</u>—but my <u>table</u>, & <u>big</u>-<u>meetings</u> &c &c! Last Wednesday Dr Lea & <u>Mol Knapp</u> came to invite us to a Pic-Nic at Jameson's Mill on Friday— we went late arrived at 12 o'clock, & returned at 4 o'clock. T'was very pleasant indeed. Your <u>Ma</u> Lea was so glad to see us—the Knapps were out in full force, & looked like they would just <u>eat the baby up</u>—one of the younger girls nursed her <u>all</u> day long. Old <u>Gabe</u> was out making eyes at the baby—she gave one grab at his whiskers, & I tell you she made the <u>tears</u> come. I was glad of it too. <u>John D</u>— was there looking as fat & hot as ever, I was sorry Alice & her baby[1] was not out. Gus Lyon says it is a little thing, but sweet & good. I wished for you to see the <u>old timey</u> dancing of the country <u>lads</u> & <u>lassies</u>—such hopping up, & down, & cutting up generally.—

I am so distressed to hear about Calvin—oh! I pray his life may be spared—do tell me about him in every letter, for I have thought of him & his little wife & daughter ever since I heard of his bad health. I do hope he is now well. There is very little sickness in our country—& the crops generally are looking well. Mr Neilson's is <u>beautiful</u>—& his tenants are doing well too. <u>Save up</u> all the funny things to tell me, which you can't write about—I'm just waiting to hear. I had a 24 page letter from <u>Bess</u>—the second I've received since she went away—she writes very few letters. She is having a pleasant time—in society all the time—the gentlemen are very attentive, & exert themselves to make her time passed agreeably. I expect she will soon go to Sophie's—they are all impatient for her to come. My dear Auntie!—I do hope the <u>cook</u> may prove of <u>real</u> assistance to her. Do tell her how much I do love her, & dear Uncle Tom. And kiss sweet Aunt Mattie for me. I'll send you another picture of the baby, if that one is lost—tell me what they all say about her <u>fine</u> suit of hair. Mrs Eager wrote me that Lide McCarty had another <u>son</u>[2]—both doing well!

Mrs Jack <u>Ussery</u>[3] has a daughter, & so has Mrs <u>Edwards</u>[4]—at Willow Cottage. Mrs Judge Sims has a <u>great boy</u>[5]—joy there! I am glad to hear about your quilt—I do no sewing except <u>mending</u>.

Cous Jennie went away <u>sick</u> with head-ache (of <u>course</u>)—I have not heard whether she is going to Mrs Hamilton[6] or not—she is again expecting an heir!

Our garden has gone to <u>weed</u>—Mr Neilson had some of the grass cut down, & planted potatoes, beans, turnips & cabbage for Fall. Since the rains the weather has been very pleasant. My tomatoes are doing well—I am going to try Catsup next week. My cucumbers are doing nothing—I wish to plant more for pickles. I'm drying okra, & think of you every time I see it.

Mr Neilson says he intended to write to you but I write so much I don't give him a chance. He was not disgusted with your letter, but highly pleased—I won't tell you what he said—you'd get vain. I am glad you have some fluting tongs—expect they will be much used on <u>T'weet-hearts</u> clothes. (I won't say a <u>word</u> about any thing you tell me—so write <u>freely</u>) I have not seen any of the Vaughan's in some time—they don't come over at all—so busy—<u>no cook</u> &c &c.

Beck nor Kate have been up in an age—Sister Mary has gone down there today, & I hope she may bring one of them home with her—<u>Beck</u> is preferred—she promised me a week. Mr Barry's health is very bad—he is in a weak laguid state like he is every summer. The morning-glory-vines in the garden are beautiful—all white with stripes of blue—These on the gallery are three colors—Blue, pink, & deep purple—I'll save some seed for Cous Mary—Mrs Eager trained the vines so prettily—Mr Neilson made me a bench, & they grow on it now—cypress, balloon-plant, & morning-glory all climbing up & looking beautifully—Moss-pinks blooming too.

No old lady Buck did not die—but is setting again—the chickens do not die much now—tho' some of the lot hens set themselves to death! Harry & Carlo are well, but are as ill-mannered as ever about barking, & running after people passing by. Little daughter grows quite excited over their deep-mouth baying. She climbs up by everything, & stands alone any time—but won't take but a few steps at a time—She is so funny in her little ways—& poor little thing gets so lonesome, & will have attention. I have now called Ed, & sent her down to the cabin to see all her colored friends, whom she adores! They are all so good to her. I have written too long a letter. I must stop now, & write a little to Lide, & congratulate her.

Our united love to our relatives, & thank them for their kindness to you. Everybody asks about you—even to Mrs Mary Vaughan[7]—saw her at the Pic-Nic. Oh! you ought to have seen how dressed up Capt Flood[8] was, & how polite—just flying around with a jug of cider. I tell you I enjoyed it.

All the colords send howdy & many wishes for your return. What has become of Aunt Gracie. Howdy to her & Linny.[9]

Heaven bless you—

Your loving
Lute.

NOTES

1. Bettie Freear Young (b. 1873), daughter of John D. Young and Alice Baskerville Young.

2. William McCarthy (b. 1873), son of Maurice McCarthy and Eliza Williams McCarthy.

3. Juliet E. Murphy Ussery (1846–83), wife of farmer John Mastins Ussery (1840–1917) and mother of Rufus Henry Ussery (b. 1873).

4. According to the 1880 census, Thomas J. Edwards and Fannie Edwards had two daughters: M. L. Edwards (b. ca. 1871) and Jessie Edwards (b. ca. 1875).

5. Henry Upson Sims (1873–1961), son of William Henry Sims and Elizabeth Louisa Upson Sims.

6. Mariah Louisa Abert Hamilton (b. ca. 1832), wife of manufacturer James Hamilton (1820–81). Mariah was pregnant with her son William Baskerville Hamilton (1873–1938). The Hamiltons were residents of Columbus in the 1860s but had moved to Wesson by 1870.

7. Mary Jane Sharp Vaughan (ca. 1832–87), widow of Wesley Earnest Vaughan (d. 1866).
8. Felix W. Flood (ca. 1833–ca. 1910).
9. Gracie and Linny worked for the Nesbitt family.

ℊᴧ

Cordele reaffirmed family ties in northern Mississippi, Bess established her social credentials in Virginia, and Lucy focused her attentions closer to home.

Lucy to Cordele

Wildwood—
Aug: 3rd/.73.

My dear Cordele—

Tis Sunday again, & finds me writing to you. I don't know that I do right to put off my epistolary pleasures until Sunday, but I think of you so constantly, there's surely not much harm in writing down a <u>few</u> of my thoughts. I am very lonely—Mr Neilson & bro James have just left for church—Mr Schaeffr[1] preaches today—& as there was no body to leave "T'weet-heart" with, I am perforce compelled to stay at home all by myself. George & Ed have gone on a visit to their <u>kinsfolk</u>—Mr Neilson put them on <u>Vicky</u> yesterday morning—with orders to Jim for <u>new</u> hats, & each 25cts to spend as they choose; & then for them to go on out to see Press, Martha & Co, & stay until this evening. I hope they will do right, & take good care of the <u>beloved</u> Vickey, & return in good time. I thought it was very kind in Mr Neilson to let them have his horse—but he said they'd been very good & useful boys this year, & he wished to favor them.

There is a "dis-tracted meeting" going on at Military Chapel,[2] & of course all the other negroes wish to attend, & I told Sarah she might go, & we'd have cold dinner today—so I gave her a lunch of biscuit, ham, & a <u>molasses cake</u>; & that's <u>all</u> the <u>whys</u> baby & I are so lonely. To day two weeks is the <u>big</u>-meeting up at Vaughan's.[3] I was over at the Captains last week & of course they are in <u>high-feather</u> over it. We intended to go to <u>Beck's</u>[4] but thought t'would be <u>safest</u> to go by "<u>Pa's</u>" (or <u>father-in-law's</u>) first to see if she was not there, & sure enough <u>there</u> she was! She insisted on hitching up & going back home, but of course we would not hear to that—so we spent the morning very pleasantly with the entire family. I delivered your message to Amanda[5]—she was quite pleased, & says <u>do</u> come back in time for the <u>big</u>-meeting! She has <u>lots</u> to tell you. Beck's baby[6] is a real nice, sprightly little thing—the image of <u>its Pa</u>!—I am to send over to her orchard for fruit to can, & jelly, & preserve. I thought as I was disappointed in getting blackberries for <u>Jam</u>—I had best fill all my jars with <u>pear</u>, & <u>quince</u> & <u>wild</u>-plum preserves. Jane says she's determined to get me some this year. I have put up eight nice bottles of Catsup—& hope to get more—tho' the tomatoes are rotting badly. I try to dry okra, & save the lima-beans—tho' tis slow work.

I took Louise in her carriage the other day, & as I was cutting the okra, she jumped up in the carriage, & reached back after the <u>handle</u>, & <u>over she</u>, <u>carriage</u> & <u>all</u> went—I was so scared & ran as fast as I could to the rescue. She was not hurt—but very much frightened—as soon as she recovered sufficiently—she turned, & <u>quarreled</u> with the carriage as hard as she could.—oh! tis too funny to hear her <u>quarrel</u>—not one word can she articulate—but the intonation of voice is perfect. She has learned to walk right well, these last few days—I wish you could see her now as she comes stepping so slowly (<u>delibly</u>), & cautiously from the couch at the fire-place to me here at the writing-table—such funny <u>wide</u> stepping! She has learned to kiss her hand at people—<u>so sweetly</u>! The other day, she was asleep, & I sitting sewing, when I heard a noise at the door, & looked up, & there stood Lily Wooldridge[7] & Virgie Ayers—came over from the Oaks to see the baby—she woke up in a little while, & oh! so delighted to have company—they had a long play, & then the little girls went back. Sister Annie, Lizzie, Minnie & Ben came over—Charlie had'ent returned but expected to next day. Lizzie & Minnie are coming Wednesday to stay some with me. Minnie has had a long bilious spell, & looks a <u>pale yellow</u>. Ben is <u>prettier</u> than ever, almost bald from measles. Sister Annie looks so well, & is right lively. Friday I went to Sister Mary's, & spent the day, while Mr Neilson went to town—such a pleasant time with her & Kate. They went down to church to day, as it was communion (at our church)—<u>Beck</u>, I reckon, will <u>come back</u>—I will be so glad to see the old girl.

After-noon.

I hear that Maj Arnold, & his sister-in law[8] were <u>married</u> the other day. Right soon! Amelia Pope & Mr Jordan[9] will be married in the Fall—the <u>cruel</u> Father has retracted his command for his not visiting her, & <u>all</u> now is sun-bright & joyous. So much for <u>marriages</u>—for <u>births</u> I have to <u>record</u> the arrival of a <u>second son</u> for Eloise Johnston <u>Bell</u>![10] A daughter for <u>Mrs William Whitfield</u> Sr.[11] Our pastor's wife is in a <u>high state of expectancy</u>![12] Ar'ent you surprised?—I thought she was too <u>sickly</u> for such performances!—Maj Armstrong[13] (of our church) is dead—he has been a sufferer for a long time—abscess of the liver! Old Dr Hall[14] is not expected to live—that Mr <u>Cole</u>,[15] who has been so long a charity patient is dead—There's a good deal of light bilious attacks, but not much fatal. Tommie Bradford has been sick, & is said to look <u>dreadfully</u>! He & Annie expected to go to <u>Shinn's</u> [Spring]—last week. Your letter of 22nd was truly enjoyed. I hope by this time you have more letters from me. We had a good laugh at what you said of the comments of the relatives on baby's picture—I'll reserve one for <u>Corrie</u>— but will wait till she writes to me. I think there <u>was</u> a <u>crowd</u> at Aunt Mattie's—I'd like to have seen our new cousins. The weather is not so very hot with us—the frequent rains cool the atmosphere, & the nights are delightful. I am going to write to Trot, & consult about <u>when</u> best for <u>you</u> to come home—when I think of your return my heart leaps up with joy!—but I don't wish to be selfish, or to run any <u>risk</u> about your coming. Tell me of your visit to Mr Alexander's.[16] I know you enjoyed it—I had only a postal card from Trot last week—she & Bess on a little jaunt—would write as soon as they returned to Staunton. Jim keeps well—Mr Neilson will go to town tomorrow, & see him. I wish you could see what a romp "Papa & Daughter" are now having on the bed!

Our best love to all. Keep well & come home rosy & fat. George & Ed have arrived all right, <u>new hats</u> & <u>all</u>! Report their folks well—except <u>Pheobe</u>. Poor old woman is always sick. Babe <u>bows</u> to every body that passes, & is fond of <u>reading</u> from books & papers. Also takes pencil, & writes to Aunt <u>Nelia</u>. Heaven bless you—Write soon to Lute.

NOTES

1. Rev. George Shaeffer (1806–86), husband of Clarissa Barry Shaeffer (1810–86) and presiding elder of the Columbus First Methodist Church (1851–54, 1856–57, 1862–64).

2. Military Chapel was located in Caledonia.

3. Mt. Pleasant United Methodist Church in Caledonia. The church was often referred to as "Vaughn's church"; in 1833 James Vaughn (ca. 1762–ca. 1844) and Susannah Vaughn (d. 1843) donated almost six acres of their land to the trustees of the Mt. Pleasant United Methodist Church.

4. Rebecca Winston Shaeffer (1848–1942), daughter of George Shaeffer and Clarissa Barry Shaeffer, married Joseph Wilber Vaughn (1846–1925) in 1872. Joseph's parents were George Wilber Vaughn and Sarah Evalina Perkins Vaughn.

5. Amanda T. Vaughn (1853–1905), daughter of George Wilber Vaughn and Sarah Evalina Perkins Vaughn.

6. Clarissa Barry Vaughn (1873–1964), daughter of Joseph Wilber Vaughn and Rebecca Winston Shaeffer Vaughn.

7. Lily Lee Wooldridge (ca. 1863–1910), daughter of Robert Wooldridge and Mary Blewett Wooldridge (1836–1915).

8. Lawyer James Mason Arnold (1838–97) married Orlie Lowry (ca. 1849–72) and, after Orlie's death, wed her sister Florence Lowry (b. ca. 1855) on July 29, 1873. During the Civil War, James enrolled as a private of Company K, Fourteenth Infantry Regiment Mississippi, and was later promoted to sergeant. He was elected to the Mississippi legislature in 1863 and returned to the army when the session was over.

9. Amelia Pope (b. ca. 1852), daughter of planter Henry A. Pope (b. 1819) and Mary A. Byme Pope (b. ca. 1832). Amelia married teacher Junius Jordan (b. ca. 1848) and moved to Pine Bluff, Arkansas, where Junius established the Jordan Academy.

10. Joseph B. Bell (1873–1905), second son of James B. Bell and Eloise Johnston Bell. Their first child was Harrison Thomas Bell (1872–1940).

11. Lucy Whitfield (1873–1941), daughter of farmer William W. Whitfield (1823–1903) and Sallie Elizabeth Whitfield (1848–1930).

12. Eleanor Chambers Boude was pregnant with James H. Boude (b. 1873).

13. James Trooper Armstrong (1825–73) owned Woodstock Plantation near Pine Bluff, Arkansas. He married Columbus resident Matilda Porter Greene (1830–95) in 1850.

14. Dr. John H. Hall (1801–73).

15. Farmer George Jefferson Cole (1836–73), who during the Civil War served as a private in Company K, Forty-first Infantry Regiment Mississippi.

16. Farmer Elias Alexander (b. ca. 1819) and his wife Mary Clementine Alexander (b. 1827) lived in Olive Branch, near Lucy's relatives the Nesbitts.

෪ð

By August there was sickness about Columbus and its surrounds. At Wildwood, Lou-Gray had a fever from cutting teeth, and John suffered from a "right stubborn bilious fever." "He several times wished for <u>you</u>," Lucy informed Cordele on August 10, 1873, "but I told him he'd be well by the time you could possibly get here."

Contending with a household of convalescing inmates, Lucy responded angrily to Lizzie's idea of extending her stay in Virginia to ensure Bess's continued cultural development. The slower pace of home life in Columbus had its charms, Lizzie assured Lucy, but could not compare to the social opportunities found in Virginia. Lucy opposed the idea and was furious that her sister could place accomplishments and connections above "heart love & yearning."

Lucy to Lizzie

Wildwood.

Aug 19th/.73.

138

My dear dear Trot—

I was hindered from writing my weekly letter to go by Monday's mail—but I hope a delay of a few days will not make you anxious. Mr Neilson's fever, when broken once, did not again return, & he has been <u>going</u> ever since—he does not feel so very well today—but will take medicine tonight, & anticipate any further trouble. I know you will be sorry to hear that Babe is sick—has had right high fever all day—she had a slight fever last week—but there was no return, & we gave her no medicine at all—this time however, the fever continues so long, we are giving broken doses of calomel—she is cutting <u>three</u> jaw teeth at once—at least, they are all thro' the skin—but not the whole tooth just the <u>points</u>. I can't help being anxious, of course, but I am quite <u>controlably</u> so, <u>as yet</u>. I have been expecting her to have fever, & know that it is so natural, that I reason myself into quiet. Mr Neilson has gone to church—the annual protracted meeting is going on at our neighboring church—I was there this morning when Louie's fever arose,—& came right home. There's a great deal of light sickness—tho' few fatal cases. I hear Dr Burt,[1] in town, is quite ill—not expected to recover. Jim came out Sunday to the big-meeting—, & staid all night & went in next morning. How much I enjoy his frequent visits—he seems to too—the baby is devoted to him, & he says he never expected to love any child as he does her. I never saw him look as well, at this season, in my life—I pray he may so continue. Lizzie Symons has been staying with me for ten days past—I took her down to Sister Mary's this morning—& must say I really begrudged her going. She is so delightful to have in the house—I enjoyed each moment of her stay. Mrs Barry & Elise[2] have been up—staid two days & a night. She was very pleasant, & seemed to enjoy herself. I have nice long letters from Cordele every week—she is so anxious to come home—still she does not write so melancholy about it as at first—I think the trip has done her good—& her heart is full of love & good feeling for the relatives. I think they appreciate her real worth. Cousin Mary compliments her by saying she will miss her as much as she did Cousin Sue when she married, & went off. Cordele has been complaining dreadfully of your's & Bess' neglect, but in her last, she was rejoicing over a "good long letter from Sister at last."

Your two letters to me descriptive of your recent jaunts were indeed treats—I was so proud of the first I could not resist the temptation of reading it aloud to Mrs Barry & Lizzie—they enjoyed it almost as much as I did, for they are both appreciative. Right upon the spot, Mrs Barry implored me to give much love to dear Lizzie & Bessie the next time I wrote.

I thank Miss Baldwin, for inviting you to make her a visit, for more reasons than one—I know I should never have received two such letters from Mrs Taylor's (too!) social-house. I do know it must be a charming retreat—so beautiful, so airy, so calm, so restful. I think of Currer Bell's description of the Pensionat of Madame Beck's—you remember what a bright, airy, sunshiny place she portrayed.[3] Ah! you make me feel a yearning to be there—but I will not allow myself even to think of nice trips, yet awhile. No, it is best I should be contented where & how I am.

Now I come to answer about Bess staying away this winter—Of course I remember she is a grown girl, quite free, & white enough—but if I've a spark of influence she'll not stay! Trot, really I am astonished at your entertaining such an idea for a moment! Do you wish the child weaned from us all entirely! Dear knows she is enough so already! What is Music, & French compared with heart love & yearning. I declare I feel real hurt! I've thought over it all, & tried to modify my feelings & expressions—but there's no use. I write with the tears streaming down my face—to think that she desires to stay away another year, & you are willing! I would'ent tell Jim for the world for he would be sure to say "I told you so"—"they have <u>both</u> in heart turned from us!" If I write too vehemently, excuse me—I will never do so again. You will perhaps think I'm making much ado about nothing[4]—I do not so consider it—Bessie is so very dear to us, we cannot give her up, for so long a time, quietly. She makes sacrifices of her feelings to please others, & I am selfish enough to wish her to make some for us—If Columbus is so distasteful—surely her family are not—her accomplishments need not be neglected—her old Prof is as good as any <u>can</u> be, & if she has an inclination for self improvement I don't see why! she could not make her <u>will law here</u>, as well as elsewhere. Oh! no Trot come home to us, & bring our child—our pride! Don't expend all the sweetness of both your lives on out-siders. We wish for you—we long for you! Have I said too much?—

The picture you send I cannot judge much on account of faintness—it is so dim—but I fear it is far too stern for my sunshiny Trot.—I really can't say whether to keep it or not—please exercise your own or Bessie's judgement. Good-night— Heaven bless you both—I do pray for your health to improve—I think you live in too much of a whirl—more quiet would be better.

Your loving
Lute.

Aug 20th—Babe has had no fever today—but exceedingly fretful from action of medicine.

Mr Neilson & Jim think Cordele can come home soon—think there will be no risk. Wrote to her to come some where between the 1st Sept, & the 10th. I will be so very glad to see her. Write soon. Tell Bess I'm going to give her a long one soon. Kiss each other for

Lute & T'Ida.

NOTES

1. Dr. William Jefferson Burt (1804–73).
2. Eliza A. Barry (b. ca. 1863), daughter of Bartley Barry and Mary Eliza Raser Barry.
3. Brontë, *Villette*.
4. William Shakespeare, *Much Ado about Nothing*.

℘ↄ

The late summer days passed pleasantly at Wildwood. Visiting friends and neighbors kept Lucy's entertaining skills in check, but a visit from the minister's large family left her wishing for Cordele's assistance.

While younger southern women such as Lucy were keen to hone their domestic skills, older women such as John's sister Sarah were less than enthusiastic about the prospect of domestic labor. Visiting relatives in Maryland, Sarah declared that her host's inability to hire a cook, coupled with her reluctance to assume that office herself, spelled an end to her stay on the Eastern Seaboard.

Lucy to Bess

Wildwood—
Aug 24th/73.

My dear old Bess—

I don't know which wrote last, you or I—but it does'ent matter much, I feel like confabing with you this afternoon, & I'll do so while Louise is out with her colored friends. I do miss your <u>frequent</u> letters so much—I love the long ones too—'pears like I would like them both long & frequent. Jim sent me out his last letters from Trot & yourself—Trot does'ent keep so well this summer, I wonder why!—I feel uneasy about her—I am glad you are so well—getting fat Trot says—why! you should grow <u>thin</u> & <u>pale</u> over the departures of your friends for foreign parts—you never would play the role of sentimental young lady fading in the spring-time of life, from a 'secret n'er confessed.'[1] Why! what will those friends think when they hear you have taken their going so comfortably? I, having passed the romantic age, am quite delighted to hear that you are so robust. You will soon go to Sophie's, I presume,—they complain dreadfully at your <u>long silences</u>. I really do think you ought, thro' courtesy, to write oftener. Lizzie left me yesterday. Two weeks since she came from home—she was sweetness & amiability itself—it is refreshing to be with one so bright, & entertaining. Minnie was here part of the time too, & she was lovely in behavior to the baby—Babe was sick when I last wrote—she had no more return of fever—but is very cross, & spoilt—she is thirteen months old today, & has twelve teeth—I think her eyeteeth are coming, & make her so fretful. She walks about so well & is very proud of the accomplishment. Mr Neilson is well, & I hope will keep so. We look for Cordele home soon—I will be so very very glad to see the old lady. Had a letter from Sissie last night—distressed at hearing of Mr Neilson's sickness—She says the Homewood folk[2] have lost their cook, & they all try their hand in the kitchen. Says she does not expect to get that office & is talking of coming home. Perhaps she may come on with you & Trot—

Sunday-night—Stopped this lovely epistle, & went over to the country S.School, & then came home via Bro James'—found Mrs Boude & her <u>four</u> daughters there.[3] With Sister Mary's <u>two</u> & our <u>one</u> there were <u>seven</u> girls—oh! horrors! Did I mention that Mrs Boude has <u>prospects</u> again?—Yes! indeed—another girl

I bet!—Mr Boude will come out tomorrow, & then next day they will come here—mercy! I feel <u>right scared</u>. I wish Cordele was here! I'm not afraid of entertaining grown people—but <u>children</u>!—when will they ever get enough to eat. Mesdame Benoit & Ottley have been planning all the summer to come out & spend a night & day with us, but the Col has been so feeble they could not come. The weather today has been extremely hot—the very hottest of the summer I think. I do not think we've had a very warm summer—only a day or two of intense weather, & then would be rain. Write & tell us of your plans—please go back to your old sweet way & write often—but if you neglect every body else, write <u>good</u>, <u>long</u>, <u>loving</u> letters to your Uncle Jim—I know you love him—& you are his darling.

Tell Trot I wrote her last week. Do excuse <u>excess</u> of stupidity. I write so rapidly, & am constantly interrupted.

My eyes ache for sight of you—my heart yearns for your spiritual presence, & my arms wait for your bodily presence—when will I be made so happy?—Heaven bless you—

your T'Ida.

NOTES

1. Lucy paraphrased "Nor thou with disappointment hear / A secret I had ne'er confessed" ("H.G.K.," "A Confession," *Blackwood's Edinburgh Magazine* [1853], vol. 74, 630).

2. Homewood was the estate of Charles Abert (1822–97), son of John James Abert and Ellen Matlack Stretch Abert, husband of Henrietta Constantia Bache Abert (1822–87), and director of the Mutual Fire Insurance Company of Montgomery County, Maryland. Henrietta was a great-granddaughter of Benjamin Franklin (1706–90). Homewood was originally located on 925 acres of woodland near Norbeck, Maryland. Charles sold several hundred acres of the land surrounding the estate during and after the Civil War.

3. Henry B. Boude and Eleanor Chambers Boude had three daughters: Caroline Boude (b. ca. 1861); Alicia Boude (1865–1923); and Katherine Thompson Boude (1871–1955).

ℬ

Cordele returned home to discover that Lucy and John had decided to lease Wildwood and relocate to Willow Cottage. As Lucy informed family and friends of the move, Cordele put the finishing touches to her quilt, to be entered into the handiwork exhibition at the upcoming town fair. With Lucy preoccupied by motherhood and Lizzie and Bess captivated by Virginian society, Cordele reaffirmed her family's standing in the community by exhibiting her genteel skills with needle and thread.

Doll quilt. Irion Neilson Collection.
Courtesy of Collection of the Museum of Mississippi History,
Mississippi Department of Archives and History.

Lucy to Lizzie

Wildwood.
Sept 27th/.73.

My dear Trot—

Your little note accompanying the enclosed letter of Bessie's came duly to hand, & arrested an incipient feeling of uneasiness on your account, for sometime had past with no word from you. I write this morning to let you know that we are <u>all well</u>, & in high expectation over the coming Fair, which begins next Tuesday. Cordele put the last stitches on her beautiful quilt yesterday—she is not expecting the premium—but we think <u>all</u> should make an effort—especially as the gentlemen have gone to the trouble & expense of building a <u>Floral</u>-Hall—for the exhibition of ladies' handiwork. It is a beautiful circular building, & quite ornamental.

I do wish you & Bess were here—not that there'll be any great sights to be seen—but then you'd see all of our world at once. I could not determine from your letters whether you had planned to go by Washington or not—Bess wrote me that she wished you would that you were <u>most</u> certainly expected, & <u>wished</u>. You said you expected to leave Staunton on 3rd Oct—will you go to W—or North Mississippi—pray don't stay a <u>whole</u> month up there—the other members of our family are on <u>stilts</u>, & say they never expect to say "<u>Come home</u>" to either of you—but I can't help expressing what my heart so longs for. Babe is just as well as she can be, altho another tooth is on the way. We wished all who love her could have seen her last night—such a romp, such a glee, she was in—her <u>dancing</u>, is too absurd.

Cordele says she will write after the Fair—she has been so busy with her quilt—has not had time to play with <u>babe</u>—except <u>Sundays</u>. Mr Neilson is <u>swamped</u> in work—building a ginhouse down at lower place & attending to Mill & <u>farm</u> here. Cordele & I will have to take charge of <u>this place</u>, while he is down at Willow Cottage ginning—I wish we could move down before winter but can't, as other people have possession of the house. When you come, we are going to bring you out to take <u>care</u> of <u>us</u>. Don't get scared we won't make you stay <u>too</u> long in the <u>country</u>. We talk of, & wish for you both <u>all</u> the time—

Heaven send you safely to your loving child

Lute—

Where shall we address our next letters?
Staunton, Va.

ॐ

Bess traveled north to Maryland to join Sarah Neilson at Homewood, the estate of Charles and Henrietta Constantia Bache Abert. Lucy penned a plea to Bess to remember that the heartstrings of home would endure long after society's sparkle had faded.

Lucy to Bess

Wildwood:
Sept 28th/.73.

My dear Bess,

Your long & affectionate letter from Homewood made my heart swell with unalloyed pleasure. You know I have been real <u>jealous</u> of your growing love of strangers, & <u>apparent</u> indifference to <u>home</u> & home-people. I am not a jealous nature, neither am I very exacting of the <u>attention</u> of friends—I have entirely <u>too</u> much trustfulness to be either the one, or the other—<u>yet</u>, "up to a certain point, you know,"[1] I was very <u>amiable</u>—but when the suspicion of <u>your</u> becoming <u>weaned</u> from us, once crossed my mind, I was aroused to <u>resentment</u> & a determination not to allow <u>any</u> circumstances to separate us, if <u>possible</u>—This sort of feeling cannot last long with me, if I meet with no response from those by whom the feeling is excited—if they remain indifferent—then my ardor cools— a slowly creeping feeling of disappointment comes, which soon turns to steely & settled coldness. I have many times regretted this, perhaps <u>unjust</u>, way I have, but I cannot help it. Imagine then my gratification when you so sweetly assured me by every <u>word</u> (& I know how sincere you are), that you are not changed in feeling towards us, & really desired to return, home—I am perfectly satisfied now, & shall make <u>no</u> more ado! But, my dear, how can you stay a <u>whole month</u> in <u>North</u> Miss?

You & Trot are the <u>first</u> of our people "who feel as birds to <u>your</u> mountains,"[2] & are the <u>very</u> last to return. It would not hurt either of you to be here right now, & go with us to the Fair next week. Not that there are such great sights to be seen there—but it is a social & unrestrained meeting of friends. I could not decide from what Trot last wrote, whether she would go to Washington for you, or you come back to Staunton—she said tho' she expected you would leave about 3rd Oct which is next <u>Friday</u>—that seems a queer day to start. Any way, I will feel that you are nearer, when you touch Mississippi-soil, & will then have to posses my soul in patience until, the spirit moves you to come further south-ward. Perhaps I may go to town tomorrow to buy a new bonnet for the Fair—you see <u>that</u> is <u>my</u> occasion of the season, in-as-much-as I will see more people than at any other time—It will be January before we can go to Willow Cottage. You don't know what a comfort it is to have Cordele back again—she is so sweet, so loving, & so helpful. Babe & she are both <u>blissful</u>—but 'Miss' does not <u>spoil</u> her as she was inclined to do before she went away. I ask so many questions about little Lucy Myers—I feel more interest in that child than any other next my own. I know you will be glad to see <u>your child</u> once again. Mr Neilson is <u>well</u> again, & <u>so very busy</u>—farm, mill, & building Gin-house all demand his personal attention. I feel real sorry for him; & wish I had Sophie Lewis' administrative powers, I'd take charge of the farm.

I know you are having a delightful time with those nice, refined, elegant people. I thank you for sparing the time to write me so sweet a letter. I rejoice with you in every pleasure, & feel thankful to Our Father for his exceeding kindness, & many mercies. Ah! my heart sings aloud in praises!—& then oh! what joy, to know that <u>you</u> do not forget the Giver in the enjoyment of the gifts. My dear child, God will always bless an humble & grateful heart! I feel that the many prayers of your sainted parents are being answered in mercies to their child.

I can never feel towards any one as I do to you—the peculiar circumstances, which surrounded your childhood, makes a feeling of <u>tenderness</u> ever hover around you—a tenderness such as is only second to that which is felt for my own little blue-eyed darling, who is now toddling around coming up every little while to give a <u>kiss</u>, or <u>ruthlessly</u> to tear my letter from my hands! I wish you could see her—she is so funny—, & her <u>dancing</u> is the extreme of absurdity! Trot sent me your letter in which you expand on the beauty, gracefulness, & fascination of <u>Ellie Abert</u>[3]—I knew you would be charmed! I did not intend to leave the impression on your mind that she was another "<u>Serene</u> Highness"[4]—I only meant she was delicately high-bred, & of consequence a highly-strung nature. I do wish to know her, & all of the sweet family—& Mr Abert reminds you of my husband—then I <u>know</u> what he must be. Oh! I shall have such a world of talk about Mrs Abert, Sophie, Rhinnie, Stannie, Charlie, Allan—Robert & Mary.[5] I do not wonder Sissie prefers their home to ours—but we will always be glad to welcome her—& will try ever to make our home feel like <u>her</u> home. I wonder if she will not return soon. I thought perhaps she would come on as far as Corinth in your good company. Mr Neilson is getting real restless at her prolonged stay.—

We have been so busy with Cordele's quilt—have it now complete, & ready for exhibition at the Fair. It is beautiful—& we all feel proud of it—& don't care at all for the premium—I expect there will be others to excell it—but <u>ours</u> is pretty enough.

Cordele says she sent Jim Hayden's[6] photo right back to you—I was sorry, for I did wish to see how <u>long-neck</u> looked with a <u>moustache</u>. He must be the happiest man on earth now that his upper lip is actually covered—how long & how assiduously he cultivated that darling moustache.—

You were real wicked in trying [to] tease me about your ivory-type—oh! how anxious I am to see it. If it is better than my last picture of you, it must be perfect. Tell my sweet old Soph I will write after the Fair, & tell her <u>of all</u> the wonders (?) which I have seen or heard or felt (?).

Tell Sissie that we delivered her message to <u>Gen</u> B— about the widower, & he enjoyed it heartily—said tho' there was one here (Mr <u>Wm Winston</u>),[7] who was making most particular inquiries of her & he believed it would be better for her to come home—marry him & settle down with us—Mr Winston rejoices in a family of <u>seven girls</u>!—Mrs Blewett has a nice fat little girl-baby of a week old— her name is Margaret.[8]

Mr Neilson says "what kind of a chair would you prefer—cushioned, cane, or split-bottomed"? He wishes to get it ready!

Keep me posted as to the welfare of <u>our</u> Costa-Rica-brave. I feel very much <u>interested</u>—but believe you are more so in <u>another</u> not so far off—<u>am I mistaken</u>?

Have not laid eyes (or hands) on Col Abert—sent word he was coming out—but don't believe him. Cous Jennie still in Wesson. Mr & Mrs Perkins have returned, & are now at their home in Artesia—Hope to see them at the Fair.

God-bless you—Your T'Ida.

De (Jones) Tomlinson has a little baby-girl—named <u>Mamie!</u>[9]

NOTES

1. George Eliot, *Middlemarch* (1871–72), ed. W. J. Harvey, 418.

2. Ps. 11:1.

3. Ellen Abert (1846–99), daughter of Charles Abert and Henrietta Constantia Bache Abert.

4. A title used to address some members of royalty.

5. Charles Abert and Henrietta Constantia Bache Abert's children: Sophia Abert (1849–1906); Maria Bache Abert (b. 1855); Constantia Bache Abert (1858–1934); Charles Abert Jr. (1852–1922); Allan McLane Abert (1865–1951); and Robert Walker Abert (1846–1928), husband of Mary Bithia Warner Abert (1843–1918).

6. James Fournier Hayden (1846–1902), son of teacher George B. Hayden (1816–78) and Louise Fournier Hayden (1823–96) of Demopolis, Alabama. James was the nephew of Lucy's sister-in-law Harriette Hayden Irion Hogan.

7. Farmer William Burton Winston (1825–99), widower of Frances Rose Winston (b. ca. 1830). The couple had seven daughters: Frances Rose Winston (b. ca. 1852); Rebecca Winston (b. ca. 1854); Mary E. Winston (b. ca. 1855); Maria C. Winston (b. ca. 1857); Nellie M. Winston (1858–1931); Jennie A. Winston (b. ca. 1862); and Annie F. Winston (1864–88).

8. Clara Blewett (1873–1937), daughter of Thomas Garton Blewett Jr. and Mary Jane Witherspoon Blewett. The couple must have changed their minds about the name of the child.

9. Mamie C. Tomlinson (b. 1873), daughter of William H. Tomlinson and Cordelia E. Jones Tomlinson.

Interlude

MISTRESS OF THE DELTA

*F*all's golden veil spread across the Yazoo-Mississippi Delta, quieting summer's death knell in its wake. Lizzie Barron always made her annual pilgrimage at this time of year, when the swamps had purged themselves of disease and the trees, with their "netted masses of vine & brambles hanging in glorious festoons," made their way free of the "seas of water, & quagmires of mud." The trip to the Barron plantation, a sprawling expanse of land near Friar's Point, involved taking a skiff across the "glossy bosom" of Moon Lake and then riding miles through messy forests and sludgy undergrowth. Delta country, as Lizzie well knew, was not for the fainthearted. A seven-thousand-mile receptacle for the springtime flooding of the Yazoo and Mississippi Rivers, the delta's silt-rich soil thrived under even the most rigorous of agricultural regimes. Dreams of abundant crops had lured hungry planters from across the South, but they often came at a price. The region may have been famous for its cotton, but it was equally well known for its outbreaks of malaria, typhoid fever, cholera, and dysentery. "This would be the most delightful country in the world," remarked one local, "if it were not for the months June, July, August, and September." Those who were able left with the first blush of warm weather and returned, as Lizzie did, in the safety of fall.[1]

Travelers were often overwhelmed by the unconquerable delta, but all who visited her agreed that the Barron plantation was a sight to behold. Perched on high ground overlooking the Yazoo Pass, it had been the home of Cullen Barron and his first wife (and Lizzie's cousin), Parthenia Thurman Barron. Its wide galleries had been a place of refuge during Lizzie's tumultuous girlhood, but Cullen had died a week after his and Lizzie's marriage, before she was able to walk its halls as mistress. In spring 1864 the plantation—valued at over sixty thousand dollars—passed to the young widow. Lizzie could not face the empty house alone, and so with the help of her brother Jim and a trusted neighbor, she managed the operation from afar. Cullen Barron's agricultural legacy, which had offered up a ready-made domestic ideal, instead provided Lizzie with mastery over an independent brand of postwar womanhood. In the hard years that followed, she made decisions about crops, overseers, finances, and contracts with freed people, throwing the dividends of plantation labor into her niece's education and a series of refined jaunts to Virginia. A whirlwind romance and marriage to farmer James Madison Watt (1814–1900), however, led to a permanent delta homecoming in September 1874. As James tried his hand at farming, Lizzie embarked on house-keeping and the task of fitting her outward-looking, all-embracing new southern femininity into the stricter confines of the postwar domestic ideal.

NOTE

1. Eliza Lucy Irion Neilson diary, 1866; Amanda Worthington to Robert Tilford, April 22, 1838, Worthington Family Papers.

Sisters and Wives

September 1874–January 1876

After three years at Wildwood, Lucy and John traded in their small country farm for Willow Cottage. Granting their neighbor Mr. G. McCown (b. ca. 1824) a lease on their former home, Lucy and John embraced the agricultural and domestic challenges that came with their new abode. Conveniently located on the outskirts of Columbus, Willow Cottage combined the best of town living and country life. It was a spacious household with ample land, quietly bucolic yet close enough to the city limits to guarantee a steady supply of farmhands and an even steadier supply of guests. After working the land at Wildwood, John now found himself at the helm of a different agricultural enterprise, where he swapped the hard labor of small farming for a managerial workload. With friends and neighbors dropping by on a daily basis, Lucy and Cordele readjusted their domestic routine to manage the expanded responsibilities of a large household with the lively buzz of Columbus life. Home, respectability, and society were intimately connected in the postwar South, and Lucy and Cordele were aware that a lapse in domestic detail had the potential to reflect badly on the family's standing more generally.

Lucy and John's relocation to Willow Cottage, however, involved more than just a set of practical adjustments. The home was, after all, an Irion family institution. Within its walls coming-of-age romances, candlelit nuptials, the cries of firstborn babies, and the last dying moments of kin had taken place; there had also been the rush of secession talk, the march of soldiers to battle, the heady days of emancipation, and the lean postwar years. Willow Cottage had become both the hub of family life and a public beacon of respectability. It was no wonder that Lucy felt overwhelmed at the prospect of taking charge of her childhood home. The domestic changes were made none the easier by Lucy's second pregnancy and Lizzie's romance with James Madison Watt. When Lizzie wed her beau in Columbus on September 17, 1874, Lucy noted the shift in family relationships. With James and Lizzie Watt embarking on a new life together, Lucy struggled with the idea that she now sat at the center of family life.

❧

Less than ten days had elapsed since Lizzie's nuptials to James Madison Watt when Lucy wrote an impassioned plea for her newly married sister to return home. Unable to tend to her sick child while preparing for the birth of another, Lucy felt more overwhelmed by the thought that she had been left at the helm of family affairs. In her note, almost childlike in tone, she hoped to remind the rightful head of her position and continued responsibilities.

Lucy to Lizzie

[Willow Cottage, September 26, 1874][1]

Dear Trot—Please come home as soon as you can. Tell Maj Watt I will both forgive, & love him all the days of my life, if he will only let you come <u>now</u>, & stay with me until my trouble is over. I have been in such <u>distress</u> for the last two nights & days about little daughter. She has been so sick—& is still unrelieved—when she had those dreadful spasms, I thought I would die—I never will forget how she looked—& oh! how I wished for you, my dear darling—so strong, so reliable! Mrs Eager has been my strong-tower. Dr Matthews is here now—& says he is glad to hear from you—& that you had so warm, & cordial a <u>reception</u> from all your new kin. But he cannot think you are very appreciative of warm-heartedness or less you would never have left here.

I was so glad to get your letters—they were so bright, so loving! I will answer at length as soon as I can—that is if you don't <u>come</u>—but please do come. Tell Maj Watt, I want him to come too. I want to know him better. Oh! Trot, if you could use your influence to come <u>nearer</u> us—don't stay down there if you can—I know you are sensible, & will not be unreasonable—but there is no use in your staying there, Maj is travelling all the time any how—Good-bye. I cannot write more—all are waiting—Do come, do <u>come</u> & <u>soon</u>. Bess was in Ithaca [New York] went [when] last heard from—well & having a good time—<u>Jim</u> Hayden with them, & they are gay!

God-bless you both. Pray for us, & especially for my darling—your Lute.

NOTE

1. Laura Eager had written the following note at the top of Lucy's letter:

My dear friend,
 I should have written to you on Friday, if Lucy had not sent for me. Will write soon.
 Lovingly,
 L.E.Eager.

୫୬

A letter from James Madison Watt provided Lucy with another opportunity to plead for Lizzie's return to Willow Cottage. A weak attempt to highlight the practical reasons for a visit did little to hide Lucy's growing fear that her sister's wifely duties took precedence over Irion family life.

Lucy to James

Willow Cottage.
Oct 4th/.74.
Maj J.M. Watt—

My dear Brother.

Your letter has just been received, & it's loving, & earnest tone has awakened an echoing thrill in my heart. I assure you, I will joyfully meet you in days advance of true friendship—such a friendship as will last 'till life's end, & will put us forever at loving ease in our future communion. I thank you for the expression of such feelings, & will ever appreciate them. It makes my heart warm towards <u>you</u> that you <u>know</u>, & <u>feel</u> what a treasure you have taken from us—therefore you can the better sympathise in our loss.

I told you <u>she</u> was the best woman God ever made—<u>best</u> in every relation of life—& I am gratified that you & your friends & family have already found my words true—& the <u>longer</u> you are blest with her presence, the <u>dearer</u> she becomes. I know I grieved selfishly over giving her up—but I felt a kind of desperation, & did'ent care if I did show <u>bad</u> feelings—I <u>encouraged</u> them. Oh! if you will only send or <u>bring</u> her home right away, I don't think I'll be <u>naughty</u> to you any more—indeed! I'll be your grateful loving little Sister—You can afford to be magnanimous for she is your's for life—& she loves you, & yours already enough to make us all terribly jealous—but I believe in a wife <u>belonging</u> to her husband. I belong to mine, & <u>glory</u> in his ownership—therefore I cannot feel jealous of her love for you. Life's so much more blest, where these <u>natural</u> ties are recognised. I am only too happy in the thought that she has married a man, who has a keen appreciation of her worth.—T'would break my heart for her to have done otherwise. I never could bear for her to go unappreciated—I was always jealous of her good qualities being fully recognised. You did not specify what time you would come—let it be as speedily as convenient—I do not wish to be unreasonable—but we have your room all in readiness, & are constantly wishing for you. We will be happy to have you with us as long as you can possibly stay— remember <u>this</u> is family-head-quarters—& must always be!

Our little daughter has been violently ill—but thank Heaven, she is well again—I felt I could not bear the sight of such suffering much longer—Our dear friend Mrs Eager came to our assistance, & oh! was such a comfort—don't you know my heart yearned for my <u>Mother-Sister</u>?—she is so strong, so helpful in all times of trouble. All are well now—& my husband is just as busy as a man can be—he gets as much as he can do with his gin & mill—which makes him feel encouraged as to <u>hard</u> times. Come & see for yourself. I won't ask you to kiss your wife for me—I feel loath to inflict such a punishment!—

Good-bye—all send best love to you both. Tell Sis Lizzie to write <u>oftener</u>. You must not stop either—Your's—

Lucy I. Neilson

ℰⓐ

Lizzie returned to Willow Cottage to assist Lucy with the delivery of her second child, John Abert Neilson Jr. (1874–1935), on October 17, 1874. "Jack" grew quickly, despite persistent bouts of colic and an outbreak of hives.

In less than a month, Lucy rose "every morning to breakfast" and had ventured out as far as the dining room to assist Cordele with sewing up a flannel shirt. "[I] will take a walk on the gallery as soon as it is right," she informed Lizzie on November 5, 1874, determined that her stint away from society would not be a prolonged one.

As the Neilsons adjusted to their expanded family, changes were also afoot in the management of Wildwood. With McCown announcing his departure from the farm, the Neilsons agreed to lease their former home to Press Barron.

Lucy to Lizzie

Willow Cottage.
Nov 16th/.74.

My dear Trot—

I am sitting by the crib where little Jack lies asleep, & while he is so pleasantly employed, I will enjoy myself a wee bit, by talking to you. What ages, & cycles have rolled their weary length along since you left, & then we have had no letter since you got to Winona—of course we hav'ent heard from the Post in days, so perhaps we have quite a full mail awaiting us. I hope so, for oh! I pine, I hunger, I thirst for news from you. I am afraid tho', if you are housekeeping, you will be so busy, there'll not be much time for <u>long</u> letters, & <u>those</u> are the kind <u>I</u> always wish from you. I like for you to give yourself plenty of time, & scope, so you can speak of the many things, you know I feel interested in.

We are all well now—I hav'ent as yet resumed entire charge of housekeeping on account of a cold, which I contracted right here in my room—being as careful as I could too—it has not affected me seriously tho' at all—only in head & chest. I felt thankful it did not settle in my breasts. No trouble in that quarter tho'—little

Jack just fills himself as full as a puppy, & then rolls over to sleep—or in the afternoon, with the colic. I wish you could see how your son fattens—Cordele says he is every bit as heavy as Mrs Ottley's baby[1] now. She does not give sufficient nourishment & has to feed it from a bottle. Cordele went to church yesterday, & stopped by to see Miss Ellen—when she returned, she brought Cousin Cornelia & Lou Ellen with her. <. . .>

Last week was very pleasantly passed, the weather was mild, & we had friends with us. Bro James came one night—then Madie, her sisters & the boy[2] came, & oh! such a very pleasant visit we did have—Madie & little Lyon spent the night— she was much like her old self, & delighted us with her sprightly conversation— Lyon is as sweet a child as I ever saw—she had no nurse but he played by himself all the time, was absorbed in Louise's numerous toys, & "sings." She was amiable too, & allow him full liberty. We had to give her quinine again—she was feverish one night—it was just about three weeks since she had had chills—she is well again now—& is real sweet—she wrote you a letter with me holding her hand— her own diction.

Col Albert came out to tea, & spent the evening with Lizzie—Jim came too. Mr Neilson had to go on a great Caledonia trip, & we sent for Jim to protect us. I hope to go to town this week for a little while—Jack sleeps right long in the morning, & I think I can run away, & leave him for a time. I wish to get Mrs Willeford to cut my new Polanise—navy-blue.

Do write us that you are sure enough coming home with Bess—& that the Maj has concluded that Columbus is as central a place as he can live in! Would I ever get done shouting, & praising the Lord for his goodness—if such an arrangement could be made! But I'll not think of such a thing—I must bear this great cross of separation from my most congenial spirit on earth! Tell Bess, I have written to her, & hope there are two or three answers to it, somewhere on the way. We are counting the days now till her return. Tomorrow is the 17th—baby a month old—what a terribly long month—it seems Jack has been with us always! I begin to long to get out—to ride, to visit, to go to church!—Tell Maj Watt to take good care of you (?) I know such advice is needed. We were wondering yesterday, if you two had gotten over the hugging & kissing period!

Mr Neilson is well, & busy—the cotton season is 'most over—he is now putting in wheat. Mr McCown is going to leave Wildwood—& Press is going to take charge—I am sorry he won't be on this place, but he wished to go to himself. Aunt Phillis is going to stay with me till Christmas.

Little Daughter blotted my letter in this unsightly manner. Write every opportunity, & don't wait for me. All send love to your entire household. God-bless you. Your loving

Lute—

1. William Ottley (1874–76), son of John King Ottley and Ellen Gertrude Williams Ottley.

2. Adair Lyon Childress (b. 1873), son of John Whitsitt Childress Jr. and Mary Adair Lyon Childress.

ℊ℈

Dispensing with angry outbursts and desperate pleas, Lucy came to the sad realization that her sister's status as head of the family had been necessarily sacrificed on the altar of wedlock and wifely submission.

Lucy to Lizzie

Willow Cottage.
Dec: 13th/.74.

My dear Trot.

So many times have I wished to answer your last precious letter, which was such a delight to us all—but you know how <u>times</u> do fly by, & leave our <u>best</u> desires unaccomplished—then too I knew you would not be uneasy, for Bess was sending you letters & P.Cs every day or two—yet, my heart has been so filled with love & earnest yearnings for you, I could not feel satisfied, & <u>now</u>, with eagerness, I seize my pen to write some sort of a letter—long or short good or bad—to assure you of my constant thoughts of you, & appreciation of the deep love expressed for us in your letter. Such out-pourings of heart-affections are worth every thing in the world—because they inspire confidence, & beget similar emotions in others. It is <u>giving</u> & <u>receiving</u>—it is expanding, & elevating—it is <u>Christian</u>—this opening of the heart, & letting its warm feelings have full sway. This, I think, is the secret of your influence upon all (with a few exceptions) with whom you are thrown. Yes, your letter was read, & reread with warmer & warmer feelings—but oh! it left an <u>aching</u> for a vanished form & a sound of the dear dear voice.

'When will we meet again,'[1] is the haunting thought of my mind day after day—it is so <u>very</u> hard to realize that you are sure enough, & <u>for life</u>, separated from us. When we all gather around the fire-side—Mr Neilson, Jim, Cordele, Bess, the children & myself—my thoughts go out to <u>you</u>, the only absent one— my heart is unsatisfied—& I feel these reunions to be almost as much pain as pleasure—But I really must not <u>write</u> such thoughts, if I do <u>have</u> them—they are so one-sided, & selfish—don't let your dear, good, generous husband know that they are written. We all love him & feel that he is one of our family—& when our <u>better-spirits</u> have sway over our hearts, we are <u>glad</u> that <u>you</u> have found so congenial a mate—& rejoice with you in the possession of such a man's love. So no more repinings over the old ways & old days—we, as a family lived too long together anyhow! But oh! can't you & Maj come home Christmas? By this time the farm will have been rented, & you can come without let or hindrance! I wish to see Maj again—I am myself now, & can enjoy him. Bess is so in love with him—she talks so much about him—that we all wish he would come back soon. The letters which she received from you both were so sweet & gratifying. She certainly did enjoy her stay with you, & will be ready to go back at any time I think. We sent her trunks in town yesterday to Mr Shattuck's, & today she staid there for the first time. She was loth to leave us—& looked right doleful as we drove off, & left her. You know how my heart yearned over her—tho' I do think she is the most self-reliant-self-sufficient person I ever knew. She has had a great deal of business to attend to since her return, & she has acted like a woman of forty years experience. Jim was perfectly satisfied with her actions & manners throughout. I questioned him particularly. I was afraid she would get excited, & become haughty, abrupt & self-opinionated—but he says she did not. I told her that her Uncle Jim was much pleased with her—& she replied "Well, I did exactly like he told me about everything—I even said the very words he used—in fact my obedience was perfect." I sympathise with you in every feeling towards the dear girl—she is your child, & she loves you as a Mother—I can't think of your separation without tears. The part of your letter regarding her is too pathetic. We have had long talks of you, & she gave us the particulars of your little party, & of course we were interested in all. I do think it was so smart of you & Polly (Ah! excuse me, Lucinda) to cook all those nice cakes—hurrah! for you—always equal to emergencies! Bess says t'was the best tasting, as well as looking, party she ever attended. We enjoyed the nice candies you sent daughter very much, & thanked you for the remembrance.

—Well! now I'll tell you a little of my 'goings on'—I have actually made four visits, & been to church once—& little Jack was only eight weeks old yesterday! First, I went to see Mrs Ottley—we had lots of fun comparing babies—weighing them, & making them lie down side by side. They weighed within a half pound of each other—hers having the advantage. Left Jack there & Cordele, Louise & I went shopping, & to see Madie Childress—then came back got Jack & Aunt Phillis, & came home. My next trip was up to see Sister Mary—now you know that was a mutual pleasure!—little Jack does splendidly—never has colic while visiting, & the motion of the carriage puts him instantly to sleep. Then last Sunday-afternoon, we packed up bag & baggage, & went in to see Cousin Jennie—who had returned a few days before. Jim laughs, & calls us 'the McCallas'[2] because it takes two vehicles to transport our family from place to place. Last Friday again, we sallied forth, & went to Sister Annie's—& today, I was thrilled with excitement by leaving little Jack & going to church. Every-body greeted me as if I had been gone to foreign parts—& so many sweet inquiries were made for the boy! (Nobody calls him baby). I wish every day—almost every hour—you could see him. He grows so astonishingly—so fair & fat & no pretty hair—Aunt Phillis is as proud of him as I am almost—She sends her kind remembrance to you, & says you ought to be here to wash him now—he is such a nice big boy! Many think him better looking than daughter—he certainly is very bright—& has begun to notice, & coo & laugh! The colic troubles him only fittfully now— the periodicity is broken, & sometimes for days he is not in pain. Cordele is growing so fond of him—we tell Louise to look out for her nose—but 'Miss' grows solemn then, & declares, she can never love another child as she does her—(as if any body thought such a thing possible). Mr Neilson is proud of him but loves his daughter best—Jim says he is a bully-boy—but loves daughter best, & oh! spoils her to death. Jack's mother loves him every second of his little life, more, & more—but she does not love daughter any less. Aunt Phillis is the only one, who can unreservedly declare she loves him best! Louise had fever again one evening last week, & became so jaundiced, we took her in town to consult a physician— she was not much sick but so very yellow—Dr Matthews was gone on a great hunt—so we took her to Dr McCabe. He was so kind—so attentive, so interested in her case—& gave her medicines which have done her so much good that she is like a different child now. I know Dr M— will hate our going to him—but I don't care. Dr McCabe asked so pleasantly of you & Maj—paid you both nice compliments. Dr Matthews was so gushing over my coming out again, to day I was right 'shamed! Louise talks constantly of you both—we asked her the other day whose wife you were—she answered quickly "Watt's wife"—then begun hugging her doll Zelle, & grunting, & saying "I love my wife so well"—we presume she has seen some such performance—has she not? Of course she is all excitement about Christmas & Santa Claus—but I beg the family not to give her much, for she is getting so spoiled with presents, she hardly appreciates anything—That is so bad for a child. I must stop—tho' I feel I have only begun! Good-bye dear Brother & Sister—do write & come to see us very very soon. All send love. God bless you.

Your loving, Lucy—

NOTES

1. "Bonny Lizzie Bailie" appeared in James Maidment, ed., *Scottish Ballads* (1859) vol. 2, 16.

2. Anne Eliza Irion McCalla (1825–92) of Corinth was Lucy's cousin. She and her husband James Moore McCalla (1814–77) had ten children.

A good supply of servants, a few years' domestic experience, and a little extra money allowed Lucy to tackle the demands of holiday entertaining with confidence. She sent a report on the festive season to Lizzie, noting the fine dinners she had assembled and the Christmas gifts she had distributed to family, friends, and servants. Looking toward domestic arrangements for 1875, Lucy wrote excitedly of her success in securing Nancy as her dry nurse and Woos as her wet nurse. Like most southern women, Lucy assumed the primary role in breast-feeding her children but relished the freedom and status afforded by a wet nurse. Town life, it seemed, offered greater opportunities to create a new brand of femininity based on the old tenets of southern paternalism.

Lucy to Lizzie

Willow Cottage.
Jan 3rd/.75.

My darling Trot—

Altho' you have not answered my last letter, I excuse your silence, (because I know you have been as busy as any woman could be) & will obey the dictates of my heart, & write again, to assure you of my constant remembrance.

Christmas, & New Year festivities are over!—It is a season when all hearts long for re-union. We missed you more than we dared express—my throat was troubled with a <u>choking</u> sensation whenever any one mentioned your absence. Jim gave his usual present of a nice large turkey, & of course our dinner had to be on Sunday, for his & his friends accommodation. Sarah & <u>Nancy</u> & <u>Woos</u> gave us a <u>delightful</u> dinner—everything was prepared, & served elegantly! Sarah had splendid success with her cake—she baked <u>four</u>—two large lady-cakes, & two jelly—she feels confidence in her capacity now, & we have no failures. Nancy helped me with the icing—the weather was bad, & we did not succeed as well as we wished—but the cakes looked very well—decorated with violets & leaves. Shall I give you our bill of fare? A nice large fresh ham (baked beautifully)—fresh sausage—rich chicken-pie;—turkey—rice—potatoes (sweet & irish) okra-jelly (quince & apple) pickle (cucumber, artichoke, & sweet)—nice bread (<u>corn</u> & <u>flour</u>). Desert—delightful mince-pies—ambrosia-cake—(lady & jelly)—wine & coffee!

Of course Jim had his <u>same company</u> the <u>Lee brothers</u>[1]—Mr Moore & Col Abert declined, with <u>many regrets</u>! Bess & Lizzie Symons were the only lady-guests. All seemed to enjoy <u>themselves</u> & <u>the dinner</u>! I thought of last year, & of <u>another Lizzie</u>!

Next day we had the family. Bro James & family—Mr Symons & family—Mrs Hopkins & Annie[2]—& Mrs Eagar—Cousin Jennie had headache & could'ent come! We all were sorry, for <u>she</u> was to have been the <u>traveled</u> heroine of the

Butter mold with the initial "N" in the press. Irion Neilson Collection. *Courtesy of Collection of the Museum of Mississippi History, Mississippi Department of Archives and History.*

day—the lion-<u>ess</u>! However headache will come at any time—especially <u>Christ-mas</u>-times! So many times you were spoken of, & wished for.

Our dinner was a success again—instead of a turkey, we had a brace of baked fowls, & <u>turkey</u>-<u>hash</u>! Nannie said, she believed <u>my</u> dinner <u>tasted</u> better than Jim's. Sister Kate was extravagant in her praises—wished to know, if Lucy got up such a dinner all by herself. "Yes, with such a cook as Sarah & plenty of <u>rich</u> material, it is an easy matter enough to get up a good dinner"—<u>said I</u>! Aunt Phillis was in <u>quiet</u> ecstasies all the time, & petted, & spoilt little son to his heart's content. The children were all good, & played with the new toys in sweet harmony—Louise & Annie are devoted to each other—& <u>Lou</u> is real sweet these days. I forgot to tell you of Louise, & her <u>Christmas</u>-gifts. She had been told of old Santa Claus months before hand, & entered fully into the mysterious romance. She had a great desire for a "<u>Tis</u>-<u>mas</u>-<u>chee</u>"—having conceived the idea from a picture in her picture-book—her Father went to the woods, & selected a beautiful little cedar-tree, & secured it to a plank about a foot square (which I covered in appropriate <u>green</u>), & all her little presents were hung upon it. We decorated it with festoons of pop-corn, & gay colored candies. The gifts were not expensive or handsome, but pretty, & suitable to the times. There was a little candle-stick,

& blue-candle which Cordele gave her; a horse, a ball, & some beautiful crystals from Pa-pa; then I gave her a tin-sett—all kinds of little cups, & spoons, & bowls, & pans—each of these were hung up, & shone quite resplendently—then a lovely red-tin coffee-pot; Aunt Bessie sent a cooking-stove, & vessels—of course her's & little brother's stockings were filled with candies, & fruits—(also Thomas' & little Phillis'). Little Brother received two rattles, & almost a third!—(Mrs Eagar having bought one for him, but hearing him so well supplied, concluded not to bring it).

Now, if you could only have seen little daughter when she came in & saw the tree! She ran in, & began calling out "oh! Tis-mas-chee—Tis-ma-chee!" Then as we handed her the little gifts, she would say "oh! han-chy (thank-you!) Santa-Taus—han-chy!" Poor little heart was so joyous! It is worth while doing anything for her, she is so very appreciative! She was so taken up with her toys, she hardly ate, or slept any that day. I am more than ever determined, always to exert myself for the entertainment of my children on Christmas—for oh! what a sweet life-time remembrance it is. She appears so well now, & is like her old self—playful & happy—rarely ever a martyr! And oh! your Son!—if you could only see how he grows, & how pretty he is—& so smart too—taking notice of every thing, & laughing so good-naturedly! Aunt Phillis & Sarah went away last Tuesday—the latter will return for the year—I never saw anyone so loth to leave as Aunt Phillis—she loves the baby dearly, & oh was so good, & faithful in every discharge of duty. We made her quite rich in Christmas-gifts. Little Son gave her a nice poplin dress—Cordele a calico-dress—& Mr Neilson & Jim each a pair of stockings. Then we had her wages all ready for her, & she went off to town on a shopping expedition.

Nancy has moved over—& Mr & Mrs Abrams[3]—will come this week. We will have no other families on the place. I hope Mr Neilson can get plenty of men. I am glad to have Nancy & Woos—they will neither be in our employ regularly—but we can get them, whenever we wish. Nancy & John Abrams have rented the land, which Jim Merritt[4] had—, & Woos will do our washing—she will live in the room next Sarah's. I can go off on a frolic anytime, & leave little brother—since Sarah is to be my dry nurse, & Woos my wet-nurse—She has a beautiful baby—great, big, fat, girl—named Bessie! Nancy has cooked this week for us, & did it very well—Sarah returned this afternoon—glad enough to get home—she said.

Jim & Bess came out last night—Bess was full of interest—she & Lizzie have had a delightful week—of which she has, or will, tell you. I know it is not very pleasant for them to come out now—our home is such a nursery—but I am wonderfully selfish, & wish them to come every Saturday-night. Jim is very happy in having Bess with him—& she is so sweet to him. I think she feels a little worried with me being so taken up with babies—& feels constantly an aching void—which Auntie alone can fill. She showed me your last letter—written hurriedly &

with pencil. I hope you may get thro' all that worry of company, & breaking-up without being made seriously sick. Pray do take every possible care of yourself & Maj too. I am sorry you both have been sick—hope <u>rest</u> will restore you. You do right, to write to Bess—whether you have time for our letters—or not—she needs constant communion with you. God-grant you may not long be separated. Cordele has not been very well recently—I am going to send her out visiting—she has been so closely at home for so long a time. My health is perfect—tho' I am rather thin. Mr Neilson is fat, & saucy—sends his love to "<u>Watt</u> & <u>Trot</u>." Don't neglect to answer his little note enclosed in my last letter.

—Cousin Cornelia Benoit wishes the <u>pattern</u> of the rag-doll (Betsy Baker) which you made Louise—she promised Katie McCarthy[5] to make her one—have you an idea where it is? If so—don't fail to send it!—

Annie Bradford married a Mr Kennedy[6] of Knoxville Tenn, & has gone there to live. I could write much more but must kiss you both good-night hoping to see you very soon. God bless you—

Your loving Lute.

NOTES

1. William Hollinshead Lee and bookkeeper Alonzo Church Lee (1843–1910).

2. Annie Hopkins (b. ca. 1854), daughter of Dr. James White Hopkins and Catherine Cabot Neilson Hopkins.

3. Malinda "Woos" Barron married John Abrams on November 20, 1873. They had a daughter, Bessie (b. 1874).

4. Freed man James Merritt (b. ca. 1842), husband of Malissa Merritt (b. ca. 1838).

5. Katherine McCarthy (b. ca. 1871), daughter of Maurice McCarthy and Eliza Williams McCarthy.

6. Annie Bradford married grocer James Kennedy (b. ca. 1834) on December 31, 1874.

℘ଈ

In December 1874 Columbus's mayoral elections were in full swing, with Republican candidate and former Union general Beroth Bullard Eggleston (1818–91) pitted against Democratic candidate Joseph P. Billups (1827–87). Concerned that the free black vote would culminate in a victory for Eggleston, the white men of Columbus circulated a handbill entitled "Bread or No Bread." "The colored man who votes for Eggleston will, as certain as fate, vote meat and bread out of the mouths of his wife and children," it declared. "We will know who you are, and it will be brought up to you the first job of work you ask for." After Billups's victory, another circular was distributed listing the names of "worthy" and "unworthy" freed men.[1]

The bitter fight to regain Democratic control over Mississippi continued into 1875. Lucy reported on the political victories that edged the Democrats closer to power.

Lucy to Lizzie

Willow Cottage.
March 5th 75.

My darling Trot—

We have heard nothing from you, since you left Memphis, & it seems so very long—altho' in actual measurement of time, no more than a week. To tell you how very often we speak of, & wonder over 'the Watts,' is impossible. I worked myself up into a right anxious state of mind last week when those dreadful storms were raging every night—I feared you might be on the river—having heard no bad news thus far, I am comforted. Another fatal accident occurred about fifteen miles from here—another hurricane swept thro' the country, & killed a whole family—the house was entirely destroyed, & the bodies of four persons found several hundred yards from where the house stood—I believe the little boy was alive—but no hope of his recovery. The country people were perfectly panic-stricken—nor do I blame them—this is the fourth time, within the memory of present citizens, that these destructive hurricanes have taken almost the same track—verging each time a quarter of mile father south. I might as well be killed out-right, as to live in such dread, as I certainly would, if my home was near there. We were down at the bridge looking at the high water, when the wagon came by with the coffins in it. T'was quite a thrilling sight watching the people swimming—I could scarcely keep from screaming out—the water was higher than it has ever been, & ran down very slowly. If this was the case in our high-lands, what must it have been in your float country. O! Trot my heart sinks lower & lower whenever I think of that dreadful, awful, horrid country! If we should need each other—how could we ever come or go! I wish I did not love you & Major then my heart would'ent ache so, in thinking of you!

We are all well—the children growing. Jack so strong & big I can scarcely hold him. A week ago today Mr Neilson let us have the carriage—we went to Sister Annie's first, & told her we would be back to dine with her, & spend the afternoon—then we went calling—paying 'little visits,' as Louise called it. Went to see Mesdames Cox—Manning—King—Mitchell—Osborne,[2] Harris, & Mit Williams. Found everybody at home & very agreeable. They admired & praised Louise & Jack to my heart's content—so you may know I was well pleased. Every-body talked of you—& oh!ed and ah!ed over you going away &—"to-the-Missis-sippi-bottom at that"!! The afternoon was spent delightfully. Sister Kate, Annie & Bess came, & you may know we had a good time laughing, & rejoicing over "the Symons being in town." Lizzie has her parlor fixed up very nicely.

We had such a treat since you left in hearing Dr Munsey![3] Oh! Trot I wish you could have heard the lectures. The sermon you did hear—I forgot—you seem to have been gone so long—so long! I did not hear the lectures either—but Lizzie & Bess remembered as much as they could & told me! Bess has written you of our voting Sunday, & the result being in our favor! I never was more surprised! I thought of course we were an "insignificant minority"—Bess & Jim came out home with us, & we had a good laugh all to ourselves. We of course will not say a word out-side—for now we can afford to be magnanimous.

This week has been quiet in everything save the weather—we've had every variety of that—no visitors—excepting Mrs Barry & Elise—& they are the quietest people that could have come. Bess & Liz say they are coming out next week to stay all week with us. Sister Mary also is coming down on a general visit. I hope to have her some—it is my "plan"!

Had a small sight of Mesdames Ottley, Benoit & Eagar on Sunday—must see them again soon. Sister Eagar's glorious black eyes did some of their prettiest shining over the result of the voting Sunday! What a very volcanic nature her's is—& such a decorous out-side! If we felt as much as she does, what would we not do & say that was inelegant, undignified, rude! Ask Major!—

Cordele has not been well at all recently—last night, she took calomel—we have also a very formidable looking bottle of bark-bitters of which all partake when feeling the effects of East-wind. Little daughter says she "likes nice, good, bitters, herself." She certainly deserves credit for taking medicine well now. I wish you could hear all her sweet prattle—she talks constantly of you & 'Watt'—"loves you so much, & will be so dad when you 'tome home." During the high water, our calves went across the bridge, & came near drowning. Woos & Cordele were down there as it happened, in time to save them—they were so frightened that they ran up the other way (towards town) as hard as they could—very soon two of them returned—but it was late in the afternoon before the third (a bull) came bellowing down the road—little daughter heard him, & said "that's our calf. I tan't see him myself, but I know his woice." Of course we all laughed for it was so funny to see, & hear her—so earnest—so confident! The idea of knowing the voice of a calf!—I could fill pages of her sayings, & doings—but I won't—I shan't. I can scarcely keep from crying when, she talks of you!—

Did you think of me on the 3rd—my birthday—Mr Neilson hoped to have the Calash in readiness as a surprise—but of course Atwater[4] failed him—

I know you will certainly write us by every opportunity—long letters, when you can, telling every detail—short letters, notes, even a line, when time is limited—we must hear often from you—or I'll imagine every united misfortune has befallen you, away down in that miserable country. The good Lord protect you both—this is my despairing prayer every time I think of you. The servants are all well, & Nannie would have many messages, if she knew I was writing. Tell

Major we all do love him—altho we get <u>mad</u> sometimes! What would I do if I did not trust him, with true earnestness—he has one of my heart's dearest treasures! Good-night to both—your loving

Lute.

NOTES

1. Handbill reprinted in Nordhoff, *Cotton States,* 83.

2. Julia Manning (1844–1902) was a neighbor of Lucy's sister-in-law Catherine Cabot Neilson Hopkins. Fannie W. King (b. ca. 1832) was wife of Andrew W. King, and Emily E. Osborne (b. ca. 1830) was wife of Dr. Richard Russell Osborne (b. ca. 1823).

3. William Elbert Munsey (1833–77), well-known Methodist preacher from Virginia who extended his ministry to several states.

4. Carriage maker Alfred E. Atwater (b. 1837), husband of Mary Sherrod Atwater (1842–1932).

᙮ᢙ

It was Cordele's turn to write to Lizzie, and she produced an epistle on domestic happenings at Willow Cottage. "Our flowers are blooming so prettily, I do wish that I could send you a bouquet, but, I cant as you live so <u>far</u>, <u>far</u>, away," she wrote on March 15, 1875. "Our place does look so pretty now the green wheat, and the orchard is in full bloom. We did have very little snow, it looked like a big frost; so Babe did not have the pleasure of "noballing. John has actually done some gardening some of the seed are coming up. He is nearly done planting corn."

Lucy added a short postscript, dismissing Lizzie's suggestion that Bess should live with her.

Lucy to Lizzie

[Willow Cottage, March 15, 1875]

Dear Trot,

Cordele has written you one of her condensed letters, which tells all concerning the family—I will add a note just because I love to have some communion with you even if it is one-sided. Your letter was so eagerly read—it was so full & satisfactory. You are getting more content you say—& making your husband happy—that's right! You struggled when you thought there was a chance of escape, but when it proved in vain, it is sweet & wifely to give up, & make the best of everything. Yes, that country always had a charm for you—but I do hope you'll not live there all your life. I hang high hopes on <u>Maj</u>! He's a <u>restless</u> man!—he can't settle down quietly in the deep back-woods—the <u>world</u> is his home. He is content <u>now</u> because there's so much to be done, & just such <u>jobs</u> as he is now engaged in suits him! I know he has managed with consummate tact to get those negroes to yield as they have done. I do admire a man who can <u>carry all</u> before him!! But I don't admire the way you both are besieging Bessie to come down there to live! I think it a down-right shame, trying by every inducement possible to get her away from us. Don't grieve & worry yourself over her living such an unprotected life. I am sure, I don't see where-in she is so very unprotected—Columbus is as quiet, & harmless as the country, & there's her Uncle Jim always with her—besides the people with whom she associates are of the most sedate & proper! I don't know what she will do—I know she will go to see you, & I think that all well enough—but not to <u>live</u> down there—<u>absurd</u>—<u>prepostrous</u>!! I told her she did'ent have to make any such promise, or arrangement—she talked <u>mighty</u> good—but I expect she'll do as pleases her best—& I fear it will please her to go! Mr Neilson says he is going down there in the <u>Fall</u> certain—I tell Cordele she can go then too, & take Louise, but send her back with her Father. She was much pleased hearing of little Grace Stratton, & Virginia Belle—But of course she asked a hundred questions as to <u>who</u> they were, & not satisfied at their being some body else's girls, & <u>not yours</u>, she was ugly, & stuck out her mouth, & said "Auntie got no little girls"—She says "do bing Watt home."

I thought perhaps it was too <u>late</u> in the season for a <u>feather</u>-<u>bed</u>, & may be. Maj would be living some-where-else by <u>next</u> winter—but we'll send it & other things as soon as your next letter comes—I wrote to ask if you did not wish some other things sent too. I do not think the mattress is <u>worthy</u> of such a trip—but will consult Mr N—. Do write by every mail—God-bless you—

Lucy—

᪥ᘮ

As Lucy celebrated her fourth anniversary, she reaffirmed her belief that a happy marriage and home life were the fulfillment of a southern woman's highest mission. Dispensing housekeeping advice to her newly married sister, Lucy had finally settled into the role and responsibilities that went with occupying family headquarters.

In contrast, Lucy noted the messy divorce case of family friend Cornelia Williams Benoit and James W. Benoit. While Cornelia's grounds for divorcing her husband are unknown, such cases were rare and often accompanied by circumstances involving violence, alcoholism, or financial neglect. "The Capt is trying all of them so much," Cordele disclosed in a letter to Lizzie dated April 30, 1875. Seemingly unaffected by the sensation the case had caused, Cornelia nevertheless brought unwanted attention to her family, including her sister, Ellen Ottley. The strain of the case and the public embarrassment took their toll on Cornelia's brother-in-law John King Ottley.

"Miss Cornelia Benoit and Lou Ellen are boarding at Mr Shattucks now," noted Cordele. "Ellen does hate [it] so much, but they thought that Miss C troubles were preying on Col Ottley mind, so much that it was telling on his health. So the move was made on that account." Lucy or one of her descendants thought the matter so sensitive that she or he made an attempt to blacken out her references to the case in the following letter.

Lucy to Lizzie

Willow Cottage.

April 20th/.75.

My darling Trot—

Your dear, sweet letter of the 13th came today, & oh! how precious was each word. You were right when you guessed you were thought of, & wished-for, on that anniversary-day—yes! indeed you were—all the time! We had a nice dinner, & our friends Col & Mrs Ottley & Mrs Benoit were with us to enjoy it, & wish us 'many happy returns.' Col.'s toast was that "we might have an hundred-returns, & a dozen children." Miss Ellen made him halve the number of children, & then we all drank with much merriment. We had invited Dr, & Mrs Gus Lyon,[1] but do you know they have left Columbus? Yes, gone to Shrevesport to settle. Are'ent you sorry? We can illy spare such people from our church, & community. I was much disappointed in not having them dine with us for a last time—but Dr was away, & Mrs Lyon was busy with her preparations to return home on a visit, & then go to her husband. All who know her are in love with her, & grieve over her departure—I am right glad now that I did not have the opportunity of know- ing her better—my heart aches so to say "good-bye" to those I love. It had been a long time since the Ottleys & Benoit's had dined with us, & they have been in such trouble about that divorce-case—& now it was purposely crowded out of this last court, & is left over for the next—three more weary months. Cousin Cornelia has concluded to take Lou-Ellen & go to St Louis as soon as she can. She is quite cheerful—more so than Mrs Ottley. They have all been subjected to some very disagreeable examinations & cross-examinations—poor Mrs Eager was on the witness-stand from 9 o'clock A.M.—until 1 o'clock P.M.—She stood the trying ordeal finely, & was much complimented upon the answers she gave— so pointed, so concise, & of course true. The examination was carried on in the bank, & not the court-room. Mrs Ottley too was questioned at length. The mean- ness of the lawyers—Beck Humphries & Bev: Matthews[2]—is noticeable in every thing—they are stirring up the events of the dead past & trying to prove things derogatory to Col O's character—this comes so hard on the old gentleman, it will put him in the grave, if they persist in so doing. Miss Ellen is doubly tender & lov- ing to him. She is hardly like herself—more abstracted, more humble than I ever expected to see—so sweet tho' & loving. She feels the mortification of the whole affair much more than Cous Cornelia. Our anniversary being on Tuesday—Mrs Eager, Lou Ellen, Johnnie nor Charlie came—all went to school. Mrs Eager however came out the Sunday before—& we had a good talk—then on Friday-evening she came again, & brought Lou-Ellen, & little <u>Laura</u>—you can imagine Louise's delight! Next day was lovely, & we all (except <u>Jack</u>) took a <u>long walk</u>. Over the bridge, along the pretty clean, grassy road by "Tom Vaughan's,"[3] then deep in the <u>budding</u>, <u>flowering</u> woods, taking the path <u>you</u> love, leading to Eggleston's Spring. I thought of, & wished for you every step of the way—if you could only have seen the children, Laura & Louise, running hither & thither picking violets, daisies, & hare-bells—they were so excited—so joyous—so determined not to leave <u>one</u> poor little flower. I thought we never would get them along—but we did finally reach the Spring, & then we went to the Pic-nic-ground, & how vividly last year's pleasures were reviewed—<u>then</u> I had <u>you</u>! <u>Now</u>!—but never mind!

Lou-Ellen is certainly a lovely girl—both in face, form, & manners—she did so enjoy <u>everything</u>, & was bright, & laughing. Mrs Eager was <u>blissful</u>. She & little Laura returned to town that P.M.—but Lou-Ellen staid until the next morning—when Mr Neilson & I took her in town in our <u>pretty new</u> carriage! I wish you could see it, & have a ride—the horses carry it so nicely, & the whole turn-out is pleasant to the eyes.

Bessie has always been a dear, sweet girl to me, but I do know this Spring she has just surpassed everything—she sent North, & got me a beautiful piece of silk (just like your wedding-dress) to make me a basque, & overskirt—then came out, & worked like a <u>slave</u> for a <u>whole</u> week—making me two as handsome skirts—(one silk & the other alpaca) as you ever saw—all kilt-plaited—shirred puffs, & ruffles, & all sorts of new-fashioned trimmings. I was going to have <u>Beck</u> Barry to help me, but she got a school up in the neighborhood of Bro James', & of course she could'ent come—so Bess took the burden, & <u>well</u> she bore it—Mrs Willeford fitted the basque, & overskirt, & I made them; & wore the suit last Sunday—my friends all complimented it, & we were quite satisfied with the <u>style</u> ourselves. Bess, & Col Abert came out to dinner with us—we had a pleasant time, & then in the afternoon, the Col proposed to take Bess up to see <u>Sister Mary</u>, & take tea & come back by moon-light—he had a beautiful horse & buggy—off they went—& did'ent return until '<u>Monday</u>-night by <u>candle</u>-<u>light</u>'—now was'ent that a frolic?—they went all around the country to Wildwood, to Beck's school &c.

We've had Sister Mary & the little girls to spend a week with us, then Cordele went home with them & staid <u>two</u> weeks. Cousin Jennie & Lizzie have been out too—so you see we have had plenty of company. Mrs Whitfield, Capt & Mrs Field brought little Harris[4] to take Louise to ride—they went to the woods, & let the little folks get out—pick flowers & <u>eat</u> cake—when they came back little Harris came up the walk with Louise's hand in one of his, & a big piece of <u>corn-bread</u>

in the other! How we all laughed—Mrs Field, with great impressment, assured me Louise had behaved like a <u>perfect little lady</u>! They have been so sociable, I am going to see them soon, & take both children.

Louise's health now seems perfect—& our boy Jack is as fine a specimen of babyhood as you ever saw—can sit alone well, & two little teeth are nearly thro'—he is never sick. Bess will write you of the kind invitation she had from a friend of her Father's, Mr Thos Miller,[5] to visit Mobile—I expect she will go next week. Jim's health is very good—he does'ent come out very regularly, & I do so miss his visits.—

I am glad to hear of any details of your home-life—the new stove, & bread-making <u>thrills</u> me with interest, & I only wish I was near to give you the benefit of my experience. I know you will learn soon to make as good bread as I do, but still I might help you some—as to cake baking—I succeed with that <u>Snow-ball</u>-receipt admirably—& that is the <u>only</u> one I ever try—have you it? I did as you advised & got <u>crushed-sugar</u>, & make beautiful cake since—Mr Neilson's birthday cake was so nice—we iced it too.

I am going to spend next <u>Friday</u> & <u>night</u> with Cousin Jennie—then Saturday I've promised Mrs Ottley. I expect to enjoy my visit very much—will have a musical-treat at Cous George's—<u>he</u> Bess & Jennie. I will leave Louise at home with her Papa, & <u>Nela</u>—how I wish you could see her playing with <u>roses</u>—so sweet, so refined—such pretty talking—says tell "Auntie & Watt '<u>tome</u> home, & she will give then some "<u>pitty woses</u>."["] We all long for you & Maj—<u>when will you come</u>?

I am glad Maj is getting on well with his plantation—, & your garden I am interested in. Mr Neilson's crop is all planted, & looks like a well-kept garden— our garden <u>proper</u> has had more attention this Spring than ever before—I hope we may have nice vegetables—we've had Sholottes, radishes, & lettuce.

Nancy says do write something of the <u>old</u> friends down there—Woos' says she is <u>mad with you yet</u>—says you write like you are too happy & content down that <u>beloved</u> swamp. Her baby is right fretful with teething & thrush—had one little tooth—beat Jack. Sarah is well, & good. Kiss Maj for us all, & write soon to your loving Lute.

Notes

1. Dr. Aurelius Augustin Lyon married Susan Winter (b. 1849) in 1874.
2. Beverly Matthews (b. ca. 1823) and William Washington Humphries Jr. (1841–1904).
3. Farm laborer Tom Vaughn (b. ca. 1836).
4. Mary Whitfield (ca. 1841–1924), wife of farmer George Whitfield (ca. 1822–1904); farmer Joseph Harris Field (1840–1915), his wife Sarah J. Field (b. ca. 1849) and their son, Joseph Harris Field Jr. (b. ca. 1873). The Whitfields and Fields were neighbors.

5. Thomas Porter Miller (1808–93), of Mobile, Alabama, owner of banking house Thomas P. Miller and Co. and husband of Eliza Emma Williams Miller (1820–1917).

ço

Promising crops were destroyed when Columbus was hit by a severe hailstorm in April 1875. "I never saw such a sight in my life," declared Cordele in a letter to Lizzie dated April 30. "Some of the hailstone were as large as a turkey egg; drifted at the end of the gallery where the gutter is. Bro John said he thought there was about ten bushels in a pile; it staid on the ground two hours. The wheat is ruined, and the fruit is all beaten off; the trees, are stripped of their leaves, and our garden is just ruined. My roses bushes are torned to pieces, but we are thankful that our lives are spared. It came when the negroes were eating dinner, and the horses were all in their stables."

As the days grew longer and warmer, the Irion family readied their calash and paid over a dozen visits to kinfolks and friends. While visiting was a mix of duty and pleasure, Lucy and John accepted it as a necessary way to reaffirm their family's reputation and standing. So too was their participation in Memorial Day activities, a tradition that originated in Columbus and held special significance to its citizens.

Lucy to Lizzie

Willow Cottage—
May 12th '75

My dear dear Trot.

I hope before this, you have received Cordele's letter, one from me, & a postal, which I wrote last week. I do not wish a week to pass without your hearing from one, or the other of us—but last week, beside the usual duties of every-day life, we had an opportunity of returning our calls—(some made a year ago)—which we did, with much pleasure. We paid sixteen—that was doing very well for us— we are not very fashionable, & indeed! we had been so long in going to see our friends, we felt like being social—then we took the children to a good many places—where we had been especially asked so to do—& of course the ohs! & ahs! over them consumed time. Every body groans & moans over your fate—& really I do think it is a melancholy one—buried alive!—oh! horrors of all horrors!! Where do you suppose Mr & Mrs H. S. Taylor have perched themselves to roost, at this time of life?—why! a way up on the highest, most-un-get-at able of the Montevallo-hills—the place where Nathan Whitfield[1] used to own. I was afraid to trust any one else to drive our precious carriage-full, but Mr Neilson, & he very considerately sympathised with my uneasiness, & one bright pleasant afternoon we set out—Cordele, Louise, Mr Neilson on front seat of Calash—Sarah, Jack,

& myself on the back, & Edward on 'Nealy' as an outrider. After much agitation on my part, for fear something might happen to us in going over the hills & hollows, we arrived safely, found Sister Taylor at home, & mighty glad to see us! Oh! how we talked & talked! She is so mad with you yet about marrying— & oh! her groans & moans are deepest, & loudest of all over your going to the bottom! She sent more messages than I could ever write! Our next call was on Sister Randolph[2] (I should say 'Aunt Bland')—She was much gratified by Johnnie's bringing his family at last (broad 'a') to see her, & we paid a long, & delightful visit—little Virginia[3] showed daughter all her 'sings,' & played with Jack so funny he laughed long, & loud—indeed! our little folks left very reluctantly. Then we went to see the Shaeffer's—Charles' new wife (Alice Witherspoon[4]—Cordele wrote you of their marriage)—she appeared very sweetly—the parlor was filled with callers, & Alice thought she certainly was in the whirl & vortex of fashionable life (?)[5] Bro & Sister Shaeffer are mighty well pleased with Charlie's choice, & were pleased by our calling so promptly.—don't get scared I am not going to give a detailed account of all the other thirteen visits we made—no! these were the work of an afternoon—Mr Neilson did not honor us with his presence on the next day's trip! We started early called 'till noon—dined at Sister Annie's—then went out again in the afternoon. No visit was more enjoyed than the one to Fannie Richards[6]—she is certainly a lovely woman—so true—so genuinely friendly. She made many inquiries of you—her baby is a beauty, & delights her anxious heart in being healthy.

Had a real nursery time up at Mrs Harris Field's—she & Capt Field, & even the statuesque Mrs Whitfield declare Jack the most splendid of boys—their little girl[7] is small & lady-like—just a good mouthful for Jack—we had serious fears of his devouring her—he is a very demonstrative fellow. Louise & Harry love each other dearly, & play so prettily together. Mrs Field says she is coming out to spend the day with us sometime.

Sister Annie has been so violently ill I did not think she could live—but she is much better now—tho' far from being in a safe condition—John Furniss is with her now. Bess is in Mobile yet, & is having a delightful time—Mr Thomas P. Miller is an old friend of bro Mc, & a distant relative of Uncle Hayden's.[8] Cordele says she remembers hearing Bro Mc speak of him. Well! it seemed he made inquiries of the family—learned of Bess' being the only one left, & wrote her a most pressing invitation to come, & make them a visit—so as they might know her—that he cherished so fond a recollection of her Grand-Father, Father, & Mother, he wished to know their child. You know it is polite to accept an invitation when it is given, if you are going to do so at all—so we thought it best & most polite for Bess to go right away—then too all her Spring out-fit was nice, new, & very stylish—so off she went, & will not return until about the 20th—tis a pleasant episode & I hope she will please her new friends & relatives.

Now I have to record an event which shocked, & for the time, paralyzied the whole place—on Tuesday 11th at noon—our black boys & young men, all went down to the creek to bathe—we had settled ourselves for our naps, when the cry of distress was given—"<u>Charles</u> is <u>drowned</u>"!!⁹ Mr Neilson ran with all his might, but oh! too late—the poor fellow had sunk to rise no more! He could not swim, & very recklessly jumped into a very deep place, & was swept in the swift current—one of the boys (William Billips)¹⁰ risked his life for him—caught hold of him—but in his struggles they both sank twice—William barely escaped. They went right to searching for the body but have not yet recovered it. Poor Charles! I know you will grieve over the poor simple negro as we do—all of his life (—with the exception of a few years) has been spent with us—every event of his baby-hood, & childhood comes to mind—& he was so faithful, as a man, in the dis-charge of his duty. Mr Neilson says he was as steady as an old man, & he certainly will be missed in the yard, & kitchen. Then it is so pitiful to think no one could help him—there right with his friends he could not be saved—& now his poor body cannot be found for decent burial. Mr Neilson has done everything that can be done, & will now have to wait until it rises. We sent Edward right away to tell poor Pheobe, & Martha—Press came down immediately with Ed, & helped all he could. His simple account of <u>how</u> the dreadful announcement was received, was really pathetic. Said he was in the field working, when all of a sudden he heard women's voices, & he <u>knowd</u>, they were in distress—then the horn began blow-ing loud, & he pitched off as hard as he could to see what was the matter—he thought Pheobe had fallen in a fit, for he left he[r] not feeling well—but before he got to the house he met Ed—who told him all! Poor Charles! I don't think had an enemy in the world—I never saw negroes so subdued, so expressive of feeling in my life. Mr Neilson sent Pheobe word, he would do all he could to recover the body, & send her word when to come. Nancy & Woos are weighed down with the thought of his unprepared state of heart. Woos' first exclamation was "oh! his poor soul—his poor soul—the Lord have mercy"! I never knew two women more burdened by the weight of souls in my life, than Nannie & Woos—their zeal is quite a rebuke to me, who am too indifferent. I have felt so awed,—so shocked by this dreadful event, I feel as frightened as a child, & cling foolishly to the strong arm of my dear, loving husband. He does'ent laugh at me, & call me foolish & silly & nervous—but tenderly protects me. What would become of me without him! Oh! I know I am putting my trust too much on him—I love, & I tremble!—I am so surrounded with love & blessings, I try to be grateful, & to love the Giver more & more—but if he should hide his smiling face, would I receive his chastening in the right spirit. I do miss you so—I long for <u>soul</u>-talks—such as cannot be written—

On Memorial-day we went to the Cemetery & decorated our grave, as usual, in pure white flowers—as I bent over it, my tears <u>rained</u> down upon it, but was my grief for the dear dead, no! the Lord forgive me, I was crying for you. Mr Neilson scolds me every time I write you a letter—he begs that I shall leave off such a wailing strain, & write cheerfully—says he knows Maj Watt hates to see my letters come in the house—but I tell him, to let me alone, & leave me to my complaints, Maj don't care—he knows I'm a spoilt child, & will only laugh, & do as he pleases! Maj knows too I love & honor & trust him—& all my complaints are selfish—but he don't blame me, for having loved you, he can sympathise. But don't stay down there too long—don't run any risk either of you—your health & lives are too precious to tamper with—then don't you Trot stay there again all alone—come up to Memphis with Maj & go out to see the Nesbitts—or else go out to the Point, & visit your friends there—or you might happen to think of Columbus! Do you remember where such a locality is?

There now! I did'ent intend to say one word about your coming home—but I have, & what is writ is writ—

Our garden is coming out some since the hail destroyed it—tho' it is a long time to wait for vegetables—Mr Neilson had to reap his wheat, & cure it for provender for his stock—we hope the Wildwood-farm will yield enough for our bread. Cordele is in high feather about her dairy, & poultry, both are doing well. Such nice golden butter—& such good cool clabber—are quite apetizing. We have nothing for our table, scarcely—but plenty of good bread, butter & milk. Our Spring-sewing lies mountain high—"when shall I ever get thro',"[11] is a question which suggests itself every-day. Aunt Phillis has been here this week, & I've had the house thoroughly cleaned—that's one big job off heart, & hand.

Louise & Jack are well, but each has light colds, in spite of all my care—the weather is so changeable. Jack has two teeth, & can almost crawl—will do so right away, when divested of long skirts—we are all impatient to see him in short-clothes—you would love him now—he is so bright, & merry. I wish you could see Louise with her new-Spring-hat on—so airy—so much of woman-nature expressed in each toss of her head. Lizzie Symons has been our milliner—Mr Bluhm brought on nice bonnets, & beautiful flowers, & I tell you, they have sold readily—I think our bonnets are very pretty & stylish.

Jim has not been well—looks badly—I wish he would come home, & rest awhile—but he won't. There has been a spelling-match in town—our little friend Virgie Ayers won one of the prizes—also a concert, & supper—none of which we attended.

Old Maj Powell is dead—has been sick for a long time. Our friend Mrs E.P. Odeneal is in very bad health—they fear she has heart-disease—Mrs Field is no better, & will not return to Mississippi until Fall. I believe I wrote you that Cos Cornelia Benoit was now boarding at Mr Shattuck's—this has occasioned so much talk, & such hard things said of Col & Mrs Ottley—I knew it would. Capt B—won't allow Lou Ellen to go to St Louis. All the family connection are well—excepting Sister Annie. Good-bye my darling old Bro & Sister—heaven protect you both. Write often, & don't wait for <u>Mother</u> Lucy I. N—

Notes

1. Farmer Nathan William Whitfield (1849–1918), husband of Laura Eloise Pickett Whitfield (b. 1851).

2. Elizabeth Bland Beverly Randolph (1804–80), wife of Capt. Edward Brett Randolph (1792–1848). The Randolphs had been friends and neighbors of John Abert Neilson's father, William Walker Neilson (1792–1869), and William's first wife, Sarah Helena Frazier Neilson (1798–1835).

3. Virginia Sherman (1865–88), great-granddaughter of Elizabeth Bland Beverly Randolph.

4. Bookkeeper Charles A. Shaeffer (1844–1941) and Alice Eugenia Smith Witherspoon Shaeffer (1844–1929).

5. Maria Susana Cummins, *The Lamplighter* (1854); see 1855 edition, 442.

6. Sarah Frances Evans Richards (1841–1925), wife of merchant William Coolidge Richards (1828–1916). The couple had a daughter, Anna Elizabeth Richards (1874–1951).

7. Bate Field (b. ca. 1875), daughter of Joseph Harris Field and Sarah J. Field.

8. James Hayden (1788–1863), husband of Mary Parthenia Irion Hayden (1794–1860). Mary was the sister of Lucy's father, McKinney F. Irion (1792–1866).

9. Charles had worked as a servant for the Irion family for several years.

10. Farm laborer William Billups Jr. (b. ca. 1854), son of William Billups (b. ca. 1818) and Matilda Billups (b. ca. 1826).

11. Lucy was perhaps paraphrasing "Oh, Heaven, sweet Heaven, when shall I see? / When shall I ever get there?," from a hymn; see Pollard, *Black Diamonds,* 34.

Bess seized upon any opportunity to visit her Aunt Lizzie, and Lucy lamented her inability to join them for a "good long talk."

Lucy to Lizzie

Willow Cottage—
June 20th '75

Trot, you sweet old story-teller, you know <u>well</u>, you did not write me any more letters or P.C— than I received—no, you may as well own-up to have <u>neglected</u> that little duty—it is so easy to <u>think</u> letters, but quite another thing to commit them to paper. I don't want you to imagine my feelings were hurt to the depth of <u>doubting</u> your love, & interest,—such a thought of <u>you</u>, I don't think, can ever even float thro' my brain, much less abide there long enough to make my heart ache in sympathy! Dear old Trotwood! What an insaitiable heart mine would be, to wish <u>more</u> evidence of your sweet, gushing <u>satisfying</u> love! I am a trustful woman, & am never unhappy for lack of faith in those of my friends, who are true & tried. Of course, I am <u>fussy</u>, about <u>you</u> especially. I don't much care if I am either—my dear old earnest, gentle husband disapproves of my '<u>carryings</u> on,' & shakes his wise head, but then you know I can scold at him & tell him 'I <u>will</u> fuss as much as I please.' He thinks me really very disagreeable on that one (?) subject—yet, if I was altogether <u>sweet</u>—would'ent too much sweetness pall on his taste—there's nothing more useful in its' way, than family-<u>spice</u>!

This is Sunday-night—we've been to church & S.School today—In S.School met friends, & interchanged pleasant greetings then a <u>colony</u> of us Presbyterian-women, headed by Mr Neilson, went over to the Methodist-church to hear Mr Harrison[1] preach a Commencement sermon to Capt Belsher's[2] boys. The discourse itself was as fine a one, as I ever heard; lacked only <u>one</u> thing of being eloquent. Mr Cason preaches his <u>last</u> sermon, as Pastor of the Baptist-church, to night. We took Louise again today—& sat in the pew with '<u>little</u> Laura'— of course they were both delighted, & had a pleasant time all during services, exchanging <u>hats</u>, fans & handkerchiefs. They were <u>fidgety</u> but quiet.

—Louise's birthday day will soon be here—she talks a great deal about it, & tells who of her numerous "fy-<u>ends</u>" she's going to invite, & what we will give them to eat. She wishes me to make her a nice-big-white-cake like Pa-pa's "<u>birf</u>-day." The other day she was in a real narrating way—said she was going to have a 'birf-day'—<u>and</u> she was going to town, & ask Mammie <u>Liss</u> to come out, & spend the day—& then she would go to the side-board, & get out a little <u>duck</u>, & <u>poke</u> it at Mammie-Liss, & she would say "Why! Louise"! Her imagination runs wild with her. Mr Neilson fears she will learn to tell <u>real</u> stories. So many times do I wish for you to hear, & <u>see</u> her—for she's a little <u>actress</u>, & throws great spirit into everything she says. Bess don't enjoy her as you would, she is thinking too constantly of the <u>clouds</u> which <u>will</u> come, to delight in the present sunshine—but you would bask in each little thread of brightness. You know one must take smiles & tears very often, <u>together</u>, in this life. Louise frequently asks me to tell her about "the old <u>mad fog</u>" which Auntie used to tell. I do the best my imitative powers can, but am never successful in giving sufficient emphasis to "the old mad <u>fog's</u>" angry denunciation of the <u>bad</u> "<u>little fog</u> that would'ent mind his ma-ma"!!! She undertook to tell it herself one day, & began by saying—"Well! one time there was a little <u>fog</u>, & he had a good Papa & Mama & <u>Auntie</u> & <u>Watt</u>"—at <u>this</u> unexpected turn I laughed out-right, & she stopped short. It is funny to see Jack playing with her—he is as fond of frolic as any child three years old—& mercy! what a great strong vigorous fellow he is—just rushes <u>ahead</u> & <u>will</u> have his own way, & takes all the play-things away from Sister—but if she cries, is ready to give the <u>widest</u>-mouth kisses & make friends.

What good long talks you & Bess can have. I told her to tell you everything—& she is a pretty good person to enter into details, <u>these</u> days. I think I have broken her into the habit. What would I not give to <u>hear</u> you talk. Cordele says she never expects to see you again—but I tell her, I look for you confidently next Fall to make a <u>long visit</u>. Bess said she intended to have Maj's promise recorded in 'black & white' to that effect—hope she will have her way. And Cousin <u>Mary</u> is married![3]—<u>she</u>, who declared nine months ago, she could not go thro' what <u>you</u> did for any man!—did'ent she encounter worse opposition? Bess was so sweet in writing us <u>all</u> about the plans & arrangements—we were very much obliged to her—now <u>you</u> must write what you think of her <u>man</u>! Bess declares you & Maj are <u>worse</u> in love than ever. Wish I could see & <u>hear</u> Maj—I love him & am so entertained by him. Tell him I know he would want to steal <u>Jack</u> now if he could see him. Hope you found everything getting on well when you returned home. Hope Daught is feeling better—wonder when I will ever know her <u>for myself</u>. I <u>love</u> her <u>spiritually</u> now, but I am so much of the '<u>earth-earthy</u>,'[4] bodily-presence is quite essential to my happiness. Mr Neilson said with so much earnestness, the other day, I do <u>wish</u> I <u>could</u> go down to see Maj & his <u>crop</u> right now! I fear he might get in the <u>notion</u> of moving, if he did. Our wheat, & oats turned out well, & we are having such seasonable rains, the corn looks beautifully—we look for easier times next year. I suppose your garden is perfection—we are having pretty good vegetables now, & are getting up pickles, putting up jam, jellies &c for the winter. Cordele is in her glory—there was such quantities of whortle-berries this season, we made <u>jam</u> of them instead [of] black-berries—Cordele has put up some twelve or fifteen jars of jam—small fruit jars. Then she made some nice jelly—& if the <u>peaches</u> will only turn out well, we will get a new supply of jars, & have a fine winter-supply. Mr Neilson believes in <u>fruits</u>, & <u>sweets</u>—I'm so glad too! Cordele is spending the week in town, she said she would be sure to write to Bess this week, & she will tell all the <u>current</u>-news. I know nothing—our friends come to see us quite frequently—but we go out very little—too much <u>farmers</u> for much visiting! We are getting our sewing done—all our things are off hand, & the children's dresses seem light work. Do write to us our dear old Darlings—I will write Bess soon. All the 'colords' would send messages, if they knew I was writing. Kiss each other, & all for us—God bless you.

Your loving Lute.

I did not say a word of Jim—because I fail to see him yesterday—he went on a trip down to Mr Ellis' Saturday, & staid all night. He is well tho', & as cheerful as could be expected for a poor forlorn <u>Uncle</u> with <u>no</u> neice to cheer him. Write long letters if you can,—tho' <u>short</u> ones & even P.C— are <u>not</u> scorned.

NOTES

1. Rev. W. S. Harrison was pastor of the Columbus First Methodist Church (1874–75).

2. Private-school teacher Thaddeus C. Belsher (1832–1901), husband of Mary Elizabeth Belsher (1847–1920).

3. Mary Nesbitt married Charles Davis on June 7, 1875.

4. 1 Cor. 15:47.

 ৯৯

By October 1875 the Democratic Party's campaign to overthrow Republican rule in Mississippi was in full swing. In actions known as the Mississippi Plan, white southerners used ritualized violence and intimidation to wrestle back the political control they had lost after the war, terrorizing African Americans in their homes in an attempt to destroy their claims to citizenship. The days of cloaked threats, such as those used in the mayoral election of December 1874, were over. Henry Buchanan Whitfield recalled that the white men of Columbus purchased cannons, which "were frequently fired by day and at night; were carried to different places in the county where there was to be public speaking, or gatherings, and often fired on the route."

Columbus's white Democratic supporters rallied in the streets on the eve of the state election. Word spread that an old shed and a stable were on fire in different parts of the town, and the crowd reacted violently. Robert Gleed (1836–1916), a former slave, the first African American city councilman, the first African American senator (1870–76) from Lowndes County, and founding director of the first African American bank in Columbus, was "charged with inciting the negroes to fire the town." The ensuing violence resulted in the deaths of four African Americans.

Not surprising, the Democratic Party swept to a resounding victory the next day. "Where the Republicans should have received fully twelve hundred (1200) votes, there were only <u>seventeen</u> (17) regular tickets voted on the day of election!!" noted Whitfield. By 1876 the Republican Party held only three southern states—Florida, South Carolina, and Louisiana. The result culminated in a flurry of courtside activity as white men threw themselves into the task of testing and overturning the preceding work of Republican lawmakers to the detriment of African Americans, workers, and women.[1]

As the violence unfolded, Lucy was away from home assisting her sister-in-law Mary Bruce Barry Neilson with the birth of her daughter Catherine Sims Neilson (1875–1960).

Lucy to Lizzie

Home—Nov: 5th '75

My dear, darling Trot—

It has been a long time since your welcome letter came, but I have had good excuses for not writing. I begun a letter long ago in Oct, but here it lies unfinished—so I will just tear it up, & begin anew, hoping this time to be more connected, & get this ready for the mail. We have been greatly exercised this week on account of the election—but things have quieted now, & we hope for peace. Last Monday-night was one of tumult, & might have been very disastrous, both as to life & property, if the white-men had not stood up for their rights, & made the negroes & carpet-baggers afraid. The town was set on fire in <u>fourteen</u> different places <u>at once</u>, & the negro-military company was out <u>in arms halting</u> passers-by—the whites then arose in their might, & ordered out the <u>fire</u> companies, & military too—then the shooting begun—the officers of the black-company were arrested, & put in the calaboos, & three others were killed, & the officers of the <u>white</u> company went to Sherriff Lewis, & told him if there was another house set on fire, <u>he</u> would have to <u>swing</u> as high as Haaman[2]—after this very <u>mysteriously</u>, & very quickly <u>all</u> the fires were put out even before the companies could get to them. No damage was done further than the burning of a few out-buildings. The negro Gleed could not be found—the men went to his house, & as they could find neither he nor his wife, they tore his house up considerably, & broke the furniture, for this, all cool-headed people are sorry—as they could not find him, they ought not have injured his property—that was <u>beneath</u> the party—but oh! how infuriated they were—& with, <u>just cause</u>, the Lord knows. We feel thankful that all is quiet now—but I fear the revenge of the <u>leaders</u> will yet be felt—I do not fear the negro left to himself. You never saw such consternation as prevails even yet—some have taken to the woods & are afraid to return. We hear that all went Democratic—but very probably Ames[3] will order another election. We have thought of, wished for, & prayed for you & Maj all the time. Does'ent it seem a long time before you will come?

I was away from <u>home</u>, during all the excitement—up at Sister Mary's helping to attend to her, & her little <u>baby</u>-girl! I suffered most <u>intensely</u> day awake all night Tuesday-night imagining ten thousand horrors—the canon was firing every fifteen minutes, & that did not help to quiet me. Next morning brother James brought me home—where I found all my precious ones safe, & well. I had left Louise with her Papa, & Nela. I know you would have <u>whipped</u> me for being so miserable—but indeed! I could not help it. Sister Mary was doing very well, & the <u>little Kate</u> is quite pretty, & bright, & <u>good</u>. I hope to go to see her again next week, & take Bess. They are so anxious to have a visit from her. Oh! you don't know how we have enjoyed <u>Bess</u>—I wish you could see how <u>splendidly dashing</u>

she looks—people open their eyes, & compliment her so heartily—I know they just can't help so expressing themselves. Bun came home with her & spent a week—he is sweeter, & lovelier than ever. You know I could'ent enjoy him much last year, but this time, I allowed nothing to keep me from him. He has written me a beautiful letter since his return—& Corrie has written too. Poor child! she is in bad health has had chills, & they finally brought on miscarriage. Her little <u>boy</u> lived only a few hours. She wrote cheerfully tho & said she hoped to be out in a few days.

Bess has been gone a week, & I feel like it had been a month. Mr Neilson saw her for a few moments Wednesday, & she said she had been <u>scared to death</u> by all this excitement—I was so sorry for her, in my mind, for you know how much afraid she's always been of <u>negro-fusses</u>. I hope she & Jim may come out tomorrow-night—for I do wish to see them so much.

Little Jack has had no chills now for three weeks—but I have to watch him constantly—he is teething all the time—does not walk yet—nor is he inclined— so cautious & so <u>fat</u>. He is said to be much better looking than Louise—& his eyes are beautiful. Large <u>changeable hazel-gray</u>—Louise is looking splendidly—so fat, & rosy. I wish for you every day to hear her talk. She is now in a great notion of visiting you—stopping on the way in Memphis, & putting up at <u>the Peabody</u>.[4] Any one to hear her talk of cars, & hotels, & omnibusses would imagine her quite traveled. She was devoted to Bun, & he appreciated her attachment, & <u>wrote</u> so touchingly of it. I don't know whether Mrs Miller's prophecy will ever come to pass, or not—that you will love Jack better than her, but she certainly is quite interesting.

Jack is beginning to show boyish shyness already—he understands every word that is said to him & not <u>one</u> syllable will he try to say. When he sees a dog, he will say <u>bow-wow</u>—& and a pig—he will grunt—"<u>umph umph</u>" a horse, he will say "whoa!—whoa!" Other things he does not deign to notice. He is devoted to his Father, & such gratification you never before witnessed. I am so glad for Louise was always so changeable, & coquettish in her manner to him—but Jack is always the same. Cordele is well except occasional toothache—she hopes to pay a visit to the Dentist soon, & get relief. She has just finished a new calico-dress—which fits beautifully—then I made her a nice over-suit of soft grey & black-plaid, to wear with a black skirt—this is a real pretty outfit—& Mrs. Willeford has made her an alpaca-dress, which she will get home tomorrow—I hope it will be stylish. For her bonnet, she only got new flowers, I think it will do nicely. For myself, I will get nothing—our cotton crop has fallen short just <u>half</u>, & there are bills, & debts (neither large nor burdensome) which must be paid before anything else is gotten.

Louise is so nicely fitted out for the winter, with her fur-suit I will not have to get her anything—& Jack had such a beautiful sacque made—given him by his

Aunt Bessie he will have enough—then you know he accommodates himself very well to all his sister's out-grown clothes. Bun gave Jack a little <u>white knife</u> for his birthday-present—& also brought me a lovely <u>butter</u>-knife, with "<u>N</u>" engraved on the handle. Now don't you know Mrs John A— & her chaps do have more given them than any folks you ever saw! "Better born lucky than rich"!

I am so glad, & thankful to hear of Daught & her <u>boy, Jim Watt</u>—I do hope she may get strong, & well now. I was glad you enclosed her letter—I love to read of people loving & appreciating <u>you</u>. I am not going to say complimentary things to you tho', for I know if ever there was a spoilt woman you are. Maj just sits up, & praises you from morning till night. Bess told me so much of you—I really felt like I had seen you. I said, "now Bess you have been to see Maj at his own home again, do you love him as much as ever"—"Yes, I do Aunt Ida—<u>more</u> than ever—& I tell you, any body is obliged to love Maj who knows him—the more intimately the better you like him." She said this with all her vim, & earnestness, & I know it is the truth—

Sarah's marriage[5] passed off well—the ceremony was performed in our hall—the bride wore a beautiful white-swiss (which I made) & the groom was resplendent in a new suit of black—refreshment <u>table</u> (the same which was used at your marriage) was set in the Office & all the cakes were iced nicely, & trimmed.

Good-bye—do write, & assure us of your safety. We were so grieved to hear of your having been sick again. Do take care of yourself & Maj, & make haste home. Every item of your home-life is interesting to us—so give as many as you can. We hope for a letter tomorrow. God bless you both. All send love. Affect—<u>Lute</u>.

NOTES

1. Henry Whitfield to Attorney General Edward Pierrepont (1875), in Bond, ed., *Mississippi*, 135–37; Feimster, *Southern Horrors*, 55; Bercaw, *Gendered Freedoms*, 181.

2. In the Bible, Esther petitioned Ahasuerus to repeal Haman's command that all Jews be put to death. Ahasuerus did so and ordered Haman to be hanged on the gallows he had prepared for Mordecai (Esther, 7).

3. Adelbert Ames (1835–1933), Republican and governor of Mississippi (1874–76).

4. Memphis's Peabody Hotel (est. 1869) and became a popular destination for the well-to-do.

5. Sarah married William Billups.

❧

In spring 1875 Bess visited the home of banking magnate and family friend Thomas Porter Miller in Mobile, Alabama. Not long after came the announcement of Bess's engagement to his son, bank clerk Frank Williams Miller. When members of the

Miller family visited Columbus, Lucy and John spared no expense to ensure that they received Willow Cottage's genteel hospitality.

Lucy to Lizzie

Willow Cottage.

Jan 12th 76

My dear, darling Trotwood—

I am hungry for a chat with you, I'm just obliged to have a word or two, even if Jack won't go to sleep. I've been waiting on his lord-ship for an hour—all the time thinking what I <u>might</u> be saying to you. He is now in a big play with his Pa-pa, & I'll begin my talk tho' I know I can't go on uninterrupted. You certainly must have felt a <u>home</u>-<u>drawing</u>, these last few days especially—for <u>we</u>,—(Cordele, Bess, & I)—have done little else than wish for you, & talk of you. Sometimes we'd get much wrought up on the subject of your coming—at others, a kind of despair (<u>born</u> of <u>impatience</u>) would settle upon us, & we'd each declare you <u>never</u> were coming—no! never!

I hope your next letter will announce when we may expect you. I was much disappointed in not getting a letter from Maj on Monday—surely there is one in the Post for me now. We've had a delightful visit from Bess—her friends, the Millers, left her last week on Tuesday—Saturday Mr Neilson, Louise & I went in, & took dinner with her, & then she came out home with us—staying until this afternoon, when she returned to town with Mrs George Whitfield—who had been out, & spent the day with us. I had not seen Mrs Whitfield for a <u>perfect</u> age until Saturday, we met in Bessie's room, when she remarked that she had planned to get Bess someday, & come out to our house for a real social <u>old</u> fashioned visit—of course, I was pleased to hear her say so, & asked her to come <u>today</u>—which she did, & we've enjoyed her very much. I never saw her so easy in manner, or more talkative. She looked pleased with her entertainment & when the coffee was served in the parlor, <u>hot</u> & <u>strong</u>, I tell you, her eyes did sparkle. Julian came with her—he is a splendid boy—both in person, & mind. Mrs Field is no better I judge, as she keeps postponing her return home—she is not expected until next Fall. <u>Henry</u>[1] will come on a visit <u>tomorrow</u>—we attribute Mrs Whitfield's <u>sudden</u> sociability to <u>that</u> fact—she wishes him to have a pleasant time with Bess!—

I think you are losing a great deal of pleasure in staying away from <u>us</u> so long—I declare it is a treat to be with Bess—she is so splendid—I do dread her getting married—I know she will have to marry, & I fear <u>away</u> from Columbus—that's the <u>distressing</u> part! She has written you an account of her <u>elegant</u> reception on New Year. If you could have seen, as I did, such evidences of love & interest shown by every lady in the boardinghouse, you would have <u>cried</u> for very <u>appreciation</u>! How they did work for her—every one—there was not a more elegantly decorated room, & table in the town, & the ladies did it all—each one working as if she was their own young lady. I was telling Mrs Ottley of it all, & she remarked with so much earnestness—"Well, Lucy, that is just a reward for Bessie's own conduct, for I never saw a young lady so considerate of <u>married</u> ladies feelings, in my life, & she has been kind & thoughtful of them & they all love her!"—Yes, they do love her, & dread to have her leave the house—real stingy of her—& <u>Jim</u>, why! he is as proud of her as any Father could be. You would have been pleased with her entertainment of Miss Miller[2]—there was not an attention which could have been paid, that was left off. Her friends, of both sexes, stood up to her thro' it all—she says she will never cease to thank <u>Mr Lee</u> & Uncle Jim for they were her right-hand-men on all occasions. Her Uncle John too was perfectly lovely & sent her the carriage <u>whenever</u> she wished it. It is such a nice little turn-out—the horses look so fat, & go so well. We did our nicest for Belle, & she was delighted out here. Her brothers[3] are such nice, pleasant young men—so affable, so gifted (in music), & so perfectly unaffected. I tell you, they are people of worth, & I am glad Bess has them for friends. I have lots more to say, but will wait, & hope for many a precious talk with you, my dear, my dearest!

Your letter to Cordele was so enjoyed—I hope you were not disappointed in any of your intended festivities. Wish I could have partaken of your elegant dinner. I was <u>sick</u> all during the holidays, & enjoyed none of the good things, now I am well, & am regretting all the time that <u>all</u> has been eaten up. Sarah tried how nicely she could have every thing—& of course I was pleased. She does the same service of last year, so does Woos. We have some new farm-hands—& Tom Barron & family have moved back.

Louise is tired of waiting for you—she grows so fast. I think you will be surprised what a great girl she is—I am sometimes sorry to see her leaving off her pretty baby ways, & effect <u>big</u>-girl manners. I don't like her growing up without you seeing her development of mind & body.

Jack is so <u>sweet</u> & <u>bad</u>, & fat, & lazy, & smart, & saucy, & rough, & boyish. All say he is fine-looking—prettier than daughter—& indeed! he has fine eyes. Do come along & see our darlings for your self! I'm not a bit jealous when you say you wish to see them more than any of us. Bro James is now in Jackson attending the Legislature[4]—I am sorry for Sister Mary—she has a young man on the place for protection—but it is dreadful for the master to be away for so long. She came to see us the other day—her little babe is pretty & good & smart. I tell Jack she will both walk & talk before he does. Sister Sallie is still with Sophie Lewis—we are expecting her here sometime soon. All your friends ask so much of you—Mrs Short especially is <u>dead</u> to see "Lizzie." Poor Miss Anna I am sorry for her—she has her brother's three children[5] here. I suppose her kinspeople will help her with them. Mrs Eagar seems so happy at Mr Shattuck's—she & Mrs Ottley came out once during the holidays. Col's health is very poor—sometimes he is entirely confined to bed. I don't know whether Cousin Cornelia has returned from Mobile or not. I wish to see her, & hear all about my dear Lide. Mrs Odeneal's health is no better. Cordele told you of Mrs Hand's[6] death—she died New Year's day—what a glorious New Year to her—she has been so long a sufferer.

Good-bye dear—John, & Cordele unite with me in love to you & husband! Write soon.

May God bless you, & send you safely to us. Your Lute

NOTES

1. James Henry Whitfield (b. 1860), son of Henry Buchanan Whitfield and Laura Young Whitfield.

2. Belle Augusta Miller (1853–1929), daughter of Thomas Porter Miller and Eliza Emma Williams Miller.

3. Frank Miller's unmarried brothers: Charles B. Miller (1851–1908); George E. Miller (1855–1928); Edward C. Miller (b. ca. 1858); and Henry L. Miller (b. ca. 1860).

4. James Crawford Neilson served in the Mississippi House of Representatives (1876–77).

5. The children of Anna Leigh Short's brother Dr. James W. Leigh (b. ca. 1829): William Leigh (b. ca. 1871); Robert Emmett Leigh (1869–1956); and Fannie Leigh (1863–89).

6. Mary Williams Hand (1803–76), widow of Dr. John H. Hand (1798–1853).

Seven

A Social Fabric

August 1876–December 1877

*O*n May 4, 1876, Bess married Frank Williams Miller. Like most postwar weddings, neighbors and friends assisted with last minute sewing, prepared flowers, baked culinary delights for the wedding table, and selected gifts for the happy couple. In contrast to antebellum times—when grand affairs were staged to enhance families' status and honor—postwar weddings were collective celebrations where both the guests and guests of honor participated in the ceremonies and reaffirmed their place in community life.

Bess and Frank did not stay in Columbus long but headed northward for an extended tour, with later plans to set up house near Frank's parents in Mobile, Alabama. Enamored with new horizons, Bess still found time to report back regularly to family headquarters. "I had a long letter from Bess yesterday," Lucy wrote Lizzie on June 23, 1876. "She & Frank are as bright & happy as the days are long. They are so in love with the Lakes above St Paul, they have prolonged their stay much longer than they intended—Have gone tho' now, I suppose, to Northampton Mass [Massachusetts]."

As Bess enjoyed a respite from the southern summer, Lucy conceded that the poor state of the crops at Willow Cottage hinted at hard times ahead. Cordele's flower patch, she noted, was "drying & dying up" to the extent that she could "scarcely get a rose for the hall-table." "Our vegetables are giving out too—before others come in," she added, "our table is real scarce." Lucy and Cordele drew upon every inch of domestic resourcefulness in order to make ends meet.

With measly crops and frugal tables, the women of Columbus cast their gaze outward to other ways of maintaining their place in society. Many, including Lucy and Cordele, threw themselves into church activities, which had undergone something of a revival since the appointment of Rev. John David McClintock (1836–81) to the ministry of the Columbus First Presbyterian Church. "I do think Mr McClintock one of the most pious, & humble Christians I ever knew," Lucy declared to Lizzie on June 26, 1876, "& then every one of his sermons are so instructive. I thank God, for sending him to us." If Reverend McClintock had lifted the spiritual tone of Columbus, his wife, Margaret Brown McClintock (b. ca. 1850), succeeded in drawing community ties a little closer around the church.

"Bright, & <u>fresh</u>" and "real stylish," Mrs. McClintock challenged the women of Columbus to affirm their standing through church fund-raisers, concerts, and Sunday school programs. After focusing so closely on their ability to create a domestic ideal out of postwar hardship, Lucy and Cordele welcomed the opportunity to work alongside their neighbors and friends in the task of community building.

𝔾ᴤ

Lizzie's report on her neighbor's lush summer garden prompted Lucy to warn her sister of the dangers of enduring the season in "that abominable, horrid, dreadful, <u>fatal</u> Swamp." "Remember you staid too long last year—why not take warning by past experience," she lectured in a letter dated June 23, 1876. "I am not speaking selfishly now," she added. "I only wish your good—if you were elsewhere, I would not say 'come home' at all." Within weeks James Watt wrote to the Neilsons informing them of Lizzie's illness.

Lucy to Lizzie

Willow Cottage—
Aug: 26th '76.

My darling Trot.

My anxiety was much relieved by Maj's last letter, saying you were so much better—still I feel restless until I know you are up again, & well enough to come <u>home</u>, if you decide it is best, to come here for medical treatment. Any how, I wish to hear frequently from you. I do not urge your coming here—you know what is best, & most convenient for yourself, & husband—yet, t'would be against nature, for me not to have <u>my own hopes</u>. My <u>most</u> earnest desire is that you may not return to the plantation until after frost. I wrote Maj so urgently on that subject, I fear he may get a little provoked, but you must kiss him on the bald-head, & tell him "it is only Lucy's foolishness." I do thank Maj so much for writing so often while you were sick. I know he was uneasy—tho' he told me <u>not</u> to be. I never heard of Castalian Springs [Tennessee] before, & I imagined you off at some way off place without even the comforts of life—from Maj's last letter, I judge it is quite a place of resort, & nicely kept. He did not explain where you were, or how come you <u>there</u>. You can't imagine what <u>crickets</u> you & Watt seem to us old settled people—you lead such active, & varied lives, you forget to explain your whereabouts, & surroundings. I will content myself tho', if <u>only</u> you will <u>write often</u>, & keep well. I know Columbus is an out-of-the-way place, & Maj's business needs his attention, so I won't tease, & worry about your coming—tho' our disappointment was very keen, when your letter came from Kosciusko saying you could not come. I was so confident you would come on every <u>next</u> train, I had cake baked, & your room put in readiness. I quite sympathised with your disappointment in John's not going to the bottom. He has been solicited by the Cotton-buyers to take the position of public-weigher of cotton this season—& he expects to be in readiness to enter upon the duties by the middle of next month. He will have to go to Mobile first, & thinks he may take <u>Greene</u> Spring [Alabama] in his route, to visit his old friends the <u>Tutwiler's</u>, & Cousin Willie Wright[1] is there now too, & they are all so anxious to see him. I beg him to go. Cordele had a letter from Cousin Mary Davis yesterday—they were all well, & very much disappointed that I was not going to visit them this fall. I do wish I <u>could go</u>, for I am better situated to go on a trip now, than I ever expect to be again until I am <u>too</u> old to have more babies. Jack is old enough to go without a nurse (with Cordele's help), & there is <u>no prospect</u> for a <u>successor</u>,—'aint you glad!

Cous Mary said she had not heard a word from you since <u>you left</u>. Poor Corrie expects to be sick <u>in</u> November.[2] Cous Mary says she is very cheerful—tho she looks badly, & old.—Cordele has kept well all thro' the hot weather, tho I was afraid she would make herself sick putting up fruits, & preserves for winter. She has a good quantity put up. We have not had a letter from Bess in nearly two weeks. Jim received the last, but he said there was nothing in it. She will be leaving Rochester [New York] now pretty soon, & I don't know where to address a letter. Oh! I have so much to talk to you about, & can't write everything. All our friends are well. Mrs Ottley thinks of going to the Centennial[3]—I have not seen her on the subject. Mrs Eagar spent several days with us last week—they are all well, & happy. Went to see Mrs Short not long ago—she is well, & sweet, & loving, & asking for you every breath.

The children are well, & lively—they do so many funny things every day, which makes me wish for you to see & hear. Jack is now begging his Father to let him <u>shave</u>—he drives "<u>Mandy</u>" as furiously as ever all over the house. The other day I was asking him his catechism, & said "Who made you Jack["]—He replied "<u>Dod</u>"—"What else did he make?"—"<u>all sings</u>"—What did he make you & all things for? "<u>Whoa Mandy</u>"!—Thus ended his catechism! He certainly does think he was made for driving horses!

Sarah keeps up yet, tho' I am expecting every day, & night for her to fall down.[4] Nancy will take her place I reckon. Bess said they wished to be back home between the <u>15th & 20th Sept</u>—if so, it won't be long before she is with us—it makes my heart ache to think she will not be with us ever again as of yore. Mr Neilson is getting his cotton out fast. He will go to ginning next week. The weather has been intense—we had a thunder-storm last evening which has cooled the atmosphere much. I dread September—but pray we may all keep well.

Good-bye my darling, take care of yourself. I am glad you have Mrs McCain[5] with you—Give her my love—also to Maj when he comes.

All send heart's full of love, & many messages. The black people were as anxious as could be, when they heard you were so ill. God keep you safe—

Your loving
Lute.

NOTES

1. Educator Henry Tutwiler (1807–84), founder of Greene Springs School for Boys of Havana, Alabama. Henry was husband of Julia Ashe Tutwiler (1820–83) and father of eleven children, including Julia Strudwick Tutwiler (1841–1916), educator, prison reformer, and advocate of educational opportunities for women. James William Abert Wright (1834–94) was a former teacher at the school.

2. Laura Corrie Nesbitt Myers was pregnant with her son George D. Myers (1876–1960).

3. While national celebrations centered on the Centennial International Exhibition (1876) held in Philadelphia, Pennsylvania, Lucy was probably referring to celebrations held in Columbus, which were to be hosted by local Granges at Jameson's Mill.

4. Sarah Billips was pregnant.

5. Possibly Jane Crutcher Topp McCain (1825–97) of Carroll County. Jane's husband, Nathaniel H. McCain (b. ca. 1812), may have been a relative of James Madison Watt's first wife, Mary S. McCain Watt (b. ca. 1814).

ॐ

After a Christmas visit to Willow Cottage, Lizzie returned to the plantation. With her sister's health restored, Lucy turned her attention to a family scandal brewing closer to home, namely Jane E. Abert and George W. Abert's decision to rent out rooms to Rev. Knowles Shaw (1834–78). A musician-evangelist of the Stone-Campbell movement, Shaw "drew great crowds to attend on his ministry, to hear him sing and listen to his unsurpassed temperance addresses." His religious credentials were not enough to temper Lucy, who feared that an irresponsible association with "Yankee Campbellites" threatened to blight the family name.[1]

Lucy to Lizzie

Willow Cottage.[2]
Jan 29th/.77.

My darling Trot.

Your <u>three</u> letters, written while en route to the plantation, were anxiously looked for, gladly received, & <u>thankfully</u> read! We all give you much credit for your thoughtfulness in writing, for you know how dreadfully we hated your going off by yourself in that miserable weather. We feel grateful for your safe arrival at Delta, & meeting your good husband. Dear Maj! I know how he must have watched & waited for your coming, & with what rapture he must have met you. I sympathise with his great joy. God grant you may both keep well, & don't forget to write us every week or ten days.

You know Trot, you told me not to forget that you & Maj were as much in God's keeping there, as you would be here—but I can't exactly realize that fact, & am constantly feeling anxious about you. I wish you to bear in mind what I told you about leaving before the high water this Spring—now you recollect, & don't you tamper with that awful river & moon-lake. Don't you get mad with me.

It is a week ago tonight when we were making preparations for your early departure the next morning. How long it seems! Cordele & I were lost for days— we really did not know what to do with ourselves. John proposed taking us to town, one bright afternoon, just to enliven us a little—he missed you as much as we did—only he did'ent howl about it. Poor little Jack went in Cordele's room for several successive mornings, & put up pitiful wails about "Aunie leave me." Louise looks so sad & lonely, whenever we say anything about your going away, we have to change the subject. Of course all your friends lift up their voices in lamentations over your departure.

Mrs Sydney Street,[3] & Miss Street came out last Saturday—they were sorry not to see you. Had such a pleasant visit from them. I like Mrs Sid very much. The Mosbys[4] have not come yet—they surely must be mad—or the horse is dead— we've had several pretty days, & yet they come not. I went in town this morning with John, to pay Cousin Jennie a visit—The Shaws have come, & Cousins George & Jennie are like people in straight-jackets. I have no patience with their putting themselves in such a muss—Yankee-Campbellites! I went in especially to cheer poor Jennie up a little—she looked so wretched yesterday at church. I tried to make her promise to come, & pay us a long visit—but she would not— says she will come—but would appoint no time. I suppose you understand that the Campbellite-preacher Shaw has been engaged to preach here for a year, & has rented Cousin George's house, & he & Jennie will remain there for awhile— board with them!

Sissie will stay with Sister Kate this week. I wish she would make haste home— we miss her dreadfully. Cousin Mary Barry wishes her next week—Mr Barry came in person to invite her. We succeeded in getting a nice supply of butter & eggs for Bess—She is well & grieved over you. One of Bob Barron's[5] little girls— Molly—caught on fire last Friday, & was so badly burned she died this morning. I am sorry for the parents, for they are both fond, & careful of their children.

I liked to have forgotten to tell of Jack's entrê into religious life—he actually went to Sunday-school yesterday, & behaved so <u>nicely</u>—sat in Pattie's class—& kissed Judge Goodwin <u>like a man</u>! [pages missing]

The black folks would have many messages if they knew I was writing. They express much interest in your welfare.

Notes

1. Lipscomb, *A History of Columbus*, 112.

2. John added a note to the letter: "Jim says the cotton cleaner was shipped several weeks ago—Write to Agent of Memphis & Charleston road at Memphis—if the cleaner is not at Delta—J.A.N."

3. Fannie Miner Beman Street (1854–1939), wife of druggist Sidney Bryan Street (1843–1929).

4. Farmers F. W. Mosby (b. ca. 1830) and Sallie V. Mosby (b. ca. 1842).

5. Mollie Barron (ca. 1867–77), daughter of Robert Barron and Lidia Barron.

ℱ⏳

As her children grew, Lucy noted the differences in rearing boys and girls. While Louise was given training in submission and piety, Lucy encouraged Jack's outspoken independence. "For mercy-sake don't advise me to train Jack up with any more decided ideas of <u>his rights</u>, else he'll be as insatiable as Bonaparte ever was," she declared in a letter to her brother-in-law James Watt on March 27, 1877. "He recognizes <u>no</u> rights now of any living creatures, but <u>his own</u>!—unless <u>he</u> chooses! then he's generous enough! makes quite a <u>blow</u> of self-condemnation about his <u>great</u> generosity too!"

In the following letter Lucy also mentioned the appointment of Republican candidate Rutherford Birchard Hayes (1822–93) to the presidency (1877–81). Pitted against Democratic candidate Samuel Jones Tilden (1814–86), Hayes failed to win the popular vote and yet refused to concede, noting that victory hinged on contested electoral votes in Louisiana, South Carolina, and Florida. In January 1877 Congress established an electoral commission to resolve the issue; they awarded Hayes all the disputed votes, thereby giving him a majority of one. Tilden did not contest the decision, and in return the Republican Party abandoned Reconstruction, making way for home rule in the South.

Lucy to Lizzie

Home—Feb 16th '77.

My dear, dear Trot.

Your bright, loving letter was received with joy, & all felt its' influence beaming over our family-circle, like a sunbeam. You surely are a happy woman—& how blest the person who is ever with you, feeling, luxuriating, in your brightness. We have received all your letters, & even the P.C. which "Watt" was unwilling you should send. The Post-Master is more particular about forwarding your letters, this year, than last—when he willfully withheld them for a whole month, thereby giving me so much anxiety. I thank him for his thoughtfulness.

We are well, & happy in our sweet little home. Last Saturday we were invited to Mr Williams' to dine—as we went into town, it was such a lovely day, & the children looked so nice we concluded to have their pictures taken—this is the result—what do you think of them? Louise, I think, is too much magnified—making her features look coarser than natural. I fear Watt will not like it so well, on that account—for he so delights in her delicate, refined look. Her hair too is not nicely combed—we have recently had it shingled, & I could not make it look as pretty as when longer. Master Jack's is very good—considering he started out saying—"won't do it"—"want a biscuit"—&c &c. I don't think it is as pretty as he is—his colored friends are all dissatisfied—declaring it "aint nigh as prutty as Jack." I am glad to have them anyhow. I know you will be glad to see even the images of your children. I don't think you need fear their forgetting you. They love you with all their earnest natures. Louise is doing so nicely with her lessons. Every morning, directly after she is dressed, I teach her catechism, & letters. I do not keep her longer than a quarter of an hour—I never wish to tire her. She is proud to know her letters, & does not dread her lessons as a task. Jack is getting more & more of a man! Actually drives the carriage nearly the whole way to town, & back. Has such a good idea of guiding the horses too. What won't he be doing by the time he is six years old.

I hope by this time you have received the nice long letter which Sister Sallie wrote you last week. Cordele also sent you another long one this week—so you see we have not neglected you, even tho' Watt did accuse us of being glad to get rid of you. Never mind! I'll whip Watt on sight, for being so saucy! We laughed heartily over his characteristic advertisement—am saving it for Jim to laugh over Sunday. La! yes, Hayes, just as well be in the chair—the Democrats virtually backed-down long ago—when they consented to a compromise! See now, I can express political opinions as well as Sallie Brooke![1] Don't tell!

Mrs Hardy is now with Bessie—she went down on Monday in company with Mrs Ottley. We've staid at home quietly this week—no visits, nor visitors. Sister Sallie has read "Head of the family"[2] to me—I like it—but it is too sorrow-ful! I am making myself some new under-wear—first since my marriage—six years ago this time I was busy with my trousseau! Six happy years!! Thank God for them!

John has every thing about the farm in perfect order, & is ploughing his cotton-lands. He is interested in all that concerns you, & Watt—& does wish to see you both so much. Cordele has made Daughter five beautiful calico-dresses—she is at a stand still about the quilt—no scraps—& Bess won't give that blue satin Polanaise—<u>stingy</u> old thing! Do write to us often, & we will do the same. God bless you both my dear Trot & Watt.

Your loving Lute. [. . .]

NOTES

1. Sarah Elizabeth Watt Brooke (1848–78), daughter of James Madison Watt and Mary McCain Watt and wife of Kosciusko lawyer Callowhill Minnis Brooke (1847–1911).
2. Dinah Maria Craik, *The Head of the Family* (1851).

෴

Lucy and John celebrated their sixth anniversary in grand family style. Later, Lucy attended Margaret Brown McClintock's fund-raising event for the Columbus First Presbyterian Church.

Lucy to Lizzie

Home—April 24th '77

My darling Trotwood—

Your last to Cordele was received yesterday—& need I say it was warmly welcomed? You've been real good since absent this time. I hav'ent had a single chance for being uneasy, so regularly have your letters come. We appreciate every effort on your part, & I am sure we've been prompt in our replies. We've kept you so well posted, we won't have a thing to tell when you come—but I reckon we can manage to kept [keep] up some <u>sort</u> of talk—don't you? You, dear old <u>Watt</u> & <u>Trot</u>, we want to see you dreadfully! The children are asking every day, when you are coming.

We all keep well & are delighted to hear how big & fat you are growing. I reckon I would fully agree with Maj in thinking you <u>beautiful</u>! I just want to kiss & hug you for both my last letters—<u>especially</u> our joint one—John's & mine—our <u>wedding</u>-day-letter! Why! it was just the perfection of a letter. I read it with delight & pride! I thank you for thinking of us, for writing to us, & above all for loving us so unreservedly! Our darling sweet Trot! The picture you drew of Willow Cottage was vivid, & life-like—except we had no '<u>neighbors</u>' to grace the occasion. For the first time since our marriage we had no guests—just our <u>home</u> folk. We had the house nice & sweet—Nancy gave us a delightful little dinner— roast duck, & Queen's Pudding. Sister Sallie came home especially to do honor to the occasion. Sully sent a lovely bouquet to the <u>bride</u>-<u>groom</u> for a <u>birthday</u>

gift, & we were dressed, & brushed & comb, & had a sweet merry time all to our little selves! Of course at dinner, toasts were proposed, to be drank in good sober buttermilk! Louise is ambitious of never being behind the foremost, so she was ready with her sentiment. Raising her glass, tossing her head to one side, she said with great airiness "there is rest for the weary"![1] This brought down the house, as you well know! The married pair, of six years, wondered if we did have such a wearied, worn-out look, that even the babes, & sucklings perceived it! We thought of our absent members, & wished for them—oh! that we were near enough to always be united on these anniversaries! Perhaps we may be neighbors yet!

I read your letter to the servants—they were so pleased—Nannie declared you "rite just like you had looked in, & seed us all—& God knows, the last of the letter is as good as any sermon that ever was preached"! Woos, & Aunt Phillis said Amen to that! So you see my dear your sweet courtesy was fully appreciated by all!

The charades came off last Friday-night—we all went, even to Jack! You never heard of an affair of the kind going off with better success! The night was beautiful, the house was well filled (Institute-chapel), & the stage-management most excellent, & the acting perfect! Had three Charades—Matrimony—Marplot—& Mistaken—then there was sweet music, & dance-songs by the little girls! I never enjoyed an evening more! Sister Sallie appeared as Mother in Marplot. Annie Hopkins & Helen Saunders[2] being her daughters—Lucy Gerdine was the old woman, & oh! if you could have seen her! All did their beautiful best, & there was nothing more to be desired. We cleared $95, & then had contributions making the amount $105. This is a nice little sum for the Mite-society[3]—is it not? We wish to have the S.School-room repaired—which you know it so much needs! Jack looked on at every thing with the interest of a well grown youth—did not think of sleep, & is now trying to sing the songs which the children sang on the stage. One about "Rueben, & Rachel."[4] I wish you & Maj could hear him! He went to town with us this morning, & drove. He likes to go so fast we called him "Watt," at which he laughed most heartily. Louise grows fast, & is a sweet little girl most all the time. She looks real cute in her little sun Norman-cap. Cordele & I have our bonnets—they are nice, & becoming I think. Cordele's polanaise is very pretty—mine not yet finished. Cordele will go to Sister Annie's tomorrow, & stay until Sunday—to attend Presbytery. I know she will enjoy herself. Our friend Mrs Gregory was in town last week, & came out home with us Sunday, & staid until night service, when we took her back to town. She is so anxious to see you! "Oh! if I could see Miss Lizzie, & have a good long talk!" I think she really would like your advice—she is right troubled as what is best to do—she is tired of her present life. She has been successful—but poor little thing! she is tired of so much publicity, & the battle of Life is wearying—altho' she is so brave—"working for Watt." She is very little changed, sweet, loving, tender, self-absorbed, or rather, <u>egotistical</u>—full of sympathy for others, & very true. Had so much to ask of Maj. You know I dilated on my "in-law." Says you & Maj must be sure <u>to stop to see her</u>—says don't pass her by—she would be so very glad to see you. We hear from Bess—she sent us some Maple-Sap by mail, but we missed it. She will come in June. Jim seems right well, & was quite lively when I saw him—he was with us Sunday. All send best love. Poor answer for your letters—not my fault but <u>misfortune</u>—no <u>ideas</u>.

Your friends are all on the qui-vive [alert] to hear of your coming. Give my love to <u>Florie</u>, & <u>hopes for her welfare</u>. Kiss Maj for us all—now I know that will be a job which neither of you will object to. God bless you both. John has gone to Wildwood and is <u>well</u>, & <u>sweet</u>.

Good-bye—
Lute.

NOTES

1. Isaiah 28:12.

2. Helen A. Saunders (b. ca. 1856), daughter of acclaimed portrait painter William Carroll Saunders (1817–1902) and Helen L. Saunders (b. 1819).

3. Children's society of the Columbus First Presbyterian Church.

4. Harry Birch and William Gooch, "Reuben and Rachel" (1871), in Studwell, ed., *Americana Song Reader*, 80.

℘ஓ

Columbus proved a popular summer retreat for family and friends. John's sister Sophie Abert Neilson Lewis and her children (Maud Lewis, Charles Abert Lewis [b. 1872], and Sylvester Creswell Lewis Jr. [b. 1874]) visited Willow Cottage in June and were followed soon after by Bess and Frank Miller.

The summer bore witness to birth, death, and marriage: Sophie decided to remain at Willow Cottage for her confinement; John's brother-in-law John Symons died suddenly; and Jim Irion introduced his fiancée, Carrie Petty Hardaway (1856–1926), to his family circle.

Lucy to Lizzie

Willow Cottage
June 28th/.77.

My dear darling Trotwood—

Your sweet affectionate letter was such a treat to us all. I read it aloud, & all appreciated it. Bess & Frank have been with us three weeks—they have enjoyed

Sophie Abert Neilson Lewis. Sarah Neilson Papers.
Courtesy of Special Collections Department,
Mitchell Memorial Library, Mississippi State University.

themselves, & so have we! Sophie & her little folks were here for the first few days, & then they went to Bro James', where they have been since—they will return Monday—then Bess, & Frank will spend a few days in town visiting, & go home. It seems a short visit for them, for the time has passed very pleasantly. Numbers of friends have called—but they have been no where except by special invitation—they seem so perfectly satisfied to stay here with us. Bess was so glad to get home. And we have had so many good ditties—I've done nothing, but sit by her side, & listen & "tell 'bout it" myself! Housekeeping is easy, for Cordele will help about the vegetables; catching the especial chicken for each meal, & the dairy of course. Woos is such a good cook, & manager too—she is never hurried or confused—& Mammy altho' she does get nervous around the table, does her duty well. I make Lide come in, & keep off the flies. We have nice vegetables, & fruits, & you know it is easy to have a good table. Frank does seem to enjoy every thing so much. He is very agreeable, & appreciative—we love him very much. The children are so fond of him. Bess looks very happy—& you would be gratified by seeing her _practice_, what you have for years _preached_, for her good. She was right sorrowful, & lost at not seeing _you_ at _home_, when she first came— said "it seemed so strange not to see Auntie at all _any where_"! She & Frank do so wish to have you & Maj visit them.

Bess is well but quite thin—weighs only 118 lbs—Frank looks so well—his weight is 161 lbs. Cousin Cornelia gave them a nice tea—had Mr & Mrs Teasdale[1] to meet them—then Sister Annie had them to dine—meeting Mrs Bradford, & Annie Kennedy. Mrs Field had them to tea all by themselves! They have had quite a number of calls, & would have had more—if they been in town. The _fashionables_ seem quite anxious to cultivate them. Mrs Gen Lee, & Mary[2] were among their first visitors. They will return to Mobile, & stay all summer, if they can, with an occasional sail over the Bay.

We were so merry, & happy at home—little Maud came down, & we (John, Sister Sallie, & I) concluded we would go to "the Institute Commencement" exercises—the night of the children's entertainment—to let our little folks enjoy it—we dressed them all sweetly, & went (_Jack_ too), we were sitting in the Chapel enjoying some _lovely Fairy-scenes_, when a messenger came to Mr Neilson saying we must come to _Sister Annie's_ that Mr Symons was _dying_! Yes! he was up town settling his last accounts with his partner Mr Moss[3]—when he was suddenly struck with death—Mr Moss was writing a notice of the dissolution of the co-partnership, when he spoke to Mr Symons once, twice, & on receiving no answer he looked up, & saw he was deadly pale, & about to fall—he rushed to him, caught him in his arms, & called for help. He was taken home as quickly as possible, but never spoke a word to any of them! Poor dear Sister Annie tried in vain to make him speak to her. He made of [a] caressing movement, but that was all! In four hours after he was taken, he peacefully breathed his last. Now did you ever hear of so sad a death! I do grieve for Sister Annie. She was such a devoted wife. Poor Mr Symons! how sweet the rest must be to him, for he had been so bowed down by business troubles. He said not long ago—He loved Sunday more than ever before in his life—t'was indeed a day of _rest_ for him—for no one could thrust bills, & duns at him—no one could talk business to him! Lizzie grieves in a heart broken way that goes to my heart—she takes trouble so hard. Can't you write to them? You certainly have a gift at saying comforting things. John Furniss is here now. The funeral services were held at the church, & oh! Mr McClintock's remarks were just the most appropriate, the most comforting that could have been said—he read the 39th Psl, & commented up each verse—dwelling especially on the 9th & 10th verses.[4] There were a great many gentlemen present, & oh! surely the most lasting impression was made!—

We are all well, & have been, with the exception of one chill which '_Miss_' had, some few weeks ago. We are so glad to hear that you & Maj keep well—do take care, my sweet old dears—such a great fear comes over me about you every now,

& then—but then I know you can be cared for there as well as elsewhere by our Father—still if you have the means, & opportunity of getting away from there—I do think you will be tempting Providence by staying. Go to Bailey. I do not urge you to come here, for I do not think it will be very pleasant for you or <u>Sophie now</u>— for she is very sensitive about her 'condition' & the <u>boys</u> are mighty <u>bad</u>! I do hope in the Fall you can come before she goes away—for I do want you to see her.

Miss Anna Short came out, & spent a good long day with us—she is <u>working</u> very hard, but is sweet, & cheerful, & longing to see "Lizzie." Mrs Ottley has returned from Iowa leaving Col at the Infirmary. I have not seen her—I do not know her plans. Mrs Weaver, Lulie Teasdale, & Mrs Theo Jones came out yesterday—they all made particular inquiries of you, & expressed their regrets that you & Maj were not here at our reunion. Your picture you drew of our meeting at your house is indeed tantalizing—can it ever be fulfilled? never! I hope to come to see you tho' some time, & will do so when I can, most certainly. I do not scorn your invitations—nor turn a cold shoulder either. I would gladly go to you, & Maj any where in the world. Now about Jim, & his girl.[5] In the first place, <u>we all</u> think that letter of yours to her, was just <u>perfection</u>! I have seen Carrie once or twice—had very little conversation with her. She is said to be a <u>lovely</u> girl, by all who know her. <u>Mary Frazee</u>[6] is intimate with her, & speaks so highly of her. Jim arranged to have Bess, & Frank go down to see her. Bess says she is a sweet blushing girl, with very little to say—but refined in looks & manners. Her mother is Mrs Smith, having married a second time, & has one little Smith-girl— <u>Melville</u>.[7] Mr Smith is an intelligent gentleman. They are a good substantial country family—have been quite wealthy, & are now <u>well-to-do</u>! It is reported in town that Carrie is worth $30,000 in her own right—at which <u>Jim laughs</u>. I am glad it is not a large family of rough country boys—no telling how they might turn out. Bess says they have a good large house nicely furnished, & kept—but with the inevitable country-stiffness about every thing! Carrie is much courted by all the country-side—there is considerable jealousy felt that a <u>town</u>-man should come in & win the prize. Mary Frazee says Carrie is right much afraid of <u>us</u>—hears we are intelligent, & fastidious—fears she will not be acceptable. She need have no fears, as Jim's wife, we will accept, & love her if she will let us. Jim seems so happy, & loving. I do feel so thankful for the change in him—he is so full of hope, & interest in life now. God grant he may not be disappointed. Tell Maj we are longing to hear him laugh, & talk. It does seem so long since we heard him. Louise says tell Auntie to kiss Uncle Watt for her. Jack says tell Auntie to "<u>turn back</u>"—there's never much variety in his messages. I wish you & Maj could see him play with his dog. It is an amusing sight. You need have no fears of the children forgetting you—they speak of you each day. The servants ask continually when you are coming.—

Sullie Matthews, & Rebecca Barry have just left they were so sweet, & pleasant, & sent love to you as I told them I was writing. Dr McCabe came the other day to pay a <u>social</u> visit to Bess—<u>which she missed</u>! He & I filled up the time talking of <u>you</u>. He is right uneasy about you staying so long on the River. He really loves you & Maj, & has your interest at heart. Cordele & John send very best love to you. Children send love & kisses. Bess and F—gone visiting.

Good-bye—God bless you both. Lovingly

Lute.

Respects to Dr Cook.[8]

NOTES

1. Store owner Howard M. Teasdale (ca. 1842–1924), husband of Tulula Weaver Teasdale (ca. 1843–1918). During the Civil War, Howard served as a hospital steward in Company B, Forty-third Infantry Regiment Mississippi.

2. Mary Blewett Harrison (1858–1915), daughter of lawyer James Thomas Harrison (1811–79) and Regina Blewett Harrison (1820–90) and sister of Regina Harrison Lee.

3. Possibly J. L. Moss (b. ca. 1836).

4. "I was dumb, I opened not my mouth; because thou didst it / Remove thy stroke away from me: I am consumed by the blow of thine hand" (Ps. 39:9–10).

5. Carrie Petty Hardaway, daughter of druggist James T. Hardaway (b. ca. 1828) and Sarah Jane Petty Hardaway Smith (1833–1917) and stepdaughter of farmer Moses B. Smith (1829–86).

6. Mary Weenonah Zuleme Frazee (1856–1936), daughter of George Frazee and Mary Jane Blair Frazee.

7. Malvina Smith (ca. 1867–1945).

8. Possibly Dr. Joseph T. Cook (b. ca. 1849), who, according to the 1870 census, lived in DeSoto County and by 1880 resided in Alcorn County.

✿

Lizzie visited relatives in northern Mississippi while her husband James made his way to Willow Cottage. With picnics to attend and fashionable people to cultivate, Lucy made a point of chiding Frank Miller about the deplorable state of Bess's wardrobe. Even in hard times, keeping up appearances still helped affirm a family's place in the social world. Bess's plain white polonaise and old scarf were hardly befitting elegant entertainments; nor were they reflective of the reputation that John and Lucy had worked so hard to maintain.

Lucy to Lizzie

Willow Cottage.
July 18th/.77.

My darling Trotwood—

I retire to the privacy of the "Office," to have a quiet little talk with you. Your <u>two</u> letters from Cousin Mary's have been received, & enjoyed. I thank you for them. Maj was very uneasy at not hearing from you—we tried to laugh him out of any such feeling, by saying you were only trying to retaliate for the way in which you had been treated on a former occasion by him—but he said "no! <u>Lizzie</u> would never do such a thing as that—she had too much feeling!" I knew if you were sick, our Nesbitt-relatives would not take it upon themselves to keep it from us—for they know by past experience what a <u>curious</u> somebody you are, when sick. Still when your letter did come assuring us of your health, & happiness, we were <u>very</u> glad. It came the morning of our <u>Pic-nic</u>-day! Yes, we did have another pic-nic in the middle of July down at Eggleston's Spring just where we enjoyed ourselves <u>three</u> years ago. And the day was delightful—we had no dust, no mosquitoes, no gnats, no snakes—& a good fresh breeze all day. Mrs Ottley, & her boys, Sully Matthews, & Lucy Gerdine joined us—beside my S.school class—<u>six</u> of the nicest girls in town, as you well know. Willie Pope, & Harry Dashield[1] were the boys in attendance. Dr Matthews could not come neither <u>did Jim</u>. Sister Sallie, & Miss Ellen wished for <u>Maj</u>—rather reproached me for not having the pic-nic before he left. I need not assure you of Miss Sully's <u>steadfast</u> remembrance of <u>you</u>, & wishes for you, & oh! Trot I do know if you had been with us your sunshine would have been felt over all the party. We had a most excellent dinner—Pig, chicken, salmon-salad—potatoe-salad—pickles, corn-pudding (<u>Nancy's best</u>), tomatoes, grated ham, white bread, <u>brown</u> biscuit, wafers, beat biscuit—then <u>cakes</u> made by Sully, which you know were most excellent—& peaches—iced lemonade, & ice-water. <u>Coffee</u> of course—Now don't you know you would have enjoyed dining with us. Nancy, Aunt Phillis, Woos, Lide, & <u>Bessie, & Ed</u> were <u>all</u> the colored help we had. Nancy declared it was the best dinner she had enjoyed since a Pic-nic "<u>Miss</u>," & Mrs Hull, & Mrs Pettit[2] &c had once down in the Bottom. The <u>girls</u> seemed to have a very pleasant time—& the children were <u>wild</u> with delight swinging, & jumping. T'was a new experience for Sophie's little ones. Mr Neilson was just <u>loveliness</u> itself that day—attentive to all. We went in the carriage for Virgie Ayers, Mary Blair, Annie Love, & Fannie Pope[3]—in the afternoon he took them back—had the two horses, & the top of the carriage thrown back—don't you know that ride was a treat for the girls? Lou Ellen, & Pauline Orr[4] came in their own conveyances.

We have been in quite a round for the past six weeks, but now we will retire from society; & await <u>Mrs Lewis'</u> entertainment. We have had so much company—<u>callers</u> I mean—& I have enjoyed them so much. I tell Cordele it will take us <u>two</u> years to pay back. Sophie's, & Bessie's friends of course came to see them, but they were <u>all</u> our friends as well. Every body wished for you. Bess seemed to enjoy the very last moment, & so did Frank. We have received some sweet letters from them since they left. Bess received a great deal of attention—such nice elegant entertainments too! But she did not have anything to <u>wear</u> at all—<u>so very</u> stingy—this is entirely <u>sub</u>-<u>rosa</u> [secret]. I made her real mad by laughing at her stinginess. She had one black grenadine polanaise made after she came—& she had <u>made herself</u>, one or two great, <u>plain</u> long backed polonaises of <u>plain</u> white linen lawn, & those were the <u>only</u> things she had! Very soon it was too warm for the grenadine, & then the <u>plain</u> old white polonaises, & that same old <u>Spanish-scarf</u>, were her <u>only</u> costumes! I was mad, & disappointed. One day I said "Frank the next time you bring Bess home, I want her to have <u>one</u> decent dress at least." He jumped like he was shot, & begun explaining how he had given her the money to have a handsome outfit, & she would not use it. I was right sorry for him. She bought <u>Alpacca</u>, & she & I made Frank a <u>coat</u>—which was a sight, (for he is so <u>peculiar</u> a form John's patterns will not fit him)—but Bess made him wear it. I whispered to him not to do it, but he did!

Cordele put up Black-berry jam, syrup, & pickle, Huckle-berries, & jelly for Bess—she paid her very liberally—she also gave me a nice little present—I don't mean to have you think she is stingy to us—<u>but to herself</u>. I do hope she will get over that foolishness. She is very thin, but keeps well.

Your description of the joy over Aunt Mattie's return was indeed very vivid. Oh! I do want to see them all so very much, & if possible this winter we will go. Poor dear Uncle Tom my heart swells in love, & tenderness for him. I do hope he may get better soon. Don't let our dear Aunts think we are ever cold or indifferent to them—we do love them. I've been right hurt with Cousin Mary, Corrie, & Bun they will <u>not</u> write to us. I wrote to Corrie, & Bun both—long letters, & Cordele did to Cousin Mary, & yet we receive no word. Did they ever get the children's pictures? I do know Cousin Mary lives delightfully—Maj told me so much about her—& he likes Cousin Davis so much too. Dear Maj—he was <u>too</u> sweet to us all! We love him more & more. He can't feel any more loving to us than we do to him. He, & Sister Sallie were <u>mutually</u> pleased—which is rare, after people have been told so much of each other. I do think they love each other dearly—such a sweet friendship too. Sister Sallie is just <u>starving</u> to see <u>you</u>! I feel so sympathetic—she is oppressed, & depressed too, by <u>many</u> surrounding circumstances, at the same time, she is doing her duty—yet she is so <u>very</u> easily affected, so <u>sensitively</u> organized; there are <u>few</u>, very few, in this rough world, who <u>can</u> or <u>will</u> understand. But she will bloom like a rose, when congenial <u>sunshine</u> comes. That sunshine she can find with you, & your husband, & I hope she may this Fall. I long for your coming. I don't blame Maj for saying Cordele is the sweetest woman in the world. I wish you could follow her in her round of daily duties. We get on so nicely—the children love each other, & play beautifully. Sophie is just, as sweet, & entertaining as she can be. Louise is quite thin—tho' she has not been sick. Jack has had no chill, since the one before Maj came. We do try to watch them carefully. I know you would love to see the <u>five</u> together. Maj was so sweet to them—they all loved him.

Our dear love for <u>Cousins Davis</u> & all

Write soon to Lute.

NOTES

1. William P. Pope (b. ca. 1861), son of planter William Elzey Pope (1834–1922) and Fannie Patterson Pope (1839–1901); Harry J. Dashiell (1861–1922), son of lawyer Thomas Rowan Dashiell (1835–76) and Fannie Howry Dashiell (1840–98).

2. Mary Elizabeth Tarpley Hull (1830–1903), wife of farmer Isaac Hull (1823–88); Jane Foster Cooper Pettit (1828–1911), wife of farmer James T. Pettit (1825–92). Both families lived in Coahoma County near the Barron plantation.

3. Mary Armistead Blair (1863–1910), daughter of David Paxton Blair and Elizabeth Armistead Pope Blair (b. 1812); Anna Love (1861–1951), daughter of Amzi Ellis Love and Edith Wallace Love (1823–72); Fannie Pope (b. ca. 1863), daughter of William Elzey Pope and Fannie Patterson Pope.

4. Pauline Van de Graaf Orr (1861–1955), daughter of Judge Jehu Amaziah Orr and Cornelia Ewing Van de Graff Orr (1833–1917).

℘᷀

Sophie Abert Neilson Lewis gave birth to a son, John James Lewis (b. 1877). Surrounded by a supportive network of relatives and friends, Sophie felt loath to comply when her husband demanded that his family meet him in St. Louis. Instead she contemplated setting up house with her unmarried sister, Sarah Dandridge Neilson.

Unlike Sophie, Laura Wright Eager was well versed in ways and means of making a living. Teaching had provided her with intellectual credit, financial independence, and a position of good standing in the community. When Franklin Academy's board left Eager out in the cold, Columbus residents rallied around their beloved educator.

Lucy to Lizzie

Home—
Sept 20th/.77.

My dear Trot.

We did not get our usual letter from you last week—which makes us feel uneasy, lest you should be sick again. I do hope not, my dear old darling! You do not [know] what a sinking of the heart I feel, when I think of you being sick away from home. I hope there is a letter from you now in the Post—we have not heard for two days, on account of the continual rain. I wish to write to Maj, but don't know where to address the letter—being in doubt whether he is still with you, or at the plantation. Cordele wrote you last week—I added a little note on business. We all keep well. The weather is so cool & damp, the children do not look well—I have them both taking Quinine to day. Sophie's little folks keep remarkably well. The baby is a bright little fellow—& looks older than five weeks. She is undecided what she will do with herself, & children the coming winter. Her brothers, & sisters wish her to spend time here with Sister Sallie at the old Belmont-place. Her husband wishes her to be [in] St Louis by the first of next month. I do not know what they will do.

We had a most excellent sermon from Dr Lyon last Sabbath—He, & Mrs Lyon & the two young ladies[1] are now here on a visit to their friends. I was very curious to hear him preach again after all these years—to see if his preaching would satisfy me as it used to—especially after hearing such sermons as I have heard for the last year from our pastor. I was not disappointed. I do think he has grown spiritually. I never heard "Christ & him crucified"[2] more earnestly preached. I remember hearing bro Mc say long ago that was his only objection to Mr Lyon's sermons—they were intellectual treats, but had not enough of "Christ, & him crucified" in them. I think if he was permitted to hear what was said Sunday, he would be much rejoiced over the change. Dr Lyon did <u>not</u> preach from <u>notes</u> either—took his text—closed his Bible, & gave all his attention to the congregation. He & Mrs Lyon both asked many questions of you. I never saw Mrs Lyon look better—she has new teeth, & fashionable clothes, & her manner is so pleasant. The young ladies are much liked—they are very stylish in appearance, & are so sweet, & unaffected. They will leave tomorrow.

Many of our people are returning from their summer's jaunts—among others—Col, & Mrs Ottley. Col is very feeble—no better than when he left last Spring. Mrs Ottley just as pretty, & bright as a rose. The School-commissioners left Mrs Eager out in the cold in their last election—(<u>political</u> pique against all her friends—) but she has promise of a good private school, to open the first of

Oct in the basement of our church. She is very cheerful, & much gratified at her friends rallying around her. Mr E. P. Odeneal is lying very low—indeed! I would not be surprised to hear of his death. Mr Neilson sat up with him Monday-night, & thought then, there was no hope for him. John, & Willie have both come to see him. Poor Mrs Sturdivant[3] is the most to be pitied—her father was such a prop, & stay to her. There is no other serious illness that I have heard of. We have much to be thankful for—I hope we are.

Do write whenever you can. We <u>all</u> hope to see you. The children so often wish for you. Dear Trot, we do love you, & <u>long</u> for you.

Do try to keep well. Kiss Maj for me, if he is with you. I will write him very soon. God bless you.

Your loving
Lute.

NOTES

1. Lucy Deaderick Lyon and Idelette DeBure Lyon (b. 1858), daughters of Rev. James Adair Lyon and Adelaide Eliza Deaderick Lyon.

2. 1 Cor. 2:2.

3. Mary Jane Odeneal Sturdivant (b. 1835), daughter of Ebenezer Patrick Odeneal and Rosamond Dearing Odeneal and widow of Charles Gray Sturdivant (1830–62).

❦

September 1877 brought heavy rains, "which will," Lucy conceded, "much injure the cotton crops." "The fields look so forlorn, as if no more beautiful white cotton will ever be gathered," she wrote James Watt on September 22. "Mr Neilson is busy ginning—he keeps cheerful altho' times are blue. The season opens so dull. Well! for my part, I will be content, if we have enough to eat, & wear, & all <u>keep well</u>."

Family plans, however, meant that Lucy had little time to ponder the struggles that lay ahead. With her husband's consent, Sophie Abert Neilson Lewis agreed to spend the winter in Columbus. "Sister Sallie is going to have her old home repaired, & they will live there," Lucy noted. In the midst of relocating Sophie and family to Belmont, the inhabitants of Willow Cottage were rocked by the news that Bess was gravely ill with bilious fever. Lucy, now pregnant again, made a desperate dash to Mobile to nurse her beloved niece back to health. When Bess was out of danger, Lucy enjoyed the sights of the city and reported back to family on the Millers' "lovely home—so complete—so well fitted up." "I can see that Bess is a <u>thorough</u> housekeeper," she wrote with motherly pride on September 29, 1877. When she returned to Columbus in October, preparations for Jim and Carrie's wedding were in full swing.

Belmont, the Neilson family home. Irion Neilson Family Papers.
Courtesy of Mississippi Department of Archives and History.

Lucy to Lizzie

Home. Oct 17th/.77.

My darling Trot.

Three years ago this day my dear son Jack was born into the world! How much I have to be thankful for—my child has been blest in mind & body—he is our pride & joy! You were with me then—I wish for you now too! (When is there a time I do <u>not</u> wish for you?) Jack had a train of cars for his <u>present</u> at breakfast, & cake, & custard for his dinner—this rejoiced the eyes, & stomachs of <u>all</u> the children! The family-connection have so many children—there is a birthday or <u>two</u> for every month in the year, except <u>Feb</u>, (& I expect that vacancy will <u>soon</u> be filled)—Sister Sallie is afraid all the children will have dyspepsia from eating so many birthday-dinners. Louise, Cress & Jack have already had their's Charlie's will follow soon—5th Nov. Our children have had a happy time all summer— their separation will soon be at hand, & oh! how they will miss each other. Sophie is now at Bro James' (with Maud & the baby) having the home at Belmont put in order—the repairing, white-washing &c have been completed, & now the house-cleaning is going on. Sister Sallie is ready to go whenever John can send her. I feel very much interested, & will do all I can to help her. Cordele is so good—she gave Sister Sallie a box of things for her pantry—two jars of whortle berries, two of apples, two of peaches—a jar of wild plum preserves, a bottle of catsup, & one of cordial. Sister Mary has also contributed some—so they will not have entirely empty shelves. I will have a ham, & loaves of bread, both white & brown, ready for their immediate use—also toasted coffee, & a package of tea. We can give them some of our fresh nice Irish-potatoes, & corn too—say nothing of turnip-greens & onions! I never saw a person so loath to leave a place as Sophie was this! We have all had a pleasant summer—& we will miss each other mutually. It speaks right well for human-nature,—(& especially woman's nature)—for four women, & six children (& one poor lone man) to live in the same small house for so long a time together, & part better friends than they ever were!

All this I've said, & no word about our wedding! Well! since I've had news of your getting on so well, & Bessie's steady improvement, I am much happier, & take the greatest interest in the coming event. The marriage will take place on the afternoon of the 23rd at 3 o'clock. There will be no entertainment at Carrie's home—just the two families—we will return home that night: but Jim, & Carrie will not come up until Wednesday-afternoon—when they will go to their room at Mrs Shattuck's. They will occupy Mrs Shattuck's room until the first of January when they will take Mrs Lee's—"The Lees" will go to housekeeping in the Wormedsdorf-cottage next year.[1] I went Monday-morning to see Mrs Shattuck, & she & I had a good long talk. I will go again tomorrow, & help arrange the room—take all those pretty things which Bess sent—I know the room will look nice, for Jim has a lovely brussels carpet (drab ground & showers of bright flowers), & new furniture. All the ladies at Mrs Shattuck's are as much interested as if Jim was their kinsman. The only thing which is lacking is pretty pillow, & bolster shams—I don't know what made me forget them—a pin cushion too Mrs Lee intended making but can't use her hand—the dressing-case is complete—(all rose & white—so lovely & bridelike)—except the cushion. I think I can get Mrs Mosby to make one yet. I thus enter into details for I know you will be interested.

Jim says he cannot come out to dine with us until the following Sunday (is'ent that tackie?), he cannot leave the store longer than two days. Of course, we will have no company! Just ourselves—Jim & Carrie! Won't it feel strange for us to have a new sister? I think of her constantly as our neice. Our friends think it scandalous that neither you or Bess will be here; & look disappointed that we are going to allow the event to pass without an entertainment. You know people have such high ideas of our devotion to each other they expect us to turn the world upside down for one another, & oh! how gladly I would open my doors (to as many of the world as could get in), & invite them to rejoice with us on this occasion! Jim is more tremulous than you would think. Everybody teases him unmercifully—but he takes it all in the most amiable manner possible. I went up in his room the other day, & got his clothes to mend, & put in order. We have made him sheets, & plain bolster-cases.

Carrie belongs to the Baptist-church, but Mr McClintock is going to perform the ceremony! Don't you think that is a bold step for Mr Jim to take right at first? I know the Baptist folks will be highly miffed.

Mrs Willeford is trying herself on Carrie's trousseau—even Mrs <u>Field</u> told me she had seen some of the things, & they were lovely! I was right astonished at her owning up to seeing them.

Mrs Field offered to give flowers to decorate Jim's room; now was'ent that sweet of her.

Not having any company at our house, & Jim's putting off until Sunday to dine with us—gives us ample time for our house cleaning. We will not be hurried at all. I hope Mrs Hunter[2] will have my dress here in time. I don't know what I shall do, unless I call on my friend Mrs Ottley. I am now <u>modestly attired</u> in her lace sacque, & imagine my self highly presentable. I am sorry Cordele can't have her new dress, for all Carrie's folks are quite dressy, but I could not help it. Her plum-color is very nice, & she has had it looped stylishly, & nicely cleaned, & her bonnet is being put in order—so I have no doubt she will look very well. I know my dress will be plain—I could'ent expect anything more for $20. Yet I hope it will look stylish. Kiss my dear Bro Watt for me—I don't know how I am to do without seeing you both until next Spring! We all wish for you, for we love you with all our hearts. Not a word about Louise or John—they both are well, & send best love. John is too busy to be like himself—looks tired & careworn.

I know you were glad to see Cous Mary—& Cous <u>Davis</u>! Do write soon! Will our things be sent C.O.D.? Try to get all in one box if you can. Let us know when the box starts.

Good-bye—God bless you both, & keep you safe.

Loving—
Lute.

NOTES

1. Lucy was probably referring to the upcoming marriage of William Hollinshead Lee to Louise Waring (1856–1907) on February 21, 1878, and the relocation of William's mother, Elvira Anne Lee, into their household.

2. Dressmaker P. J. Hunter (b. ca. 1854).

🙰

Jim married Carrie in a quiet country ceremony, surrounded by family and friends. Unable to indulge in lavish food, finery, and entertainment in an effort to impress guests and garner prestige, postwar southerners instead joined with their guests to reaffirm community ties. Cordele and Lucy represented the family, and their friends worked diligently to ensure that the bridal party received proper congratulations.

Lucy to Lizzie

Home—Oct 25th/.77.

My darling Trot—

The event which has absorbed us for sometime is over, & <u>well</u> over. The morning of the 23rd dawned upon us, bright & beautiful. In good time our family (John, Cordele, Louise, Jack, myself, & <u>Ed</u>) were in our little carriage èn route for the wedding. The children were excited with the importance of the occasion, & Jack was wondering "<u>what</u> they were going to <u>have</u>"—["]alas! poor human nature." The ride was long but the day was so lovely, we all enjoyed it—there was just enough frostiness in the air, to make our <u>spirits</u> high. On the way, Jack grew weary of so much riding, & concluded he had rather go back home to see his (dog) <u>Ponto</u> than to go to Uncle Jim's wedding—such a sentiment drew down such a storm of reproachful ohs! & ahs! the little fellow looked <u>almost</u> ashamed of having expressed his innermost feelings so publicly—his <u>Ed</u> was the only one who gave him the comfort of a <u>smile</u>. We got to Mr Smith's in good time for me to lie down, & rest. Mr, & Mrs Smith I had before known, & liked very much—then we were presented to Mrs Smith's two sisters—Mesdames Baldwin & Williams[1]—the former a widow, with no children, living not far off, with their father <u>Mr Petty</u>. Mrs Williams has a nice husband, Dr Williams, & <u>three</u> children—two of whom are off at school—one little boy at home. These, with a little girl of Mrs Smith's named Mellie, compose Carrie's family. There [they] are nice people too—people who live well, & know what to do—a little reserved, as most people are, who live in the country. Mrs Baldwin is real <u>dashy</u>—quite handsome, & intelligent. They are <u>nicer</u> people than expected. They have a good home, well furnished. There were some of the neighbors present—a few of Carrie's young married friends. Then came Mrs Lee, & her two sons—this was all the company. Mr McClintock's ceremony was as appropriate as words could make it—not as long as when Bess was married, but equally as beautiful. Carrie looked so pretty—her fair young face was the reflex of her character—modest, & refined. Her dress was lovely—drab silk with soft fleecy rouches & white flowers at throat, & sleeves. Her hair is always beautiful—wavy, & golden. She conducted herself with great ease, & dignity—was not at all overcome with embarrassment as I thought—I was glad too. I never saw Jim look as handsome, & oh! <u>his</u> face was also a reflex of what his heart felt. I never saw a sweeter expression of coun- tenance. Mrs Lee was his Mother, & walked up, & gave him a sweet kiss—she was so interested, from <u>first</u> to <u>last</u>, as if Jim was her son—she, of course, has taken Carrie under her wing.

After the kissing, & handshaking, & congratulations—we were invited out to refreshments. Everything was nice, & good, & very abundant—the cakes were elegant both in <u>quantity</u>, & quality. The turkey, pig, & salads splendid. Two kinds of wine, & all the fruits of the season. <u>Jack</u> was delighted with "<u>what they had</u>"— he & Ed ate their's out in the yard. Louise has been dissatisfied ever since that I did not let her have as much as she wished—says "Ma-ma did not let her <u>enjoy</u> the <u>party</u> as much as she wanted." Both the children behaved well, & attracted much attention. Jack seems to understand perfectly about the marriage—says "Aunt Carrie belongs to Uncle Jim now." We had to start home as soon after refreshments as was polite—the Lees, Mr McClintock & ourselves. Jim, & Carrie staid, of course. We bade good-bye with many promises of sociability between families. Arrived at home about 7½ o'clock P.M.—I was <u>dead</u> tired—for I had Louise in my lap most of the way—Jack in Cordele's. We looked upon it tho' as a day full of enjoyment.

All this time, I've said no word about my <u>nice</u> dress, which came the day before, & which <u>pleased</u> me in all respects. For <u>which</u> you, & Mrs Hunter will accept my thanks. It is just the kind of dress, I wished, & is so comfortable, & made me look quite genteel in <u>figure</u>!

I think Cordele's dress is lovely, & will have it made as soon as I can. I thank you very much for your care, & trouble—I am sorry you felt worried about not sending it in the same box with mine. You ought not to have thought of paying the extra express. You spoke of children's flannel—none came, & what flannel do you mean?—they have enough for the winter I think; any how until <u>you</u> come.—

Well! now to the wedding folks again! Next morning John went off on busi- ness, & Cordele, Louise, Jack & myself went in the carriage to Mrs Shattuck's, & then sent Ed on for Jim & Carrie—Fred also with the cart for baggage. We went to work at Jim's room—to put the finishing touches. Every lady in the house added her little ornaments, & beautifying touches, & by the time all was arranged. I wished most heartily for you, & Bess! Mrs Lee was in her <u>glory</u>—so was Mrs Thompson[2]—fixing baskets of grasses, & vases of the loveliest flowers, looping the beautiful lace curtains with pretty blue ribbons; hanging fancy watch cases against the wall, & pretty card receivers on the mantel-piece. Jim's furniture is very pretty, & every thing is in such sweet taste. Mrs Lee, & her sons gave a most elegant present—a pair of silver goblets—<u>gold lined</u>, & genuine. Mr Cox gave a beautiful wash-stand sett—white & gold-bands. Bessie's, & Frank's pres- ents were the very things needed. Cordele gave a pair of vases to match Frank's toilet-sett—pink & white. Mrs Lee asked Mrs Humphries[3] for flowers, & she sent around the loveliest, rarest collection I ever saw! A great dish that covered the table. There were flowers every where—looked more like May, than Oct.

Just as all was in readiness, we looked out, & saw the carriage! All was now pleased excitement—Cordele & I went to the door to meet the bride & groom, but lo! only Mary Frazee, & a Mr Fitzpatrick (Carrie's cousin) who came to say that Carrie had had a severe chill, & fever, & was quite unable to come. What a disappointment! I don't believe I ever felt one more acutely—not so much for us, who had fix[ed] the room, as for Mrs Shattuck, who had prepared a most <u>elegant</u> tea. I took the young folks in to see the room—& when they left, went to tell the sad news. Every face showed interest & disappointment. We persuaded Mrs Shattuck to put up all her nice things for the next evening, when they would come. We then came home. Next day we sent the carriage again & this time they came. John & Cordele went in to meet them. Every thing, & every body was in readiness—more fresh flowers had been sent in from Mrs Field's—& every thing bright, & inviting. Carrie was not very well, but went thro' the reception, & introductions with great credit to herself—so John said. All were in the parlor to receive her before tea—which was nice, & not at all like a boarding-house. Then they went out to tea. <u>And</u> such a table! John says it was like a party-table for fifty people, & such <u>elegant</u> things—salads, sardines, pickles, wafers, most beautiful breads,—great snowy cakes, & foaming bowls of Charlotte-russe, nuts & fruits. Now thats what Jim's friends did for him! And he will fully appreciate every thing.

They will dine with us Sunday—we hope to have Mrs Thompson, & Mr & Mrs Shattuck to come also—no one else. I have my cakes baked, & iced—am very well pleased. We'll have a turkey, & a brace of ducks. Hope every thing will be nice. My days for dinings, & company are few—I <u>am a sight</u> to myself.

Oh! I do wish to see you! I have not arrived at the <u>tearful</u> period yet—but will soon, & then I shall <u>cry</u> for you—<u>yes</u>! <u>I will too</u>!

I hope you are better—don't go to the plantation as long as you feel badly. Come home rather!

I must close. Kiss dear Watt, if he is with you—& ask him if he ever received my letter.

Do you, & Walker Irion[4] keep up your correspondence yet?—if so, tell him all about Jim's wedding. <...>

All send love—the chaps are asleep.

God bless you both.

Your loving Lute.

1. Mary M. Petty Boulding (b. ca. 1838) and Virginia Pidgeon Petty Williams (b. 1835) were the daughters of farmer Ralph Blakeney Petty (1807–83) and Frances Rice Petty (1816–68). Virginia was married to Dr. Henry Lawrence Williams (1830–1911) and was mother of Lillie M. Williams (b. ca. 1861), Henry Petty Williams (1866–1922), and Samuel Williams (1869–1908). The family lived in Pickens County, Alabama.

2. Mary Shell Curtiss Thompson (1820–96), mother of Melissa Elizabeth Curtiss Shattuck.

3. Rebecca A. Humphries (b. ca. 1828).

4. Dr. John Walker Jones Irion (1860–1945), son of Lucy's brother Dr. John Lewis Irion (1828–1904) and Anne Elizabeth Griggs Irion (ca. 1840–97).

ℱ

The Grange movement's popularity had begun to decline by 1877. Still, John Abert Neilson remained committed to the cause. When he decided to attend a Grange meeting in Holly Springs, Lucy noted that while her pregnancy would prevent her from traveling, the organization's decision to let "wives & families of Grangers . . . pay their own expenses" would have resulted in the same outcome.

As they struggled to make ends meet, Lucy relished John's decision to join the Presbyterian church.

Lucy to Lizzie

Home. Dec. 5th/.77.

My darling Trot.

Your letter came safely, & quite relieved my anxiety—I am so glad to hear you are getting on so well. Oh! that you could be with us. We so often speak of you having been with us this time last year. Mr Neilson will start next Saturday for the State Grange which will meet in Holly Springs. I expect he will go right on to Bailey Station to see Cousin Mary, & perhaps spend Sunday with her—he cannot make any definite plans for he does not know about the Rail Road connections on that road. He will be obliged to get to Holly Springs Monday to meet a very important committee. I wish him to see all the relatives while he is gone, & regret, more than words can tell, my inability to go with him. Besides my condition— the wives & families of Grangers have to pay their own expenses this year—which amounts to their being left at home. I do wish Cordele, & Louise could go any-how, but John made only a half cotton-crop, & you know our expenses are always heavy. John can't tell whether he will go to see the relatives before or after the meeting of the Grange. He would have more time <u>after</u>. I wish you, & he could meet at Cousin Mary's.

What do you think? John has transferred his membership from the Methodist-church to <u>ours</u>! Yes! indeed!—it took the breath out of me! I did not know he had an idea of such a change, until he showed me his letter. Mr Wadsworth[1] has gone back to Georgia—Mr Neilson was much attached to him—he said he thought it a good time for the change, before a new preacher came. The Methodist[s] are quite grieved—they had just elected him to a new office in their church. I do not think they ought to begrudge him to our poor old church, for we certainly do need help. Mr McClintock continues to be the beloved of our town. He asked Kate Barry if she had seen me, since <u>the</u> change—he said—"I know her face wears a broader smile now than ever." I wish you could <u>see Cordele</u>. She is like one <u>freshly revived</u>. We do not make a <u>great ado</u>—all rejoice in an orderly-<u>Presbyterian</u>-way—which you know is always <u>nice</u>, & dignified. <u>Louise's</u> little face brightened like an angel's, when I told her, & she said "O! Papa! I am so glad you are going to join <u>in</u> our church!" We did not think of her comprehending the situation.

I am glad Bro Watt received my letter at last—tho' it must have been <u>months old</u>. I do wish I could see him. Frank, & Bess sent us an oyster-treat Sunday—Jim, & Carrie came out to enjoy it with us. They were both well, & look so sweetly content. Carrie will join our church next Sunday—she brought her letter up with her from the church in the country. She has been home to spend a week.

We will have some change with our servants—we cannot keep so many. William & family, Uncle Noah & Aunt Phillis will go off together somewhere. I am sorry for <u>Mammy</u>—she does not want to go. I do not know what Woos will do. Nan wishes to go on a visit to <u>Lizzie</u> & <u>George</u>. All send love.

Do write soon.

Your own Lute.

Cordele resents that I did not mention <u>Jack</u>. He is just the <u>brightest biggest</u> boy in all the country. Goes to town with <u>Ed</u> on the cotton-wagon. He sends his love, & says bring him a <u>sling-shot</u>. Louise sends a letter written by her own hand.

NOTE

1. Rev. Willard W. Wadsworth (1851–1916), pastor of the Columbus First Methodist Church (1876–77).

℘ဆ

*Christmas 1877 was a modest celebration where new family members were wel-
comed to the table and distant kin were remembered with love. Carrie and Jim,
noted Cordele, were a picture of wedded bliss. "We like her [Carrie] ever so much,"
Cordele disclosed in a letter to Lizzie dated November 9, 1877. "She says she will
learn how to be sisterly, she seem to like me and confides in me. . . . Bud Jim seem
perfectly happy. Poor fellow I am glad to see him so."*

*An unexpected gift from her Sunday school class reminded Lucy of her place in,
and contribution to, the task of community building in the New South.*

Lucy to Lizzie

Home. Dec 26th/.77.

My darling Trot.

You are so good & thoughtful—how can we thank you sufficiently for your
kindness in remembering us these holidays. The box arrived just in time—on
Christmas-eve. We <u>all</u> went into town to our S.school <u>Christmas</u>-tree last night,
& found the box awaiting us at the Express Office. We <u>all</u> return thanks, & if you
could see the children, you would feel repaid for your trouble. Louise was wild
over her tea-sett—just "<u>like</u> I wanted it Ma-ma—<u>real</u> big cups & tea-pot, & sugar
bowl—& oh! the dear little spoons, & sugar-tongs!" Then the little kerchief is
just <u>her</u> color—how her eyes do sparkle over it! Jack is beside himself with his
<u>driving</u>-<u>reins</u>, & a riding-stick (with horse's head) & whip! We can hardly make
him look at his beautiful kerchief, or a lovely copy of the "<u>Nursery</u>"[1] which I gave
he & Louise jointly—nor will he take time to eat or do his <u>duty</u> in other things.
Cordele is as proud as a Queen of her elegant neck-tie, & so am I. John laughed
very heartily over the cravat. I know Carrie will appreciate her presents more
than any thing you could have sent—for she has but one sett for her bed, & was
deploring her need of fresh ones for Christmas. She made Jim an elegant dress-
ing-gown, & he gave her a lovely pin-cushion, & <u>tidy</u> (I believe). Bess wrote me
of her nice present from you—she is very proud of it. The Christmas-tree was
beautiful last night. I wish you could have seen how sweetly Louise behaved whenever her name was called out. She received several presents—a pretty doll, sent
from Mobile by Katie McCarthy—a picture prettily framed, & a card-receiver.
Jack got very impatient for his name to be read, & when it was, he walked up like
a man—he received a <u>rabbit</u> & a <u>tin horn</u> (!) that blows most <u>awfully</u>! Cordele
received a beautiful blue pin-cushion with a lace cover. John a <u>bag of candy</u>, &
Jim a bag of <u>pea</u>-<u>nuts</u>. My S.school class gave me an elegant pair of Parian-marble
<u>roses</u>, & <u>brackets</u>! I was so surprised, & my heart is full of thanks to the dear girls.
I will be with them only one more Sabbath. When you return from the bottom—
you must come <u>right on here</u>. I will need you then. Our dear love to Maj—<u>all</u>
send hearts of love to you both! We do long to see you.

Have you heard of the death of <u>Nelia Hardy</u>.[2] Yes, she was buried last week. I will write particulars next time.

God bless you—take care of you, & send you safely to us.

Your loving & thankful
Lute.

NOTES

1. Lucy had probably purchased a copy of *The Nursery: A Magazine for Young Readers.*

2. Cornelia Hardy (1859–77), daughter of Maria Clifford Hardy and Dr. Cornelius Hardy.

Interlude

Patron of the Unwed

*W*inter's canopy draped over the avenue of young magnolias that joined the northern and southern grounds of Columbus's Friendship Cemetery. The hallowed spot, set high on a bluff overlooking the Tombigbee River, was the final resting place for hundreds of Union and Confederate soldiers, most of whom had spent their last desperate hours on the bloodied fields of Shiloh. At the time, the citizens of Columbus had been overwhelmed by the grim work of burying the dead; they expanded the northwestern boundaries of the cemetery for Confederate patriots, procuring a separate allotment for the internment of federal soldiers. After the war they faced the equally daunting task of maintaining the cemetery. A group of four enterprising women, known for their tireless efforts tending the graves and decorating them with flowers, roused the town into action. The inaugural Decoration Day, which commemorated the sacrifices of both northern and southern soldiers, was held on April 25, 1866. Cordele Irion probably joined the procession that made its way into the cemetery grounds that day and participated in the following years when she made wreaths with Lucy and joined the townsfolk in the "imposing & solemn" memorials.

Cordele's temporary relocation to Wildwood had robbed her of membership in this strong community of women and the town that nurtured their involvement in cultural and religious affairs. Nestled at the juncture of the Tombigbee and Luxapalila Rivers, Columbus had been built on the genteel plantation ethos of the Old South. While cotton may have furnished the town with more than its share of stately homes, flush planters had also developed its educational and religious reputations. Franklin Academy and the Columbus Female Institute welcomed students from across the South, providing teachers with an alternative to marriage and motherhood. Cordele never equated paid employment with single blessedness, but she did derive great pleasure from a cultural landscape that turned, in part, on the intellectual programs of its academies. With her Sunday school class at the First Presbyterian Church and her steadfast attendance at religious services and conferences, Cordele moved through Columbus with a self-assurance that came from owning her place in the world. Her return to Willow

Cottage had been met with sweet relief, and she wasted no time in plunging headlong into the work of single blessedness—a life filled with family responsibilities, intellectual pursuits, devotional purpose, and community endeavors. Columbus's vibrant intellectual and religious life and its ranks of progressive postwar women made it possible.

Eight

United in Grief

January 1878–September 1883

*H*ard times demanded strict measures of domestic economy. Lucy greeted 1878 with her mind set on trimming the household budget while maintaining the semblance of gentility she had worked so hard to attain. The practical consider-ations of pregnancy provided her with some assistance; expecting another child afforded Lucy a sensible excuse not to indulge in the frills and furbelows of the season and a reason to pare down the frenetic social calendar at Willow Cottage.

Nevertheless, balancing domestic and family responsibilities with the de-mands of society left Lucy somewhat pressed for time. Either her letter writing or her ability to save her correspondence suffered as a result. Between 1878 and 1883 Lucy saved letters to record news of a more critical nature, in particular to inform Lizzie and Bess of the deaths of relatives, leaders in the community, and members of their immediate family circle. Lucy had always noted, in passing, the loss of a church member, a friend's neighbor, or a former servant—an update on the subtle shifts in community membership.

But death did not always appear as a footnote embedded among town hap-penings. When a neighbor, a friend, a family member, or a servant died, Lucy pieced together a detailed account of the departed's final moments. When death was expected and prepared for and came in a lucid, prayerful moment among family and friends, the loss of a loved one was tempered by the consolation of witnessing his or her passage into heaven. In 1862 Lucy had drawn comfort from her brother McKinney's "blessed blessed death-bed," which was not on a lonely battlefield but rather in the family home, where he "bade [family and friends] farewell, & exhorted [each one] to meet him in Heaven!"[1]

Not everyone was offered a peaceful passage or was given time to repent sins and declare a willingness to die. When their servant Charles drowned and John Mauger Symons collapsed under the weight of debt-ridden stress, Lucy wrote disconcertedly about unexpected death, which snaffled the opportunity for spiritual preparation. In an account of John Symons's death, Lucy relayed her sister-in-law's desperate attempts to rouse her dying husband. Robbed of his last words, John's salvation became uncertain and unaccounted for.

Death and its associate rituals strengthened the bonds of community. Family and friends offered support to the dying by taking turns to sit or pray with them. They bore witness to death and retold accounts of the death-bed scenes. They also participated in the rituals of burial and mourning, where remembrance was woven into both the fabric of community life and family reputation.

ℰ

Heavily pregnant and beset with thoughts of her own mortality, Lucy was overcome upon hearing the news that her sister-in-law Mary Bruce Barry Neilson had died of pneumonia on January 13, 1878. Mary had been eight months pregnant.

Lucy to Lizzie

Home Jan 14th/.78.

My darling Trot.

I have sad news to write this time, our dear Sister Mary Neilson is <u>dead</u>! Oh! yes, & you know how I grieve for her as indeed! I may, for she was one of my best friends on earth. On last Thursday Mr Neilson, & Cordele took the two children, & went up to see how they were all getting on, for Bro James had left home a few days before to attend the Legislature. Sister Mary complained then of cold, but was not sick. They took dinner with her, & came home soon after,— soon she felt badly, & lay down, & that night she grew so bad, the Doctor had to be sent for—she had pneumonia in its most acute form. We did not hear of it until Friday-afternoon when Mrs Eager, & Mrs Ottley came out, & told us Dr Matthews was quite anxious about her, especially as she was <u>eight</u> months in pregnancy. Saturday-morning we sent a messenger to hear how she was, & if we were needed; Sophie Lewis had sat up with her that night, & wrote that she had had a bad night, but was comfortable that morning—said she would let us know, if Cordele or Mr Neilson were needed. Dr Matthews went up that morning, & staid until late in the afternoon, when he left her free of fever, & talking & feeling quite naturally. He had not been home more than half an hour, when he was sent for again—her lungs were completely congested, & she suffered agony until she died, about 11 o'clock Sunday-morning! Labor pains came on too, & she sank immediately. Her mind was perfectly clear, & she assured them of her readiness to die—her only desire being to live until her husband could reach home. Oh! I can hardly realize this terrible affliction! Poor Bro James arrived this morning, only in time to look upon the cold cold clay, & see it laid to rest. He is completely crushed, as you may well imagine—such a wife as she was to him, & how he loved her! I feel so afflicted myself I dread to see him. I try to control myself, for my own, & my unborn babe's good, but oh! it is hard. There never were two sisters who had sweeter intercourse, than we have had for nearly seven years. She was every thing to me in the first years of married life, when I was so inexperienced. Her love, her sympathy, her interest, & her deeds of kindness were untiring. But why need I enumerate to you, who know so well how I loved, & depended on Sister Mary! And now to think she has gone, & I could not be with her in her last days, to administer one little comfort, of word or deed! I dare not think of those three orphan girls—thank God, the babe died with the mother—it never knew a separate existence. Just before Christmas, she came, & spent a week with us. Such a sweet time we had together too—I shall always be so thankful she came. We had so many merry laughs, & jokes about our Motherly conditions, & called our babes, the twins! I told her she had treated me badly, for it was not her time at all—but mine, & what would I do without her—she had spoilt me. One day during the holidays, she wrote for us to come, & dine with her—all met at her house, & what a delightful day we had. Nine little cousins, under the age of nine, were together, & such harmony you never saw! We parted with promises of meeting again, as soon as circumstances would permit. She & I exchanged prayers for each other's safe delivery! That was my last sight of her. Do you wonder I feel so stunned! so shocked. I wonder I can write all these details, & yet I must tell you, my darling! And now comes your letter, saying you cannot come! Well! I know you would, if it was possible—but my heart, & hope sank when you left Memphis. I will try to be brave, & with God's help, I will pass thro' the deep waters. I do not feel nervous about myself, because Sister Mary died. I feel that if it is best, I will be safely delivered, & if not, I trust it is not presumption in me feeling, I have a Savior! If things should go ill with me—remember, I love you next to my husband, & children, & if you cannot live here, that you will come for Cordele, & let Sister Sallie come to her brother, & his children. This may seem cruel at first, but I know it will be for the best in the future. I mean the greatest kindness to all concerned! I trust you to carry out my wishes!

I am anxious about your health. I cannot help it. Oh! if it was possible for us to be together.—We are all well, & all disappointed. The children can't understand why you can't come. Louise's face took on it's pathetic look, when I told her you were not coming. I am afraid Jack will forget you—we talk of you constantly, & try to keep you in his memory—he remembers his Uncle Watt perfectly, but it has been a long year since he saw you. They nearly break my heart about their "Mamie." Bess said in her last letter that she had not heard from you for three weeks. I hope my Christmas letter was not lost. I addressed to Delta. I have Woos for cook, & Lide for maid—Mamy Phillis went off in a flood of tears—begging me to send for her, when I got sick. Nancy is so good & attentive & knows so much more about babies, I don't think I will need Mamy, & then Aunt Mary is here too, always ready for a job! Sister Annie will be with me too, & if she is not,

I will send for Sophie—she is equal to any doctor. Don't be uneasy about me—only write, write, write!! If my mind is easy about you I can do my whole duty in a much more satisfactory manner. I hope Tot-Neanie will be a good, healthy little girl, & not cause much trouble. I wrote you immediately upon receipt of your letter of Dec 30th—hope you have it now. We have had cold, disagreeable, weather, but no snow. I have not seen Jim or Carrie for two weeks—it is a long time—but we have no extra horse now—Will Lee bought Jim's horse, & buggy. I love Carrie more & more—she is so much more practical, & helpful than I feared she would be. I wish her to know you, & Maj. I know Maj would feel like petting her. Tell Maj I trust him to take care of himself & you, even if he does have to live in that God-forsaken country. I know he will bring you out as soon as he can. I do not wish you to come, & leave him!

God bring us together soon. John, & Cordele unite in love, & prayers—

Your loving Lute.

I send you a notice of Nelia Hardy's death. I wrote you some of the particulars.

NOTE

1. Eliza Lucy Irion Neilson diary, undated recollections, 1862.

℘

On February 11, 1878, Lucy gave birth to Elizabeth "Lizzette" Cornelia Neilson (1878–1958). With two growing children and a baby to care for, Lucy put aside her journal for the period 1878–79.

On July 11, 1878, Lucy's niece Bess gave birth to a daughter, Frank Miller.

On December 2, 1879, John's brother James Crawford Neilson married Catherine Elizabeth Barry. "I thank God for blessing me with a good wife, abundant crops, health & strength," he wrote in his diary days after his marriage. Catherine was the sister of James's first wife, Mary Barry Bruce Neilson. In 1881 Catherine gave birth to a son, James Crawford Neilson Jr. (1881–1942).[1]

By 1880 Lucy was pregnant again, and on October 4 she gave birth to Sophie Abert Neilson (1880–82). Lucy's sister-in-law Carrie added to the troupe of girls, giving birth to Mellie Gray Irion (1881–1960) on February 20, 1881.

Lucy saved a few brief letters for the period 1880–82. On January 3, 1882, she made up for short notes by composing a sixteen-page letter to her sister-in-law Sarah Dandridge Neilson. The letter relayed particulars on the death of Rev. John David McClintock, pastor of the Columbus First Presbyterian Church. Lucy noted that while McClintock had been given a blessed deathbed, his loss had been keenly felt by

Catherine Elizabeth Barry Neilson. Sarah Neilson Papers.
Courtesy of Special Collections Department,
Mitchell Memorial Library, Mississippi State University.

all. *Without a spiritual guide, Columbus residents felt a loosening of the religious ties that bound faith and community together.*

Lucy to Sarah

Home. Jan 3rd/1882.

My dear Sister.

I feel really ashamed that your letter of greeting should have been written & received before mine was even begun. I <u>think</u> of you & Sophie so much, it is right hard, sometimes, for me to convince myself, that I have not <u>written</u> some of my thoughts, & sent them, as an assurance of my unceasing love, & interest.

Now that a quiet time has come, I so eagerly avail myself of it, & will write interminably I expect, for so many things come to mind of which I would like to tell you. First, is to tell the particulars of the sickness & death of our dear pastor—as you seemed desirous of hearing. He & Mr Neilson went to Synod, as you know. His health had not been as good as usual for weeks, & he had been in a dreadful strain, owing to the sickness of his wife, & infant[2]—then he was sick himself, & got out of bed to nurse his wife thro' a <u>second</u>, & very serious spell of sickness. We all hoped the trip would rest him body, & mind, & he seemed very eager to go. I shall always be glad that Mr Neilson went with him, for he was very desirous of his companionship. Mr Neilson said he seemed to enjoy himself very much in Vicksburgh, & met some old friends—which to one of his loyal nature, is always exquisite pleasure. On his way home he stopped in Jackson, & preached two sermons for Dr Hunter's[3] people. Those sermons were said to have been splendid, & all were edified. At the Dêpot, as he was coming home, he got his feet wet, & I suppose staid wet for the night. At Meridian, Dr Bardwell joined him—bringing the remains of Mrs Christian[4] to Columbus for burial. On reaching town, he assisted in the funeral services—then went to the Cemetery, & walked all over it with Dr Bardwelll—then during the day, he & Dr Bardwell took another <u>long</u> walk around the town. That night he came near choking to death with croup. And he was never well afterwards—he struggled against his sickness, & the last sermon was preached in a very labored manner. But oh! how lovingly he laid his hands in blessing upon our dear little Crawford—& how sweetly the innocent thing looked into his face, & coo-ed! He was sick next week—tho' not confined to bed—the next Sabbath, he wrote a note of deep regret, to Mr Neilson, saying he could not hold services that day.

Tuesday following, we went in to dine with Mrs Col Richards to meet Annie Hopkins Ross—Mr Neilson met Dr McCabe, & he told him how <u>very</u> ill Dr McClintock was—Mr Neilson hurried around to see him—, & he had no more hope for him. He did not die until the next Monday—, & all was done that mortals could do—but the Father took him! And oh! Sister, his death was in beautiful harmony with his life—his dying message to his people was "For I know whom I have believed, and am persuaded that he is able to keep that which I have committed unto him against that day."[5] O! our poor stricken church! We grieve for him as friend, pastor, but most of all, as our <u>pure spiritual</u> Guide! What we will do now, we cannot tell. The session feel deeply the great responsibility of making another call, & yet how important to have the church opened for worship. It seems the Lord will blot us out—another member died last week old Mr Hildebrand—, & one of the Misses Miller had a partial stroke of paralysis the other day. Who will be next.—

The whole community was grieved at Dr McClintock's death—men who apparently had no feeling, expressed the deepest regret. Every respect, every honor that could be paid, by an afflicted people, was paid to his dear memory. Perhaps you have had the particulars written more connectedly, more concisely than I have written them—I hope Sis Lizzie did, for I heard her say she had a letter for you, but did not know your address. Mr Neilson sent you a money order on the 23rd or 4th—& was a little surprised that you had not received it—you have, doubtless, by this time. I am glad you did'ent have any Christmas money, for I know how liberal hearted you are—& also hold in remembrance the box which you & Sophie sent last year—my heart ached over that box, for more reasons than one.

[. . .] Now for our own household! We thought best to let the children have a little tree, & receive their presents Saturday-night—so there would not be so much stir & delay Sunday morning—You know we have a Superintendent now to get off to S.School. Well, Bro Watt, & Sister, & Carrie, & little Mell came out Saturday afternoon, & we had everything in readiness—bright fires in all the rooms—especially in the parlor, where stood the tree ready for any kind of strange fruit. Mysterious brown-paper parcels were smuggled from the carriage, & after the happy greetings were over the children retired to my room for some games,—while the grown folks stepped across the hall to help Santa Claus. Of course, the presents were simple, & no attempt was made to ornament the tree other than the display of the gay colored toys—but it was real pretty. Santa Claus was very generous in tin wares—their bright coloring together with the gay bandannas for the colored friends, made quit[e] a show. There was a dressing-case (containing comb, brush, & hand glass) for Louise from Aunt Carrie—a hood of bright warm color from Mama—a box of paint from Neana—a mug from Papa, & some other trifles from Santa Claus—Jack rejoiced in a foot ball, a set of garden tools, a new cap, a slate, & book, & some trifles from Santa Claus. Lizzette, of course, had a doll—a beautiful one from Frank Miller—a housekeeping sett from Aunt Carrie—a cup & saucer from Lide (the nurse), &c. Dear little Sophie had a beautiful dress, & handsome sacque from Mrs McClintock—a new pair of shoes—some new stockings—dolls, tin ware in abundance. Little Mell had an elegant cup, saucer, & plate from Mrs Shattuck—sent all unbeknown to Carrie—& then dolls & little things fit for a baby to break, given by my children—Jack's present was a little tin horse—so like a boy! The colored friends were remembered with handkerchiefs & sweet soap. Lide, Bettie, & Thomas with numerous little things from the children. Frank Miller had her name called out too—& was the recipient of some very expensive tin ware. Now, altho the presents were of very little value as far as money went—yet to see the delight, the wide-eyed wonderment of the little folks when the bell rang, & the door was thrown open, was beautiful to behold! It is worth all other kinds of enjoyment to me, as a fond Mother to see the sweet, eager faces—so filled with happiness, & content. I wish you could have seen & heard Tot. 13th [page]—oh! dear me!

She was so perfectly delighted—"oh! she said" "Santa <u>Taus</u> came in here while we were at supper, & put all these things on this <u>chee</u>. When I meet him in town, I am going to say "Thank you <u>Santa-Taus</u>," and Sophie will have to say "<u>ta-ta</u>"!! She is still in the enjoyment of the sweet old delusion of a <u>real</u> personage. Louise was so proud of her letter, & card from Charlie—she begun answering last night, but I told her she must wait until Saturday to write.

[...] Tell Sophie, she would not be at all ashamed of her name sake, could she see how cute, & sensible she is. Sis Lizzie declares she is the <u>most lovely</u> baby I ever had—or anybody else in her opinion. Yes, I think Crawford is very like <u>you</u> & <u>Lou</u>. You know Lou was always like you, & so is Crawford. He is a magnificent boy—big as <u>Jack</u> was at his age—out growing all his clothes. Louise & Jack staid all night with Annie, & Kittie, & such happy birds, they all were. Lou is very pretty, & getting real <u>dignified</u>, & like a grown up girl. She is perfectly simple in her manner—no airs—no pretentions. You are well paid for writing me to write you a long letter. Don't let anyone know how many pages I have inflicted upon you. John would send love & say "<u>come</u> home," but he is not at home. God bless you all this New Year!!

Lute.

Bring this letter home with you. It will save me writing a description of Christmas 1881 in my Journal for the children. Excuse such a request—but I am pressed for <u>time</u>.

NOTES

1. James Crawford Neilson diary, December 1879, Lillian Neilson Papers.
2. Paul Brown McClintock (1880–81), son of John David McClintock and Margaret Brown McClintock.
3. Rev. John Hunter (1824–99), pastor of the Jackson First Presbyterian Church.
4. Arabella C. Christian (1820–81).
5. 2 Tim. 1:12.

ℰ๖

On February 6, 1882, Bess gave birth to a second daughter, Hattie Hayden Miller (b. 1882). Lizzie, who attended the birth, relayed particulars to Lucy and family in Columbus. "What a world of interest the little <u>thing</u> awakens," remarked Lucy in a letter to her sister dated February 14, 1882. "We are <u>crazy</u> to see her. I imagine her very much like Frank." "What a generation of <u>girls</u> our family are <u>raising</u>," she added. "Where will the <u>husbands</u> come from—for, of course, they must be very <u>choice</u>, or else we'll [have] none of them."

While Lucy dreamed of watching her family grow, she knew all too well that children trod a precarious path to adulthood—and many, including Lucy's daughter Sophie Abert Neilson, did not survive. Three days after her daughter's death, Lucy wrote to Lizzie and Bess.

Lucy to Lizzie and Bess

Home. July 16th/.82

My darling Sister, & Neice.

I come to you with an over-flowing heart—not <u>all</u> of sorrow, for there's much of praise too. Our little one, our precious one, is so safe, so free from pain, or suffering—so <u>securely</u> nestled in the loving Savior's bosom—how can we wish her back! We grieve for our own loneliness—our heart's cry out at the breaking of the <u>tenderest</u> bond—but could we to sin, & pain, call her soul back again? No dearest Savior! no!—

It came upon us so suddenly—her sickness was so short—we can scarcely realize that it is not all a dream, from which we will soon, rejoicingly awake! You know Sis Lizzie, she had not been well for some weeks—cutting her four worst teeth. We had been so very careful to watch every change of the weather— making suitable changes in her clothing—had fires too every cool morning— even omitting the usual head washing on last Saturday, for fear of cold. She was not very well Saturday-afternoon—& that night I gave her a powder, because I thought she was a little feverish—next morning she was well, & after rubbing her with quinine, she was bright, & lively. We went to S.School, & came back, finding she had had her nap, & was bright & loving as usual. All day Monday she was her own little merry self. Monday-night, I was awakened by her breathing rather heavily—as if her nose was obstructed. I got up rubbed her with a little liniment—put a suet-plaster on her chest—gave her some glycerine & potash— after this her head seemed to clear, & she breathed naturally, & I went back to sleep. Tuesday, she was quite <u>hoarse</u>—but just as bright & lively as she could be. The Lee family dined with us—brought their little girl,[1] & oh! how Sophie did love her, & how prettily the three little girls played together. They were right with us all day. I was anxious about Sophie's hoarseness, & gave her toddy, & glycerine several times thro' the day to break up the phlegm. She had three very hard coughing spells—Cousin Mary Barry was here too, & I asked her several times—please to listen to Sophie's breathing, & see if there was any sound of <u>croup</u>—she did listen attentively, & Sophie patted her so lovingly on the face, as she put her ear down on her chest to listen. Cousin Mary could hear nothing that indicated croup. But toward's night Mr Neilson proportioned calomel, & ipeac, & we begun giving her that. All this time she was just as good, & bright, with <u>no</u> distress of countenance, or fretfulness at all.

When our friend's were gone I put her to bed—she slept profoundly until about 10 o'clock, when she awaken with great difficulty of breathing, & dryness of cough—we sent immediately for Dr McCabe—he came so promptly, & relieved her, & staid until her breathing was natural—left explicit directions, & said we must send him word in the morning if she was not entirely relieved—which we did, & he came promptly. He did not try to deceive us as to the severity of the attack—but we all went to work. All day Wednesday she was bright & playful—the calomel had good effect—but the <u>breathing</u> was still obstructed. The Dr came again in the afternoon, & said he would come again at night, & watch with us. She went to sleep at her usual time, & awakened between 8 & 9 o'clock.

She was so bad, we sent for the Dr anyhow—tho' he was coming as fast as he could. All that fearful night we fought death—The Dr was oh! such a friend!—God bless him for the comfort, & support he was to me that night. Thursday was not such suffering—her mind was perfectly clear—she could ask for anything she wished. She was loving, & clinging to the last—& would even <u>thank</u> us for giving her water. The end was calmness, & peace. God gave us strength in the supreme hour to bow in <u>sincere</u> submission to His will! What a blessing was that!—

Such a sweet little life to look back upon!—We, every one, appreciates her loveliness—indeed! "<u>Lovely</u>" was my little pet name for her. We have no cause of <u>regret</u>—we did all we had <u>knowledge</u> to do. Sister Sallie was, a tower of strength to us. Friends flocked to our aid—& all that tenderness, & love could do—was done. The children all grieved—but there was a <u>peculiar anguish</u> in Tot's cry for her little sister.

I dwell upon the particulars—not to excite your emotions—but because, I feel that you wish to hear. My dear Sister, must nerve herself, & bow her heart in submission—Tis from the Lord! Be still!! I never had a trouble in my life, I did not wish to <u>fly</u> to you with it, but this time, I thanked God, you were away—, & you must not give way to your grief, & injure your health—for oh! remember how precious your life is to us all. We hope, & pray you both, & the little children, keep well. None of us are right well. The weather is too cool night, & morning—like September.

Jim, & Maj were both with us—but Carrie & little Mell were down in the country. Mrs Ottley, & Cousin Mary Barry, & <u>Nan</u>—dear faithful Nan—performed the last service. Mr Stainback read appropriate verses at the grave. There was a large attendance of friends. Every body so good, so thoughtful. Our friends Messrs Cox, Lee, Topp & Hale² bore the little white casket to it's last resting place. We have had everything to make us grateful. Now oh! that <u>each</u> of <u>us</u> may gain a <u>spiritual blessing</u>, thro' our temporal loss! May our little One be the means of <u>fixing our hearts</u> on high.

Do take every care of yourselves & write us as often as you can. We were sorry not to hear from the Post today—we expect letters are waiting there.

Miss Lizzie Blair sent me a sweet loving note. Mr Neilson went, & presided over the S.school as usual—a great trial to him tho'. Cordele, & I felt we could not go. Woos, & Lide looked lost this morning. They missed their baby. Aunt Phillis & Nan watched all night with us. We all send love. We <u>do</u> love each other. God take care of you all, & send you safely back.

Lovingly,

L.I.N.

NOTES

1. Anne Louise Lee (1879–1944), daughter of William Hollinshead Lee and Louise Waring Lee.

2. Probably W. W. Topp Jr. (1851–1908) and Charles Harrison Hale (1847–80).

෯෨

Dazed by the events of the previous two weeks, Lucy drew comfort from recounting the story of Sophie's death. Wrapped in the innocence of childhood, her daughter was "<u>redeemed</u> by the blood of the precious Savior." "We are blest in having had such a sweet life to look back upon," she wrote Lizzie and Bess on July 20, 1882. "And now Heaven does seem more <u>real</u> with her sweet spirit there."

As Lucy and John grappled with their loss, the bonds of family and community tightened around them. "Our friends are unremitting in their kindness & attention," Lucy wrote, and "Sister Sallie is such a comfort to us all—she rejoices that she is with us in our time of trial."

Lucy to Bess

Willow Cottage.

July 29th/.82.

My darling Bess—

Your dear, sweet letters filled my heart with love, & gratitude. Such unselfish love blesses any life, that it shines upon. I have never had one second's uneasiness about your loyalty. From earliest childhood, you have clung to us with wonderful closeness. You might have been attracted by the gloss & glitter of the world—but you were ever as true as the needle to the Pole.[1] How <u>safely</u> I <u>trusted</u> in you. That's the <u>best</u> feeling after all. We have always had the most delightful intercourse, & what a source of happiness it has been. We feel that we are sure of each other's love. I am impatient for your sympathy in love, & sorrow. Sister Sallie was astonished that I could <u>write</u> to you & Sis Lizzie while my heart was so sorely torn—I told her, I had been so used to go to you with every thing—I could not rest until I did pour out my heart to you. Mr Neilson received Sis Lizzie's dear letter today, & I did thank God for the <u>quiet</u> which pervaded it. Oh! you know Bess—how sadly how constantly, we miss our sweet one—It seems impossible sometimes to realize that we will never look into those eyes again—or fold that dimpled form in our arms. It seems as if we must hear those little pattering feet—or hear that sweet fresh voice. She was snatched from us so suddenly—we have felt half paralized. I do not wish Sis Lizzie to torture herself with the thought of Cordele or me breaking down. No—thank God—we can grieve without any fear of that. We pray not to grieve in a sinful, & repining manner. At night, I suffer most!— my arms are so empty. I am as conscious all thro' my sleep of her <u>loss</u>, as I used to be of her precious bodily presence. When we have had much company, & Tot would sleep with me—I did'ent once, even in half conscious moments, mistake her for my little Lovely. No, that feeling of <u>loss</u> is with me always. Yet, we do not mourn in tears all the time. We all talk of her sweet, winsome ways—& the children speak of her constantly, & wish for her in their plays, & repeat her little <u>sayings</u> in the happiest way. Tot says the precious Savior is <u>keeping</u> care of Sophie now. They have had <u>no</u> shrinking of my room, or the parlor since her sickness or death—every thought, & feeling towards her is love, & tenderness. They would fondle her little hands, & feet, as she lay white & still. When we went to town we took the little casket in the carriage with us, to the church, where the procession formed, & the pall-bearers took it in their carriage—even this close contact seemed to please them. You don't know how thankful I am they feel thus, & have had no nervous fears—as I used to have when a child. We have had many friends to visit us—everyone has shown the tenderest love—Love, & sympathy is sweet.

Theodoric Lyon has written a very sweet "In Memoriam" which I enclose.[2] We will be very <u>lonely</u> now, Sis Sallie left this morning, with the children. Sophie Lewis was impatient for them to come—she feared the scarlet fever for John James—his throat is his weak point. We do not much fear the fever out here—we have not allowed the children to go to town, even to S.School. They will be very lonely—for they have had a happy time with their Cousins. Sister Sallie hated dreadfully to go—she has been such a sweet comforter to Cordele & I.

Mrs Bradford has spent a night with us—she was so kind, & sympathetic. Mr Neilson saw Maj on the train this morning en route for Corinth. I do not know when he will return. Carrie has returned from the country—but we have not seen her. We are very anxious to see her, & especially Mellie. [pages missing]

Your loving T'Ida

Howdy to Adeline. Woos up yet?[3] Don't you think Sis Lizzie writes too much—so many, & such long letters—it must tax her strength. Writing is quite a strain. She must confine herself to P.Cs. I am very unselfish in saying this, for her letters have been such a pleasure to us all. All the coloreds ask to be remembered.

NOTES

1. Barton Booth, "Sweet Are the Charms of Her I Love," in Benjamin Victor, *Memoirs of the Life of Barton Booth* (1733), in Cleveland, ed., *English Literature*, 418.

2. A copy of the clipping is included in the diary transcript.

3. Malinda Barron was expecting her second child, Nannie Barron (b. 1882).

℘ℨ

With meals to be prepared and Sunday school classes to attend, Lucy struggled to return to life without Sophie. Salvation's promise, which had loomed large in July, waned as the search for answers began. Like many evangelical women, Lucy scrutinized herself, fearing that Sophie's death was retribution for her devotion to earthly, not spiritual, things. Lucy's anxiety was compounded by the realization that she was pregnant again.

Lucy to Lizzie

Home.

Aug 7th/.82

My darling Trot.

I wrote you a P.C this morning, just by way, of quieting your fears as to any of us being sick. Your letter yesterday was so nice, & cheering—I read it time, & time again. You don't know how glad I feel, when I think of you as being quiet in heart. I know how willingly you would bear every trouble, & sorrow for me—but that cannot, & ought not to be. I have been most tenderly guarded & protected all my life—but God is a loving Father, & He does not chasten except in wisdom.[1] Perhaps He saw, I looked upon my child as a gift, & not a loan—He took His own, to remind me of my mistake. It is very hard to feel entirely willing to be as nothing. We sing that little hymn "O! to be Nothing—nothing"![2]—but is it not, most of the time, only lip-service. If there is anything on earth that a Mother feels is her very own, it is her baby—her nursling. But when the stern fact is forced upon her, that it is not—oh! an utterly helpless feeling possesses her torn heart. But will not this very helplessness, make her fly to the Rock that is higher than she.[3]

O! for a blessing—a lasting spiritual blessing to flow from this affliction! Mrs Lyon wrote me a most beautiful Christian letter—she said among other exalted things—"Think what an honor to be the Mother of a Saint in Heaven." I had never thought of that—all my thoughts were of my unworthiness to be entrusted with her here on earth.—I wish you, & Bess could see all of our loving, tender letters—which have come from friends—north, south, east, & west. Every body has tried in every way to show their sympathy.

I went to S.school yesterday for the first time—I almost wished I had staid at home. I put a great strain on my feelings, but at last had to succumb, & was so over come, I was unfitted for any duty. I hope next time it will be less a trial. The fright about scarlet fever is over—we allowed the children to go to s.school yesterday. They had become right restless at staying away so long. Tot said Saturday—"Well! tomorrow is Sunday, I want to go to church, & I'm going too!" She is so bright, & loving—she has seemed to try to be sweet & good—whenever she sees me weeping—she will come, & throw her arms around my neck, & beg me not to cry. She will be so glad to see Frank, & Hattie.

We begin already to count the time of your return—does it not seem long? Maj drove out yesterday to see us—we enjoyed his visit. He is well, & in good spirits. Had a letter from the Dr—which he said he was going to send you. I will be glad when the Dr returns—Jim Irion says he has no business going a courting even in the summer time.

Had a most satisfactory visit from Anne Ross⁴—she was very interesting—, & filled with longings to see you & Bess. She & Charlie love each other devotedly, & are very happy—despite poverty. Anne will teach this next term in her Mamma's school. She says she will be happier for something to do—she has no prospects of family, & is well, & rested, & she goes to work with vim. She will teach only in the mornings. Lizzie Hale is in town now, visiting Anne—she will come out here the latter part of the week. Anne will go home Thursday. Rebecca Barry, & Elise go over to Starksville this afternoon to make the Friersons⁵ a visit. Rebecca gives Elise the trip. Quite an era in her life. It is reported in town, that Mrs Ottley has gone to Denver to marry Mr Campbell.⁶ We wonder from whom she can be running away! Cousins Cornelia, & Lou Ellen promise to come out this week—but I don't know. Cordele is getting over her cold, but has lingering touches of toothache now, & then to remind her of it. Mr Neilson has been absent all day—attending the meeting of Supervisors. We miss him very much. He has been away from home, as little as possible, since our affliction. Is'ent he just the loveliest man—so different from other men, who would avoid all that was sad, or gloomy. He certainly does fill my heart, & life with a wealth of love.

Louise has been very lonely since Maud left—I am going to let her visit some, for she has been at home so closely. She studies some, every day, when not interrupted by company. Jack is so lonesome without John James, that Mr Neilson has to excuse <u>Tommie</u> from the field to play with him sometimes. Woos is up yet—but will retire from the kitchen tomorrow I expect. Nan will take her place. Woos seems very strong, & well.

I had a letter from Bun—poor Auntie—how worse than death is her case! How nobly Corrie is standing up to duty. Who would ever have thought that she, with her highly nervous nature, could help take care of a person afflicted as Auntie. Why Corrie used to be afraid of her own shadow. Beside this living trouble—her heart is broken on account of her darling Sister's death.[7] Bun says she is perfectly overcome by it.

Tell Bess to write when she can, & I will do the same. Kiss the children for each of us. What does Frank <u>talk</u> about these days. I am hungry for some of her bright sayings. I wish I could see the baby. Carrie will come out this week. Little Mell was mighty sweet yesterday. God bless you all. Lute.

Notes

1. Heb. 12:5–6.

2. Georgiana M. Taylor and R. George Halls, "Oh, To Be Nothing" (1869), in Hobbs, *American Hymnody*, 88.

3. Ps. 61:2.

4. Annie Hopkins married lawyer Charles Coffin Ross (b. 1850) on July 14, 1881. Charles was the son of Rev. Frederick A. Ross (ca. 1796–ca. 1882) and teacher Frances R. Ross (b. ca. 1821).

5. The family of Rev. Samuel Reese Frierson (1818–80) and his wife Mary Evelyn Barry Frierson (1829–88) of Starkville.

6. The marriage did not take place.

7. Possibly Mary Nesbitt Davis. Laura Corrie Nesbitt Myers's other sister, Elizabeth Nesbitt Eddins, was alive at this time.

ℬ

Lucy gave birth to James Furniss Neilson (1883–1924) on January 18, 1883. With Lizzie visiting Margaret Brown McClintock in Kentucky, Lucy relished the time spent nursing babies, attending church, and visiting with friends. The bonds of community, which had embraced her in her time of trial, now tightened ever closer in a celebration of new life.

Lucy to Lizzie

Willow Cottage—
May 28th/.[1]883.

My dear darling Sister—

We have received your letter from Daught's—also your <u>little</u> note 'on the cars,' & now await one announcing your arrival at Mrs McClintock's—meanwhile I will write a little, for I feel so constrained to have a talk with you. We imagine you, & Sister Mc, having nice long confabs, & this afternoon, I will draw my chair up, & join you. There are many little home, & town items, which may interest you both, & I will write in a free, dis-jointed way, which you will excuse. I am thankful to say, 'all is well' with us as a family—the weather is lovely—my 'gude man' busy having his <u>wheat</u> cut.—the sound of the <u>reaper</u> is heard in the land, on all sides— the crop promises fair. Soon we will have nice fresh Graham flour, & sweet bread. Yesterday was a beautiful Sunday—Cordele did not feel well—so she & Furniss staid at home—but the faithful Superintendent went early—followed later on, by myself & the children in the new carriage (with new nickel-plated harness which <u>Sophie</u> Lewis bought for us in St Louis—& is beautiful)—The Sunday School was well attended—the church services delightful—there was a good congrega- tion, & Mr McAlpine[1] glowing in his earnestness on the great work of Christ's church—foreign missions-text—"Go ye unto all the world"[2] &c. Jim, Carrie, & Mellie—also Kate Neilson Annie & Kittie came home with us. We had a pleasant social talk in the afternoon—as we <u>nursed</u> babies together. You have doubtless heard of the case of scarlet-fever in the Augusta Seminary, & of Miss Baldwin's prompt action in the matter—She telegraphed to each parent, & asked their intentions as to what best [to] do for the girls—Of course, <u>our</u> Dr dispatched for his dear darling[3] to <u>come</u>, as fast as steam could bring her. He then called in his friends Mesdames Harrison & Sykes[4] to put his home in exquisite order—while he took the first train to meet Passie. "It is said," he was so determined every thing should be looking it's 'beautiful best' for her sweet eyes to look upon—that he actually <u>telegraphed</u> to Mrs Sykes, <u>please</u> to see that the <u>flowers</u> were all well sprinkled!!! Ha! ha! ha!! I will laugh Trot—I don't care if you do shake your head at me. <u>You</u> know, your <u>Beloved</u>, <u>is</u> a perfect old maid—now don't you? Mrs Ottley told me about the <u>flower sprinkling</u> & I told her—I was bound to write you of it—& oh! how she enjoyed the thought!! Passie is said to be looking remarkably well—she was at church yesterday, with her Father—but of course, <u>I</u> did'ent see her. Mrs Harrison, Mrs Sykes, Mrs Fort & the children[5] went to the dêpot to meet her, which attention seemed very gratifying to her—for they said she was very <u>gushing</u>. You also know that the Musical Conservatory at Cincinnati[6] is under <u>Small Pox</u> Quarantine. Poor Minnie can't get home now—& poor dear Sister Annie is almost frantic—She has telegraphed Minnie to let her know if she is sick, & she keeps her trunk packed, ready to go to her at a moment's warning. I am so sorry for her—poor anxious Mother!

Little John Hale[7] has been so very ill with bilious pneumonia—he is better now—but looks wretchedly. I fear Lizzie will be ill herself for she goes to school now even before she has had any rest from nursing John. Sister Annie came back from Selma when she heard of John's sickness—we felt so thankful she did—I was so powerless to help Lizzie—with my little baby so young.

Mr Neilson has been taking me round visiting—last week, we made eight good visits. Among others, we went to see Carrie Eager—found her very glad to see us—but very lonely without her husband—two of her little children[8] were sick in bed—you know my heart went out in sympathy to her. My friend Mrs Fitts has been in town—You may know, we had a meeting, & a show of children!![9] We had not seen each other since my marriage! Lide declared, I looked just as young as ever! Mrs McAlpine has come home with her two little girls[10]—she looks very well. Mr McApline spent a day with us last week—he was so pleasant. Elise was here, & was glad to meet him. Elise has helped me with three dresses—I am very much pleased with the fit, & style—think you would be too!—it is real good to have that much work off hand, & on body!! It is a pleasant feeling to have some nice new clothes too—I have been without so long. Cordele is making Lizzette's little home dresses so nicely—& I am going to make her a pretty white dress this week—ready for the Examination exercises next week. Tot went with her Mamy to the colored "zamination," & enjoyed herself very much—said "The drum beat so, it made my heart beat—but I liked it tho!"

The children do miss you so much. Every day they speak of it—& as for Cordele & John & I—words fail! But oh! we are so glad you have this precious friend to go to, & we feel so safe, in having you with her—if you do get sick—which we pray you may be spared—You have a better start this year, & oh! may you return to us in the Autumn—fresh & bright as the days are long. You must know, after you had been gone about ten days, Furniss had a hoarseness, which made us feel uneasy—all our sorrow of last year was brought to mind—but God spared us & our little one seems bright & well—altho' still a little hoarse. We have been to the Cemetery recently—carried lilies to dress our little grave—put some also on dear Mr McClintock's, & little Paul's. Tell Mrs McClintock, she would be glad to see, what nice order her graves are in—the flowers were blooming beautifully—especially the white verbena—with her permission we will transplant a sprig of it on Sophie's grave, as we have lost all of ours. I always associate our three loved ones together in that bright world.—

Saw Minnie Mills[11] yesterday—she comes in to Sunday School, & has taken her old class again—it looks quite natural to see her. Tell the boys[12] Jack still loves them better than any friends he ever had—he would be so glad to have them here with him. Louise & Lizzette send their love to all. Cordele will write soon. Mr

Neilson would have <u>lots</u> of love & good wishes to send if he knew I was writing. Our united love to Mrs Mc—Miss Lyde[13]—yourself, & the Judge.

Your loving Lute.

Your colored friends make many & anxious inquiries of you. They send best respects. I enclose one of Jack's <u>enigmatic</u> epistles. Tot wishes to write a letter to Auntie <u>too</u>—but I can't this time. Kiss little John for me. <u>Furniss</u> is <u>so pretty</u>.

NOTES

1. Rev. Robert Brown McAlpine (1848–1920), pastor of the Columbus First Presbyterian Church (1883–87) and husband of Mary Elvina Craig McAlpine (1857–1946).

2. Mark 16:15.

3. Passie Fenton McCabe (1868–1940), daughter of Dr. Fenton Mercer McCabe and Passie Butler McCabe (1838–70).

4. Julia Randolph Whitfield Harrison's daughter Caroline Dyer Harrison had married lawyer Edward Turner Sykes (1838–1922). Julia was living with her daughter at this time.

5. Louisiana Victoria Harrison Fort and her sons, Robert Wallace Fort and Julian Harrison Fort (1874–1917), were living with Louisiana's sister Caroline Dyer Harrison Sykes at this time.

6. The Cincinnati Conservatory of Music was founded in 1867 by Clara Baur (1835–1912).

7. John Symons Hale (b. 1878), son of Charles Harrison Hale and Elizabeth Symons Hale.

8. Charles Christian Eager (1850–1909), son of Charles Prince Eager and Laura Emily Wright Eager and husband of Carrie Hargrove Eager (1855–1903). Charles and Carrie had three children at this time: Mollie Eleanor Eager (1876–1954); Laura Eager (b. ca. 1878); and Ebenezer Hargrove Eager (1879–1948).

9. Eliza "Lide" Watt Fitts and William Aylett Fitts had four children at this time: Cornelia Fitts (b. ca. 1868); Margaret Fitts (1870–1957); William Aylett Fitts Jr. (1871–1967); and Olive Aylett Fitts (b. 1878).

10. Rev. Robert Brown McAlpine and Mary Elvina Craig McAlpine had two daughters: Laura Craig McAlpine (1881–1971) and Mary Kirk McAlpine (1883–1968). Mary had just returned from Selma, Alabama, where she had given birth to Mary Kirk.

11. Mary Hunt Mills (1854–1921), daughter of Willard Curtis Mills and Cyrenthia E. Hunt Mills.

12. Wallace Cecil McClintock (b. 1872), George B. McClintock (1875–1939), and John David McClintock Jr. (b. 1879), sons of Rev. John David McClintock and Margaret Brown McClintock.

13. Eliza Brown (b. ca. 1852), daughter of Judge George N. Brown (b. 1822) and Maria Brown (b. ca. 1929) of Catlettsburg, Kentucky, and sister of Margaret Brown McClintock.

꧁

When John injured himself in a carpentry mishap, Lucy used the incident to educate her daughters on the finer skills of domestic care.

Lucy to Lizzie

Home—June 5th/.83

My dear Sister—

I <u>did</u> write you a long letter, which ought to have reached you the day after you arrived at Mrs McClintock's—<u>where</u> it has gone, I can't imagine. Cordele & Carrie have both received your P.Cs, & on each, you expressed great disappointment at not hearing from home. I am so sorry for I thought how nice it would be to get news from home so soon—& now I have only time for a short note. We are all well—last Saturday Mr Neilson sprained his ankle right severely. He was up on the Gin House steps—nailing them (for they were much needing mending)—when on[e] side gave way—he sprang to the ground (a height of <u>ten</u> feet), & in jumping more weight rested on the left ankle—which <u>turned</u> under him. He was brought to the house by the men—luckily, I did not see them—'till Mr Neilson called to me, that he was not hurt much. Of course you know, <u>what</u> a rush of feeling came over me, when I saw my dear husband being brought in the arms of the men—& his dear face so white with pain! But I did not loose all self-control—we sent for the Dr—who came <u>so</u> promptly—& examined <u>so</u> carefully—& then pronounced no bones broken—no dis-location—a severe sprain tho'. When he first came he said "your <u>leg</u> is right much swollen is'ent it"? Mr Neilson replied—"<u>not</u> at all, Sir—that's the natural size!" "Goodness! what a leg!"—said the Dr!—Mr Neilson said afterwards to me—The Dr was so astonished at my leg—what would he have done—if it had been a <u>woman's</u>!!—So you see we had our fun even if my poor man was hurt. But you know how my heart sung for joy that it was no worse. He went to town yesterday—he & Jack—for it was <u>Supervisor</u>-day—on the return the <u>buggy broke</u> down—right by the grove, in front of Mr Green's, Jack took Charlie from the buggy—<u>mounted</u> him, & came home for the carriage. To think the buggy should have held out all this time, & then break down with my poor lame man. He got home all right tho'—& we had another laugh. Lizzette of course begged to go in the carriage <u>for</u> Papa. When Mr Neilson was first hurt—the children were all in a state of excitement—Jack's eyes filled with tears—he rushed right out of the house—got on a <u>mule</u>, & took a ride! (How like a man!)—The <u>girls tho</u>, hung around him all after-noon—waiting on him in every <u>possible</u> way—so like <u>dear sweet women</u>!! This is the <u>last</u> excitement in our family—the Lord preserve us from any more dangerous ones. Louise has been so wrought up about her Examination—she had to get sick over it—she is so ambitious. She had a chill Sunday—she has taken remedies, & will be well again, & ready for school tomorrow. Letter from Bess—says she has written to you—all well—over the Bay—having a <u>real</u> nice time—<u>cool</u> & breezy. Minnie Symons was expected home last night. Mrs Ottley bloomed forth in a $25—<u>bonnet</u> Sunday—lovely, & very becoming. Kiss dear Sister Mc a thousand times, & thank [her] for being so sweet to my Darling. All send love, & more messages than I can write—

Good-bye. God bless you—Tell the boys—I wish they could hear Jack say his <u>speech</u>. All the coloreds send love

Your Lute

♄

On the anniversary of Sophie's death, Lucy reflected on the loss of one child, the birth of another, and the faith that had sustained her on her journey through motherhood. James's happy baby sounds could not fill the silence that had permeated Willow Cottage after Sophie's death, but his presence had helped to lessen Lucy's grief.

Lucy to Lizzie

Home. July 11th/.83

My dear, darling Sister—

This afternoon is so lovely—so calm—so golden—I have come out on the gallery, after dressing for the evening, & as I look around me, the sweet home-scene, makes my thoughts, & heart turn to one, who is not at home—& altho' my work-basket sits by, <u>loaded</u> with work, which ought to be done,—I push it aside, & will write you a <u>short</u> letter anyhow. My heart is too full of longing, & loving, & sweet, & sad memories to allow me to sew on "band, gusset, & seam"[1]—this day, one year ago,—our darling Sophie was with us, & this night one year ago, she grew so ill—then begun our dreadful fight with death. Should I grieve that the battle went against all our poor human efforts—for else, my child would not have known this whole year of glory, with her blessed Savior—think, only think, what she would have been deprived of, by staying with us. O! Lord make me truly glad that my baby, my darling is safe for <u>all</u> eternity! Having <u>known</u> her, & felt that she was <u>our's</u>, makes it very hard to be unselfish enough to say <u>we</u> are <u>glad</u> to have her gone—for was she not lovely—was she not a child to feel proud of having given birth to? It was hard to realize that such a short life was given, so strong, so happy a child. To us, it seemed that she was fitted for long life on this earth. Bessie sent me such a beautiful piece of poetry—called "<u>my jewel</u>"—I know she has been thinking of our darling, & of us. I will send you the little poem sometime, when I can spare it. The children all think, & speak of their little sister so often—

They are devoted to their little Brother—he does not take Sophie's place, of course,—but would'ent home be very desolate without a baby? He is so bright, & loving—gives real wide-mouth kisses, & <u>means to kiss</u> too. I think he will soon have some teeth—I was hoping he would not begin so early. He does not seem sick at all—but you know what a goose I've always been about him. Maj Watt took quite a fancy to him. I do not think he liked us saying he favored Walker— for you know, Maj never fancied Walker for some <u>unknown</u> cause.

Jim Irion has actually made up his mind to take a month's vacation—& he will leave this evening for Mobile—going across the Bay to see Frank, & Bessie. He would not <u>commit</u> himself as to length of stay—but we are only too glad to have him go, even for a short while. Mr Neilson, Cordele, & Lizzette have gone to bring Carrie & Mellie Gray to stay with us, while he is away. I am expecting them back now in a short time, & will be better satisfied, when I hear that Jim has truly started on the cars. I don't think he has been on the cars, since he went to Meridian for you, when you were so ill—how many years ago? Lizzette was very happy in having a little <u>Japanese</u> tray, & a <u>long</u> letter to send to Frank for her birthday–which is <u>today</u>—you know. Cordele is going to see what Dr Reynolds[2] will say for her comfort.

Mr Neilson can go without his crutch a little now, & of course, he is out <u>all</u> the time—which makes me uneasy—for fear of his hurting his ankle over again. He constantly speaks of writing to you—for he certainly does love you dearly—but not a line has he written to either of his Sisters. I tell him I am ashamed to send any more messages for him. He has been enjoying reading—first—Charles Kingsley, & now "Life of Mrs Prentiss."[3]

Tell Cecil, George, & John that Jack is the happiest boy I know, at present— he is the proud owner of a pretty little "<u>Billy-goat</u>." Ben Symons sent him word, he had one for him—& poor Jack was on his head until his Papa had the wagon hitched up to go over to Millwood for it. I could not allow so good an opportunity pass, for paying a visit to Sister Anne, & Lizzie, & Minnie, so my two daughters, & myself jumped into the wagon, & went as far as Fairoaks.[4] We had such a cordial reception, as you well know. Had a delightful visit—met Mrs Fort there—she was in one of her pleasantest moods, & sent messages, full & free, to you—Says she is still waiting for a companion letter from you, to lay alongside the one you wrote her last year.

Minnie spent several days with us last week—she is very interesting in her account of her life at the Conservatory. Maj says—"I tell you Lucy, there's <u>stuff</u> in that <u>gal</u>, & she'll make a fine woman when fully developed." I think so too—if Lizzie was not satisfied with the song Minnie sang—before the Press

Convention—<u>Mr Teasdale</u> persuaded her to sing a simple Italian ballad—instead of her <u>showy echo</u> song—Lizzie says, she remembers how he used to treat Bessie, & every other person <u>not</u> his own pupil. Lou Ellen sang splendidly, <u>both</u> nights of the Convention, & at church last Sunday. Claudia[5] was sick, & Mr Teasdale played for us—so it seemed quite like old times to have the <u>two</u> back in the choir. I suppose you have seen the papers descriptive of the proceedings of the Press &c. I believe tho', I'll send you our last one any how. I have Mrs Snell's address of welcome too—if you have not already seen it. It is not much of itself—but it was beautifully & <u>gracefully</u> recited. We heard Pauline for the first time, & we were electrified. She recited Kentucky Belle.[6] We have so much to tell you—so many little nothings. I have never told you what a delightful day we had when the Richard's, & Mrs Evans came. How we all wished for you. Maj was here—& in time for dinner too. He seemed to enjoy the day very much. Mrs Evans <u>lived</u> in the past. I never saw her seem to enjoy herself more—she walked around & looked at all the old familiar places, & noted all the changes. Mrs Richards, of course, was charming—& the <u>Col</u>—his old quisical self. Well! they have come back—Jim was left at Dêpot—don't reckon he will come back from Artesia. Carrie & Mell well—Cordele says, Dr Reynolds says she must wait another <u>month</u>.

Louise has written you another letter—says she wont count letters with you. She has written a good many letters this vacation—I encourage her to write—she is reading Dickens' Child's History of England.[7] All the colords ask a great deal about you. Maj started west, told us to direct to <u>Kosciesco</u> [Kosciusko] (never knew how to spell it). Carrie says, she is jumping Furniss while <u>I</u> write—All send love to you, Sister Mc & Miss Lyde. God bless you—Your loving

Lute.

NOTES

1. Thomas Hood, "The Song of the Shirt" (1843), in Black, ed., *British Literature,* 57–58.

2. Dr. Nelson Reynolds (b. ca. 1827–83), dentist.

3. Charles Kingsley (1819–75), English author and clergyman; Elizabeth Prentiss and George Lewis Prentiss, *The Life and Letters of Elizabeth Prentiss: Author of Stepping Heavenward* (1882).

4. The home of Elizabeth Symons Hale.

5. Claudia Maer (1866–1961), daughter of Samuel T. Maer (1828–74) and Susan Casement Maer (1837–1906).

6. Constance Fenimore Woolson, "Kentucky Belle," *Appleton's Journal* (September 6, 1873), vol. 10, 289–90.

7. Charles Dickens, *A Child's History of England* (1851–53).

ॐ

Alabama belles Mary and Anne Dawson visited Columbus in August 1883. In a few short weeks the sisters sparked a social revival among the town's finest families. "Wont they have a good opinion of the society of Columbus," Cordele remarked to Lizzie on July 21, 1883, after providing her sister with a long list of the visits, parties, and other genteel entertainments enjoyed by the "Misses Dawson." The town's residents enjoyed the fashionable interlude that provided them with reminiscences of young womanhood in the antebellum era.

Closer to home the hard work of making a life in the New South continued. Lucy noted that John's niece Annie Hopkins Ross had entered the ranks of the teaching profession.

Lucy to Lizzie

Willow Cottage
Aug 13th/.83.

My dear, darling Sister—

Your letter of 8th of Aug, & your note of 9th—were duly received, & I cannot resist the temptation of sitting down, <u>Monday</u>—as it is—to answer. [. . .] We are all well. Cordele wrote you about Furniss being baptized, & how sweetly <u>he</u> (& <u>all five</u> of the children) behaved. Our little man looked so pretty in his <u>fine</u> lace robe. Sulley's boy[1]–is very fine looking—he was in short clothes. All <u>three</u> of our babies (Mrs McAlpine's) "spoke out in <u>meetin</u>," in their sweet little <u>coos</u>. Ah! how well I remembered the last time we stood there, with our <u>now</u> sainted <u>three</u>! Tell my dear Sister McClintock we have ties both on earth, & in Heaven, which will bind our hearts forever. Mr McAlpine was looking pale & worn by the hot weather—but he has now gone on to Va—& I hope he will return invigorated. Our dear little Mrs McAlpine looks sweet, & calm, & <u>resigned</u>. Her little children are not well, & are very troublesome. She has a brother, & a girl-cousin[2] staying with her while her husband is gone. She has <u>Lou Hendrick</u> (Zack's wife)[3] as her maid of all works. Lou carried the baby up in church, & held her, until she was baptized, then Mrs McAlpine took her—the father baptized his own child. Maj was right about Lou Ellen—she is as round as a ball—poor little thing![4] I can't help feeling uneasy about her. She seems very well, & bright, & cheerful. When we had no organist the last Sunday—she <u>raised</u> all the hymns for us—in her sweet clear voice—(she was not able to play the organ herself). I could scarcely keep from crying, as I listened to her. I hope she may come out to see us this week, & I will ask all her plans.

You say you are rejoiced that the Dawson-girls have had such a nice time— why! they are <u>all the fashion</u>. The young gentlemen just follow them around. The

Hopkins had them to spend a week at their house. Wattie[5] exerted herself, in a most pleasing manner, for their entertainment. Will[6] _was_, & _is_ lovely to them! They have now gone back to Fairoaks—from there to Bro James', & then next week, <u>here</u> again. They are perfectly charmed with Columbus, & vicinity. Mary, is a combination of Mary Lyon & Bessie Irion—as <u>girls</u>—I think—very dashing, & sparkling. Annie, is more quiet—but so well "up" in all society ways. I read them one of your's, & one of Sister Sallie's letters—& told them they missed seeing our <u>brightest</u> stars. They are very regretful, & say they must know you.

You ask of Charlie & Annie Ross. Well!—<u>Ma</u>-<u>ma</u> Ross has sold her Seminary in Huntsville (since old Mr Ross' death) & has been <u>elected Principal</u>, of the <u>Syn-odical</u> Female College[7] of Rodgersville Tenn, for <u>five</u> years. So Charlie, & Annie go there with her to help her carry on the school. They find the Buildings & grounds very desirably located, & in good order, & as there are no <u>free</u> schools, in that part of the world, they hope to make a success of the school. Any way the school is under the care of the church, & the salaries are not entirely depen-dent upon number of pupils. After Annie got settled up there, she wrote for her Mother to come, & make her a visit—& so Sister Kate has gone, & I do hope will enjoy her liberation from all household cares,—which seem, at times, so onerous to her. Sister Annie says, she thinks, Sister Kate will look out for something to do for herself, while gone—as <u>matron</u> or something of that kind. I do not think she would be happy away from Columbus—even if she could get a <u>good place</u>—do you? I think she magnifies her home troubles.

I saw Judge Lyon the other day, & he says Madie Childress wishes you <u>to visit</u> her before you leave that part of the world. It would be nice for you to see Madie—but, of course, you will not go on that vague sort of invitation. I hope you can go to Louisville to the Exposition[8]—some of our people have gone. <u>Mr & Mrs Scruggs</u>[9] among others. I wish Mr Neilson & Jim could both go—but Mr Neilson feels that he has already lost so much time by his lameness, he must stay at home, & see after his work. He is having material hauled for building a new Gin House—& of course, can't leave. Where is he going to locate it?—down in the field by the big trees—<u>south</u> of the present position—I do not like it—but he threatened to put it nearer the house—on the side next the creek—if I objected. He has been busy on country business for a week—but then he gets paid, & times are very dull now—this is his last day—until next month.

Louise is now up at Bro James'—Annie spent last week with her. They seem to enjoy every moment of the time. I wish the boys could see the play house, they have made under the Grape-Arbor. They have up-stairs, & down-stair-rooms & dining-room, & kitchen. Such making of <u>mud</u> cakes, & pies they have. It was really very pretty to see the busy little <u>house</u>-<u>keepers</u>, & hear their different places, & opinions. Our children have kept so well, & been so happy all vacation. Their pleasures have been simple, but so enjoyed.

Mrs Fannie Richards has invited Louise to make her little girl a visit, & I hope she can do so—I like for my child to be thrown with such nice, refined people. Mrs Ottley did the nice, polite thing for the Dawson girls—she took them to ride in her handsome Bret—& then had them to stop at her house to a <u>surprise tea</u>!— Yes, she had her table beautifully set in china, silver, & glass—had an elegant tea, & young gentlemen invited to meet them—all without their dreaming of any attention, except the drive—now was'ent that sweet of her—the whole family felt obliged to her—& the girls were so appreciative.

Lizzette is as bright as a bird—& says so many things that I wish her <u>apprecia-tive</u> Uncle Watt could hear. I know he would enjoy her. I am going to write to him right away—& trust to his getting the letter some time, some where! Jack has had <u>goat</u> on the brain so long, I told him I did'ent believe he would know "B—" from "Billie-goat"—so this morning he seemed at a loss what to do—I had him bring his Arithmetic, & say his <u>tables</u>—he knew them every one, with scarcely an hesitation! Furniss is just lovely—he is the brightest, quickest little wiry fel-low. <u>Understands</u> so much that we say—knows when we call "<u>Lide</u>," & looks all around for her—he loves her dearly. He has two teeth, & wants to eat so much we are obliged to give him bread-crumbs, & gravy—& when he sees <u>fruit</u>, he smacks his lips, in the most appetizing manner, & looks like he will take a fit, until we let him have a <u>suck</u>! Cordele is so lonesome about putting up fruit—she has made some nice pear-preserves—& now only looks forward to <u>wild</u> plums—& Scup-ponong grapes as her last chance. Annie Bradford Kennedy & <u>husband</u> are out at Tom's on a visit—<u>Mr K</u>—a perfect helpless <u>invalid</u>. I can't write you a short letter. God bless you all.

Lute.

The girls were delighted with George's letter, & Louise will answer when she returns. <u>Coloreds</u> all send respects & many messages. <u>Ask</u> Sister Mc about <u>boys</u> <u>shirt waist</u>. You have never done as I asked you to find out <u>where</u> she <u>gets</u> them for her boys.

NOTES

1. Sanders B. Bradford (1882–1916), son of Thomas B. Bradford and Mary Sullie Matthews Bradford.

2. Mary Elvina Craig McAlpine had two brothers: James T. Craig (b. ca. 1859) and George H. Craig (b. ca. 1866); her cousin was probably Nannie Coleman (b. 1868), who at this time lived in the home of Mary's father, Benjamin Hogan Craig (1835–1907).

3. Seamstress Louise Ann Hendricks (b. ca. 1840), wife of Zack Hendricks (b. ca. 1830).

4. Lucy may have suspected that Lou Ellen Benoit was pregnant at this time. She mar-ried Otto Maer (b. 1860) on January 1, 1883.

5. Virginia Watkins Young Hopkins (1855–1944), wife of clerk Edward Randolph Hopkins (1855–1942). Edward was the son of Catherine Cabot Neilson Hopkins and Dr. James White Hopkins.

6. Clerk William B. Hopkins (1858–1913), son of Catherine Cabot Neilson Hopkins and Dr. James White Hopkins.

7. The Rogersville Synodical College was established in 1849 as a Presbyterian school for girls.

8. The Southern Exposition, showcasing products from across the South, was held in Louisville, Kentucky (1883–87).

9. Rev. John H. Scruggs (b. 1848), pastor of the Columbus First Methodist Church (1883–86), and his wife Ludia M. Paine Scruggs (b. ca. 1848).

ℱ๑

With Lizzie enjoying the therapeutic benefits of Bailey Springs, Lucy informed her sister of John's alterations to the gin house, the health of her children, and the thunderstorm that prematurely ended an impromptu family reunion.

Lucy to Lizzie

Home—Sept 5th/.83.

My dear, dear Trot,

Your letter from old Bailey was so gladly received—I felt like answering immediately—but it was Cordele's week to write, & I wrote, instead, to Miss Lide Brown. Was'ent it lovely of her to write of your departure?—it was a very sprightly, & gracefully worded letter, & I did so appreciate her thoughtfulness. How they do love you, & how they do lament your leaving! You certainly have the art of attracting & holding the love of all, with whom you are thrown. I look upon it as a gift from God—which you have appreciated & made useful to others as well as your self! How thankful we do feel [for those] dear friends you have just left. I wrote to Miss Lyde, & then I thought I would wait a few days, & write to Mrs McClintock.

I do hope dear, good, old Bailey will prove as beneficial as it did years ago, & send you home fat, & well. O! God grant you may escape an attack of illness—& have strength for the winter. I would not care so much for flesh. La! your letter made me laugh, & I could so well picture, the old place. I have very pleasant associations connected with the place—despite its' faults. Wonder if some of the visitors from Columbus will not soon find it dull, & go elsewhere—hope so—if not, do be careful. I was on my way to pay some visits up on the hills—but first, went by the Post, & got your letter—of course, I went to see Mrs Field first, & she espied your writing, & right away wished me to read it to her—which I did. We had a little laugh over our Gin-house secret. She very much enjoyed being in our secret, & said "all of us women have our little annoying secrets—don't we?" She was truly glad to see me, & to hear from you. I think I must have staid there three hours—but oh! can you ever get away from her under less time? Said she was going to write to you. You know, Capt Field has bought the Blair-lot & is going to build! Yes, the lot is Mrs Field's—bought, & made over to her. I do not know whether she is glad or not. I then went over to see Corinne's wonderful baby.[1] Mrs Orr met us (Lizzette & I) so cordially—& Pauline was so nice. Corrinne looked serenely happy over her great big boy! I do believe tho' there was more gush about her than I ever before noticed. The baby is like her—even asleep, & they say—he has her eyes. After a very pleasant half-hour with them—we went down to see Mollie Short Lanier, & her new little boy.[2] Mollie is like her old self, & asked after you & Bessie before I had hardly taken my seat. She has a very nice little baby—small—tho'—like Furniss.

Lou Ellen came out last Friday-evening, & staid until Sunday—she was lovely. I do think she grows in manner much like Lide McCarthy. I never noticed it before. She will remain in Columbus till after her affair—which will come off in November. She is bright, & as cheery as a bird. Louise missed seeing her, for she was in town—spending the week with Laura. She has gone tonight to spend with Wenona Spillmann[3]—who will have some of the neighbor-children come in, & help celebrate her tenth birthday. Poor little Tot deplores her extreme youth every time her sister is invited out. She shakes her head, & threatens the growing community with the retaliatory measures, she is going to take when she gets grown up! I declare she is a curious little creature. So willful, & so defiant—yet so sweet, & cheery, & easy to control when the reins are pulled in. Mary Dawson is much amused at her—& declares she is a little old woman of an hundred years—so quai[n]t—so smart.

Yesterday Lizzie Hale wrote us all to come over, & spend the day, to meet Bro James' family. We could not go over until the afternoon. Mr Neilson was in town on Supervisor business—but he gave us Gentry to drive us over those roads. We started a little before three o'clock—O! it was intensely hot—so hot, I would not take Furniss. We had to go very slowly—& before we got there we heard a peal of distant thunder—by the time we reached the house, there was a very threatening cloud—& wind & soon it began raining. Kate, & her family were there—the house was full to overflowing—nineteen white folks. Sister Annie, & Lizzie both delighted & beaming! What a merry party we were, despite the wind, & clouds, & rain. But you know my heart was turning homeward to my little man. Kate said she must go, & go in the rain too—for it was growing so late, & dark. We said, we must go too—I did wish I had taken the baby, for I would never have ventured out in such weather, if he had not been at home. You can just picture us! We would'ent have cared for the rain—but oh! so much electricity! But I will do myself the credit of saying, I behaved handsomely! You know how dreadfully afraid Cordele is of storms—she was very pale, & the children excited, & scared. But I told them, we must just trust in the Lord—He would take care of us—then Gentry was a good driver, & the carriage, & harness good, & strong! This quieted them more than I expected. I tried to be calm myself—but oh! how the lightning did flash right in our faces, & how the terrific thunder did peal on every side. Then <u>those</u> hills. But Gentry drove with such a steady hand—& the clouds went <u>all</u> around us—it rained only in dashes—we kept perfectly dry, & got home all right—tho' it was real dark, & had only time to shelter the horses, & carriage—before the rain came down in torrents—& the lightning & thunder was dreadful! I don't know when I have been as excited—I could not get to sleep for sometime after going to bed—altho' I was safe at home with my husband, & children, & 'all <u>was</u> well'—yet I had exercised so much self-control, I was real nervous, without knowing it. Furniss was so glad to see us—had been missing us, & crying softly, & clinging to his Mamy. At the first sound of our voices—he raised his head, & begun laughing, & reaching out his arms to come to the house. Mr Neilson was glad to have us home safely—but was <u>astonished</u> we had <u>gone</u>. (There was no sign of a cloud, even as big as a man's hand, when we started.)

Lizzie Hale wished a grand family re-union before the Dawson girls left—& this was <u>why</u> we did try to go on <u>that</u> especially <u>hot</u> afternoon—so we <u>did</u> go—& <u>did meet</u>—& <u>did get</u> home safely—altho 'most <u>scared</u> to death! Heard from Kate, & her children today—they got home so late Bro James had eaten his supper,—supposing they were going to spend the night at Lizzie's. They got home tho' before the <u>big</u> rain came.

The Dawson-girls will leave Friday-afternoon, & Sister Anne will go home with them, & stay <u>three</u> weeks—return in time to take charge of Lizzie's house, & children. She thinks she will stay at Fairoaks this winter—Lizzie board in town, & go home Fridays. Cousin Mary Barry will probably <u>board</u> out there with her—while Kate will take care of Mr B— & Elise go to Florida for the winter—this is their present plan—they do not know what they may do eventually. Elise has made Cordele a very pretty linen-lawn. It fits nicely, & looks stylish. Dr Reynolds has sent her word to come in <u>next week</u>.

We are well up with out work now—but of course, there is plenty ahead of us—if you see any pretty children's patterns, do try to get them for me—<u>aprons</u> for Tot, or dresses for both girls. The Gin House stands most conspicuously—I will try to have some trees <u>planted</u> around about there this winter—& hope for their branches to veil the offended vision. Perhaps they may stretch out their friendly arms by the time, the girls are grown. Don't let's say any more about it—will we?

Where is Maj?—I wrote to him at Carrolton. I hope he is well—Give him our love.

I told <u>Mrs</u> McAlpine of your loving inquiries—she seemed quite pleased—Mr McAlpine has not yet returned. Mrs Ottley has gone with her boys—John for Clarksville [Georgia], & Eugene[4] for water-cure. Do write a letter to Cousin Cornelia, if you can. We do not hear often from Bess—do you? She seems very far off. I will not say one word about your coming home—but oh!—

Colored friends wish to see you so much—Woos says she <u>misses</u> you <u>all</u> the time. All send love—God keep you. Your loving

Lute.

I don't believe I mentioned <u>Jack</u>—& he said so much too before he went to bed about your coming home. School will open the 24th. Children are beginning to look over their text books. They remember very well. Good-bye.

NOTES

1. Franklin Orr Harris (b. 1883), son of Franklin Harris (1856–1936), and Martha Corine Orr Harris (1861–1946).

2. Osborne Lanier (b. 1883), son of city marshal Henry M. Lanier (1849–1905) and Mollie Short Lanier (1853–90).

3. Winona Spillman (b. ca. 1874), daughter of Dr. John W. Spillman (1830–1900) and Yandaloo Frazee Spillman.

4. Eugene McLaran Ottley (1876–1907), son of John King Ottley and Ellen Gertrude Williams Ottley.

Afterword

Nearer Home

*I*t seems fitting that Lucy closed her journal while thinking about the trees she would plant around the gin house and the preparations she had under way for the recommencement of school. Her compendium of correspondence contains only three additional letters. The first, composed by John on April 13, 1891, was an anniversary greeting to Lucy reflecting on their twenty years of marriage. "They have been happy years to me," he wrote his wife. "Years full of effort— full of hope—full of confiding love—full of blessings—with mingled failures— disappointments—sorrows, griefs. . . . Years, which in their steady march—have brought us nearer Home—nearer God." The remaining two were written by Lucy during a visit to the Greenwood home of her daughter Lizzette in September 1911. No letters remain to mark the death of her sister Lizzie in March 1911 or the death of her brother Jim in December of the same year.

Lucy died on November 17, 1913, at seventy years of age. John survived his wife by almost nine years; he died of heart failure just weeks short of his eightieth birthday, on February 25, 1922. "He left us with something of inestimably greater value than silver and gold," noted his daughter Lizzette, "the priceless heritage of a stainless name."[1]

Lucy's postwar life bore the hallmarks of a new southern domesticity built upon a companionate marriage, hard work, and careful measures of gentility. She looked outward to accomplish the standards she set at home, garnering support for John's campaign for sheriff, for example, in the hope that such a position would provide her family with greater respectability and financial stability. Paid employment was never considered and intellectual improvement was sidelined as she kept her eyes firmly fixed on marriage and motherhood, hearth and home. Lucy's sister Lizzie used her financial independence to nurture the social and intellectual pursuits she had been deprived of in adolescence, turning to the domestic ideal only after her marriage to James Madison Watt. Cordele embraced the vocational purpose of single blessedness, creating a rubric of usefulness within the household and the community. Bess basked in the glow of a new southern gentility, founded on her Virginia education and coming out. Unlike many young women, Bess was never asked to make a choice between society and paid employment. Instead, Lizzie's financial status underwrote Bess's social agenda, which culminated in an advantageous marriage and a domestic ideal of Bess's own.

Lucy, Lizzie, Cordele, and Bess sat at different life stages and different points on postwar womanhood's new continuum, and they worked together at the task of rebuilding their lives and the social credit of their family name. Their individual stories played within the collective bonds of family and community. By celebrating both traditional and nondependent ideals of womanhood, each made a dynamic contribution to the creation of a New South.

NOTE

1. "Capt. Neilson Crosses the River," newspaper clipping.

BIBLIOGRAPHY

Manuscript Collections

Columbus Dispatch Pictorial and Industrial Edition, 1905, Newspaper Collection, Special Collections Department, Mitchell Memorial Library, Mississippi State University, Mississippi State, Mississippi.

Harriett Beecher Stowe Papers, Clifton Waller Barrett Collection, Albert and Shirley Small Special Collections Library, University of Virginia, Charlottesville, Virginia.

Irion Neilson Collection, Collection of the Museum of Mississippi History, Mississippi Department of Archives and History, Jackson, Mississippi.

Irion Neilson Family Papers, Mississippi Department of Archives and History, Jackson, Mississippi.

Lillian Neilson Papers, Special Collections Department, Mitchell Memorial Library, Mississippi State University, Mississippi State, Mississippi.

Sarah Neilson Papers, Special Collections Department, Mitchell Memorial Library, Mississippi State University, Mississippi State, Mississippi.

T. C. Wier Family Papers, Special Collections Department, Mitchell Memorial Library, Mississippi State University, Mississippi State, Mississippi.

Worthington Family Papers, Mississippi Department of Archives and History, Jackson, Mississippi.

Published Works

Alcott, Louisa May. *Little Women.* Ed. Elaine Showalter. Harmondsworth, U.K.: Penguin, 1989.

Bate, Jonathan, ed. *Elia; and, the Last Essays of Elia.* Oxford: Oxford University Press, 1987.

Bell, Alan, ed. *The Sayings of Sydney Smith.* London: Gerald Duckworth and Company, 1993.

Bercaw, Nancy D. *Gendered Freedoms: Race, Rights, and the Politics of Household in the Delta, 1861–1875.* Gainesville: University Press of Florida, 2003.

Black, Joseph, ed. *The Broadview Anthology of British Literature.* Toronto: Broadview Press, 2009.

Bond, Bradley G., ed. *Mississippi: A Documentary History.* Jackson: University Press of Mississippi, 2003.

Brontë, Charlotte. *Jane Eyre* (1847). Ed. Q. D. Leavis. Harmondsworth, U.K.: Penguin, 1985.

———. *Villette* (1853). Ed. Mark Lilly. Harmondsworth, U.K.: Penguin, 1985.

Bulwer-Lytton, Edward George Earle. *The Caxtons: A Family Picture.* Edinburgh: William Blackwood and Sons, 1849.

———. Earle. *My Novel* (1850–53). London: Routledge, Warne, and Routledge, 1859.

Bulwer-Lytton, Edward Robert. *Clytemnestra, The Earl's Return, The Artist, and Other Poems*. London: Chapman and Hall, 1855.

Bulwer-Lytton, Rosina. *The Peer's Daughters: A Novel*. New York: Stringer and Townsend, 1850.

Carter, Christine Jacobson. *Southern Single Blessedness: Unmarried Women in the Urban South, 1800–1865*. Urbana: University of Illinois Press, 2006.

Cashin, Joan E. *A Family Venture: Men and Women on the Southern Frontier*. Baltimore: Johns Hopkins University Press, 1991.

Censer, Jane Turner. *The Reconstruction of White Southern Womanhood, 1865–1895*. Baton Rouge: Louisiana State University Press, 2003.

Church Publishing, *The Book of Common Prayer: And Administration of the Sacraments and Other Rights of the Church*. New York: Church Publishing Inc., 2001.

Clarke, Erskine. *Dwelling Place: A Plantation Epic*. New Haven, Conn.: Yale University Press, 2005.

Cleveland, Charles Dexter, ed. *A Compendium of English Literature: Chronically Arranged, from Sir John Mandeville to William Cowper*. Philadelphia: E. C. and J. Biddle, 1865.

Cobb, James C. *The Most Southern Place on Earth: The Mississippi Delta and the Roots of Regional Identity*. New York: Oxford University Press, 1992.

Cornford, Stephen, ed. *Night Thoughts*. Cambridge: Cambridge University Press, 1989.

Cox, Karen L. *Dixie's Daughters: The United Daughters of the Confederacy and the Preservation of Confederate Culture*. Gainesville: University Press of Florida, 2003.

Crawford, Richard, ed. *The Civil War Songbook: Complete Original Sheet Music for 37 Songs*. Minola, New York: Dover, 1977.

Cummins, Maria Susana. *The Lamplighter* (1854). Boston: John P. Jewett and Company, 1855.

Davis, Herbert, ed. *Pope: Poetical Works*. Oxford: Oxford University Press, 1978.

Dickens, Charles. *Great Expectations* (1861). Ed. Margaret Cardwell. Oxford: Oxford University Press, 1993.

———. *Oliver Twist* (1838). Ed. Kathleen Tillotson. Oxford: Oxford University Press, 1999.

———. *The Posthumous Papers of the Pickwick Club* (1836–37). Ed. Robert L. Patten. Harmondsworth, U.K.: Penguin, 1986.

Edwards, Laura F. *Gendered Strife and Confusion: The Political Culture of Reconstruction*. Urbana: University of Illinois Press, 1997.

———. *The People and Their Peace: Legal Culture and the Transformation of Inequality in the Post-Revolutionary South*. Chapel Hill: University of North Carolina Press, 2009.

———. *Scarlett Doesn't Live Here Anymore: Southern Women in the Civil War Era*. Urbana: University of Illinois Press, 2000.

Eliot, George. *Middlemarch* (1871–72). Ed. W. J. Harvey. Harmondsworth, U.K.: Penguin, 1994.

Erbsen, Wayne, ed. *The Bluegrass Gospel Songbook*. Asheville, N.C.: Native Ground Books and Music, 2006.

Farnham, Christie Anne. *The Education of the Southern Belle: Higher Education and Student Socialization in the Antebellum South.* New York: New York University Press, 1994.

Faust, Drew Gilpin. *Mothers of Invention: Women of the Slaveholding South in the American Civil War.* Chapel Hill: University of North Carolina Press, 1996.

Feimster, Crystal N. *Southern Horrors: Women and the Politics of Rape and Lynching.* Cambridge, Mass.: Harvard University Press, 2009.

Ferguson, N. L., and M. J. Percival, eds. *The Oasis: Or, Golden Leaves of Friendship.* Boston: Dayton and Wentworth, 1855.

Feuchtwanger, E. J. *Bismarck.* London: Routledge, 2002.

Foner, Eric. *Reconstruction: America's Unfinished Revolution, 1863–1877.* New York: Harper and Row, 1988.

Fox-Genovese, Elizabeth. *Within the Plantation Household: Black and White Women of the Old South.* Chapel Hill: University of North Carolina Press, 1988.

Friend, Craig Thompson, and Lorri Glover, eds. *Southern Manhood: Perspectives on Masculinity in the Old South.* Athens: University of Georgia Press, 2004.

Gardner, Sarah E. *Blood and Irony: Southern White Women's Narratives of the Civil War, 1861–1937.* Chapel Hill: University of North Carolina Press, 2004.

Glymph, Thavolia. *Out of the House of Bondage: The Transformation of the Plantation Household.* New York: Cambridge University Press, 2008.

Henry, Mellinger Edward, ed. *Folk-Songs from the Southern Highlands.* New York: J. J. Augustin, 1938.

Hobbs, June Hadden. *'I Sing for I Cannot be Silent': The Feminization of American Hymnody, 1870–1920.* Pittsburgh: University of Pittsburgh Press, 1997.

Hutchinson, Thomas, ed. *The Complete Poetical Works of Percy Bysshe Shelley.* London: Oxford University Press, 1927.

Jabour, Anya. *Scarlett's Sisters: Young Women in the Old South.* Chapel Hill: University of North Carolina Press, 2007.

Janney, Caroline E. *Burying the Dead but Not the Past: Ladies' Memorial Associations and the Lost Cause.* Chapel Hill: University of North Carolina Press, 2008.

Kinsley, James, ed. *Burns: Poems and Songs.* London: Oxford University Press, 1971.

———, ed. *The Poems of John Dryden.* Oxford: Clarendon Press, 1958.

Lipscomb, William Lowndes. *A History of Columbus, Mississippi during the 19th Century.* Ed. Georgia P. Young. Birmingham, Ala.: United Daughters of the Confederacy, Mississippi Division, Stephen D. Lee Chapter No. 34; Dispatch Printing Company, 1909.

Lohrenz, Mary Edna, and Anita Miller Stamper. *Mississippi Homespun: Nineteenth-Century Textiles and the Women Who Made Them.* Jackson: Mississippi Department of Archives and History, 1989.

Lounsbury, Thomas R., ed. *Yale Book of American Verse.* New Haven, Conn.: Yale University Press, 1912.

MacDonald, George. *Adela Cathcart.* London: Hurst and Blackett, 1864.

Maidment, James, ed. *Scottish Ballads and Songs.* Edinburgh: Thomas George Stevenson, 1859.

Massey, Mary Elizabeth. *Bonnet Brigades.* New York: Knopf, 1966.

McGann, Jerome J., ed. *Lord Byron: The Complete Poetical Works*. Oxford: Clarendon Press, 1980.

McMillen, Sally G. *Motherhood in the Old South: Pregnancy, Childbirth, and Infant Rearing*. Baton Rouge: Louisiana State University Press, 1990.

Nordhoff, Charles. *Cotton States in Spring and Summer of 1875*. New York: D. Appleton and Company, 1876.

Opie, Iona, and Peter Opie, eds. *The Oxford Book of Children's Verse*. Oxford: Clarendon Press, 1973.

Orgel, Stephen, and Jonathan Goldberg, eds. *John Milton*. Oxford: Oxford University Press, 1990.

Ott, Victoria E. *Confederate Daughters: Coming of Age during the Civil War*. Carbondale: Southern Illinois University Press, 2008.

Pollard, Edward Alfred. *Black Diamonds Gathered in the Darkey Homes of the South*. New York: Pudney and Russell, 1859.

Quinn, Arthur Hobson, ed. *The Complete Poems and Stories of Edgar Allan Poe with Selections from His Critical Writings*. New York: Alfred A. Knopf, 1964.

Rable, George C. *Civil Wars: Women and the Crisis of Southern Nationalism*. Urbana: University of Illinois Press, 1989.

Randolph, Vance, ed. *Religious Songs and Other Items*. Vol. 4. Columbia: University of Missouri Press, 1980.

Ravitch, Michael, and Diane Ravitch, eds. *The English Reader: What Every Literate Person Needs to Know*. New York: Oxford University Press, 2006.

Rhys, Ernest, ed. *The Poems of Charles Kingsley*. London: J. M. Dent and Sons, 1927.

Richardson, Samuel. *Clarissa Harlowe* (1747–48). Ed. Angus Ross. Harmondsworth, U.K.: Penguin, 1985.

Ricks, Christopher, ed. *Tennyson: A Selected Edition Incorporating the Trinity College Manuscripts*. Berkeley: University of California Press, 1989.

Roberts, Giselle. *The Confederate Belle*. Columbia: University of Missouri Press, 2003.

Rosen, Hannah. *Terror in the Heart of Freedom: Citizenship, Sexual Violence, and the Meaning of Race in the Postemancipation South*. Chapel Hill: University of North Carolina Press, 2009.

Scott, Anne Firor. *The Southern Lady: From Pedestal to Politics, 1830–1930*. Chicago: University of Chicago Press, 1970.

Scudder, Horace E., and George Monteiro, eds. *The Poetical Works of Longfellow: Cambridge Edition*. Boston: Houghton Mifflin, 1975.

Shakespeare, William. *Hamlet*. Ed. Ann Thompson and Neil Taylor, 1.2. London: Arden Shakespeare, 2006.

———. *Othello*. Ed. E. A. J. Honigmann, 2.1. London: Arden Shakespeare, 1997.

Smith-Rosenberg, Carroll. "The Female World of Love and Ritual: Relations between Women in Nineteenth-Century America." *Signs: A Journal of Women in Culture and Society* 1 (fall 1975): 1–29.

Stephan, Scott. *Redeeming the Southern Family: Evangelical Women and Domestic Devotion in the Antebellum South*. Athens: University of Georgia Press, 2008.

Stowe, Steven M. *Intimacy and Power in the Old South: Ritual in the Lives of the Planters*. Baltimore: Johns Hopkins University Press, 1987.

Studwell, William Emmett. *The Americana Song Reader*. New York: Routledge, 1997.

Swain, Charles. *English Melodies*. London: Longman, Brown, Green and Longmans, 1849.

Tardy, Mary T., ed. *Southland Writers: Biographical and Critical Sketches of the Living Female Writers of the South*. Philadelphia: Claxton, Remsen and Haffelfinger, 1870.

Vance, Randolph, ed. *Ozark Folksongs*. Columbia: University of Missouri Press, 1980.

Watts, Isaac. *Divine and Moral Songs* (1715). New York: Hurd and Houghton, 1866.

Weiner, Marli F. *Mistresses and Slaves: Plantation Women in South Carolina, 1830–80*. Urbana: University of Illinois Press, 1998.

West, Jane. *Letters to a Young Lady; In Which the Duties and Character of Women are Considered, Chiefly With a Reference to Prevailing Opinions*. London: Longman, Hurst, Rees and Orme, 1806.

Whites, LeeAnn. *The Civil War as a Crisis in Gender: Augusta, Georgia, 1860–1890*. Athens: University of Georgia Press, 1995.

———. *Gender Matters: Civil War, Reconstruction, and the Making of the New South*. New York: Palgrave Macmillan, 2005.

Williams, Wallace E., and Douglas Emory Wilson, eds. *The Collected Works of Ralph Waldo Emerson: Volume IV, Representative Men: Seven Lectures*. Cambridge, Mass.: Belknap Press of Harvard University Press, 1987.

INDEX

Neilson, Jim, 33, 130

Neilson, John Abert (JAN): business interests of, 82, 91; and Civil War, 19; as cotton weigher, 224; and courtship, 1, 18–21; death of, 282; and fatherhood, 148, 176, 196; finances of, 65, 82, 247–48; and Grange, 155, 157, 247; health of, 43, 51, 60, 71, 112, 177, 271, 273; on Irion family estate, 74–77; manages Wildwood, 19–20, 77, 79–80, 82, 100, 108, 112, 162, 172, 183; manages Willow Cottage, 214, 224, 228, 240, 268, 276; marriage of, 2, 31, 35–36, 53, 65, 107, 110, 116, 119, 122–23, 134, 191, 205, 229–30, 266, 282; move to Willow Cottage, 183, 189; and postwar masculinity, 1, 19–20, 77, 122–23; and religion, 89–90, 152, 174, 178, 247–48, 263; and sheriff campaign (1871), 36–38, 44, 51, 65, 82

Neilson, John Abert Jr.: birth of, 192; childhood of, 196, 211, 213–14, 220, 227–28, 230, 241, 259, 273, 276–77; health of, 207, 211, 217

Neilson, Louisa Abert, 61, 106, 112, 151, 171, 180, 198

Neilson, Louisa Gray: birth of, 147–49; childhood of, 171, 175, 180, 198–99, 202, 213, 220, 228, 230, 259, 276–77; education of, 271–72; health of, 164, 177–78, 183, 190–93, 207, 211, 217; naming of, 150–51, 154–56

Neilson, Louisa Pinckney Abert, 19, 150n2, 151, 154

Neilson, Mary, 32

Neilson, Mary Bruce, 61, 106, 110–12, 115

Neilson, Mary Bruce Barry: death of, 254–55; and domesticity, 101, 220, 242; and entertaining, 94, 146, 151, 154, 175, 178; friendship with ELIN, 126, 140, 147, 149, 195, 254–55, 262–63; marriage of, 75n18; and motherhood, 30n1, 110–12, 115, 170n7, 215–16, 255; and visiting, 61, 136, 162, 165, 169, 171–72

Neilson, Sarah Dandridge: friendship with ELIN, 20, 32–33, 228, 255; moves to Belmont, 238–42; and religion, 230; travels of, 40, 55, 61, 65, 101, 106, 142, 180, 183, 185, 220; and visiting, 25, 29, 229, 233, 264

Neilson, Sarah Helena Frazier, 212n2

Neilson, Sophie Abert, 256, 259, 261–67, 272–73

Neilson, Will, 10

Neilson, William Walker, 19, 212n2

Nesbitt, Demsey, 27n1, 56n11, 165n2

Nesbitt, James A., 165, 217–18, 237, 267

Nesbitt, Malinda, 60, 161, 165, 172

Nesbitt, Mary. See Mary Nesbitt Davis

Nesbitt, Matilda, 27n1, 56n11, 142, 161, 165, 165n2, 172, 175, 237, 267

Nesbitt, Robert D., 165

Nesbitt, Thomas, 60, 165, 169, 172, 237

Nichols, Josephine Bobo, 40n3

Nichols, Robert Foster, 37

Noah (servant), 248

No Name (Collins), 59

Odeneal, Ebenezer Patrick, 61n5, 168, 211, 240, 240n3

Odeneal, Rosamond Dearing, 61n5, 168, 221, 240n3

Odeneal, Willie Blanch. See Willie Blanch Odeneal Perkins

"Oh, To Be Nothing" (Taylor and Halls), 265

Okolona, 82, 91

Oliver Twist (Dickens), 85

"Only a Year" (Stowe), 72

Orr, Cornelia Ewing Van de Graaf, 238n4

Orr, Jehu Amaziah, 39, 238n4

Orr, Pauline Van de Graaf, 236

Osborne, Emily E., 201

Osborne, Richard Russell, 203n2

Othello (Shakespeare), 105

Ottley, Charles William, 39, 71

Ottley, Ellen Gertrude Williams: and Benoit divorce, 204–6, 211; clothing of, 272; and entertaining, 27, 53, 68, 79, 115, 153, 167–68, 277; family of, 34n12, 42n23, 194n1, 281n4; friendship with ELIN, 39, 97, 101, 114, 118, 126, 127, 220, 262, 268; and motherhood, 193, 195; travels of, 46, 234, 239, 281; and visiting, 33, 71, 144, 181, 228, 254

Ottley, Eugene McLaran, 281

Ottley, John King: and Benoit divorce, 204–6, 211; family of, 42n23, 194n1, 281n4;

white children: death of, 110–12, 145, 217, 261–63; health of, 101, 106, 149, 177–78, 183, 190–93, 196, 207, 269

white men: and Civil War, 12–13, 19; contracts with African Americans, 17–18, 84, 95, 98–99, 159–60, 248; and politics, 36–38, 200, 215–16, 220; and postwar masculinity, 1, 3–4, 17, 19–20, 77, 122–23. *See also* Army of the Confederate States of America

white women: and Civil War, 11–15; and clothing, 46, 60, 64–65, 102, 115, 117, 129, 133, 135, 184, 206, 211, 235, 237, 243–45, 272; and coming out, 11, 14, 52, 60, 72, 76, 96, 124, 129, 135, 158–60, 172, 177–79, 216–17; and courtship, 1, 10, 18–21, 53–54, 59–61, 78–79, 88, 108; and divorce, 204–6, 211; and domesticity, 2–4, 16–18, 20, 32–33, 38, 59, 87, 93, 100, 122–23, 132, 137–39, 141, 158, 207, 211, 237; and education, 3–4, 8–11, 34, 38–40, 48–50, 58, 64, 97, 102, 124, 135, 139, 143–44; and entertaining, 46–47, 63, 76, 80–81, 92–93, 97, 117, 135–36, 153–54, 171, 180–81, 197–99; female friendships of, 5, 8–9, 27, 32–33, 39, 46, 52–53, 126, 167; and marriage, 2, 35–36, 53, 91, 106, 116, 127, 133–34, 154, 162, 166–68, 175, 191, 200, 203–4, 214, 222, 242, 244–46; and memorial work, 4, 210, 251; and motherhood, 145–57, 161, 192, 216; and mourning, 111–12, 115, 261–67, 271–73; and nondependent ideal, 3–4; and politics, 36–38, 82, 202, 216, 228; and pregnancy, 59, 84, 87, 92–94, 96–97, 105–6, 113, 117, 124–27, 130, 134, 138–42, 224, 254–55; and religion, 9, 70, 80, 86, 89–90, 140, 146–47, 152, 159, 165, 167, 175, 195–96, 236, 239, 249, 266, 269; on servants, 17–18, 32–33, 44, 55, 65, 73, 95, 98, 100, 108, 114, 128–29, 131, 133, 137–39, 145, 149–50, 180, 210; and single blessedness, 50, 124, 251–52; and society, 39–40, 117–19; as teachers, 8–9, 53, 65, 68, 102, 106, 140, 206, 238–40, 269, 276, 280; and visiting, 45–46, 60, 73–74, 78, 114, 117–19, 162, 166–69, 195–96, 201, 208–9, 226, 269, 278–80; and watershed debate, 2–5

Whitfield, Croly, 142

Whitfield, George, 207n4

Whitfield, Henry Buchanan, 60, 215, 221n1

Whitfield, James Henry, 219

Whitfield, Laura Eloise Pickett, 212n1

Whitfield, Laura Young, 60, 119, 221n1

Whitfield, Lucy, 175

Whitfield, Mary, 206, 209, 219

Whitfield, Nathan William, 208

Whitfield, Sallie Elizabeth, 175

Whitfield, Theodore, 38

Whitfield, William W., 177n11

Wildwood: description of, 24; isolation of, 29, 58, 70, 86, 120; mill at, 79–80, 100, 108, 183–84. *See also* Press Barron, Cornelia A. Parthenia Irion, ELIN, JAN

Willeford, Mary Kirk, 46, 193, 206, 217, 243

Willeford, Rueben, 47n7

Williams, Charles, 71

Williams, Eliza L., 103n10

Williams, Henry Lawrence, 244

Williams, Henry Petty, 244

Williams, Isaac, 103n10

Williams, Lillie M., 244

Williams, Mary A. E., 42n25, 120n7, 167, 201

Williams, Mary Agnes, 118

Williams, Samuel, 244

Williams, Virginia Pidgeon Petty, 244

Williams, Wiley H., 40, 44, 120n7, 167–68, 228

Willow Cottage: description of, 11, 203; employment of African Americans at, 17–18, 80, 95, 98, 114; Hayden life at, 7; Irion life at, 11–21; managed by Edwards family, 166–67, 169. *See also* Press Barron, James William Gray Irion, JAN

Winston, Annie F., 185

Winston, Frances Rose, 186n7

Winston, Frances Rose (daughter), 185

Winston, Jennie A., 185

Winston, Maria C., 185

Winston, Mary E., 185

Winston, Nellie M., 185

Winston, Rebecca, 185

Winston, William Burton, 185

Wood Lawn, 7, 11

Wood Lawn (Tenn.), 5–6

Wooldridge, Lily Lee, 175